Health of South Asians in the United States

Leading scholars and practitioners come together in this contributed volume to present the most current evidence on cutting edge health issues for South Asians living in the United States, the fastest growing Asian American population. The book spans a variety of health topics while examining disparities and special health needs for this population. Subjects discussed include cancer, obesity, HIV/AIDS, women's health, LGBTQ health, and mental health.

Health of South Asians in the United States presents evidence-based recommendations to help determine priorities for prevention, diagnosis, treatment, education, and policies which will optimize the health and well-being of South Asian American communities in the United States.

Although aimed primarily at health professions students, healthcare professionals, and policy makers, this book will also prove to be useful to anyone interested in the health and well-being of the South Asian communities in the United States.

Memoona Hasnain is a Professor and Associate Department Head for Faculty Development and Research in the Department of Family Medicine, College of Medicine at the University of Illinois at Chicago.

Punam Parikh is a Project Manager in the Division of General Internal Medicine, School of Medicine at the University of California, Los Angeles.

Nitasha Chaudhary Nagaraj is a Senior Research Associate in the Milken Institute School of Public Health at the George Washington University.

Health of South Asians in the United States

An Evidence-Based Guide for Policy and Program Development

Edited by

Memoona Hasnain,
Punam Parikh, and
Nitasha Chaudhary Nagaraj

Routledge
Taylor & Francis Group

LONDON AND NEW YORK

First published 2017
by Routledge
4 Park Square, Milton Park, Abingdon, Oxon OX14 4RN

Simultaneously published in the US
by Routledge
605 Third Avenue, New York, NY 10017

First issued in paperback 2023

Routledge is an imprint of the Taylor & Francis Group, an informa business

British Library Cataloguing-in-Publication Data
A catalogue record for this book is available from the British Library

---

Library of Congress Cataloging-in-Publication Data

Names: Hasnain, Memoona, editor. | Parikh, Punam, editor. | Nagaraj, Nitasha Chaudhary, editor.
Title: Health of South Asians in the United States : an evidence-based guide for policy and program development / [edited by] Memoona Hasnain, Punam Parikh, Nitasha Chaudhary Nagaraj.
Description: Boca Raton FL : CRC Press, 2017. | Includes bibliographical references and index.
Identifiers: LCCN 2016043381 | ISBN 9781498798426 (hardback : alk. paper) | ISBN 9781315366685 (ebook : alk. paper)
Subjects: | MESH: Asian Americans—ethnology | Health Status | Policy Making | United States—epidemiology | Asia, Southeastern—ethnology
Classification: LCC RA448.5.A83 | NLM WA 300 AA1 | DDC 362.1089/95073—dc23
LC record available at https://lccn.loc.gov/2016043381

ISBN: 978-1-4987-9842-6 (hbk)
ISBN: 978-1-315-36668-5 (ebk)
ISBN: 978-0-367-22413-4 (pbk)

DOI: 10.1201/9781315366685

Typeset in AGaramondPro
by diacriTech, Chennai

Publisher's Note
The publisher has gone to great lengths to ensure the quality of this reprint but points out that some imperfections in the original copies may be apparent.

DEDICATION

To our Parents,
who believed in the value of education and in raising empowered daughters,
we are thankful to them for their encouragement, love, and guidance,
and for providing us the gift of educational opportunities that
many girls and women in South Asia are deprived of.

Shireen Hasnain and Brigadier Syed Hazur Hasnain, SJ & Bar
Memoona Hasnain

Kalpana Parikh and Jay Parikh
Punam Parikh

Anju Grover Chaudhary and Jawahar Lal Chaudhary
Nitasha Chaudhary Nagaraj

Contents

Foreword

I am pleased and honored to write the foreword for *The Health of South Asians in the United States: An Evidence-Based Guide for Policy and Program Development.* This book focuses on revealing, through updated research, education, and policy studies, the health disparities and challenges that South Asians in the United States continue to encounter. This book also emphasizes that new, emerging health research on South Asians can better inform policy decisions made at all levels of the government. It includes chapters on a wide variety of topics, such as cancer, diabetes, and HIV/AIDS. No doubt this collection of chapters will contribute important new analyses and program and policy recommendations to optimize the health and well-being of South Asian communities in the United States.

The opportunity to write this foreword resonates with me dearly. First and foremost, as a 1.5 generation immigrant from India, I witnessed the common newcomer challenges my family experienced assimilating in the United States. I remember my mom navigating the limited food choices for vegetarians, and both my parents shied away from the regular doctors' visits and preventive screenings recommended by health officials in the United States.

Second, as the executive director of the White House Initiative on Asian Americans and Pacific Islanders (Initiative), I believe it is important for critical issues and concerns of Asian American and Pacific Islander (AAPI) communities to be analyzed and understood by academics, advocates, and federal policymakers. The Initiative, which President Barack Obama reestablished by Executive Order 13515 in 2009, works to improve the quality of life and opportunities for AAPIs by facilitating increased access to and participation in federal programs where these populations have been underserved. Throughout my tenure as the executive director, the need to highlight and promote greater awareness of health disparities in AAPI communities, improve access to healthcare services for underserved AAPIs, and increase health data on specific AAPI populations has remained the set of priorities of the Initiative.

The AAPI community is the fastest-growing racial group in the United States. Yet, the AAPI community—including the South Asian community—is one of the most understudied populations in the United States. Further, the socioeconomic diversity of ethnic groups within the AAPI community can be significant, making the need for disaggregated data to understand the needs and priorities of this community an ongoing critical concern.

The contributors to this book clearly understand this concern and have taken the important step to address the critical gap in health research on South Asian communities. To promote the progress of understanding and learning about AAPI communities, it is important to publish new and emerging scholarship that analyzes the needs of South Asian communities facing preventable but chronic health conditions, lifestyle, and health interventions, and the unique concerns of special populations. Yet, throughout the book, the need for more disaggregated data to help health providers understand how best to address the health needs of South Asians emerges as a common theme.

This compilation of health research first calls attention to noncommunicable chronic health conditions that affect South Asian communities and the need to improve medical interventions that could promote the diagnosis, treatment, education, and prevention of these health conditions. Within the South Asian community, preventable health disparities, such as cardiovascular disease, diabetes, and certain cancers impact the community, but it is unclear if current healthcare practices are properly identifying and treating South Asian patients with these conditions. For example, according to the Agency for Healthcare Research and Quality (AHRQ), South Asians have the highest rates of cardiovascular disease among all ethnic groups.* Indeed, I can attest to the impact that cardiovascular disease has had on my own family, having never met any of my grandparents, who passed away in their 50s from this disease. Moreover, AHRQ acknowledges the need to improve research on effective and sensitive medical practices by reporting that cultural and religious beliefs regarding body image, gender roles, and cultural identity can prevent many South Asians from adopting lifestyle changes that could significantly reduce their chances of developing cardiovascular disease.

Researchers contributing to this book next tackle important lifestyle and healthy behaviors impacting the South Asian community, including nutrition, obesity, tobacco use, and HIV/AIDS infection rates. Previous studies on these health factors have concluded that the diversity within the South Asian community makes identifying, understanding, and developing appropriate interventions for adverse behaviors difficult. For example, a publication of the South Asian Public Health Association, *The Brown Paper*, included analyses of research on the dietary practices of South Asian immigrants and its impact on their risk of chronic disease. The recommendations concluded by stating, "Geographic

---

* http://www.ahrq.gov/news/newsletters/research-activities/13sep/0913ra26.html

and climatic variations and a heterogeneous population within each country make South Asian dietary practices unique and diverse. Thus, when examining diet and nutrition of South Asians to assess their health risks, it is important to determine country and region of origin."* A similar study on tobacco control interventions for South Asians found a "need to disaggregate data for South Asians and suggest that tobacco control interventions should target specific segments of the population."†

Finally, the authors focus on the health needs of special and vulnerable populations within the South Asian community, especially women, the elderly, and sexual minorities. These populations can face additional barriers to receiving appropriate medical care due to stigma, cultural biases, and lack of visibility. Once again, the ability of these populations to receive accurate, accessible, and culturally and linguistically sensitive health care tailored to help each patient understand the health disparities, risks, and appropriate preventive care that they face is limited by the data available to healthcare providers and policymakers.

Understanding the language, cultural, and other barriers that prevent AAPI communities from fully accessing and utilizing our healthcare system is critical to addressing and eliminating these barriers. That is why, since the Initiative was re-established in 2009, working with community leaders and federal health officials to promote access to healthcare and eliminate chronic health disparities within AAPI communities quickly emerged as a leading priority. Prime examples of these efforts are the US Department of Health and Human Services' *Action Plan for the Prevention, Care and Treatment of Viral Hepatitis*‡ and implementation of the *Affordable Care Act (ACA)*.

Indeed, the ACA is a historic step taken to improve access to healthcare for all Americans. The Initiative has worked diligently to ensure that AAPI communities are benefiting from the ACA and enrolling in the health insurance marketplace by developing in-language resources, holding educational webinars, and hosting community outreach and education events around the country. In fact, ACA's enrollment efforts include planning a series of outreach events tailored for the AAPI community. It remains an important goal to ensure that patients receive the highest quality of care.

The Initiative has also sought to address the need for disaggregated data on AAPI communities by working closely with Data.gov, the home of the US government's open data, to launch Data.gov/AAPI. The first web resource of its kind focused on a key constituency, Data.gov/AAPI is a robust data hub

---

* http://www.sapha.org/adminkit/uploads/files/BrownPaper-Nutrition.pdf
† http://www.ncbi.nlm.nih.gov/pubmed/18821101
‡ http://www.hhs.gov/ash/initiatives/hepatitis/

that allows visitors to search datasets and reports from nearly 50 federal, state, county, and city sources pertaining to Asian American, Native Hawaiian, and Pacific Islander communities. It is the Administration's goal to make federal data more accessible to the public so that it can assist federal agencies, policymakers, and researchers in better understanding and addressing disparities in AAPI socioeconomic status, educational attainment, health status, and other areas of importance.

This compilation of research and analyses on critical health conditions is an important contribution to identifying the future priorities, policy recommendations, and preventive actions that academics, community leaders, healthcare providers, and policymakers can take to improve the overall quality of healthcare that our communities need. Congratulations to the editors and authors for publishing this research, an important resource that the South Asian and public health communities can use to learn about and address the health and well-being needs of this growing population.

Kiran Ahuja is former Executive Director of the White House Initiative on Asian Americans and Pacific Islanders. Ms. Ahuja received support for this foreword from the Initiative's Director of Intergovernmental Affairs, Christine Harley. Ms. Ahuja currently serves as Chief of Staff at the US Office of Personnel Management in Washington, DC.

Editors' Note

There is a long road in the journey of taking an idea from the phase of conceptualization to completion. An immense amount of effort has gone into this work, which has truly been a labor of love. When we initially thought of a book on the health of South Asian Americans, we had no idea how much time and effort it would take to make the dream of an evidence-based book on the health of South Asian Americans a reality.

As educators, practitioners, and researchers, we recognize the impacts of growing health disparities nationally and globally, that continue to marginalize minority and underserved communities. The idea for this book came from our collective awareness of the need for more information, education, and evidence to guide efforts aimed at understanding and addressing the health needs of South Asian communities in the United States.

We thank the numerous people without whose invaluable contributions this work would not have been possible: the authors, for sharing their expertise in writing the chapters and responding to our requests for revisions; the peer reviewers, for their wisdom and meticulous review of chapters, which enabled us to enhance the quality and rigor of this work; our committed and able editorial assistants, Sejal Patel, MPH, Asra Azam, MPH, and Alexandra Green-Atchley, MPH, for their hard work and diligence in coordinating the monumental editorial process; Ms. Kiran Ahuja, for writing the foreword; the leadership of the South Asian Public Health Association, particularly the Research Committee members, for their support of this book; and our publisher, Routledge-Taylor & Francis, for recognizing the value of this work.

Last but not the least, we thank our families for their patience and unwavering support during the preparation of the book when each of us took precious personal and family time during evenings and weekends to work on the book. To the readers, this work comes to you with the acknowledgment that there are additional topic areas that we wanted to include in the book but were unable to, due to time and resource limitations. We hope the information in this book advances your learning, teaching, research, policy and program development, and facilitates any other work you are doing to improve the health and well-being of South Asian Americans.

Editors

Memoona Hasnain, MD, MHPE, PhD, is a tenured professor and associate department head, Faculty Development and Research, in the Department of Family Medicine, University of Illinois at Chicago (UIC) College of Medicine. The primary focus of Dr. Hasnain's work is at the intersection of medicine and public health, with an emphasis on interprofessional education, service, and research. Dr. Hasnain has a special interest in humanism, empathy, and social justice as core values in the teaching and practice of medicine. Addressing the social dimension of health and the gaps in health systems and policies that disadvantage vulnerable groups remain a unifying theme in her work. Dr. Hasnain is a board member of the South Asian Public Health Association and chair of the Research Committee. She is past chair of the Group on Faculty Development for the Society of Teachers of Family Medicine. Dr. Hasnain has served as Assistant Vice President for Education and Co-Director of FAIMER Institute with the Foundation for International Medical Education and Research (FAIMER), which is a non-profit foundation established by the Education Commission for Foreign Medical Graduates (ECFMG). Her work has been consistently externally funded and published in peer-reviewed journals. She is a reviewer for federal grants and several scientific journals. Dr. Hasnain has received numerous accolades for her research and teaching, including the Teaching Recognition Award by the UIC Council for Excellence in Teaching and Learning, the Health Policy and Administration Distinguished Alumni Achievement Award from UIC School of Public Health, and the Susan La Flesche Picotte, MD Health Equity Pioneer Award from UIC College of Medicine. She is a recipient of the prestigious Macy Faculty Scholars Award from the Josiah Macy Jr. Foundation. Dr. Hasnain received her medical degree from Dow Medical College, Karachi, Pakistan, and trained as an obstetrician/gynecologist. She earned her master's in health professions education and her doctorate in public health sciences from UIC.

Punam Parikh, MPH, is a project manager in the Division of General Internal Medicine & Health Services Research, the David Geffen School of Medicine at the University of California, Los Angeles (UCLA). The primary focus of her current work is quality improvement of healthcare, specifically reduction of preventable hospital readmissions, stroke care, cancer surgical outcomes, and improving the accuracy of patient demographic data. Ms. Parikh has a special interest in working with minority communities. She has managed several diabetes prevention initiatives in East Harlem, New York, and has evaluated cancer control and asthma education efforts among predominantly Black and Hispanic communities. She has published several peer-reviewed papers on this work.

Ms. Parikh has a special interest in the health of the South Asian American community. She helped conduct the first health needs assessment of South Asians in Southern California and organized a media campaign to educate South Asian women about breast and cervical cancers. Ms. Parikh served as vice president on the Board of the South Asian Public Health Association and co-chaired the Research Committee.

Ms. Parikh earned a master's degree in public health specializing in community health sciences from the Fielding School of Public Health, UCLA.

Nitasha Chaudhary Nagaraj, DrPH, MPH, is a research scientist and an adjunct faculty member at the George Washington University (GWU) Milken Institute School of Public Health. Dr. Nagaraj earned a bachelor's degree in healthcare administration and information systems from the University of Maryland, Baltimore County, in 1999, and a master's degree in public health from GWU. It was at GWU that she realized her passion for working with marginalized communities in the United States.

Her work at GWU is specific to the evaluation and monitoring of programs related to the health of women and children in the United States and globally. In her role at GWU, she has evaluated programs on domestic violence, family violence, and girls' education.

Dr. Nagaraj has worked with GWU to conduct a national needs assessment of the health of South Asians in the United States. She has supported projects, which have allowed her to create substantial relationships with community leaders and community-based organizations working with South Asians in the United States. Most recently, she supported projects that worked to better understand child sexual abuse, family violence, and type 2 diabetes among South Asians living in the United States.

Prior to joining GWU, Dr. Nagaraj worked on public health preparedness projects at the local, state, and federal levels.

Dr. Nagaraj is currently on the Board of the Global India Fund and on the Girl Rising US–India Advisory Board. She resides in Maryland with her husband and 2-year-old daughter.

Contributors

Sudha Acharya, MA, is the executive director of the South Asian Council for Social Services (SACSS) in Queens, New York, and has been active in the community for the past 35 years. She has held various leadership positions in community-based organizations. Ms. Acharya currently serves as the executive director of SACSS, after serving as the founder–president for the first 2 years. She has served on city and state healthcare coalitions. Ms. Acharya was awarded the Gandhi Community Award, Indo-Caribbean Network Award, and the Federation of Indian Associations Award. She has received numerous additional awards, including the Union Square Award for her work with SACSS in 2003, the Pravasi Bharatiya Community Service Award from Global Organization of People of Indian Origin (GOPIO) in 2006, the India Abroad Gopal Raju Award for Community Services in 2010, and the Sri Swami Vivekananda Award for Community Service in 2011. Ms. Acharya has her master's in English literature and financial management from Pace University in New York.

Neelum T. Aggarwal, MD, is co-leader of the federally funded Clinical Core at the Rush Alzheimer's Disease Research Center and an associate professor of Neurological Sciences at Rush University Medical Center in Chicago. She is also a former South Asian Public Health Association (SAPHA) board member and a member of the board of the global health nonprofit organization, Arogya World.

Dr. Aggarwal's research career focuses on how communicable diseases and other health conditions associated with aging affect cognitive function, physical activity, and mental health across an individual's lifespan. She is an expert on strategic design and execution of activities, both of which require rigorous research and clinical investigations in large population-based samples, and home-based research evaluations performed in Chicago's racially and ethnically diverse neighborhoods.

Dr. Aggarwal earned her medical degree from the Rosalind Franklin University of Medicine and Science in North Chicago, completed her neurology residency at Henry Ford Hospital in Detroit, Michigan, and completed an aging and neurodegenerative disorders fellowship at the Rush Alzheimer's Disease Center.

Smita C. Banerjee, PhD, is a behavioral scientist in the Department of Psychiatry and Behavioral Sciences at Memorial Sloan Kettering Cancer Center in New York. With an interest in the science of health communication, Dr. Banerjee's research seeks to gain a better understanding of persuasive message framing for cancer prevention and control. Specifically, her research focuses on developing a better appreciation of how to design persuasive messages regarding health risk behaviors and health promoting behavior change that can serve as the foundation for more effective media campaigns, health education, and interventions to ultimately improve cancer prevention and control outcomes. Dr. Banerjee is developing a growing track record as a funded investigator, including a recently funded R21 grant from the National Cancer Institute (of the National Institutes of Health) to examine a potential mechanism (empathic communication) to decrease perceived stigma, reduce patients' psychological distress, improve satisfaction with physicians' communication skills, and increase adherence to referral to psychosocial services and/or a Tobacco Cessation Program. She received funding from the National Institute on Drug Abuse (of the National Institutes of Health) and Center for Tobacco Products (within the Food & Drug Administration) in 2013 for an R03 grant to describe tobacco industry advertising strategies and analyze young adult perceptions of non-cigarette tobacco product advertisements. Dr. Banerjee's research also has received philanthropic funding from Goldstein Foundation in 2010, Nuffield Foundation in 2008, and Alcohol Education and Research Council in 2008. She has authored or coauthored over 65 peer-reviewed articles and book chapters establishing experience in the study of health communication, specifically health message design, narrative interventions, and tobacco control. Dr. Banerjee completed her B.S. in Home Science (with specialization in Child Development) from Lady Irwin College, University of Delhi, India; M.S. in Communication Media for Children from Srimati Nathibai Damodar Thakersey (SNDT) University, Pune, India; and Ph.D. in Health Communication from Rutgers University, New Brunswick, New Jersey.

Swagata Banik, MSc, PhD, is an associate professor in Public Health at Baldwin Wallace University in Berea, Ohio. He also serves as director of the undergraduate program in public health and the director of the Center for Health Disparities Research and Education (CHDRE) at Baldwin Wallace University. Dr. Banik's research includes examination of heterosexism among university students; examination of the intersection of sexual identity and HIV risk behavior among sexual and gender minority communities in the United States and India; and examination of factors that contribute to HIV/STI health disparities among vulnerable populations in the United States and South Asia. He has been working with men who have sex with men (MSM) and transgender communities in India for more than a decade. In a cross-cultural study, Dr. Banik and his team were the first to compare the risks associated with Internet usage among Indian MSM compared with their US counterparts. He is currently examining the preliminary effects of a stigma reduction intervention among healthcare providers in India in order to enhance healthcare access in male to female transgender communities in India. Dr. Banik utilizes mix-method and community-based participatory approaches in his research.

Sehrish Bari, MPH, is a research associate at Columbia University's Center on Globalization and Sustainable Development. She was previously a Research and Outreach Specialist with the Immigrant Health and Cancer Disparities Service at Memorial Sloan-Kettering Cancer Center. Ms. Bari has a background in public health and social science research and has worked on emerging issues in South Asian health in the United States for years. Her current focus is on economic development and global health issues in sub-Saharan Africa. Ms. Bari has her master's in public health from New York University.

Monideepa Bhattacharya Becerra, DrPH, MPH, is an assistant professor in the Department of Health Science and Human Ecology, College of Natural Sciences, California State University, San Bernardino. Dr. Becerra spearheaded a needs assessment program for domestic violence survivors in Inland Southern California and served as a population health data analyst for 23 nonprofit hospitals, where she conducted the Community Health Needs Assessment mandate of the Patient Protection and Affordable Care Act.

Dr. Becerra was recently awarded a fellowship as part of the US Department of Veterans Affairs National Diversity Internship Program and is currently a research consultant in the Department of Research at William S. Middleton Memorial Veterans Hospital. Dr. Becerra also teaches undergraduate and graduate courses in public health, is the faculty advisor for Eta Sigma Gamma Honorary Society, Delta Delta chapter, and coordinator for the Health Scholars Program. Dr. Becerra also serves as a research mentor, with several students publishing in peer-reviewed journals and a recent student winning the Robert Friis Best Student Public Health Practice Award for research on determinants of dietary practices among Asian Americans. She is a current board member for the South Asian Public Health Association. As a health disparities researcher, Dr. Becerra continues to address chronic disease epidemiology and the interplay between clinical risk factors and social determinants of such health outcomes, resulting in several peer-reviewed publications. Some of her recent research has highlighted the relationship between acculturation and cardiovascular risk behaviors, the comorbid conditions of asthma and obesity, and premature diabetes risk in the South Asian population.

Dr. Becerra earned her doctorate in public health, health education from Loma Linda University, California, and also has her master's in public health, health policy and leadership.

Neetu Chawla, PhD, MPH, is a research scientist at the Division of Research, Kaiser Permanente Northern California. Dr. Chawla uses both quantitative and qualitative methods in conducting cancer-related health services research. Her interests include quality of cancer-care delivery, patient–provider communication, provider-care delivery patterns, and care coordination between providers in managing cancer patients. She is also interested in disparities in patient experiences and outcomes and assessing care-delivery patterns among patients with multiple chronic conditions.

Dr. Chawla earned her bachelor's in English literature from the University of California, Berkeley, and her MPH and PhD degrees from the Fielding School of Public Health, University of California, Los Angeles. She completed a three-year postdoctoral fellowship at the National Cancer Institute in cancer prevention and control.

Ken Russell Coelho, MSc, DHSc(c), is a commissioner on the Alameda County Public Health Commission and also serves on the board of Goa Sudharop, a service organization that promotes the continued development of Goa, India.

Mr. Coelho is the author of several peer-reviewed publications in healthcare and has worked for local health departments and hospitals in the public sector for more than 8 years. He was recently appointed as a site visitor for the Public Health Accreditation Board (PHAB), a non-partisan accreditation agency responsible for accrediting health departments in the United States.

Dr. Coelho attended the University of California, Berkeley, and the University of California, San Francisco.

Sadhna Diwan, PhD, is a professor in the School of Social Work at San Jose State University and Director of the Center for Healthy Aging in Multicultural Populations (CHAMP) in San Jose. Dr. Diwan's research focuses on understanding the use of home- and community-based services and case management, particularly in older adults with dementia, depression, and chronic illnesses, and understanding factors related to the physical and psychological well-being of older immigrants. Her research has been funded by the National Institute on Aging, the John A. Hartford Foundation, the California Endowment, the Centers for Disease Control and Prevention, and others. Dr. Diwan has published extensively on health and mental health among older South Asian immigrants and has collaborated with the City of Fremont's Department of Human Services to develop curricula and provide training for the Community Ambassadors for Seniors Program.

Dr. Diwan serves on two Advisory Boards, Sourcewise, the Area Agency on Aging in Santa Clara County, and SVCN, the Silicon Valley Council of Non-Profits. She previously served on the Ethnogeriatrics Committee of the American Geriatrics Society and is a member of the Council of Ethnogeriatric Specialists at the Stanford Geriatric Education Center at Stanford University.

She has her master's in social administration and a PhD in social welfare from Case Western Reserve University. Dr. Diwan completed a postdoctoral fellowship from the National Institute on Aging at the University of Michigan.

Ami Gandhi, JD, has served as executive director of the South Asian American Policy & Research Institute (SAAPRI) since 2011. SAAPRI is a non-profit, non-partisan organization established in 2001 to improve the lives of South Asian Americans in the Chicago area by using research to formulate equitable and socially responsible public policy recommendations. SAAPRI's work has included initiatives on civic engagement, language access, healthcare access, prevention of violence and hate crimes, immigration reform, and immigrant integration.

Ms. Gandhi is an attorney who is passionate about advocating for minority and immigrant communities. She frequently writes, teaches, and speaks on racial justice and civil rights issues. She was named as the 2012–2013 Balgopal Lecturer on Human Rights and Asian Americans by the University of Illinois at Urbana-Champaign. In 2014, she was honored as an everyday "she-ro" by the National Asian Pacific Women's Forum.

Ms. Gandhi also works with a broad spectrum of organizations across Chicago. She serves on the Advisory Council for the city of Chicago's Office of New Americans, the State of Illinois Task Force on Language Access to Government Services, and the Task Force on Opportunities for DREAMers at the University of Illinois at Chicago. She serves as the board chair of Common Cause Illinois and as a board member of the American Civil Liberties Union of Illinois. She is a volunteer attorney for Coordinated Advice and Referral Program for Legal Services (CARPLS), which runs a legal aid hotline for low-income residents of Cook County. Ms. Gandhi is a member of the Illinois State Bar Association.

Ms. Gandhi earned her law degree from the George Washington University Law School and her bachelor's in psychology and cognitive science from Indiana University.

Anisha D. Gandhi, PhD, MPH, is a postdoctoral fellow at the HIV Center for Clinical and Behavioral Studies at Columbia University and the New York State Psychiatric Institute. As an epidemiologist, her research focuses chiefly on the interplay between structural forces, social environments, and sexual and reproductive health outcomes. Dr. Gandhi's previous work has highlighted the shifting demography of immigrants in the United States and its implications for accessing critical health services as well as the relationship between mobility and sexually transmitted infections (including HIV) among marginalized racial/ethnic minorities.

Francesca Gany, MD, MS, is the founding chief of the Immigrant Health and Cancer Disparities Service and the Center for Immigrant Health and Cancer Disparities at Memorial Sloan Kettering Cancer Center, New York City. She has served as the principal investigator (PI) on a number of innovative immigrant health studies in the areas of cancer, language access and cultural competence, health, healthcare access, and cardiovascular disease. Dr. Gany has a strong interest in cultural responsiveness in medicine and has created a medical interpreting research lab in order to build the knowledge base on linguistically competent research and care. Her research has led to the development of long-term immigrant health policy and programmatic changes.

As a result of the significant health disparities facing the large and growing South Asian population in the United States, Dr. Gany spearheaded the development of the South Asian Health Initiative and has been an investigator on several NIH-funded studies examining cancer and cardiovascular disease risk reduction in South Asian communities. Most recently, Dr. Gany served as the PI on the NIHMD-funded R13, "Cardiovascular Disease and Cancer Risk in South Asians: From Research to Practice and Policy," with partners in California and Chicago. This initiative brought national and international experts together to develop a consensus-driven research blueprint for addressing South Asian health disparities.

Dr. Gany has her bachelor's from Yale University, her medical degree from Mount Sinai School of Medicine, and her master's in health policy and management from the New York University Wagner Graduate School of Public Service.

Bindu Garapaty, holds a doctorate degree in clinical psychology (PsyD) and is the co-founder of an executive coaching company, The Happy Leader, LLC. Her research has focused on leadership development, cultural identity and self-awareness. Her pioneering training model incorporates identity development, sustaining well-being, leadership style, and mentorship. The training curricula focus on increasing happiness, improving performance, overcoming adversity and enhancing the human experience of resiliency for youth and adults. Dr. Garapaty's presentations have included both national and international forums in areas of leadership, education, and women's health.

As a Maternal/Child health consultant, Dr. Garapaty has worked with University of Illinois at Chicago and NorthShore University HealthSystems to advance public awareness and understanding of perinatal mood disorders. She has worked on a statewide innovative model in perinatal mental health, supported by Federal and State funding agencies. She has also served as an executive board member on 2020Mom and Post Partum Support International, organizations dedicated and influential in improving healthcare delivery for women's mental health.

Navkiranjit Gill, MPH, is a current research associate with the David Geffen School of Medicine, Department of Family Medicine at the University of California, Los Angeles. Ms. Gill's research experience is in HIV, tuberculosis, substance abuse, mental disorders, stigma, and cardiovascular diseases. Her interest lies in using social media and technology in health dissemination in order to change health behaviors.

Ms. Gill earned her bachelor's in anthropology and psychobiology and master's degree in public health from the College of Natural Sciences, California State University, San Bernardino.

Deepika Goyal, PhD, RN, FNP-C, is a professor of nursing at the Valley Foundation School of Nursing, in the College of Applied Sciences and Arts at California State University, San José.

As a family nurse practitioner, Dr. Goyal has worked in several areas including women's health, family practice, and occupational health. Currently, Dr. Goyal maintains a clinical practice caring for childbearing women in an OB/GYN office in Mountain View, California. In her academic role, Dr. Goyal teaches undergraduate, graduate, and doctor of nursing practice coursework in the areas of maternal-child health, research methods, proposal writing, and diversity.

The primary focus of Dr. Goyal's research is in the area of well-being and timely identification and treatment of postpartum depression among diverse childbearing families. Her current research emphasizes postpartum depression rates and risk factors among Asian Americans with a specific interest in identifying the role that cultural values play in mental health help-seeking behavior. Dr. Goyal has several peer-reviewed research publications in the areas of rates and risk factors of postpartum depression among diverse women; the role of cultural values in mental health help-seeking behavior; and the risk of sleep disturbance and infant temperament on developing postpartum depression.

Dr. Goyal earned her bachelor's and master's degrees in nursing from San José State University, José where she also earned certification as a family nurse practitioner. She earned her doctorate in nursing with a minor in education at the University of California, San Francisco.

Memoona Hasnain, MD, MHPE, PhD, is a professor and associate department head for Faculty Development and Research in the Department of Family Medicine, College of Medicine at the University of Illinois at Chicago (UIC). The primary focus of Dr. Hasnain's work is at the intersection of medicine and public health, with an emphasis on interprofessional education, service, and research. Dr. Hasnain has a special interest in humanism, empathy, and social justice as core values in the teaching and practice of medicine. As a medical educator and public health scientist, addressing the social dimension of health and the gaps in health systems and policies that disadvantaged vulnerable groups remain a unifying theme in her work. Dr. Hasnain's work in health disparities and health professions education converges on developing scholars and leaders, and finding effective ways to ensure quality care, particularly for vulnerable populations. Her key contributions to science are interlinked and collectively aim to improve patient-centered care and address health disparities. In addition to research advocacy and individual mentoring and guidance, she have developed and implemented academic programs organized in four themes: interprofessional collaborative education and practice; civic role, service learning, and community engagement; cultural sensitivity, competency, and inclusiveness; and wellness, resilience, and student success. These themes are woven into successful ongoing programs for undergraduate, graduate, and continuing education, with a special focus on building the health workforce pipeline.

Dr. Hasnain is the principal architect of several educational innovations, including UIC College of Medicine's longitudinal Patient-centered Medicine Scholars Program and Interprofessional Approaches to Health Disparities. Over the past 13 years, Dr. Hasnain has developed and taught a course titled International Women's Health: Current and Emerging Issues for PhD and master's students at the UIC School of Public Health. She is past chair of the group on Faculty Development for the Society of Teachers of Family Medicine. Dr. Hasnain has served as Assistant Vice President for Education and Co-Director of FAIMER Institute with the Foundation for International Medical Education and Research (FAIMER), which is a non-profit foundation established by the Education Commission for Foreign Medical Graduates (ECFMG).

Dr. Hasnain's work has been consistently externally funded and published in peer-reviewed journals. She is a reviewer for federal grants and several scientific journals. Dr. Hasnain has received numerous accolades for her research and teaching, including the Teaching Recognition Award by the UIC Council for Excellence in Teaching and Learning, the Health Policy and Administration Distinguished Alumni Achievement Award from the UIC School of Public Health, and the Susan La Flesche Picotte, MD Health Equity Pioneer Award from the UIC College of Medicine. She is also a recipient of the prestigious Macy Faculty Scholars Award from the Josiah Macy Jr. Foundation. This award is given to select educators nationally to accelerate needed reforms in health professions education to accommodate the dramatic changes occurring in medical practice and health-care delivery.

Dr. Hasnain earned her medical degree from Dow Medical College, Karachi, Pakistan, and her master's in health professions education and doctorate in public health sciences from UIC.

Susan L. Ivey, MD, MHSA, is an adjunct professor at the University of California, Berkeley (UCB) School of Public Health. She is the director of research for Health Research for Action, a UCB research center that translates research into action, particularly for Asian American populations. Dr. Ivey is also a family physician and medical director for the City of Berkeley's clinic system. In addition to her doctorate in medicine (board-certified in Family Medicine), she also has a master's in health services administration (MHSA). Dr. Ivey has two years of postdoctoral research training in health services and health policy.

Satya S. Jonnalagadda, PhD, MBA, RD, is director of Global Nutrition at the Kerry Health and Nutrition Institute in Beloit, Wisconsin. Dr. Jonnalagadda is responsible for leading Kerry's internal and external nutrition positioning, while staying abreast of proposed food regulations and identifying new nutrition opportunities. She has more than 20 years of experience in nutrition. She recently served as principal scientist for the Bell Institute of Health and Nutrition at General Mills. She has also held various roles in global research and development for Novartis Nutrition Corporation, was an associate professor at Georgia State University, Atlanta, and a clinical dietitian and later adjunct associate professor of nutrition at the University of Minnesota, Minneapolis. Dr. Jonnalagadda holds a master's in science nutrition from Case Western Reserve University, an MBA from Augsburg College, Minneapolis, Minnesota, and a PhD in human nutrition and foods from Virginia Polytechnic Institute and State University in Blacksburg. Dr. Jonnalagadda completed her dietetic internship program at Georgia State University and is a registered dietitian.

Alison Karasz, PhD, is a cross-cultural and clinical psychologist and member of the research faculty of the Department of Family and Social Medicine at the Albert Einstein College of Medicine, New York. She has been conducting research on South Asian health and mental health for the past 25 years. Dr. Karasz earned her bachelor's from Harvard University and PhD in clinical psychology from the City University of New York. Her dissertation, *Role Strain in Pakistani Immigrant Women*, supported by an NIMH grant, was a mixed methods study of women's health and mental health in a mosque community in Queens. Dr. Karasz served as a postdoctoral fellow at Rutgers Institute for Health, Healthcare Policy and Aging Research. She joined the Department of Family Medicine at the Albert Einstein College of Medicine in 1999, where she has conducted numerous studies in the areas of health and mental health, particularly related to primary care populations. Much of her research has focused on examining conceptual representations of mental disorder across cultures, using Leventhal's Illness Representation model. She has been the principal investigator on five NIH research grants, two of which focused on depression and other common mental disorders among South Asian immigrant women. Dr. Karasz has published 50 articles in the scientific literature and is the author of nearly a dozen papers on South Asian health and mental health. In 2007, she was awarded a planning grant to partner with Bangladeshi women in the Bronx and develop new models for treating depression. In 2008, in order to meet the needs of women in the community she co-founded Sapna NYC, a nonprofit organization serving South Asian women in New York City to improve health, enhance economic empowerment, and help build a collective voice for change. Today, Sapna's innovative, award-winning programs serve over 400 women per year. Dr. Karasz is also a psychotherapist with a private practice in Brooklyn, New York.

Sundes Kazmir, MD, is a pediatrics resident at the School of Medicine. Dr. Kazmir earned her medical degree from New York University School of Medicine. She has a bachelor's degree in Arabic and Middle East Studies from Bryn Mawr College and has been involved in South Asian student groups at both the undergraduate and graduate levels. She is considering both primary care and subspecialty interests within pediatrics, but has a particular interest in working with immigrant and underserved populations.

Sindhura Kodali, MD, is a pediatrics resident at the University of California, San Francisco. She completed her medical training at the University of Michigan and also earned a master's in public health at the Harvard School of Public Health with concentrations in quantitative methods and public health leadership.

Prior to her medical training, Dr. Kodali was a fellow at South Asian Youth Action (SAYA) in Queens, New York. She helped launch a mentoring and counseling program for recently immigrated South Asian youth. She earned her bachelor's from Dartmouth College in Asian and Middle Eastern studies with a focus on South Asia. She has also worked closely with Valarie Kaur and the Groundswell Movement to advocate for civil rights for South Asians and Sikh Americans and bring attention to health disparities among South Asians. Her research interests include mental health among South Asians, particularly youth, strengthening healthcare systems in underserved areas, and increasing healthcare access for immigrant communities. She has coauthored articles for scholarly journals and the media on the social determinants of health and health disparities affecting South Asians.

Rashmi Kudesia, MD, is a reproductive endocrinologist and infertility specialist at Reproductive Medicine Associates in Brooklyn, New York. Her clinical and research interests include polycystic ovary syndrome (PCOS), as well as expanding access to and reducing disparities in fertility knowledge and treatment. These areas of inquiry all relate to her ongoing projects investigating the prevalence and phenotype of PCOS in ethnic groups that are believed to be at high risk, namely Latinas and South Asians. This body of work was partially a result of her longstanding involvement in the South Asian American community, during childhood and throughout her training as president of multiple student organizations, a volunteer at SAKHI for South Asian Women, in New York City, NY, and a member of various groups and listservs addressing the needs of the South Asian American community. Dr. Kudesia is currently exploring methods for reducing morbidity in PCOS among South Asian women in the United States, a population at elevated risk for diabetes and cardiovascular disease due to both ethnicity and PCOS diagnosis.

Dr. Kudesia attended Brown University and the Duke University School of Medicine. She completed her residency in Obstetrics and Gynecology at the New York Hospital/Weill Cornell Medical College in New York City, NY and a fellowship in reproductive endocrinology and infertility at the Montefiore Medical Center/Albert Einstein College of Medicine in the Bronx. She has presented research abstracts at national and international conferences, including the American Society for Reproductive Medicine, the Society for Gynecologic Investigation, and the American College of Obstetricians and Gynecologists. Dr. Kudesia has also received grant funding to support her work and has published a number of peer-reviewed articles.

Jennifer Leng, MD, MPH, is a faculty member at the Immigrant Health and Cancer Disparities Service at Memorial Sloan Kettering Cancer Center in New York City. Dr. Leng attended Tufts University School of Medicine where she completed degrees in medicine and public health. She has extensive experience working with the South Asian immigrant community, with early exposure to the vulnerabilities and needs of the South Asian immigrant population during her medical training. While in medical school, Dr. Leng spent a year working in Dhaka, Bangladesh, examining the impact of women's work in the garment industry on the health and well-being of their children.

As a researcher in the Immigrant Health and Cancer Disparities Service, Dr. Leng has been a principal investigator or an investigator for a number of studies addressing the needs of the South Asian community, with numerous publications.

Kasuen Mauldin, PhD, RD, is an assistant professor in the Department of Nutrition, Food Science & Packaging at San Jose State University (SJSU) in California. She earned her PhD in molecular and biochemical nutrition from the University of California, Berkeley, and completed her clinical dietetic internship at the University of California, San Francisco Medical Center. Dr. Mauldin was trained in metabolic biology with a focus on lipoprotein homeostasis.

Dr. Mauldin's work on triglyceride metabolism has provided insight into possible mechanisms for targeting prevention and treatment strategies in cardiovascular disease. In addition to basic science research, Dr. Mauldin conducts clinical studies aimed at better understanding the relationship between diet and metabolism, and identifying specific dietary interventions that improve metabolism in individuals with chronic diseases.

Dr. Mauldin is a passionate educator, interested in effectively teaching science curriculum in dietetics education. Her honors include the 2014 California Dietetics Association Excellence in Research Award and the 2015 Academy of Nutrition and Dietetics Outstanding Dietetics Educator Award. She is an active member of the Nutrition and Dietetics Educators and Preceptors (NDEP) practice group, and the SJSU Center for Healthy Aging in a Multicultural Population (CHAMP).

Kala M. Mehta, DSc, is an assistant professor in the Department of Epidemiology and Biostatistics at the University of California, San Francisco. She has devoted her career to racially and ethnically diverse older adults. Her publications span several important topics on aging, including functional limitation, depression/anxiety, cognitive impairment, and Alzheimer's disease/dementia. Dr. Mehta has received accolades for teaching and mentoring, and her research on race/ethnic disparities in Alzheimer's disease has been quoted in *The New York Times*. Dr. Mehta also teaches clinical research design to medical students, residents, fellows, and international faculty using cutting-edge online education technologies. She earned her doctorate in epidemiology from the Erasmus University Medical School in Rotterdam, the Netherlands, and acquired postdoctoral specialization at The Johns Hopkins Bloomberg School of Public Health.

Mary V. Modayil, PhD, MSPH, currently works on improving upstream determinants of health within primary health care in Alberta, Canada. She previously worked as an epidemiologist and principal biostatistician with the Institute for Population Health Improvement at the University of California Davis Medical Center. Her research interests focus on interventions addressing health disparities, epidemiology and media interventions. Dr. Modayil has worked on a number of projects related to South Asians, including the California Tobacco Control Program to adapt and evaluate CDC communities of excellence indicators in order to improve tobacco control strategies at the state and community level. She also created, tailored, and evaluated campaign messaging for policy-makers and the general public. She has worked with California's statewide mini-grants program to provide outreach to California communities at risk for tobacco disparities. This includes quantifying the extent of alternative tobacco products used, effective tobacco control strategies and increasing outreach to South Asian populations. She has published several peer-reviewed manuscripts examining strategies to close gaps in tobacco control policy in order to reach vulnerable populations. Dr. Modayil earned a master's degree in public health in population health studies from the University of Alberta, Canada and a PhD in cancer epidemiology from the University of South Carolina.

Anita Mudan, MD, is an emergency medicine resident at the University of Pennsylvania. Dr. Mudan earned her medical degree at New York University School of Medicine. She also has a bachelors degree in Biochemistry from New York University. Throughout medical school, Dr. Mudan worked with Dr. Amitasrigowri Murthy on research involving diabetes in South Asian immigrants in NYC, with a focus on gestational diabetes and dietary risk factors.

Arnab Mukherjea, DrPH, MPH, is an assistant professor of Health Sciences (Public & Community Health) at California State University, East Bay, California. He also maintains formal research affiliations with the University of California, San Francisco and the University of California, Davis. His research interest include analyzing how cultural contexts, behaviors, and identity play a direct role in disparate health outcomes, particularly among South Asians in the United States and other understudied minority populations. Dr. Mukherjea has published peer-reviewed academic journal articles and presented scientific research examining the nexus between culture and behavior among South Asian Americans. He has received research funding from the National Cancer Institute (of the National Institutes for Health), Centers for Disease Control & Prevention, Office of Minority Health, and state of California's Tobacco-Related Disease Research Program. Dr. Mukherjea serves on the Research & Data Subcommittee of the Asian Pacific Partners for Empowerment, Leadership, & Advocacy. He is a Core Member of the Asian American Research Center on Health, an affiliated researcher with Health Research for Action at the University of California, Berkeley School of Public Health, and represents South Asian health interests for the California Health Interview Survey (CHIS). Dr. Mukherjea has taught undergraduate and graduate public health classes at the University of California and California State University systems since 1998. Dr. Mukherjea earned a doctorate of public health in applied health disparities research, a master's degree in public health in health & social behavior/multicultural health, and a bachelor of arts degree in molecular & cell biology (neurobiology; minor in education) from the University of California, Berkeley.

Amitasrigowri Murthy, MD, MPH, FACOG, is the director of the Reproductive Choice Service at Bellevue Hospital, and the division director of Family Planning at New York University (NYU) Langone Medical Center in New York City. After earning her medical degree at SUNY Health Science Center at Brooklyn (Downstate), Dr. Murthy completed her residency in obstetrics and gynecology at Boston University School of Medicine. She completed a fellowship in family planning and clinical care research at the University of Pittsburgh. Dr. Murthy is a board-certified obstetrician/gynecologist and has been director of the Reproductive Choice Service since joining the department in 2010. She is also an assistant professor at NYU School of Medicine and has been director of the Fellowship in family planning at NYU since 2012. Previously, Dr. Murthy was an assistant professor at Albert Einstein School of Medicine in the Department of Obstetrics, Gynecology and Women's Health. She was also the director of family planning at Jacobi Medical Center, as well as the medical director of the Title X clinic at Jacobi. Her specific interests in family planning include issues surrounding obesity and efficacy of contraception, intrauterine devices, and timing related to completion of pregnancy as well as the reproductive health of immigrants.

Dr. Murthy has published multiple articles in peer-reviewed journals, as well as various chapters in textbooks, and has completed a number of research projects related to contraception and reproductive health. This research included evaluation of a new program of post-placental IUD insertion at Bellevue Hospital, completion of a project investigating side effects of doxycycline in women undergoing medication abortion, and evaluation of the opinions of Spanish-speaking women regarding the website Bedsider.org. Dr. Murthy is also involved in creating a curriculum to teach medical students how to recognize patients who may be sexually exploited for commercial gain.

Minal Patel, PhD, MPH, is a Cancer Prevention Fellow at the Behavioral Research Program of the Division of Cancer Control and Population Sciences at the National Cancer Institute. Her career in cancer prevention and control research spans over a decade with a broad spectrum of research interests, including a particular focus on the impact of social, built, and policy environments on lifestyle behaviors and their relation to cancer. Dr. Patel utilizes a unique interdisciplinary research approach while working with both the Health Behaviors Research Branch and the Tobacco Control Research Branch to explore and better understand contextual factors related to cancer on vulnerable populations including young adults, adolescents, and underserved communities.

Dr. Patel has been involved in several projects focusing on South Asian health. These include a health needs assessment of underserved South Asian subgroups to evaluate tobacco use among Asian Indians. She also works with community groups, including Saath in California, to create culturally relevant cancer-related prevention and diagnosis intervention programs. She has consulted with the South Asian Network on projects related to tobacco utilizing community-based participatory research (CBPR) methods. Dr. Patel is involved in various community advocacy efforts. He served as vice chair for the Los Angeles County Tobacco Free Coalition and the APHA API Caucus and SAPHA, which provide a voice for Asian American health issues.

Dr. Patel earned her bachelor's in psychology from the University of California, Berkeley, and her master's in public health from San Diego State University, with a specialization in health promotion and behavioral sciences. She completed her PhD in public health in the Department of Community Health Sciences, with a minor in urban planning at the University of California, Los Angeles.

Viraj Patel, MD, MPH, is an assistant professor of medicine, clinician–investigator in the Division of General Internal Medicine at the Albert Einstein College of Medicine/Montefiore Health System, in the Bronx. He is also on faculty in the Primary Care/Social Internal Medicine residency program for Albert Einstein. His research centers on innovative community-engaged approaches to HIV prevention with gay, bisexual, and other same gender loving men and transgender communities in both the United States and India.

Dr. Patel's current work focuses on developing technology-based behavioral interventions, including social media and mobile apps, to reach and engage these "hidden" communities, as well as to leverage online social networks to promote behavior change. Dr. Patel also teaches in the primary care/social internal medicine residency program and instructs medical students in the care of LGBT populations. Dr. Patel is active in community-based settings and serves in an advisory capacity for an India-based nonprofit organization that works to promote the health and human rights of LGBT communities in India. He also serves on various civic committees related to improving the health of marginalized communities in New York City.

Dr. Patel earned his medical degree from the Medical University of South Carolina and completed his residency training at Montefiore Health System in the Primary Care/Social Internal Medicine program. He later completed a clinical and public health research fellowship in the Department of Social Medicine and earned his master's degree in public health at the Albert Einstein College of Medicine, with a focus on community-based participatory research.

Lakshmi Prasad, MPH, is the program manager for the Ohio Perinatal Quality Collaborative. She earned her master's in public health from The Johns Hopkins University. She was previously based at the Immigrant Health and Cancer Disparities Service at Memorial Sloan Kettering Cancer Center (MSKCC), where she coordinated the South Asian Health Initiative (SAHI) and the Taxi Network, with the goal of bridging health disparities and focusing on oral cancer, diabetes, high blood pressure, and high cholesterol. Ms. Prasad conducted field research in New Delhi, India, surveying rural and remote villages to determine social determinants impacting access to reproductive health in India's most disenfranchised communities.

Padma Rangaswamy, PhD, is the cofounder of SAAPRI (South Asian American Policy and Research Institute), a historian, and author of several works on the Asian Indian immigrant experience. Among her major works are *Namaste America: Indian Immigrants in an American Metropolis* (2000), a comprehensive study of Indian Americans, and *Indian Americans: The New Immigrants Series* (2007*)*, a secondary level reader chronicling the achievements and struggles of Indian Americans in North America. Dr. Rangaswamy has coauthored a pictorial history, *Asian Indians of Chicago* (2003), and contributed several encyclopedia and journal articles on the South Asian diaspora and American immigration in major publications including *Immigrants in American History* (2013), *Asian American History and Culture* (2010), and *Encyclopedia of Diasporas* (2006).

Dr. Rangaswamy has taught courses on world immigration and South Asian history at Chicago area universities and colleges. As an active and involved member of Chicago's Asian Indian community, she has served on the boards of many nonprofit organizations and helped found the Indo-American Heritage Museum (www.iahmuseum.org). Her research interests include the worldwide South Asian diaspora, the Chicago Asian-Indian community, and preservation of the history of South Asian American immigration. She has her PhD in history and her master's in English from the University of Illinois at Chicago.

Zul Surani, BS, is the executive director for community partnerships at the University of Southern California's (USC) Health Sciences Campus where he directs partnerships that enable community development activities in underserved communities surrounding the campus. He has been an ardent advocate for health and research in the South Asian community for over a decade. He is passionate about cancer education, research, and advocacy and is even more dedicated to the cause after losing his mother to cancer.

Mr. Surani has a bachelor's in public administration with a specialization in health care administration from USC and is currently working on his master's in public health, also at USC. He has served as the community coinvestigator on several research studies involving South Asian communities and has coauthored articles reporting the results in various publications and at national conference presentations. Through these studies, cancer prevention and control needs of the various South Asian communities were identified, including those within specific subgroups. Research was conducted in partnership with

UCLA's Division of Cancer Prevention and Control Research and Claremont Graduate University.

Mr. Surani has also been involved in the development and testing of health education interventions in South Asian communities. He cofounded the Community Health Action Initiative at the South Asian Network in Artesia, California where he served on the board and helped build the agency's health programs. He then went on to develop many other health programs benefiting South Asians, including a Bollywood-style fotonovela to educate South Asian women on breast cancer early detection. Mr. Surani also cofounded Saath USA, an organization that contributes to new research and the development of many new prevention education interventions to benefit the community. Most recently, he served as chair for the Asian and Pacific Islander National Cancer Survivors Network.

Divya Talwar, MPH, is a doctoral student in the Division of Health Education at Texas A&M University. Her research interests include cancer prevention, genomics, autism, and health disparities. She possesses unique multidisciplinary training with a degree in public health, clinical dentistry, and research experience in hospitals, civic centers, and local communities. Ms. Talwar currently works at the Health Promotion and Genomics Lab with a focus on genomics, cancer prevention, and autism spectrum disorder. She has presented her research at international, national, and state levels. She has also published articles in high impact factor journals.

Ms. Talwar has worked on various research aspects, including formulating appropriate research design (qualitative, quantitative, and mixed-methods), survey development, preparation of institutional review board (IRB) protocols, data collection and analysis, and interpretation of results. She is the chair of the student section for the American Public Health Association and was selected for a service award for outstanding commitment and contribution. Ms. Talwar earned her bachelor's in dentistry from India and her master's in public health from Texas A&M University.

Rajiv Ulpe, MPH, BDS, is a predoctoral student in the Department of Biobehavioral Health at Pennsylvania State University. His research focuses on the young adult cancer survivor population, specifically those coping with survivorship and lifestyle adjustments following cancer treatment.

At the University of Maryland, Mr. Ulpe worked on tobacco cessation intervention planning for Asian sub-groups in Montgomery County, with research focused on alternative tobacco products. He has also worked at the Cancer Institute of New Jersey (CINJ) (now part of Rutgers University) as a community health educator examining health issues for the South Asian population living in the New York metropolitan area. Mr. Ulpe coordinated a National Cancer Institute-funded project on alternative tobacco products used by South Asians. As the study coordinator, he helped strengthen CINJ's connections with local South Asian communities.

Mr. Ulpe earned his master's in public health in community health education from the University of Maryland, College Park and his bachelor's in dentistry from India.

BACKGROUND 1

Chapter 1

South Asian Americans: A Demographic and Socioeconomic Profile

Padma Rangaswamy, Ami Gandhi,
Anisha D. Gandhi, and Memoona Hasnain

Contents

Abstract

Objective: To provide key sociodemographic information about South Asian Americans (SAAs), including a historical overview and evolution of this population over time. Available data and statistics are also linked to key public health concerns in order to guide and facilitate the development of appropriate interventions aimed at improving the health and well-being of the South Asian community in the United States.

Key Findings: SAAs are a large and diverse community and one of the fastest-growing minority groups in the United States. Although they are among the most highly educated and highest income earners in the country, their success is not evenly distributed. There is a lack of detailed, disaggregated data available to reveal the unique characteristics of each subgroup of South Asians. There is, however, ample evidence to suggest that, while some SAAs are highly successful and have integrated well in the United States, other members of this population face a variety of obstacles, including difficulty in accessing and utilizing healthcare due to linguistic, cultural, economic, educational, social, and immigration-related issues.

Recommendations: Given the dearth of disaggregated data that would help to guide the development and implementation of culturally appropriate services, for SAA subgroups broad recommendations are offered that can be applied to SAAs as a whole. This includes raising awareness of and addressing the health needs of SAAs through more affordable healthcare coverage and development of more inclusive health policies and culturally appropriate services. Finally, there is need for more in-depth research to identify and address the unique needs of this fast-growing population.

Introduction

According to the 2010 U.S. Census, there are more than 3.4 million South Asians in the United States, making the South Asian American (SAA) population one of the fastest-growing ethnic groups in the country (U.S. Census Bureau, 2010). Over the years, the patterns of immigration for this population have varied widely, creating an ethnic community with remarkable socioeconomic diversity. The heterogeneity of the South Asian diaspora in the United States is largely based on immigration history and policies, as well as on evolving immigration patterns.

One element of this diversity is the difference in their countries of origin. These include Bangladesh, Bhutan, India, Maldives, Nepal, Pakistan, and

Sri Lanka. The number of Indian and Pakistani immigrants to the United States far outnumbers the other South Asian subgroups. Immigrants from India are known as "Indian Americans" but referred to as "Asian Indians" by the U.S. Census and other data sets. Other immigrants are referred to as "Hyphenated Americans" based on their country of origin, such as Pakistani-Americans, Bangladeshi-Americans, and so on.

The diversity in the SAA population is further enhanced by the varying histories of the immigrants. There are those who arrived in the United States over the course of more than two centuries and those of South Asian descent who came to the United States from other parts of the world, such as Africa, the Caribbean, Canada, Europe, and the Middle East. These families have immigrated one or more times and carry their own histories of discrimination or persecution from their various homelands of adoption. These histories, in turn, influence their social and economic integration into American society. Different motivations for migrating can also deeply and differently affect their sense of place (or displacement) as well as their mental and physical well-being.

There are an estimated 450,000 undocumented Asian Indians in the United States (Pew Research Center, 2014). Because they are less likely to be included in the U.S. Census count, their existence often goes unrecognized in official policy and is even denied by some South Asians who prefer the image of their community to be a model minority that does not include a contingent living and working in the United States without authorization (Hoefer, Rytina, & Baker, 2012).

The vast linguistic and cultural diversity of South Asians—and the corresponding wide range of health needs and priorities—present substantial challenges in providing culturally appropriate and effective health services. Thus, in order to more fully examine the health concerns of the SAA population, it is important to rely not only on decennial census data, but also on interim data from the *American Community Survey* produced by the U.S. Census Bureau to provide vital information on a yearly basis (U.S. Census Bureau, n.d.). These data are based on estimates and also provide the most recent figures on the community's demographic and socioeconomic characteristics. A study of these data reveals the need for more broad-based and inclusive public health research and policies. An obvious example is the need to go beyond the Affordable Care Act, which is a boon to citizens and permanent residents, but is not available as a resource for the substantial number of undocumented immigrants and holders of certain types of immigrant visas.

An Early History of Struggle and Survival

Though the majority of South Asians arrived in the United States after 1965, as discussed further in the next section, their presence in America dates as far back as the late nineteenth century. The first official record of a South Asian immigrant is of a solitary Indian admitted to the United States in 1820. Between 1820 and 1900, a total of 715 more South Asians came as adventurers, merchants, and seamen. It is believed that they either returned home or were absorbed into the local population (Jensen, 1980). The first substantial immigration of South Asians to the United States took place in the first two decades of the twentieth century, when more than 7,000 Punjabi farmers who were displaced by British land reforms left India to seek their fortune in the Pacific Northwest. They were lured by the promise of economic opportunity in the logging, construction, and railroad industries. Many eventually settled into agricultural careers in California but, like other Asian Americans, they were banned by discriminatory federal and state laws from owning land, acquiring citizenship, or marrying Caucasian women. Subsequently, many of the Punjabi immigrants married Mexican women and raised families in a unique Punjabi-Mexican culture (Leonard, 1992).

Between 1920 and the period leading up to World War II in 1939, discriminatory federal legislation, formulated in response to nativist pressure, virtually cut off any new immigration to the United States from South Asia. The Immigration Act of 1917, also known as the Asiatic Barred Zone Act, created a Barred Zone that prohibited immigration from several Asian countries, including the countries of South Asia. In 1923, the U.S. Supreme Court ruled that Indians were not "free, white persons" and were therefore ineligible for citizenship (U.S. Supreme Court, 261 U.S. 204—United States v. Bhagat Singh Thind, 1923). The Immigration Acts of 1921 and 1924 set up a national origins quota system based on the composition of the U.S. population in 1890. It was not until Congress passed the Luce–Cellar bill in 1946, allowing Asian Indians to acquire citizenship and sponsor their family members, that new immigration from South Asia resumed (Rangaswamy, 2000).

Opening the Gates

The Immigration and Nationality Act of 1965 was the most important legislative milestone for the resurgence of immigration from South Asia. It enabled South Asians to arrive in record numbers and settle in urban areas throughout the country. It also laid the foundation for the SAA population of the twenty-first century. The 1965 law ended the policy of national quotas and allowed the immigration of professionals whose skills were in high demand in the U.S. labor market. These included physicians, engineers, scientists, and academics.

The 1980 Census was the first to identify Asian Indians as a separate ethnic category within the Asian American population. The remaining South Asian groups were still aggregated in the "other Asian" category until 1990. Asian Indians remain the largest subgroup of South Asians in the United States, though in recent years their relative size as a proportion of the entire SAA population has decreased from 89% in 1990 and 2000 to 83% in 2010 (South Asian American Policy and Research Institute [SAAPRI], 2005—Making Data Count). From 2000 to 2010, the smaller Bangladeshi, Bhutanese, and Nepali populations saw more growth than the Asian Indian population (SAAPRI, 2005—Making Data Count).

After 1965, the wave of young, educated, professional South Asian immigrants was radically different from prior immigrants. This new group quickly attained economic success. By 1970, they began to use the family reunification provision of the 1965 law to sponsor the immigration of less-skilled relatives, thus adding to the socioeconomic diversity of the community. In fact, by the 1980s, nearly 80% of Indian immigrants to the United States were admitted under the "relative preferences" category, one of the channels that expanded family-based immigration (Rangaswamy, 2000). In 2000, 73% of Pakistani immigrants arrived through the relative preferences categories (SAAPRI, 2005—Making Data Count).

Information Technology Sector

The 1990s saw a boom in the information technology sector and, once again, highly skilled professional South Asians were recruited in large numbers. This time, however, they arrived under H-1B temporary work visas. This placed some restrictions on the employment opportunities for them and their spouses but, eventually, they were allowed to acquire legitimate immigrant status. According to U.S. State Department figures, the number of H-1B visas issued to people from India rose from 2,697 in 1990 to 15,228 in 1995 and 55,047 in 2000 (Ling & Austin, 2009). These figures continued to rise. By 2012, 86,477 H-1B visa petitions for initial employment had been approved for immigrants from India, while 851 were approved for immigrants from Pakistan and 932 were approved for immigrants from Nepal (Department of Homeland Security, 2013). In the current climate of uncertainty surrounding visa and immigration policies, South Asians could be adversely affected through reduced opportunities for income generation, limited access to healthcare and other social and legal restrictions.

Healthcare Sector

The number of South Asian healthcare professionals in the United States has grown over the years. Increases followed the Health Professionals Reauthorization

Act in 1992, which gave foreign medical graduates greater access to acquiring licenses to practice in the United States (Association of Physicians of Pakistani Descent of North America). In 1974, of the 46,000 Indians who were employed in the United States, 7,000 were physicians. By 2007, nearly 60,000 U.S. practicing physicians, or 5% of all physicians in the United States, received their medical training in India or Pakistan (Poros, 2013).

The SAA population is also well represented in the allied health professions— as pharmacists, dentists, nurses, and other healthcare providers—although exact figures are not readily available. The size of the South Asian healthcare professional workforce suggests that now, more than ever, there is strong potential for community advocates and healthcare providers to work together to develop culturally appropriate services aimed at addressing barriers to health services access and delivery faced by underprivileged and vulnerable SAAs.

Regional Variations

The states with the largest populations of South Asians include California, New York, New Jersey, Texas, and Illinois (U.S. Census Bureau, 2010). California has an older, more established population originated by Punjabi Indian immigrants, although farming interests gradually decreased with the migration of young professionals from all over South Asia. In New York and New Jersey, South Asian groups have formed enclaves based on communities or regions of origin. Gujaratis, for example, settled in large numbers in New Jersey, where they tend to be insular and adhere strongly to their homeland traditions (Rangaswamy, 1997). Meanwhile, Indo-Caribbean immigrants in New York are of mixed heritage who may be identified as South Asians but may also be of African descent (Prashad, 2001). Bangladeshi Americans are mostly concentrated in New York, but are much younger and more economically vulnerable than other subgroups (U.S. Census Bureau, 2000; SAAPRI, 2005— Making Data Count). In Illinois, emerging Bangladeshi populations grew 153% between 2000 and 2010 and in Los Angeles, this population grew 122% during those 10 years. The Bhutanese community experienced the most significant growth during his time period, jumping a staggering 8,255%. Many Bhutanese have immigrated as refugees and have settled in Dallas, Atlanta, and Houston. Table 1.1 further illustrates the growth of South Asian subgroups in the United States between 2000 and 2010.

The growth of South Asian immigrant communities in other areas such as Washington, DC, Texas, Minnesota, and the mid-Atlantic states shows that the South Asian population continues to broaden. Technological companies such as Microsoft, Intel, and Apple have contributed to large increases in the number

Table 1.1 Changes in the SAA Population: 2000–2010

	Single Ethnicity Reported			Single and Multiple Ethnicity Reported		
	2000	2010	Percent Change	2000	2010	Percent Change
Bangladeshi	41,280	128,792	212%	57,412	147,300	157%
Bhutanese	183	15,290	8,255%	212	19,439	9,069%
Indian	1,678,765	2,843,391	69%	1,899,599	3,183,063	68%
Maldivian	27	98	263%	51	127	149%
Nepali	7,858	51,907	561%	9,399	59,490	533%
Pakistani	153,533	363,699	137%	204,309	409,163	100%
Sri Lankan	20,145	38,596	92%	24,587	45,381	85%
TOTAL SOUTH ASIANS	1,901,791	3,441,773	81%			

Source: Asian American Federation (AAF) and South Asian Americans Leading Together [SAALT], *A Demographic Snapshot of South Asians in the United States: July 2012 Update.* Retrieved from www.saalt.org/wp-content/uploads/2012/09/Demographic-Snapshot-Asian-American-Foundation-2012.pdf, 2012, using information from U.S. Census Bureau, 2010 Census and 2000 Census.

of South Asians living and working in the Pacific Northwest and Silicon Valley of Northern California (SAAPRI, 2005; SEWA-AIFW (Asian Indian Family Wellness), 2014—Sahat Project Report).

South Asian Classification in U.S. Decennial Census

As reported in the *Brown Paper*, published by the South Asian Public Health Association (SAPHA 2002), data on South Asians in the U.S. Census were gathered inconsistently for many years. In fact, through 1970, Asian Indians and other South Asians were classified as White in the Census, which drastically curtailed the ability to assess disparities in resources available to or utilized by these groups. In the 1980 Census, six response categories were added for Asians, including Asian Indians. It was not until the 2000 Census, however, that a separate "other Asian" response category was introduced, allowing immigrants from Bangladesh, Bhutan, Nepal, Pakistan, Sri Lanka, and elsewhere to write in their specific country of origin. Additionally, for the first time, the 2000 Census allowed respondents to select more than one race category, thereby recognizing the growing population of multiracial individuals.

Unfortunately, even today, various South Asian subpopulations are often miscounted in Census data (Asian American Federation [AAF] & South Asian Americans Leading Together [SAALT], 2012). This is due to several factors, including non-Indian individuals who are required to write in their ethnicity on Census forms, as well as the fear among certain populations, particularly undocumented immigrants, about participating in government surveys. When discussing the South Asian community in aggregate, AAF and SAALT, in their demographic snapshot of the SAA population (2012), use "single ethnicity" response data in order to avoid double counting individuals and to evaluate trends with previous data sets that had fewer race classifications. Due to the growing importance of biracial and multiracial populations among Asian Americans and SAAs, however, more recent research by the SAAPRI, and other institutions, include data on the SAA population "alone and in combination" when feasible. SAALT and AAF caution that all demographic resources should be used to provide a baseline for understanding the populations of interest. They suggest that these then be combined with community-based research to provide a more comprehensive profile with specific attention given to the health needs and priorities that are unique to specific multiracial and multiethnic groups.

Current Key Demographic Characteristics of the SAA Population

More than 3.4 million South Asians live in the United States, with Indians comprising the largest segment of the population, followed by Pakistanis, Bangladeshis, Nepalis, Sri Lankans, Bhutanese, and Maldivians (U.S. Census Bureau, 2010) (Table 1.2). According to the 2013 American Community Survey nearly 4.3 million South Asians live in the United States (SAALT, 2015) between 2000 and 2010, the South Asian community as a whole grew by 81%, far exceeding the growth rates of Asian Americans (43%), Hispanic Americans (43%), and non-Hispanic Whites (1.2%). Among Asian Americans, Indians and Pakistanis are the third and seventh largest ethnic groups, respectively, while among the SAA population, the Bhutanese have experienced the most significant growth in recent years. In some states, such as Illinois, SAAs make up the largest subgroup of Asian Americans (SAAPRI, 2013—Making Data Count). Metropolitan areas with the largest South Asian populations are New York City, Chicago, Washington, DC, Los Angeles, and San Francisco–Oakland. The greatest growth of South Asians, however, has

Table 1.2   Selected Demographic Characteristics by Ethnic South Asian Group, 2010

	Asian Indian	Pakistani	Bangladeshi	Nepalese	Sri Lankan	Bhutanese	Total South Asians
Total population	2,843,391 (82.6%)	363,699 (10.6%)	128,792 (3.7%)	51,907 (1.5%)	38,596 (1.1%	15,290 (0.4%)	3,441,675
Male	1,476,387 (51.9%)	191,242 (52.6%)	67,661 (52.6%)	28,593 (55.1%)	19,734 (51.1%)	7,791 (51.0%	1,791,408 (52.1)
Female	1,367,004 (48.1%)	172,457 (47.4%)	61,131 (47.5%)	23,314 (44.9%)	18,862 (48.9%)	7,499 (49.0%)	1,650,267 (47.9%)
Under 18 years	691,684 (24.3%)	110,181 (30.2%)	37,926 (29.4%)	10,983 (21.2%)	8,026 (20.8%)	4,061 (26.6%)	862,861 (25.1%)
18–64 years	1,978,280 (69.5%)	235,666 (64.8%)	86,006 (66.8%)	39,997 (77.1%)	27,603 (71.5%)	1,051,991 (68.7%)	2,378,063 (69.1%)
65 years and over	173,427 (6.1%)	17,852 (4.9%)	4,860 (3.8%)	927 (1.7%)	2,967 (7.7%)	718 (4.7%)	200,751 (5.8%)
Median age (years)	32.0	29.5	31.1	28.8	36.3	26.3	

Source: From U.S. Census Bureau, *2010 Census Data*, 2010. Retrieved from www.census.gov/2010census/data/. Table DP-1 Profile of General Demographic Characteristics: 2010.

Note: The Maldivian population numbered only 98 and did not meet the 100 count threshold for SF2 Table.

occurred outside of these metropolitan areas. In fact, the largest growth in the SAA population was in Charlotte, NC, followed by Phoenix, AZ; Richmond, VA; Raleigh, NC; San Antonio, TX; Seattle, WA; Stockton, CA; Jacksonville, FL; Harrisburg, PA; and Las Vegas, NV. Finally, it is important to note that SAA communities are also very diverse. Table 1.2 indicates that the Pakistani-American population has a higher percentage of youth than the other South Asian subgroups, while the rapidly growing Nepali subgroup has the lowest ratio of females in its population. These are factors that affect the social organization of a community and should be taken into consideration when developing policies and programs to address the health needs of communities.

Socioeconomic Characteristics

While detailed socioeconomic statistics for the South Asian population, using the decennial U.S. Census of 2010, are yet to be published as Summary Files, there is a wealth of information that can be gleaned from American Community Survey reports published in the years between the decennial Censuses. These reports are based on estimates, and they provide the level of detailed and disaggregated data that can be mined for purposes of policy and planning in order to meet the needs of minority groups. Table 1.3 presents socioeconomic characteristics of the four largest South Asian populations in the United States. Among these, the Bangladeshi and Nepalese populations have significantly lower educational attainment, English proficiency, income levels, and health insurance coverage as well as higher proportions of people living in poverty.

Analysis of the gender, age, income, and educational distributions of South Asian subgroups can help to guide the development and delivery of more focused culturally appropriate and effective services to the most underserved segments of the SAA population. The overwhelming majority of all South Asians are foreign-born, which highlights the need for culturally and linguistically specific outreach and services to help those who are less acclimated or who have limited English proficiency and ability to navigate through the increasingly complex U.S. healthcare system. Other vulnerable subgroups of the South Asian population include persons with disabilities (ranging from 4.6% among Asian Indians to 6.3% among Bangladeshis) and those without health insurance (ranging from 11.6% among Asian Indians to an alarming 29.9% among Nepalese) (Table 1.3). Women also represent a vulnerable subgroup. For example, disaggregated data show that in Illinois, where South Asians overall have a high level of education, nearly twice as many South Asian women have less than a high school education, as compared to South Asian men (SAAPRI, 2013—Making Data Count). This difference can inform both the content and design of public health interventions that assist the most vulnerable in the SAA community.

Table 1.3 Select Socioeconomic Characteristics of the Top Four South Asian Populations

	Asian Indian Alone	Bangladeshi Alone	Pakistani Alone	Nepalese Alone
Total population	3,049,201	146,612	366,407	86,775
Male	51.8%	51.4%	53.4%	54.9%
Female	48.2%	48.6%	46.6%	45.1%
Median age (years)	32.8	30.8	29.2	28.8
Average family size	3.49	4.26	4.50	3.88
Married (population 15 years and older)	69.3%	66.0%	62.6%	64.5%
Bachelor's degree or higher (population 25 years and older)	72.2%	44.7%	54.1%	45.7%
Place of birth and citizenship				
Foreign born	71.4%	72.9%	66.2%	88.5%
Foreign born; Naturalized U.S. citizen	49.2%	51.2%	60.4%	17.3%
Language spoken at home and ability to speak English (for population 5 years and older)				
English only	20.7%	6.3%	12.0%	6.7%
Language other than English	79.3%	93.7%	88.0%	93.3%
Speak English less than "very well"	20.5%	45.9%	27.1%	52.0%
Employment (for population 16 years and older)				
In labor force	69.4%	60.4%	60.3%	70.1%
Employed	65.0%	55.4%	54.9%	62.8%
Unemployed	4.4%	5.0%	5.3%	7.3%

(Continued)

Table 1.3 Select Socioeconomic Characteristics of the Top Four South Asian Populations (*Continued*)

Income over the past 12 Months (in 2012 inflation-adjusted dollars)				
Households	977,213	36,208	90,192	22,635
Median household income (dollars)	96,782	44,293	69,042	48,260
Per capita income (dollars)	41,249	18,791	25,851	19,664
Health insurance coverage (civilian noninstitutionalized population)				
With private health insurance	78.3%	43.5%	52.8%	43.7%
With public coverage	13.5%	42.5%	26.8%	28.7%
No health insurance coverage	11.6%	17.8%	22.8%	29.9%
Poverty rates for families and people whose poverty status is determined	8.1%	27.9%	16.4%	29.5%
Housing tenure				
Occupied housing units	977,213	36,208	90,192	22,635
Owner-occupied housing units	54.2%	38.7%	52.6%	29.7%
Renter-occupied housing units	45.8%	61.3%	47.4%	70.3%

Source: From U.S. Census Bureau. *American Community Survey (ACS).* Retrieved from www.census.gov/programs-surveys/acs/about.html. S0201: Selected Population Profile in the United States: 2012 American Community Survey 1-Year Estimates.

Note: Data for other South Asian population subgroups, including Bhutanese, Sri Lankan, and Maldivian, were not available since they did not reach the thresholds for this table.

Labor market statistics also show that South Asians are engaged in a variety of small business enterprises, including taxi-driving, and working in hotels or motels, gas stations, restaurant chains, convenience stores, and newspaper stands (Rangaswamy, 2010). In 2000, the rate of foreign-born self-employed Indian Americans was 12.8% (Zhao & Park, 2013). The 2005 SAAPRI report "Healthcare for All" calls for affordable healthcare coverage for small business owners including those who are self-employed.

Religious, Cultural, and Linguistic Diversity

South Asians have strong religious, cultural, and linguistic traditions. These traditions persist in varying degrees depending on country of origin, length of time in the United States, and their experience as immigrants. All of the major religions of the world are represented among South Asians and they can belong to any one of dozens of language groups and numerous dialects of the region. India alone has 22 official languages recognized in its constitution. In the course of developing their new identity in the United States, South Asians may identify themselves along racial, religious, ethnic, national origin, or linguistic lines.

The major religions practiced among South Asians include Buddhism, Christianity, Hinduism, Islam, Jainism, Judaism, Sikhism, and Zoroastrianism. The proliferation of temples, mosques, *gurdwaras*, and other religious places of worship throughout the United States attests to the importance placed by South Asians on religion. These buildings serve not only as places of worship but also as social gathering spots where communities come together and new cultural identities and support networks are formed. Religion and culture are intertwined entities, and related beliefs and practices have a profound influence on health behaviors, health-related attitudes, beliefs, and practices (Koenig, McCullough, & Larson, 2001; Lee & Newberg, 2005; Winkelman, 2009). For example, a study of Muslim women found that the lack of understanding of a patient's religious and cultural identity by healthcare providers impedes patient-centered care (Hasnain, Connell, Menon, & Tranmer, 2011). Faith-based institutions play an integral part in the lives of SAAs and their role in the delivery of social services and health care should be taken into account when formulating policies, services, and programs.

Several studies of South Asian groups in metropolitan areas show that the most common South Asian languages spoken in the United States are Hindi, Urdu, Gujarati, Punjabi, and Bengali. The major South Indian languages—Tamil, Malayalam, Kannada, and Telugu—are also well represented (Rangaswamy, 2000). Whatever connection exists between native language preservation and English proficiency, Census data indicate that there are increasing numbers of South Asians with limited English proficiency defined as "speaking English less than very well" (see Table 1.3; SAAPRI, 2005). In fact, approximately one in four SAAs fall into this category. This trend may be connected to the increasing number of low-income, newer immigrants who tend to stay within South Asian enclaves in metropolitan areas where they are able to get by in their own language but may have difficulty accessing English classes as a result of cutbacks in government services.

Neither the history of South Asian immigration nor the socioeconomic data of the current population support the notion of a homogenous, uniformly successful South Asian community. Instead, they reveal gaps that clearly indicate a need for an inclusive, progressive, and hands-on approach to acknowledging and identifying the heterogeneity of the South Asian community in the United States, in order to more effectively address their health needs.

Impact on Political Discourse

South Asians are fast becoming a powerful segment of the American electorate—with an increase in U.S. citizens of voting age ranging from 99% for Asian Indians to 471% for Bangladeshis since 2000. The population of non-U.S. citizens of voting age has also increased since 2000. This includes green card holders who may become U.S. citizens in the future and will thus add to the growing electorate. As this trend continues, the South Asian community has greater potential to influence elections, policies, and public discourse. Under the Obama administration, SAAs have a record number of political appointments, including the U.S. Surgeon General, Vivek Murthy, who was appointed in 2015.

It is becoming increasingly important to better understand the SAA community's socioeconomic characteristics including income, poverty, education, limited English proficiency, immigration status, small business ownership, and other factors. SAAPRI's 2013 "Making Data Count" and "Voting Trends and Access" reports on SAA in Illinois, along with other resources, such as the National Asian American Survey, AAPIData.com, and Asian Americans Advancing Justice's Community of Contrasts, provide models for future research related to the characteristics and perspectives of SAA.

The Model Minority Label

Perhaps the greatest hindrance to a realistic and meaningful approach to addressing the health concerns of South Asians is the myth that they do not really need help. The most touted statistics refer to South Asians, in combination with other Asian Americans, as the group with the highest education, the highest income, and the highest number of physicians and entrepreneurs.

While the statistics are valid, and the community should take pride in the achievements and success of its own members, such figures can also overlook the diverse experiences of SAAs. These include vast numbers of underprivileged and vulnerable SAAs who face obstacles in accessing and utilizing healthcare services. In fact, a significant number of South Asians living in the United States live below the poverty line (ranging from 8.1% for Asian Indians to 29.5% for Bangladeshis) (Table 1.3). They lack the resources to "pull themselves up by the bootstraps," an exhortation that is commonly made by those who see themselves as the "model minority." In reality, the SAA population across all regions of the United States reflects many of the same disparities in age, education, income level, and language skills that are seen in other immigrant and minority communities.

Ethnic media has given extensive coverage to high-level appointments, electoral successes, and academic achievements of South Asians but made little mention of poverty levels or percentages of uninsured, uneducated, and unemployed South Asians. The idea that there are undocumented immigrants, and immigrants with HIV/AIDS and mental health issues, is glossed over by the general South Asian population, as well as the media at large (India West, 2015, p. A8). The complacency generated by the notion that "all is well" with the South Asian community can be harmful because it diverts attention from appropriately identifying problems and addressing the health and socioeconomic needs of the underprivileged and vulnerable South Asians in the United States. It also discourages honest discourse, activism, and political participation, while creating divisiveness along class lines.

An additional danger of the model minority myth is that it alienates other groups with whom South Asians need to align in order to advance public policy initiatives that would benefit the largest numbers of immigrant and minority Americans. There is much to be gained by partnering with other minority groups, such as African Americans and Latinos who share many of the same challenges, but have a more substantial voice due to larger populations and a longer history in activism (Prasad, 2001).

Healthcare Access

According to research by SAALT, approximately one in five SAAs lacks health insurance (2013). A usual source of care is lacking in 20% of Asian Indians and 21% of "other Asians" (The Henry J. Kaiser Foundation, 2008). One study showed that the employer-based insurance rate for South Asians did not increase as it did with other ethnic groups while, at the same time, privately purchased insurance had declined (Brown, Ojela, Wyn, & Levan, 2000). Recent changes in the healthcare system have been crucial for this community, as many stand to benefit from the Affordable Care Act. Still, assistance via the Affordable Care Act and other public programs may have different implications for different communities. For example, it is believed that one in five Bangladeshis will likely benefit from Medicaid expansion (APIAHF and White House Initiative on Asian Americans and Pacific Islanders, n.d.).

Barriers to healthcare access include income, language, culture, transportation, residential segregation, and other factors. In order to contextualize South Asian health, it is important to understand not only data about demographics and health insurance, but also the effects of acculturation, social support, and gender roles (Sahat Project Report).

Recommendations

The following recommendations for the development of policies and health services that address the specific health needs of South Asians incorporate suggestions made by other groups, including SAAPRI and SAALT:

- Enhance the availability of disaggregated data by adding categories and/or write-in options on surveys to allow South Asian respondents to accurately indicate their ethnic origin.
- Collect, review, and disseminate available disaggregated data from hospitals, clinics, health systems, and surveillance and research institutions.
- Incorporate findings from community-based research that may provide a more nuanced and comprehensive profile of South Asian residents of the geographic region in question.
- Provide fair access to affordable healthcare coverage for all individuals, regardless of length of time in the United States, immigration status, or employment status.
- Develop health policies that take into account age, gender, education, occupation, and income levels. This will benefit the broader population and enable the South Asian community to provide better, more targeted healthcare to its own population.
- Increase linguistic and culturally tailored services, as well as services that focus on mental health, reproductive health, sexual identity, and HIV/AIDS. Recognize that acculturation, social support, and gender roles may affect access to and acceptability of health services.

■ Acknowledge the role of faith-based institutions in delivering health and social services.

■ Appoint individuals who are qualified to address the health needs of the SAA population to high-level decision-making groups so they are able to better influence health-care delivery at the federal, state, and local levels.

Conclusions

SAAs are an extremely diverse group of people with a rich culture and heritage. Their history and evolution as an immigrant group in the United States are dynamic. Based on historical evidence and the most recent demographic indicators, the SAA population is poised to be an ever-increasing minority group who will continue to make a significant impact on the social, economic, and political fabric of their adopted country. Understanding the unique characteristics of this population is critical to ensuring the overall health and well-being of this community.

Although passage of the Affordable Care Act in 2010 increased access to health care, its future is uncertain, and various barriers remain for the SAA population. In addition to SAAPRI, SAALT, SAPHA, and other organizations mentioned in this chapter, other groups such as the Asian and Pacific Islander American Health Forum and the Illinois Coalition for Immigrant and Refugee Rights are working to articulate and address the unique barriers to access faced by immigrant and minority communities during the implementation of the Affordable Care Act.

The information presented in this chapter highlights the need for ongoing work to provide clear, understandable, and disaggregated data for the SAA population in order to guide the development of effective policies and programs that better meet the unique health needs of this population.

References

Asian American Federation (AAF) & South Asian Americans Leading Together (SAALT). (2012). *A Demographic Snapshot of South Asians in the United States: July 2012 Update.* Retrieved from www.saalt.org/wp-content/uploads/2012/09/Demographic-Snapshot-Asian-American-Foundation-2012.pdf

Asian Health Coalition of Illinois. (2005). *Health Care for All: Health Access Recommendations for Asian Americans in Illinois by Asian Americans in Illinois.* Retrieved from www.saapri.org/content/wp-content/uploads/2013/03/Health-Care-for-All-Full-Report.pdf

Asian Pacific Islander American Health Forum & White House Initiative on Asian Americans and Pacific Islanders. (n.d.). *The Health Care Law and You: How Does the ACA Help Asian Americans, Native Hawaiians and Pacific Islanders?* Retrieved from www.apiahf.org/sites/default/files/The%20Health%20Care%20Law%20and%20 You_0_0.pdf

Association of Physicians of Pakistani Descent of North America (APPNA). Retrieved from www.appna.org

Brown, E. R., Ojela, V. D., Wyn, R., & Levan, R. (2000). *Racial & Ethnic Disparities in Access to Health Insurance & Healthcare.* Retrieved from www.kaiserfamily-foundation.files.wordpress.com/2013/01/racial-and-ethnic-disparities-in-access-to-health-insurance-and-health-care-report.pdf

Department of Homeland Security. (2013). *Characteristics of H1B Specialty Occupation Workers: Fiscal Year 2012 Annual Report to Congress.* Retrieved from www.uscis.gov/sites/default/files/USCIS/Resources/Reports%20and%20Studies/H-1B/h1b-fy-12-characteristics.pdf

Hasnain, M., Connell, K. J., Menon, U., & Tranmer, P. A. (2011). Patient-centered care for Muslim women: Provider and patient perspectives. *Journal of Women's Health (Larchmont)*, 20(1):73–83. doi: 10.1089/jwh.2010.2197.

Henry J. Kaiser Family Foundation. (2008). *Race, Ethnicity & Health Care: Fact Sheet.* Retrieved from www.apiahf.org/sites/default/files/APIAHF_Factsheet04_2008.pdf

Hoefer, M., Rytina, N., & Baker, B. (2012). *Estimates of the unauthorized immigrant population residing in the United States: January 2011.* Washington, DC: DHS Office of Immigration Statistics. Retrieved from www.dhs.gov/xlibrary/assets/statistics/publications/ois_ill_pe_2011.pdf

Jensen, J. M. (1980). East Indians. In S. Thernstrom, A. Orlov, & O. Handlin (Eds.), *Harvard Encyclopedia of American Ethnic Groups.* Cambridge, MA: Harvard University Press.

Koenig, H. G., McCullough, M. E., & Larson, D. B. (2001). *Handbook of Religion and Health.* Oxford, England: Oxford University Press.

Lee, B. Y., & Newberg, A. B. (2005). Religion and health: A review and critical analysis. *Zygon, 40*: 443–468.

Leonard, K. (1992). *Making Ethnic Choices: California's Punjabi Mexican Americans.* Philadelphia, PA: Temple University Press.

Ling, H., & Austin, A. (Eds.). (2009). *Asian American History and Culture. An Encyclopedia,* (pp. 333–335). New York, NY: M. E. Sharpe.

Pew Research Center. (2014). *Hispanic Trends: Unauthorized Immigrant Population Trends for States, Birth Countries and Regions.* Retrieved from http://www.pewhispanic.org/2014/12/11/unauthorized-trends/

Poros, M. V. (2013). Asian Indians and Asian-Indian American, 1940–Present. In *Immigrants in American History. Arrival, Adaptation and Integration, Vol. 2* (ABC-Clio, 2013) 736; American Medical Association website, Retrieved from www.ama-assn.org//ama/pub/about-ama/our-people/member-groups-sections/international-medical-graduates/imgs-in-united-states/imgs-country-origin.page (last visited on May 19, 2014).

Prashad, V. (2001). *The Karma of Brown Folk.* Minneapolis, MN: University of Minnesota Press.

Rangaswamy, P. (1997). Gujaratis. In *Encyclopedia of American Immigrant Cultures*. New York, NY: Macmillan.

Rangaswamy, P. (2000). *Namaste America. Indian Immigrants in an American Metropolis*. University Park, PA: The Pennsylvania State University Press.

SEWA-AIFW (Asian Indian Family Wellness). (2014). *Project SAHAT (South Asian Health Assessment Tool)*. Retrieved from nebula.wsimg.com/928d28f8d1bb378a6 bde77a2f63bd231?AccessKeyId=04AEF55388781ABCE21C&disposition=0&all oworigin=1

South Asian Americans Leading Together (SAALT). (2015). A *Demographic Snapshot of South Asians in the United State* (Dec 2015). Retrieved from http://saalt.org/wp-content/uploads/2016/01/Demographic-Snapshot-updated_Dec-2015.pdf

South Asian Americans Leading Together. (2013). *"Obamacare": The Affordable Health Care Act, A Factsheet for South Asians*. Retrieved from www.saalt.org/wp-content/uploads/2013/06/ACA-Fact-Sheet-for-SAs.pdf

South Asian American Policy & Research Institute (SAAPRI). (2005). *Making Data Count: South Asian Americans in the 2000 Census with Focus on Illinois*. Retrieved from www.saapri.org

South Asian American Policy & Research Institute & Advancing Justice—Chicago. (2013). *South Asian Americans in Illinois: Making Data Count*. Retrieved from advancingjustice-chicago.org/wp-content/uploads/2015/10/SAAPRI-2013-Making-Data-Count.pdf

South Asian Public Health Association. (2002). A *Brown Paper: The Health of South Asians in the United States, 2002*. Retrieved from http://joinsapha.org/resource-list/the-brown-paper/

U.S. Census Bureau. (1980). *1980 Census Data*. Retrieved from www.census.gov/mp/www/cat/decennial_census_1980/

U.S. Census Bureau. (2010). *2010 Census Data*. Retrieved from www.census.gov/2010census/data/

U.S. Census Bureau. (n.d.). *American Community Survey (ACS)*. Retrieved from www.census.gov/programs-surveys/acs/about.html

U.S. Supreme Court, 261 U.S. 204. (1923). *United States v. Bhagat Singh Thind*.

Winkelman, M. (2009). *Culture and Health: Applying Medical Anthropology*. San Francisco, CA: Jossey-Bass.

Zhao, X., & Park, E. J. W. (Eds.). (2013). *Asian Americans: An Encyclopedia of Social, Cultural, Economic and Political History*, p. 558. Westport, CT: Greenwood Publishing.

NONCOMMUNICABLE CHRONIC CONDITIONS

Chapter 2

Cardiovascular Disease

Monideepa Bhattacharya Becerra and
Navkiranjit Gill

Contents

Abstract

Objective: Cardiovascular disease (CVD) is the leading cause of death among South Asians in the United States. This chapter examines the current literature on the burden of CVD, risk factors, and associated health behaviors among South Asian Americans (SAAs). The role of acculturation is also examined as it relates to cultural and behavioral outcomes associated with cardiovascular health.

Key Findings: The literature suggests a heightened CVD risk among South Asian, Americans (SAAs) as well as an increase in intermediate clinical risk factors such as diabetes, hypertension, and obesity. Negative health behaviors, including smoking, alcohol use, unhealthy diet, and physical inactivity, have also been shown to be significant concerns within the SAA population. The role of acculturation has also emerged as a potential risk factor for poorer CVD outcomes and associated negative health behaviors. Although the reviewed literature highlights CVD as a significant public health concern among SAAs, there is limited evidence-based research conducted to fully understand the cultural and behavioral outcomes as they relate to cardiovascular health.

Recommendations: More research needs to be focused on SAAs, in particular, population-based health surveys. Preventive strategies should include community health workers who can provide the South Asian American population with education on cardiovascular health, access to services, and regular screening for intermediate clinical risk factors. In addition, culturallybased dietary and physical activity recommendations should be routinely advocated by clinicians serving the South Asian American population.

Introduction

In the South Asian American (SAA) population, cardiovascular disease (CVD) is the leading cause of death (Palaniappan, Wang, & Fortmann, 2004; Palaniappan et al., 2010b). SAAs are also one of the fastest-growing minority populations in the United States (South Asian Americans Leading Together [SAALT], 2012). Despite these two facts, little cumulative assessment exists on understanding the prevalence and risk factors of CVD among SAAs. Such research is imperative to guide the development of more public health interventions that can better serve this growing population.

This chapter aims to summarize the current empirical evidence on CVD trends, risk factors, and associated health behaviors among South Asians in the United States. The literature reviewed for this chapter has been primarily limited to studies conducted in the United States since the publication of *The Brown Paper* 2002 (South Asian Public Health Association [SAPHA], 2002). All relevant records in English, resulting from a query run in several databases, were assessed in addition to pertinent organizational websites. A summary of these studies demonstrating the burden of CVD among South Asians is presented in Table 2.1.

Table 2.1 Characteristics of Studies Addressing CVD Burden among South Asians in the United States

Study	South Asian Subgroup	Location	South Asian Sample Size
Amin et al. (2009)	Asian Indian	Illinois	28
Balasubramanyam, Rao, Misra, Sekhar, and Ballantyne (2008)	Asian Indian	Texas	143
Banerjee et al. (2014)	Asian Indian, Pakistani, Bangladeshi	New York metropolitan area	39
Baweja et al. (2004)	Asian Indian	Georgia	1046
Becerra, Herring, Marshak, and Banta (2013)	–	California	1352
Becerra, Herring, Marshak, and Banta (2014)	–	California	1352
Becerra and Becerra (2015)	–	California	132
Chandalia et al. (2003)	Asian Indian	Texas	82
Changrani, Gany, Cruz, Kerr, and Katz (2006)	Asian Indian, Bangladeshi	New York metropolitan area	138
Dodani and Dong (2011)	Asian Indian	Georgia, Kansas, Missouri	159

(Continued)

Table 2.1 Characteristics of Studies Addressing CVD Burden among South Asians in the United States (*Continued*)

Study	South Asian Subgroup	Location	South Asian Sample Size
Ghai et al. (2012)	Asian Indian	California	602
Holland, Wong, Lauderdale, and Palaniappan (2011)	Asian Indian	California	5154
Ivey, Mehta, Fyr, and Kanaya (2006)	Two surveys (South Asian, Asian Indian)	California	1073 (pooled sample)
Ivey et al. (2004)	Asian Indian	California	57
Iwamoto et al. (2012)	–	California	128
Jonnalagadda and Diwan (2005)	Asian Indian	Atlanta metropolitan area	226
Kanaya et al. (2010)	Asian Indian	California	150
Misra, Endemann, and Ayer (2005)	Asian Indian	California	56
Misra et al. (2010)	Asian Indian	Seven U.S. urban cities	1038
Mohanty, Woolhandler, Himmelstein, and Bor (2005)	Asian Indian	United States	555
Mooteri, Petersen, Dagubati, and Pai (2004)	Asian Indian	United States	527
Mukherjea et al. (2012)	–	Illinois, California	88
Mukherjea, Underwood, Stewart, Ivey, and Kanaya (2013)	Asian Indian	California	38
Oza-Frank, Ali, Vaccarino, and Narayan (2009)	Asian Indian	National	1357
Palaniappan et al. (2004)	Asian Indian	California	4452

(Continued)

Table 2.1 Characteristics of Studies Addressing CVD Burden among South Asians in the United States (*Continued*)

Study	South Asian Subgroup	Location	South Asian Sample Size
Palaniappan et al. (2010b)	Asian Indian	California	4452
Shah, Hernandez, Mathur, Budoff, and Kanaya (2012)	Asian Indian	California	150
Silbiger et al. (2011)	Bangladeshi	New York	75
Silbiger et al. (2012)	Asian Indian-Guyanese	New York	198
Silbiger et al. (2013)	–	New York	520
Thomas and Ashcraft (2013)	Asian Indians	Texas	37
Venkataraman, Nanda, Baweja, Parikh, and Bhatia (2004)	Asian Indian	Atlanta metropolitan area	1046
Vyas, Chaudhary, Ramiah, and Landry (2012)	Indian, Pakistani, Bangladeshi, Nepali, Sri Lankan, Afghanistani, other	Washington, DC metropolitan area	709
Wu, Wang, and Chung (2012)	Asian Indian	Michigan	273
Ye, Rust, Baltrus, and Daniels (2009)	Asian Indian	National	534

Note: Research reports, commentaries, reviews, and book chapters not included in table.

(-) South Asian subgroup unspecified.

While this chapter primarily aims to highlight the heightened CVD burden among South Asians living in the United States, the authors acknowledge the limited literature on South Asian subgroups, including those with ancestry from Bangladesh, Nepal, Pakistan, and elsewhere. Thus, most literature presented is limited to Asian Indians living in the United States. When feasible, discussion of other South Asian subgroups is included.

Cardiovascular Disease among South Asians

CVD is a group of diseases of the heart and blood vessels. It includes coronary heart disease (CHD) resulting from coronary artery disease (CAD) (American Heart Association [AHA], 2014), cerebrovascular disease, and congenital heart disease (World Health Organization [WHO], 2012). Between 1990 and 2000, South Asian American women experienced a 5% increase in CHD mortality, as compared to other ethnic groups. The literature further shows that Asian Indians in the United States overall have two to three times higher CHD prevalence and mortality rates, as compared to the general population (Holland et al., 2011). More recently, Hastings et al. (2015) evaluated the leading causes of death among Asian Americans from 2003 to 2011. They demonstrated that for both Asian Indian men and women, heart disease remained the leading cause of death, whereas aggregated South Asian American data showed the leading cause of death to be cancer (Hastings et al., 2015). Cumulatively, such studies demonstrate that CVD continues to remain a significant burden among the South Asian population.

Summary of Evidence

Prevalence of CVD

Current empirical evidence indicates that South Asians residing in the United States have a heightened risk of CVD and associated mortality. In the United States, the *National Health Interview Survey* (NHIS) (Centers for Disease Control and Prevention, 2015) provides the only source for a nationally representative Asian Indian sample. An assessment of the Family Core and Sample Adult Core components of the 2004–2006 NHIS (Barnes, Adams, & Powell-Griner, 2008) showed that Asian Indians were more likely to have heart disease as compared to other Asian American subgroups in the study. For example, the prevalence of age-adjusted heart disease among Asian Indians was approximately 9%, whereas it was 6.5% for all Asian/Native Hawaiian and Pacific Islanders (Barnes et al., 2008).

Furthermore, CAD is the most common type of heart disease and occurs when the arteries that supply blood to the heart muscle become narrowed and hardened. In the United States, a higher prevalence of premature CAD, which in turn can lead to CHD, has been reported among Asian Indians, as compared to Blacks and Hispanics (Amin et al., 2009). Amin et al. (2009) found that 50% of Asian Indians had premature CAD, compared to 20% of Hispanics and 30% of Blacks.

Of the few studies that have looked at the prevalence of stroke among South Asian Americans, the results have shown a higher prevalence among men as compared to women. A study published in 2004 noted approximately 4% prevalence of stroke among men, compared to 2% among women (Venkataraman et al., 2004). For women in general, however, South Asian Americans have been reported to have the highest CAD prevalence and mortality rates when compared with all other races (South Asian Heart Center, 2011).

In addition to prevalence of CVD, the average age of onset for CVD and associated risk factors is younger for South Asian Americans than those of the general U.S. population. Overall, South Asian Americans typically experience heart disease 10 years earlier than other populations, (Enas & Kannan, 2005) and often without warning (South Asian Heart Center, 2011). Evidence also shows that South Asian Americans are more likely than Whites (33% vs. 22%) to have either clinical aggression and pronounced angiographic extensiveness of the disease, or three-vessel disease where the three coronary arteries that are essential for blood flow are blocked (Silbiger et al., 2013). Among specific South Asian populations, Bangladeshis have twice the rate of three-vessel CAD compared to Whites (56% vs. 26%), whereas the Indo-Guyanese population has one and a half times the rate (35% vs. 24%) (Silbiger et al., 2011, 2012).

CVD Risk Factors

The current empirical evidence highlights several risk factors for CVD among South Asians living in the United States. These include intermediate clinical risk factors (Balasubramanyam et al., 2008; Ivey et al., 2004; Kanaya et al., 2010; Misra et al., 2010; Venkataraman et al., 2004), such as obesity, type II diabetes, and hypertension. In addition, there are behavioral risk factors, including tobacco use, poor diet, and physical inactivity (Becerra et al., 2014; Ghai et al., 2012; Ismail et al., 2004).

Intermediate Clinical Factors

Several studies have shown a rising prevalence of CVD risk factors among South Asians living in the United States. Studies across the United States have shown a high prevalence of overweight or obese South Asian Americans, ranging from 34% to 63% (Balasubramanyam et al., 2008; Ivey et al., 2004; Misra et al., 2010; Office of Minority Health, 2012; Wu et al., 2012). Additional studies have reported hypertension ranging from 11% to 78%, and type II diabetes ranging from 20% to 55% (Balasubramanyam et al., 2008; Ivey et al., 2004; Kanaya et al., 2010; Misra et al., 2010; Silbiger et al., 2013; Venkataraman et al., 2004; Wu et al., 2012).

Although the wide range of prevalence of such clinical risk factors may be attributable to the study population selection, the data cumulatively demonstrate a significant risk for CVD among the South Asian American population. Empirical evidence has further shown a 35%–65% prevalence of hypercholesterolemia (Ivey et al., 2004; Misra et al., 2010; Wu et al., 2012)—again cumulatively highlighting the higher prevalence of intermediate clinical risk factors among South Asian Americans, as compared to the overall U.S. population. Researchers have also found that Asian Indians in the United States are nearly three times more likely to have diabetes than non-Hispanic Whites (Mohanty et al., 2005; Oza-Frank et al., 2009) and twice as likely to have diabetes than other Asian Americans (Barnes et al., 2008). In a recent study utilizing electronic health records, Pu et al. (2014) demonstrated that Asian Indians are nearly twice as likely as non-Hispanic Whites to report insulin resistance. Similarly, evaluation of age of diagnosis of type II diabetes has demonstrated that, in comparison to non-Hispanic Whites, South Asian Americans were diagnosed on average 10.5 years earlier with type II diabetes (Becerra & Becerra, 2015).

Current literature in the United States also indicates a gender-specific prevalence of risk factors. For instance, the prevalence of hypertension, hypertriglyceridemia, elevated fasting glucose, and hyperhomocysteinemia are all higher among South Asian American men whereas abdominal obesity, total body fat, subcutaneous fat, increased total cholesterol, C-reactive protein, and lipoproteins have been reported to be higher among South Asian American women (Misra et al., 2010; Shah et al., 2012). In addition, results from the INTERHEART study (Yusuf et al., 2004), examining myocardial infarction in 52 countries, demonstrated that nine major risk factors accounted for more than 90% of all attributable risk in populations including South Asians. Among these risk factors were smoking, high levels of ApoB/A1 ratio (apolipoprotein B to apolipoprotein A1 ratio, which signifies the metabolic relation of triglyceride to cholesterol and is used as a predictor for CHD), type II diabetes, hypertension, abdominal obesity, and even psychological stress (Yusuf et al., 2004). Conversely, Yusuf et al. identified protective factors including a regular intake of healthy foods, such as fruits and vegetables, and physical activity.

Unfortunately, there remains a significant limitation in the literature—utilization of the Framingham Risk Score (FRS) Model to assess CVD and

CAD risk (Eichler, Puhan, Steurer, & Bachmann, 2007). Such a scale is primarily focused on Whites of European descent and its applicability to South Asian Americans remains uncertain. Thus, the true burden of CVD among South Asians Americans may be significantly underreported.

Biological Factors

In a comparison of Asian Indian men and Caucasian men of similar age and body fat composition, Chandalia et al. (2003) found that Asian Indian men had higher insulin resistance and elevated C-reactive protein levels. These results are indicative of a pro-inflammatory state among Asian Indians, which, in turn, is associated with elevated type II diabetes and CVD risk. Several biomarkers have also surfaced that indicate elevated CVD risk among South Asians (Eapen, Kalra, Merchant, Arora, & Khan, 2009). These inflammatory biomarkers include C-reactive protein (Anand et al., 2004) and interleukin 6 (Deepa et al., 2006). Moreover, vascular cell adhesion molecule 2 (Deepa et al., 2006) has also been utilized to monitor CVD risk status. Such biomarkers may be used in tandem with traditional risk factors to provide comprehensive recommendations for South Asians in CVD treatment and prevention.

In recent years, researchers have also found shorter telomeres (protective structures at the end of a chromosome) to be associated with CVD risk factors. In fact, studies have shown that South Asians with diabetes have shorter telomeres, demonstrating an early marker of CVD risk among this population (Adaikalakoteswari, Balasubramanyam, & Mohan, 2005; Harte et al., 2012). Still, much of the biological assessment of CVD risks among South Asians has been conducted outside of the United States in recent years, highlighting the need for such research and identification of critical biomarkers to take place within the South Asian population living in the United States.

Diet and Physical Activity

Several behavioral risk factors among South Asian Americans can also pose a significant public health concern as a result of their association with CVD outcomes. Multiple studies have demonstrated poor dietary and physical inactivity practices among South Asians (Ghai et al., 2012; Thomas & Ashcraft, 2013; Vyas et al., 2012; Ye et al., 2009). In one study, Ghai et al. noted that 70% of Asian Indian men of healthy weight reported consuming less than five servings of fruits and/or vegetables a day, as compared to 63% of their non-Hispanic White counterparts (2012). They also found that among healthy and overweight or obese participants, a higher proportion of Asian Indians reported a lack of moderate-to-vigorous physical activity, compared to non-Hispanic

Whites (Ghai et al., 2012). In fact, nearly 47% of Asian Indian men who were overweight or obese reported no physical activity, compared to 37% of non-Hispanic Whites of similar weight status (Ghai et al., 2012). In addition, in an assessment of Asian Indian immigrants, Thomas and Ashcraft noted that nearly 68% of participants reported physical activity of less than 3000 metabolic equivalent units per week, demonstrating a sedentary lifestyle (2013). Similarly, a systematic review by Daniel and Wilbur (2011) found at least 40% prevalence of physical inactivity among the South Asian population.

It is not surprising that the rates of physical activity among South Asians living in the United States are low. One study found that South Asian women report limited knowledge of the amount of physical activity required for improved cardiovascular health (Sriskantharajah & Kai, 2007). For healthy adults, the American Heart Association (2014) recommends 150 minutes a week of moderate-intensity physical activity, or 75 minutes a week of vigorous-intensity aerobic activity, or a combination of two (Haskell et al., 2007). Such recommendations, however, are primarily based on Caucasian populations, and thus may not be generalizable to South Asians. Recognizing this, as well as the increased burden of CVD in the South Asian American population, an expert panel modified these recommendations, promoting 60 minutes of physical activity per day for healthy Asian Indian adults (Misra et al., 2012). This difference further demonstrates the need for South Asian–specific health promotion initiatives.

Cumulatively, given the importance of a healthy diet and physical activity in lowering CVD risk, it seems plausible that the current literature demonstrating the low rates of such healthy behaviors among the South Asian population can be attributed to the increased CVD risk in the population.

Tobacco and Alcohol Use

The link between tobacco use and CVD is well established (Conroy et al., 2003; Erhardt, 2009; Yusuf et al., 2004) and confirms that any utilization of tobacco can further increase CVD risk among South Asians living in the United States. Tobacco is consumed among SAAs through various methods, including cigarettes, cigars, bidis, and hookah, as well as betel quid or in paan, and other smokeless tobacco variants (Gupta & Ray, 2003; Mukherjea, Morgan, Snowden, Ling, & Ivey, 2011). Estimates of tobacco consumption vary among studies and have traditionally been relatively low for SAAs, ranging from 5% to 21% (Ivey et al., 2006; Ye et al., 2009), though it is noteworthy that tobacco use among this population remains a hidden behavior. In fact, other studies point to the plethora of tobacco products used by South Asians, all over the world with the types of product used differing among countries of origin (Gupta & Ray, 2003). *Naswar*, for example, is a smokeless product that is primarily used by Pakistanis and Indians, whereas *zarda* is common among Bangladeshis and Indians. In addition, users reported several health benefits of tobacco products (Mukherjea et al., 2012), emphasizing again the need for public health efforts to better educate South Asians and alleviate the misconceptions of health benefits of such products.

In addition to tobacco use, any use of alcohol has been associated with CVD (Ivey et al., 2006). As a result, whereas South Asians in the United States consume alcohol less often than non-Hispanic Whites (Ghai et al., 2012), the use of alcohol in this population has been associated with CVD risk factors. Alcohol consumption prevalence rates vary from 4% in all Asian Indians (Balasubramanyam et al., 2008) to 61% among South Asian men only (Misra et al., 2005), with significant studies lacking on the age and/or sex stratified analyses of such behavior.

Cumulatively, the literature highlights several CVD risk factors among South Asian Americans, in addition to the high prevalence of obesity, type II diabetes, and high cholesterol. Further, the literature highlights the notion that South Asians are less likely to meet current dietary and physical activity recommendations. Similarly, the use of alcohol, particularly among men, and the variety of tobacco products used in the community, both pose significant public health concern.

The Role of Acculturation

Acculturation is the process by which an immigrant adopts the views, attitudes, culture, and ways of the host nation (Berry, 2003; Castro, 2003). Empirical evidence demonstrates a significant association between acculturation and increased odds for CAD, hypertension, diabetes, and intermediate markers for atherosclerosis among South Asians (Dodani & Dong, 2011; Mooteri et al., 2004). Specifically, the increased duration of residency in the United States, a proxy measure of acculturation, has been associated with increased risk of CAD, hypertension, diabetes, physical inactivity, alcohol consumption, and a nonvegetarian diet among Asian Indians (Mooteri et al., 2004).

Studies have shown that second-generation Asian Indians living in the United States are more likely to be nonvegetarians and current or former smokers, as compared to those foreign-born (Ghai et al., 2012). For South Asian Americans considered to be third generation and beyond, reports have shown them likely to consume more fast food than their foreign-born counterparts, and also found an increase in risky behavior (Becerra et al., 2014; Ghai et al., 2012). Another study among adult Asian Americans in California found that an estimated 83,462 South Asians participated in binge drinking in the past

12 months (Becerra et al., 2013). The study found that those born in the United States (with both parents being foreign-born) were three times more likely to binge drink compared to their foreign-born counterparts (Becerra et al., 2013).

The relationship between tobacco use and acculturation remains inconsistent in the literature. Whereas some researchers have reported higher prevalence of current and former smokers among second-generation Asian Indian men (Ghai et al., 2012), others have shown that immigration to the United States was associated with cessation of some tobacco products (Banerjee et al., 2014). Still another study found that, upon immigration, Asian Indians were more likely to switch from a tobacco product that was not socially acceptable in the United States, such as paan, to a lesser known tobacco product, such as *gutka* (Changrani et al., 2006).

The current literature, though limited and often using differing proxy measures of acculturation (different scales and/or questions), is indicative of the role of increased acculturation to the U.S. on South Asian cardiovascular health and behavioral outcomes. Given the growing South Asian population, particularly second- and subsequent generation U.S. residents, the putative risk factors for increased CVD associated with acculturation will likely continue to rise in the future. These include increased binge drinking and higher calorie diets, making even more important the call for healthcare and public health professionals to implement early preventive strategies.

Recommendations

President Obama's Executive Order addressing the health of Asian Americans (The White House, 2009) further highlights the importance of focusing on the health and behavior patterns among the South Asian American population in order to better develop and implement culturally tailored initiatives. The current empirical findings discussed in this chapter provide the scope for several research and practice recommendations, which may help to alleviate the CVD burden among the South Asian population in the United States.

Recommendations for Research

Disaggregated data among Asian Americans remain limited and even fewer data exist for specific South Asian subgroups. Therefore, recommendations include the following:

- ■ Improve sampling strategies for better representing South Asians and South Asian subgroups in national-, state-, and local-level population-based health surveys.

- Develop policies that call for more representation of South Asians in such samples in order to provide results that can be generalized to the South Asian population in the nation, and in turn provide grounds for improved targeted funding and resource allocation. Although the current policies under Section 4302 of the *Patient Protection and Affordable Care Act* call for disaggregated data collection (U.S. Department of Health and Human Services, 2011), Asian Indians are the primary South Asian subgroup noted. The South Asian population, however, is diverse and includes those with ancestry from Bangladesh, Bhutan, Maldives, Nepal, Pakistan, and Sri Lanka.
- Utilize the *Asian American Multidimensional Acculturation Scale* (Chung, Kim, & Abreu, 2004) to better assess acculturation among the South Asian population.
- Develop South Asian–specific acculturation scales, in addition to testing novel models of acculturation (such as the operant model) among South Asians (Flannery, Reise, & Yu, 2001; Landrine & Klonoff, 2004).
- Use culture-specific dietary practices to address changes in behavior upon acculturation. Unfortunately, much of the current evidence of dietary practices among South Asians is limited in that they do not capture diversity in cooking practices related to culture. For example, use of ghee (clarified butter), which is known to increase premature heart disease (Ismail et al., 2004), and the consumption of native fruits and vegetables (Bainey & Jugdutt, 2009; Ghai et al., 2012) are often lacking in study questionnaires.
- Conduct quasi-experiment and/or randomized controlled trials addressing the reintroduction of whole grains traditionally used in South Asian cooking, such as brown rice, barley, amaranth, millet, and sorghum. This would be beneficial in reducing the CVD burden in the population (Dixit, Azar, Gardner, & Palaniappan, 2011).
- Evaluate interventions that assess the role of culturally relevant interventions, such as replacing ghee with healthier alternatives (The American Association of Physicians of Indian Origin, 2011) in changing biological markers of CVD, such as telomerase activity, reduction of the ApoB/A1 ratio, and C-reactive proteins.

Recommendations for Practice

Studies among various ethnic groups have shown that there is an association between the early presence of nonoptimal cholesterol levels and an increased risk of coronary calcification later in life (Pletcher et al., 2010). Screening among children and young adults with a family history of CVD may provide a preliminary foundation for primary prevention; however, such measures alone are not sufficient to reduce the current CVD risk (Ritchie et al., 2010). This demonstrates a need for early screening. Given the increased premature CVD risk among South Asians, several clinical recommendations exist, as presented in Table 2.2:

Table 2.2 Recommendations for Research and Practice to Improve Cardiovascular Disease Health among South Asians in the United States

Recommendations for Research	*Recommendations for Practice*
• Improve representation of South Asian subgroups in population-based surveys	• Implement early preventive screening among those with family history of cardiovascular disease and associated risk factors
• Develop, implement, and test South Asian–specific acculturation scale, including assessment of novel models	• Incorporate routine screening for cardiovascular disease risk among South Asians, including central adiposity, ApoB/A1 ratio, metabolic syndrome, etc.
• Conduct longitudinal studies addressing if and how acculturation affects health behaviors among South Asians	• Promote cultural and linguistic competencies among clinicians to recommend South Asian–specific nutritional and physical activity guidelines
• Develop and evaluate South Asian culture–specific assessment of dietary and physical activity practices	• Improve health literacy programs to disseminate guidelines among at-risk groups, such as women
• Conduct quasi-experiments and/ or randomized controlled trials assessing efficacy of culturally based health promotion interventions	• Implement community health worker–led culturally relevant programs to improve cardiovascular health behaviors and outcomes at early age
• Utilize epigenetic and molecular epidemiologic data to address the biological predisposition to cardiovascular risk	

■ Conducting early screening, particularly among those with a family history of CVD and associated risk factors, this must be promoted to ensure early detection of subclinical characteristics.

■ Consider the assessment of individual factors in evaluating CVD risk among South Asians, given the concerns of abdominal obesity, hyperglycemia, and inflammation among South Asians, as well as the lack of such measures in the FRS.

■ Implement routine screening for fasting glucose, complete lipid profile, and assessment of metabolic syndrome (Gupta, Singh, & Verma, 2006).

Previous research of South Asians in Western nations have highlighted barriers that South Asians face when changing dietary practices upon chronic disease diagnosis, including fears of alienation from culture (Lawton et al., 2008). Moreover, current classification of food items is not consistent with Western norms of proteins, carbohydrates, and so on, and is instead based on cultural and religious practices (Mukherjea et al., 2013; Mu'Min Chowdhury, Helman, & Greenhalgh, 2000). Thus, additional recommendations promoting vigilance among clinicians to identify at-risk South Asians are needed (see Table 2.2), including:

■ Policies to promote cultural competencies among clinicians who serve the South Asian population.

■ Implementation of culturally relevant dietary guidelines, such as use of the *American Association of Physicians of Indian Origin* (2011) guide to Asian Indian food, which would be valuable for practitioners serving the South Asian community.

In today's healthcare and public health arena, the role of community health workers is unparalleled (Pérez & Martinez, 2008). Of note, Islam et al. (2012) reported that many South Asians living in the United States showed interest in participating in community health worker–led programs to improve at-risk behaviors. Likewise, Ivey et al. (2004) found that Asian Indians reported limited access to CHD information, further demonstrating the need for culturally and linguistically targeted health information. Recommendations in this area include the following:

■ Train public health professionals to incorporate the key characteristics of the *Racial and Ethnic Approaches to Community Health (REACH)* initiative (CDC, 2013) and also involve various community-based organizations to address such disparities.

■ Form collaborations between clinicians, culturally competent nutritionists, and community-based organizations to synergistically implement public health efforts to improve South Asian health through integrated efforts. This is essential in an era where the healthcare system paradigm shifts from volume to value in care, and individual to population health.

Conclusions

When examining the high prevalence of CVD and risk factors among South Asian Americans, and comparing to other Asians as well as the general U.S. population, there are several factors that should be considered influential. While most of South Asian research in the U.S. has been limited to Asian Indians, the empirical evidence supports the heightened CVD risk among the overall South Asian population, including premature CAD, type II diabetes, hypertension, and more. Biologically, the higher prevalence of insulin resistance, proinflammatory markers, and other genetic factors all contribute to the increased risk for CVD in this population, though studies evaluating biological predisposition to heightened CVD risk among South Asians in the United States remain limited. As noted previously by researchers (Palaniappan et al., 2010a), the need to better understand the Asian American population as disaggregated subgroups is critical in addressing their heterogeneity in CVD risk and associated behaviors among South Asians. These data, however, remain limited and can often mask the true burden of CVD among high-risk populations. Lifestyle changes associated with acculturation, including increased binge drinking and higher calorie diets, further contribute to the CVD burden in this population. Additionally, the lack of knowledge within the South Asian community of information regarding tobacco products and their negative health outcomes has further added to the accumulating health disparities among South Asians Americans.

Cumulatively, the literature demonstrates the increasing CVD risk among South Asian Americans and the imperative need for public health efforts to mitigate this burden.

Acknowledgments

We thank Benjamin Becerra for reviewing the manuscript. We are also grateful to the SAPHA editorial team and the anonymous reviewers for their feedback in ensuring that this chapter helps to expand the current literature on the CVD risk among South Asians in the United States.

References

Adaikalakoteswari, A., Balasubramanyam, M., & Mohan, V. (2005). Telomere shortening occurs in Asian Indian Type 2 diabetic patients. *Diabetic Medicine, 22*(9), 1151–1156. http://doi.org/10.1111/j.1464-5491.2005.01574.x

The American Association of Physicians of Indian Origin. (2011). In *Indian Foods: AAPI's Guide to Nutrition, Health, and Diabetes* (2nd ed.). Retrieved from http://aapiusa. org/uploads/files/docs/APPI_Guide_To_Health_And_Nutrition__2nd_Edition.pdf

American Heart Association. (2014). Coronary Artery Disease—Coronary Heart Disease. Retrieved from http://www.heart.org/HEARTORG/Conditions/More/ MyHeartandStrokeNews/Coronary-Artery-Disease---Coronary-Heart-Disease_ UCM_436416_Article.jsp

Amin, A. P., Nathan, S., Evans, A. T., Attanasio, S., Mukhopadhyay, E., Mehta, V., & Kelly, R. F. (2009). The effect of ethnicity on the relationship between premature coronary artery disease and traditional cardiac risk factors among uninsured young adults. *Preventive Cardiology, 12*(3), 128–135.

Anand, S. S., Razak, F., Yi, Q., Davis, B., Jacobs, R., Vuksan, V., . . . Yusuf, S. (2004). C-reactive protein as a screening test for cardiovascular risk in a multiethnic population. *Arteriosclerosis, Thrombosis, and Vascular Biology, 24*(8), 1509–1515. http:// doi.org/10.1161/01.ATV.0000135845.95890.4e

Bainey, K. R., & Jugdutt, B. I. (2009). Increased burden of coronary artery disease in South-Asians living in North America. Need for an aggressive management algorithm. *Atherosclerosis, 204*(1), 1–10. http://doi.org/10.1016/j. atherosclerosis.2008.09.023

Balasubramanyam, A., Rao, S., Misra, R., Sekhar, R. V., & Ballantyne, C. M. (2008). Prevalence of metabolic syndrome and associated risk factors in Asian Indians. *Journal of Immigrant and Minority Health/Center for Minority Public Health, 10*(4), 313–323. http://doi.org/10.1007/s10903-007-9092-4

Banerjee, S. C., Ostroff, J. S., Bari, S., Agostino, T. A. D., Khera, M., Acharya, S., & Gany, F. (2014). Gutka and tambaku paan use among South Asian immigrants: A focus group study. *Journal of Immigrant and Minority Health/Center for Minority Public Health, 16*(3), 531–539. http://doi.org/10.1007/s10903-013-9826-4

Barnes, P. M., Adams, P. F., & Powell-Griner, E. (2008). Health characteristics of the Asian adult population: United States, 2004–2006. *Advance Data*, (394), 1–22.

Baweja, G., Nanda, N. C., Parikh, N., Bhatia, V., & Venkataraman, R. (2004). Prevalence of stroke and associated risk factors in Asian Indians living in the state of Georgia, United States of America. *The American Journal of Cardiology, 93*(2), 267–269.

Becerra, M. B., & Becerra, B. J. (2015). Disparities in age at diabetes diagnosis among Asian Americans: Implications for early preventive measures. *Preventing Chronic Disease, 12*, E146. http://doi.org/10.5888/pcd12.150006

Becerra, M. B., Herring, P., Marshak, H., & Banta, J. E. (2013). Association between acculturation and binge drinking among Asian-Americans: Results from the California health interview survey. *Journal of Addiction, 2013*,248196. http://doi. org/10.1155/2013/248196

Becerra, M. B., Herring, P., Marshak, H. H., & Banta, J. E. (2014). Generational differences in fast food intake among South-Asian Americans: Results from a population-based survey. *Preventing Chronic Disease, 11*, E211. http://doi. org/10.5888/pcd11.140351

Berry, J. W. (2003). Conceptual approaches to acculturation. In K. M. Chun, P. Balls, & G. Mar (Eds.), *Acculturation: Advances in Theory, Measurement, and Applied Research* (pp. 17–37). Washington, DC: American Psychological Association.

Castro, V. S. (2003). *Acculturation and Psychological Adaptation* (Vol. xii). Westport, CT: Praeger Publishers/Greenwood Publishing Group.

Centers for Disease Control and Prevention. (2013). Racial and Ethnic Approaches to Community Health (REACH) Home. Retrieved from http://www.cdc.gov/nccdphp/dch/programs/reach/

Centers for Disease Control and Prevention. (2015). NHIS—About the National Health Interview Survey. Retrieved from http://www.cdc.gov/nchs/nhis/about_nhis.htm

Chandalia, M., Cabo-Chan, A. V., Devaraj, S., Jialal, I., Grundy, S. M., & Abate, N. (2003). Elevated plasma high-sensitivity C-reactive protein concentrations in Asian Indians living in the United States. *Journal of Clinical Endocrinology & Metabolism*, 88(8), 3773–3776. http://doi.org/10.1210/jc.2003-030301

Changrani, J., Gany, F. M., Cruz, G., Kerr, R., & Katz, R. (2006). Paan and gutka use in the United States: A pilot study in Bangladeshi and Indian-Gujarati immigrants in New York City. *Journal of Immigrant & Refugee Studies*, 4(1), 99–110. http://doi.org/10.300/J500v04n01_07

Chung, R. H. G., Kim, B. S. K., & Abreu, J. M. (2004). Asian American multidimensional acculturation scale: Development, factor analysis, reliability, and validity. *Cultural Diversity & Ethnic Minority Psychology*, 10(1), 66–80. http://doi.org/10.1037/1099-9809.10.1.66

Conroy, R. M., Pyörälä, K., Fitzgerald, A. P., Sans, S., Menotti, A., Backer, G. D., . . . Graham, I. M. (2003). Estimation of ten-year risk of fatal cardiovascular disease in Europe: The SCORE project. *European Heart Journal*, 24(11), 987–1003. http://doi.org/10.1016/S0195-668X(03)00114-3

Daniel, M., & Wilbur, J. (2011). Physical activity among South Asian Indian immigrants: an integrative review. *Public Health Nursing*, 28(5), 389–401.

Deepa, R., Velmurugan, K., Arvind, K., Sivaram, P., Sientay, C., Uday, S., & Mohan, V. (2006). Serum levels of interleukin 6, C-reactive protein, vascular cell adhesion molecule 1, and monocyte chemotactic protein 1 in relation to insulin resistance and glucose intolerance—The Chennai Urban Rural Epidemiology Study (CURES). *Metabolism: Clinical and Experimental*, 55(9), 1232–1238. http://doi.org/10.1016/j.metabol.2006.05.008

Dixit, A. A., Azar, K. M., Gardner, C. D., & Palaniappan, L. P. (2011). Incorporation of whole, ancient grains into a modern Asian Indian diet to reduce the burden of chronic disease. *Nutrition Reviews*, 69(8), 479–488. http://doi.org/10.1111/j.1753-4887.2011.00411.x

Dodani, S., & Dong, L. (2011). Acculturation, coronary artery disease and carotid intima media thickness in South Asian immigrants—Unique population with increased risk. *Ethnicity & Disease*, 21(3), 314–321.

Eapen, D., Kalra, G. L., Merchant, N., Arora, A., & Khan, B. V. (2009). Metabolic syndrome and cardiovascular disease in South Asians. *Vascular Health and Risk Management*, 5, 731–743.

Eichler, K., Puhan, M. A., Steurer, J., & Bachmann, L. M. (2007). Prediction of first coronary events with the Framingham score: A systematic review. *American Heart Journal*, 153(5), 722–731, 731.e1–8. http://doi.org/10.1016/j.ahj.2007.02.027

Enas, E. A., & Kannan, S. (2005). *How to Beat the Heart Disease Epidemic among South Asians: A Prevention and Management Guide for Asian Indians and Their Doctors.* Downers Grove, IL: Advanced Heart Lipid Clinic.

Erhardt, L. (2009). Cigarette smoking: An undertreated risk factor for cardiovascular disease. *Atherosclerosis, 205*(1), 23–32. http://doi.org/10.1016/j.atherosclerosis.2009.01.007

Flannery, W. P., Reise, S. P., & Yu, J. (2001). An empirical comparison of acculturation models. *Personality and Social Psychology Bulletin, 27*(8), 1035–1045. http://doi.org/10.1177/0146167201278010

Ghai, N. R., Jacobsen, S. J., Van Den Eeden, S. K., Ahmed, A. T., Haque, R., Rhoads, G. G., & Quinn, V. P. (2012). A comparison of lifestyle and behavioral cardiovascular disease risk factors between Asian Indian and White non-Hispanic men. *Ethnicity & Disease, 22*(2), 168–174.

Gupta, M., Singh, N., & Verma, S. (2006). South Asians and cardiovascular risk: What clinicians should know. *Circulation, 113*(25), e924–e929. http://doi.org/10.1161/CIRCULATIONAHA.105.583815

Gupta, P. C., & Ray, C. S. (2003). Smokeless tobacco and health in India and South Asia. *Respirology (Carlton, Vic.), 8*(4), 419–431.

Harte, A. L., da Silva, N. F., Miller, M. A., Cappuccio, F. P., Kelly, A., O'Hare, J. P., . . . McTernan, P. G. (2012). Telomere length attrition, a marker of biological senescence, is inversely correlated with triglycerides and cholesterol in South Asian males with type 2 diabetes mellitus. *Experimental Diabetes Research, 2012*(895185), 7 p. http://doi.org/10.1155/2012/895185

Haskell, W. L., Lee, I.-M., Pate, R. R., Powell, K. E., Blair, S. N., Franklin, B. A., . . . Bauman, A. (2007). Physical activity and public health: Updated recommendation for adults from the American College of Sports Medicine and the American Heart Association. *Circulation, 116*(9), 1081–1093. http://doi.org/10.1161/CIRCULATIONAHA.107.185649

Hastings, K. G., Jose, P. O., Kapphahn, K. I., Frank, A. T., Goldstein, B. A., Thompson, C. A., . . . & Palaniappan, L. P. (2015). Leading causes of death among Asian American subgroups (2003–2011). *PloS one, 10*(4), e0124341.

Holland, A. T., Wong, E. C., Lauderdale, D. S., & Palaniappan, L. P. (2011). Spectrum of cardiovascular diseases in Asian-American racial/ethnic subgroups. *Annals of Epidemiology, 21*(8), 608–614. http://doi.org/10.1016/j.annepidem.2011.04.004

Islam, N. S., Tandon, D., Mukherji, R., Tanner, M., Ghosh, K., Alam, G., . . . Trinh-Shevrin, C. (2012). Understanding barriers to and facilitators of diabetes control and prevention in the New York City Bangladeshi community: A mixed-methods approach. *American Journal of Public Health, 102*(3), 486–490. http://doi.org/10.2105/AJPH.2011.300381

Ismail, J., Jafar, T. H., Jafary, F. H., White, F., Faruqui, A. M., & Chaturvedi, N. (2004). Risk factors for non-fatal myocardial infarction in young South Asian adults. *Heart, 90*(3), 259–263. http://doi.org/10.1136/hrt.2003.013631

Ivey, S. L., Mehta, K. M., Fyr, C. L. W., & Kanaya, A. M. (2006). Prevalence and correlates of cardiovascular risk factors in South Asians: Population-based data from two California surveys. *Ethnicity & Disease, 16*(4), 886–893.

Ivey, S. L., Patel, S., Kalra, P., Greenlund, K., Srinivasan, S., & Grewal, D. (2004). Cardiovascular health among Asian Indians (CHAI): A community research project. *Journal of Interprofessional Care, 18*(4), 391–402.

Iwamoto, D., Takamatsu, S., & Castellanos, J. (2012). Binge drinking and alcohol-related problems among US-born Asian Americans. *Cultural Diversity and Ethnic Minority Psychology, 18*(3), 219.

Kanaya, A. M., Wassel, C. L., Mathur, D., Stewart, A., Herrington, D., Budoff, M. J., . . . Liu, K. (2010). Prevalence and correlates of diabetes in south Asian Indians in the United States: Findings from the metabolic syndrome and atherosclerosis in south Asians living in America study and the multi-ethnic study of atherosclerosis. *Metabolic Syndrome and Related Disorders, 8*(2), 157–164. http://doi.org/10.1089/met.2009.0062

Landrine, H., & Klonoff, E. A. (2004). Culture change and ethnic-minority health behavior: An operant theory of acculturation. *Journal of Behavioral Medicine, 27*(6), 527–555.

Lawton, J., Ahmad, N., Hanna, L., Douglas, M., Bains, H., & Hallowell, N. (2008). "We should change ourselves, but we can't": Accounts of food and eating practices amongst British Pakistanis and Indians with type 2 diabetes. *Ethnicity & Health, 13*(4), 305–319. http://doi.org/10.1080/13557850701882910

Misra, A., Nigam, P., Hills, A. P., Chadha, D. S., Sharma, V., Deepak, K. K., . . . Physical Activity Consensus Group. (2012). Consensus physical activity guidelines for Asian Indians. *Diabetes Technology & Therapeutics, 14*(1), 83–98. http://doi.org/10.1089/dia.2011.0111

Misra, K. B., Endemann, S. W., & Ayer, M. (2005). Leisure time physical activity and metabolic syndrome in Asian Indian immigrants residing in northern California. *Ethnicity & Disease, 15*(4), 627–634.

Misra, R., Patel, T., Kotha, P., Raji, A., Ganda, O., Banerji, M., . . . Balasubramanyam, A. (2010). Prevalence of diabetes, metabolic syndrome, and cardiovascular risk factors in US Asian Indians: Results from a national study. *Journal of Diabetes and Its Complications, 24*(3), 145–153. http://doi.org/10.1016/j.jdiacomp.2009.01.003

Mohanty, S. A., Woolhandler, S., Himmelstein, D. U., & Bor, D. H. (2005). Diabetes and cardiovascular disease among Asian Indians in the United States. *Journal of General Internal Medicine, 20*(5), 474–478. http://doi.org/10.1111/j.1525-1497.2005.40294.x

Mooteri, S. N., Petersen, F., Dagubati, R., & Pai, R. G. (2004). Duration of residence in the United States as a new risk factor for coronary artery disease (The Konkani Heart Study). *American Journal of Cardiology, 93*(3), 359–361. http://doi.org/10.1016/j.amjcard.2003.09.044

Mu'Min Chowdhury, A., Helman, C., & Greenhalgh, T. (2000). Food beliefs and practices among British Bangladeshis with diabetes: Implications for health education. *Anthropology & Medicine, 7*(2), 209–226. http://doi.org/10.1080/713650589

Mukherjea, A., Morgan, P. A., Snowden, L. R., Ling, P. M., & Ivey, S. L. (2012). Social and cultural influences on tobacco-related health disparities among South Asians in the USA. *Tobacco Control, 21*(4), 422–428. http://doi.org/10.1136/tc.2010.042309

Mukherjea, A., Underwood, K. C., Stewart, A. L., Ivey, S. L., & Kanaya, A. M. (2013). Asian Indian views on diet and health in the United States. *Family & Community Health, 36*(4), 311–323. http://doi.org/10.1097/FCH.0b013e31829d2549

Office of Minority Health. (2012). Obesity and African Americans. Retrieved from http://minorityhealth.hhs.gov/templates/content.aspx?ID=6456

Oza-Frank, R., Ali, M. K., Vaccarino, V., & Narayan, K. M. V. (2009). Asian Americans: Diabetes prevalence across U.S. and World Health Organization weight classifications. *Diabetes Care, 32*(9), 1644–1646. http://doi.org/10.2337/dc09-0573

Palaniappan, L. P., Araneta, M. R. G., Assimes, T. L., Barrett-Connor, E. L., Carnethon, M. R., Criqui, M. H., . . . Wong, N. D. (2010a). Call to action: Cardiovascular disease in Asian Americans: A science advisory from the American Heart Association. *Circulation, 122*(12), 1242–1252. http://doi.org/10.1161/CIR.0b013e3181f22af4

Palaniappan, L., Mukherjea, A., Holland, A., & Ivey, S. L. (2010b). Leading causes of mortality of Asian Indians in California. *Ethnicity & Disease, 20*(1), 53–57.

Palaniappan, L., Wang, Y., & Fortmann, S. P. (2004). Coronary heart disease mortality for six ethnic groups in California, 1990–2000. *Annals of Epidemiology, 14*(7), 499–506. http://doi.org/10.1016/j.annepidem.2003.12.001

Pérez, L. M., & Martinez, J. (2008). Community health workers: Social justice and policy advocates for community health and well-being. *American Journal of Public Health, 98*(1), 11–14. http://doi.org/10.2105/AJPH.2006.100842

Pletcher, M. J., Bibbins-Domingo, K., Liu, K., Sidney, S., Lin, F., Vittinghoff, E., & Hulley, S. B. (2010). Non-optimal lipids commonly present in young adults and coronary calcium later in life. *Annals of Internal Medicine, 153*(3), 137–146. http://doi.org/10.1059/0003-4819-153-3-201008030-00004

Ritchie, S. K., Murphy, E. C.-S., Ice, C., Cottrell, L. A., Minor, V., Elliott, E., & Neal, W. (2010). Universal versus targeted blood cholesterol screening among youth: The CARDIAC project. *Pediatrics, 126*(2), 260–265. http://doi.org/10.1542/peds.2009-2546

SAALT. (2012). About the South Asian Community. Retrieved from http://www.saalt.org/pages/About-the-South-Asian-Community.html

Shah, A., Hernandez, A., Mathur, D., Budoff, M. J., & Kanaya, A. M. (2012). Adipokines and body fat composition in South Asians: Results of the Metabolic Syndrome and Atherosclerosis in South Asians Living in America (MASALA) study. *International Journal of Obesity, 36*(6), 810–816. http://doi.org/10.1038/ijo.2011.167

Silbiger, J. J., Ashtiani, R., Attari, M., Spruill, T. M., Kamran, M., Reynolds, D., . . . Rubinstein, D. (2011). Atheroscerlotic heart disease in Bangladeshi immigrants: Risk factors and angiographic findings. *International Journal of Cardiology, 146*(2), e38–e40. http://doi.org/10.1016/j.ijcard.2008.12.175

Silbiger, J. J., Stein, R., Roy, M., Nair, M. K., Cohen, P., Shaffer, J., . . . Kamran, M. (2013). Coronary artery disease in South Asian immigrants living in New York City: Angiographic findings and risk factor burdens. *Ethnicity & Disease, 23*(3), 292–295.

Silbiger, J. J., Stein, R., Trost, B., Shaffer, J., Kim, J.-H., Cohen, P., & Kamran, M. (2012). Coronary angiographic findings and conventional coronary artery disease risk factors of Indo-Guyanese immigrants with stable angina pectoris and acute coronary syndromes. *Ethnicity & Disease, 22*(1), 12–14.

South Asian Heart Center. (2011). Heart Disease Prevention | Heart Disease Risk Factors. Retrieved from https://southasianheartcenter.org/

South Asian Public Health Association. (2002). A Brown Paper: The Health of South Asians in the United States, 2002. Retrieved from http://joinsapha.org/resource-list/the-brown-paper/

Sriskantharajah, J., & Kai, J. (2007). Promoting physical activity among South Asian women with coronary heart disease and diabetes: What might help? *Family Practice, 24*(1), 71–76. http://doi.org/10.1093/fampra/cml066

Thomas, A., & Ashcraft, A. (2013). Type 2 diabetes risk among Asian Indians in the US: A pilot study. *Nursing Research and Practice, 2013,* e492893. http://doi.org/10.1155/2013/492893

U.S. Department of Health and Human Services. (2011). U.S. HHS Implementation Guidance on Data Collection Standards for Race, Ethnicity, Sex, Primary Language, and Disability Status. Retrieved from http://aspe.hhs.gov/datacncl/standards/ACA/4302/index.shtml

Venkataraman, R., Nanda, N. C., Baweja, G., Parikh, N., & Bhatia, V. (2004). Prevalence of diabetes mellitus and related conditions in Asian Indians living in the United States. *American Journal of Cardiology, 94*(7), 977–980. http://doi.org/10.1016/j.amjcard.2004.06.048

Vyas, A. N., Chaudhary, N., Ramiah, K., & Landry, M. (2012). Addressing a growing community's health needs: Project SAHNA (South Asian Health Needs Assessment). *Journal of Immigrant and Minority Health/Center for Minority Public Health.* http://doi.org/10.1007/s10903-012-9655-x

The White House. (2009). Executive Order 13515—Asian American and Pacific Islander Community | The White House. Retrieved from http://www.whitehouse.gov/the-press-office/executive-order-asian-american-and-pacific-islander-community

WHO. (2012). WHO | Cardiovascular Diseases (CVDs). Retrieved from http://www.who.int/mediacentre/factsheets/fs317/en/index.html

Wu, T.-Y., Wang, J., & Chung, S. (2012). Cardiovascular disease risk factors and diabetes in Asian Indians residing in Michigan. *Journal of Community Health, 37*(2), 395–402. http://doi.org/10.1007/s10900-011-9456-5

Ye, J., Rust, G., Baltrus, P., & Daniels, E. (2009). Cardiovascular risk factors among Asian Americans: Results from a National Health Survey. *Annals of Epidemiology, 19*(10), 718–723. http://doi.org/10.1016/j.annepidem.2009.03.022

Yusuf, S., Hawken, S., Ounpuu, S., Dans, T., Avezum, A., Lanas, F., . . . INTERHEART Study Investigators. (2004). Effect of potentially modifiable risk factors associated with myocardial infarction in 52 countries (the INTERHEART study): Case-control study. *Lancet, 364*(9438), 937–952. http://doi.org/10.1016/S0140-6736(04)17018-9

Chapter 3

Cancer

Minal Patel, Neetu Chawla, and Zul Surani

Contents

Abstract

Objective: Little is known regarding cancer prevention behaviors among South Asians who have immigrated to the United States. This chapter synthesizes

---

This chapter was prepared by Minal Patel in her personal capacity. The opinions expressed in this chapter are the author's own and do not reflect the view of the National Institutes of Health, the Department of Health and Human Services, or the United States government.

current research regarding South Asian Americans (SAAs) and their behaviors as they relate to cancer prevention and control. The objective of this chapter is to review current literature within the last decade regarding cancer risk, cancer prevention and screening, and related resources for SAAs.

Key Findings: Cancer rates among Asian Americans and Pacific Islanders (AAPIs) are generally lower than those in other racial and ethnic subgroups. Despite gains in research among SAAs, little research has been conducted on a large scale that targets this population. On the basis of the limited available research, cancer incidence rates among South Asians who have immigrated to the United States have been steadily increasing over time. This includes many common cancers such as colorectal, prostate, thyroid, pancreas, lung, and breast cancer, as well as non-Hodgkin's lymphoma. SAAs have higher incidence rates compared to their counterparts in India, with breast cancer in women being the most prevalent type of cancer. There is limited information available on the extent of cancer education and awareness programs that target SAAs. Considerable gains, however, have been made in the past decade with regard to community outreach and research involving SAAs.

Recommendations: More epidemiologic research is needed to better understand trends within subgroups of Asians and SAAs in order to better serve the community. Disaggregated data are needed to understand the differences between subgroups within the SAA population. Further research is also needed to understand cancer survivorship and treatment among this group of immigrants. Community-based initiatives that involve key stakeholders in conducting proper evaluation of existing and future programs can help to reduce gaps in cancer prevention and survivorship resources for the SAA community.

Introduction

Cancer among South Asian Americans (SAAs) remains relatively understudied. Advances in disaggregation of data have, however, allowed for a more nuanced examination of cancer incidence, prevalence, and mortality among this Asian subgroup. This chapter examines cancer incidence, prevalence, screening, risk factors, and existing community initiatives among the SAA population. Despite progress in research, these data are still limited. In fact, most incidence and prevalence data for SAAs are gleaned from larger studies of Asian Americans.

This chapter focuses on cancers that have been found to be the most prevalent among the SAA population, including breast, cervical, colorectal, and oral cancers. Preventive behaviors for cancer and evidence-based screening practices among SAAs are also discussed. Literature was reviewed using PubMed, with an emphasis on newer research published within the past 10 years. Information regarding community-based initiatives was acquired using several methods, including personal correspondence, literature reviews, and online searches.

Cancer among Asian Americans and Pacific Islanders

Cancer incidence rates among Asian Americans and Pacific Islanders (AAPIs) are generally lower than those of other racial and ethnic subgroups (Office of Minority Health [OMH], 2014). They do, however, have higher incidence rates of stomach, liver, and bile duct cancers than non-Hispanic Whites in the United States (Ward et al., 2004). Although it is known as the "model minority," many disparities exist among AAPIs, some of which are masked by aggregated data (Gomez et al., 2013; McCracken et al., 2007). As a heterogeneous subgroup of AAPIs, the SAA population is also susceptible to the "model minority" myth. For example, much of the cancer data on SAAs are derived from larger studies on AAPIs. Thus, there is a great deal of variation among AAPIs in terms of cancer incidence, prevalence, and mortality rates, according to limited information separated by subgroups.

Cancer among South Asians in the United States

Existing research suggests that cancer incidence rates among SAAs have been steadily increasing over time. This rate of cancer incidence and prevalence differs from other Asian subgroups, including South Asians who are living internationally. A comparison of cancer incidence rates among South Asians living in India, the United States, Singapore, and the United Kingdom found that for many common cancers (i.e., colorectal, prostate, thyroid, pancreas, lung, breast, and non-Hodgkin's lymphoma), South Asian immigrants living in Singapore and the United Kingdom had higher incidence rates when compared to their counterparts living in India (Rastogi et al., 2008). Details of cancer incidence rates can be found in Table 3.1 based on research by Rastogi et al. (2008). Interestingly, findings from this study suggest that patterns of cancer incidence among SAAs appear to be more similar to the White population living in the United States than to the South Asian population living in Singapore or India. In fact, Rastogi et al. found that SAAs had cancer rates higher than South Asians living in India, with the exception of cancers of the oral cavity, esophagus, larynx, and cervix uteri. Disaggregated data from the *Surveillance, Epidemiology, and End Results* (SEER) program between 1990

Table 3.1 Cancer[a] Incidence in India and South Asian Subgroups

Cancer	India[b] 1993–1997		Singapore Indians 1993–1997			U.K. South Asians 1999–2001			U.S. Asian Indians/Pakistanis 1999–2001					
										Rates[c] and Standard Error[d]				
	Counts	Rates[c]	Counts	Rates[c]	Standard Error[d]	Counts	Rates[c]	Standard Error[d]	Counts	Lower Bound[e]	Standard Error	Upper Bound[e]	Standard Error	
A. Males														
All cancers	404,309	99.0	649	101.5	4.0	4,919	172.9	2.5	2,508	151.6	3	175.8	3.5	
Colon and rectum	19,508	4.7	56	8.3	1.1	484	17.3	0.8	230	13.0	0.9	15.0	1.0	
Liver	9,153	2.3	50	7.9	1.1	186	6.6	0.5	68	4.2	0.5	4.9	0.6	
Pancreas	5,711	1.4	16	2.3	0.6	162	6.0	0.5	57	3.5	0.5	4.1	0.5	
Lung and bronchus	35,495	9.0	68	10.0	1.2	617	22.4	0.9	252	16.8	1.1	19.5	1.2	
Prostate	16,789	4.6	65	9.9	1.2	891	33.7	1.1	696	47.4	1.8	54.9	2.1	
Urinary bladder	12,444	3.2	33	5.4	0.9	186	7.0	0.5	105	6.8	0.7	7.9	0.8	
Thyroid	4,361	1.0	–f	—	—	38	1.2	0.2	52	2.0	0.3	2.3	0.3	
Non-Hodgkin's lymphoma	13,900	3.2	19	3.1	0.7	347	11.3	0.6	156	8.3	0.7	9.6	0.8	
B. Females														
All cancers	447,592	104.4	554	131.7	5.6	5,119	179.2	2.5	2,464	142.2	2.9	164.4	3.3	

Cancer	India[b] 1993–1997		Singapore Indians 1993–1997			U.K. South Asians 1999–2001			U.S. Asian Indians/Pakistanis 1999–2001				
										Rates[c] and Standard Error[d]			
	Counts	Rates[c]	Counts	Rates[c]	Standard Error[d]	Counts	Rates[c]	Standard Error[d]	Counts	Lower Bound[e]	Standard Error	Upper Bound[e]	Standard Error
Colon and rectum	13,555	3.2	53	14.9	2.0	333	12.1	0.7	168	10.2	0.8	11.8	0.9
Pancreas	3,506	0.8	–	–	–	102	3.9	0.4	35	2.3	0.4	2.7	0.5
Lung and bronchus	8,046	2.0	17	5.4	1.3	189	7.3	0.5	113	7.3	0.7	8.5	0.8
Breast	82,951	19.1	167	36.7	2.8	1,894	64.6	1.5	918	50.6	1.7	58.2	1.9
Thyroid	8,686	1.9	22	3.5	0.7	120	3.6	0.3	130	6.2	0.5	7.1	0.6
Non-Hodgkin's lymphoma	7,389	1.7	12	2.5	0.7	247	8.7	0.6	89	5.5	0.6	6.4	0.7

[a] Selected cancers from Rastogi et al. (2008).
[b] As estimated by Globocan 2002, IARC; standard errors not calculated because actual national India counts are not available.
[c] Rates per 100,000, age-adjusted to the 1960 Segi world population.
[d] Standard error estimated as the rate/square root (count) (3).
[e] Lower and upper bound estimates for U.S. Asian Indian/Pakistani cancer incidence rates are presented because the U.S. 2000 Census provides two values for this population (either Asian Indian or Pakistani alone, or in combination with another ethnicity).
[f] Dash indicates statistic not shown, rate based on less than 12 cases.

and 2008 also provide insights into the SAA population with regard to cancer incidence rates (Gomez et al., 2013). Results from this national surveillance program indicate that SAA men (Asian Indian and Pakistani men only[*]) had a 2.2% annual increase in the incidence of prostate cancer in the 1990s, followed by a 3-year decline (–11.1%), and another increase from 2006 to 2008 (11.1%) (Gomez et al., 2013). Gomez et al. (2013) also reported that SAA men experienced increases in rates of lung cancer (2.9%) from 1990 to 2008, with nonsignificant increases observed for bladder (1.1%) and non-Hodgkin's lymphoma (0.8%) during this same period. In SAA women, a significant annual increase in breast cancer (3%) and uterine cancer (3%) was found between 1990 and 2008 (Gomez et al., 2013).

In California, which has one of the largest SAA populations in the United States (Hoefel, Rastogi, Kim, & Shahid, 2012), an increase in the incidence of colorectal cancer (2.8%) was found among SAA women from 1998 to 2007 (Giddings, Kwong, Parikh-Patel, Bates, & Snipes, 2012). This increased incidence in the United States indicates a need for more research among SAAs in order to better understand the nuances specific to this population.

In SAA women, breast cancer is the most prevalent type of cancer and the leading cause of cancer mortality (Deapen, Liu, Perkins, Bernstein, & Ross, 2002; Jain, Mills, & Parikh-Patel, 2005). Oral cancers are also prevalent among this subgroup, despite evidence that the use of Western forms of tobacco such as cigarettes and cigars are lower among Asian Indians living in the United States than the general U.S. rates of smoking (Delnevo, Steinberg, Hudson, Ulpe, & DiPaola, 2011; McCarthy et al., 2005; Mukherjea, Modayil, & Tong, 2011; Mukherjea, Wackowski, Lee, & Delnevo, 2014; Patel & McCarthy, 2011).

It is important to note that oral cancers among SAAs are likely to be high due to the popularity of alternative tobacco products, including *paan, paan masala, gutka, bidi,* hookah, betel leaf quid, *supari, mishri,* and areca nut chews (Ahluwalia, 2005; Changrani, Cruz, Kerr, Katz, & Gany, 2006; Divan, 2002; Mukherjea et al., 2011; Mukherjea & Modayil, 2013; Rastogi et al., 2008). The use of alternative tobacco products is culturally relevant given their presence at cultural and religious events in the South Asian community. Researchers assessing oral cancer risk among SAAs in New York City have shined the light on the growing significance of this disease in SAAs and suggest that oral cancer poses "a serious public health problem" for this population (Ahluwalia, 2005).

---

[*] Asian Indians and Pakistanis were combined into one group by S. L. Gomez et al. (2013) due to SEER coding rules already in existence. Other South Asian subgroups were aggregated in the larger "other Asian" subgroup category, and data could not be disaggregated.

Primary and Secondary Cancer Prevention among South Asians

In recent years, more research has been conducted among the SAA community on various cancers and related behaviors. Still, little is known regarding cancer prevention behaviors. Cancer prevention can be separated into primary and secondary prevention. Primary cancer prevention refers to lifestyle-related factors that can prevent the development of cancer. These can include behaviors related to nutrition, physical activity, and tobacco use (Dos Santos Silva, 1999; Spratt, 1981). Risk factors that can affect primary cancer prevention include smoking, physical inactivity, and poor dietary behaviors.

Although more research is needed to understand the diet of the SAA population, it is likely that the adoption of a Western diet may be related to cancer incidence. This was seen among Chinese women who adopted a Western diet that was heavy in meat and sugar (Cui et al., 2007). Similarly, the lack of physical activity is also correlated with the risk for several cancers, including colon, breast, and lung cancers (Ballard-Barbash, Friedenreich, Slattery, & Thune, 2006; Bianchini, Kaaks, & Vainio, 2002; I. Lee & Oguma, 2006; Slattery, 2004; Tardon et al., 2005). Although little research has been conducted involving SAAs in the area of physical activity (Thune & Furberg, 2001), given the comorbidities of heart disease and diabetes among SAAs, it is important to address physical inactivity and its correlation to cancer risk.

Unlike dietary habits and physical activity, there is clear evidence that links smoking to cancer. It is well documented that the use of tobacco increases the risk of lung cancer, the most preventable form of cancer (American Cancer Society, 2014). One of the most widely studied areas of cancer prevention is oral cancer. Within the South Asian population, there are culturally specific tobacco products such as *bidis* and chewing tobacco, as well as traditional tobacco products.

In addition to primary prevention, secondary prevention includes screenings that have been instrumental in the early detection of cancer. The most widely used screenings include mammography for breast cancer, Papanicolaou test (Pap test, known previously as Pap smear) for cervical cancer, and colonoscopy for prostate cancer (Spratt, 1981). One of the issues in focusing solely on secondary prevention, however, is that many SAA men and women face barriers regarding access to care, affordability, and cultural constraints. This is further detailed in the following sections, along with the type of cancer, detection strategies, and barriers that prevent early cancer detection in the SAA population.

Breast Cancer

Although SAA women have lower incidence rates of breast cancer compared to other women, available research has documented a number of cancer disparities faced by this population. This includes presentation at later stages, poorer survival rates, and suboptimal rates of breast cancer screening (Bottorff et al., 1998, 1999; Gomez, Tan, Keegan, & Clarke, 2007; Keegan, Gomez, Clarke, Chan, & Glaser, 2007; Moran, Gonsalves, Goss, & Ma, 2011; Parikh-Patel, Mills, & Jain, 2006; Ponce, Gatchell, & Brown, 2003; Rashidi & Rajaram, 2000; Rastogi et al., 2008). These disparities apply to SAA women from all socioeconomic levels, including those who are highly educated, are English-speaking, and have relatively higher incomes (Bottorff et al., 1998; Gomez et al., 2007; Jain et al., 2005; Keegan et al., 2007; Moran et al., 2011; Parikh-Patel et al., 2006).

Despite these factors, rates of mammography in the SAA population remain well below national recommendations and objectives promoted by *Healthy People 2020*, specifically that 81.1% of women aged 50–74 years should have received a mammogram within the past 2 years (Menon, Szalacha, Prabhughate, & Kue, 2014). Studies have found that in the United States, Asian Indian women are significantly less likely than White women to participate in mammography screening. In a convenience sample of SAA women above the age of 40 living in New York City, 55.8% reported having received a mammogram in the past 2 years, compared to 71% in a White population (Islam, Kwon, Senie, & Kathuria, 2006). Research by Hasnain and colleagues (2014) explored breast cancer screening practices among immigrant Muslim women living in Chicago, of which, 49% were South Asian, and 51% were Middle Eastern. Among this mixed sample, 70% of the women reported having had a mammogram at least once; however only 52% had had one within the past 2 years. (Hasnain et al. 2004). Another study found that only 39% of SAA women received timely mammograms, which was significantly lower than that in all other Asian groups, as well as White women, of whom 66% received timely mammograms (Pourat, Kagawa-Singer, Breen, & Sripipatana, 2010). Pourat et al. (2010) noted that possible explanations for their findings could include access-related factors, such as insurance status and having a usual source of care, and acculturation barriers to screening, such as time spent in the United States and English proficiency.

A national study in the United States found that 63% of SAA women reported having had a mammogram in the past 2 years and that those least likely to do so included women who were less than age 50, unemployed, or noncitizens (Gomez et al., 2007). More recently, research found that cancer screening among Asian Indians living in the United States could be positively associated with higher educational levels, the number of years living in the United States, access to health care, and a family history of cancer (Misra, Menon, Vadaparampil, & BeLue, 2011). Still, limited research has examined the potential causes of breast cancer disparities among SAA women or identified factors that may influence care-seeking behaviors, the types of resources they seek, or the sources of support available to them in their community.

Cervical Cancer

Rates of cervical cancer screening vary among SAA women but use of the Pap test among this group remains well below *Healthy People 2020* recommendations. In one study, researchers examined breast and cervical cancer screening among a community-based convenience sample of South Asian immigrants living in Chicago (Menon, Szalacha, & Prabhughate, 2012). In this group of women, they found that approximately two-thirds of the sample (65.5%) reported ever having a mammogram and only one-third (32.8%) reported ever having a Pap test or vaginal examination. Several predisposing factors, including country of birth, years in the United States, acculturation, age, and other acknowledged barriers to screening, were identified as significant predictors of breast and cervical screening, whereas only past screening behavior was an enabling factor (Menon et al., 2012).

In contrast, another study used in-person interviews among a convenience sample of SAA women living in New York City and found that 67% reported having previously received a Pap test (Islam et al., 2006). In California, a state-wide survey found that 73% of SAA women aged 18 years and older reported receiving a Pap test within the previous 3 years, which still remains approximately 20% below the *Healthy People 2020* objectives (Pourat et al., 2010). Notably, the sample from this study had a substantially higher income and was more likely to be insured, as compared to the sample from the study conducted by Menon et al. (2012) in Chicago. Taken together, these studies indicate that there are lower cervical cancer screening rates across the socioeconomic gradient among SAA women. They also highlight the heterogeneity of this population as well as the need for targeted interventions based upon socioeconomic status, access-related factors, English proficiency, time spent in the United States, religion, and geographic location among SAAs.

Colorectal Cancer

Several studies have documented disparities among SAAs related to colorectal cancer, including increased incidence and low rates of colorectal cancer screening (Bharmal & Chaudhry, 2012; Giddings et al., 2012; H. Y. Lee, Lundquist, Ju, Luo, & Townsend, 2011; Menon et al., 2014). Menon et al. (2014) found that language acculturation and medical mistrust were significantly associated with completion of stool blood tests, whereas English proficiency, higher income, living in the United States more than 5 years, perception of colorectal cancer risk, and past stool blood tests significantly predicted whether they underwent endoscopy for screening. Another study found that even among highly educated SAAs, the use of colorectal cancer screening was very low, at approximately 50% (Bharmal & Chaudhry, 2012). Lee et al. (2011) conducted a study in California that combined three cycles of data from the *California Health Interview Survey* (CHIS). They found that SAAs had a 42.3% lower likelihood of getting colorectal cancer screening, as compared to 57.7% among non-Hispanic Whites.

Oral Cancer

Despite the increased risk of oral cancer among SAAs, barriers preventing access to oral health services do exist and the regular use of dental care remains suboptimal within this population. Qiu and Ni (2003) examined data from the *National Health Interview Survey* (NHIS) and found that Asian Indians in the United States were less likely to have seen a dentist over the previous year as compared with other Asians or Whites (56.6%). This limited utilization of oral health services provides an important opportunity for intervention among the SAA population in order to help reduce the risk of developing oral cancer and increase awareness of the negative effects related to the use of alternative tobacco products.

Cancer Information and Education Programs

There is limited information available on cancer education and awareness programs specifically targeting the SAA population. In fact, the majority of studies or programs that focus on cancer awareness among South Asians were conducted outside of the United States. Table 3.2 provides a snapshot of various programs that have been developed for the SAA community and shows that progress is being made in introducing cancer prevention resources to the SAA community. Of note, however, is that the educational materials and programs developed nationwide over the past 10 years have not been thoroughly evaluated or tested in terms of their efficacy or effectiveness. In fact, a lack of proper evaluation can lead to ineffective interventions and can have negative consequences, including wasted resources, dissemination of ineffective materials, and possibly even harm to the community. The majority of available cancer prevention materials and programs focus on breast cancer, leaving out other leading cancers that affect the SAA population and excluding the SAA male population entirely, along with potential cancer risks facing them. In addition, given that disparities do exist among various SAA subpopulations, special efforts to target these subpopulations have not been made, particularly in areas with high concentrations of Bangladeshis, Pakistanis, and Nepalese (Glenn, Chawla, Surani, & Bastani, 2009).

Table 3.2 Examples of Cancer Information and Education Programs Targeting South Asians at the Community Level

Program	Targeted Cancer(s)	Targeted Population	Geographic Location	Program Information	Additional Information
American Cancer Society	Breast cancer	SAA women	States with large SAA populations across the United States, including New York and New Jersey (SAPHA, 2002).	• Increased awareness about cancer by providing educational materials, up-to-date research, and an opportunity to conduct workshops specific to the South Asian community. • Workshops offered free screening programs using mobile mammography units at faith venues such as mosques, temples, and *gurdwaras*.	• Earliest known cancer education effort targeting South Asian communities in the United States. • Partial program results shared at the American Public Health Association's Annual Meeting in 2000, and gave precedent to future intervention work in the United States targeting South Asians.

(Continued)

Table 3.2 Examples of Cancer Information and Education Programs Targeting South Asians at the Community Level (*Continued*)

Program	Targeted Cancer(s)	Targeted Population	Geographic Location	Program Information	Additional Information
Breast cancer evaluation at grocery stores (Sadler et al., 2001)	Breast cancer	Asian Indian women	Southern California	• Evaluation through grocery stores to determine breast cancer knowledge, attitude, and screening behaviors specifically with Indian women in 2001 (Sadler et al., 2001). • Educational program regarding access to breast cancer screening services and information on free screening available to lower income women through the Breast Cancer Early Detection Program.	• Pre-post study design, at follow-up, 34.4% of women aged 40 and above said that they had set up a breast cancer screening exam. • 85.7% of women who set up screening exams did so with their doctors and an additional 9.5% went to a clinic (Sadler et al., 2001). • Effective in informing women about breast cancer and improving intention to screen and changing behaviors.

Program	Targeted Cancer(s)	Targeted Population	Geographic Location	Program Information	Additional Information
					• No evidence if program was adopted by communities or organizations reaching Indian women.
South Asian Network's (SAN) Community Health Action Initiative (CHAI) (Surani, Baezconde-Garbanati, Bastani, & Montano, 2003)	Breast and cervical cancer	SAAs	Southern California	• Partnership with the Asian American Network for Cancer Awareness, Research and Training at UCLA's Jonsson Comprehensive Cancer Center and the National Cancer Institute's (NCI) Cancer Information Service at USC Norris Comprehensive Cancer Center. • South Asian community leaders used science-based materials from NCI and adapted them into South Asian languages.	• No evidence if workshops sustained or what their impact was in the community.

(Continued)

Table 3.2 Examples of Cancer Information and Education Programs Targeting South Asians at the Community Level (*Continued*)

Program	Targeted Cancer(s)	Targeted Population	Geographic Location	Program Information	Additional Information
				• Breast cancer awareness workshops implemented using community-based participatory research methods.	
Saath USA (Saath-USA, 2008).	Breast, cervical, colorectal, and ovarian cancers	SAA women	California	• In collaboration with UCLA's Jonsson Comprehensive Cancer Center and support from the California Breast Cancer Research Program. • Using community-based participatory research methods, evidence-based health education strategy conducted to increase breast cancer awareness among South Asian women, aged 40 and above, and to inform community of available breast health services, targeted at low-income and uninsured families.	• Program proven successful and currently being implemented by Saath-USA in Southern and Northern California (Surani, Agustin, Lally, Kashiwagi, & Barnett, 2012).

Program	Targeted Cancer(s)	Targeted Population	Geographic Location	Program Information	Additional Information
				• Main components: culturally and linguistically appropriate photo novella, outreach interviewing by trained lay health advisors using motivational interviewing, and "change talk" to help women navigate barriers toward obtaining and keeping mammography screening appointments. • Translated into several South Asian languages, available on website (Saath-USA, 2008).	
South Asian Total Health Initiative (Mehrotra, 2010).	Breast cancer	SAA women	New Jersey	• Cancer awareness module developed and delivered through collaborations with local community organizations, radio and television shows, and faith communities.	

(Continued)

Table 3.2 Examples of Cancer Information and Education Programs Targeting South Asians at the Community Level (*Continued*)

Program	Targeted Cancer(s)	Targeted Population	Geographic Location	Program Information	Additional Information
				• Advocates for and conducts research on South Asian health with the goal of improving community wellness, improving health literacy, and increasing delivery of culturally competent health care.	
The Smokeless Tobacco Product Prevention and Awareness Network through the South Asian Health Initiative (SAHI).	Tobacco-related cancers	Gujarati and Bangladeshi immigrants (Changrani et al., 2006).	New York	• Ongoing education regarding oral cancer is offered through religious and community organizations, health fairs coordinated through SAHI (SAHI, 2015).	• SAHI is part of a larger NIH-funded initiative to reduce health disparities in the U.S. South Asian population, through a multidisciplinary program coordinated by Memorial Sloan Kettering (Napolitano, 2013).

Program	Targeted Cancer(s)	Targeted Population	Geographic Location	Program Information	Additional Information
The Pink Pashmina Project through the Metropolitan Asian Family Services and the Asian Health Coalition funded by the Susan G. Komen Foundation (Asian Health Coalition, 2012).	Breast cancer	SAA American women	Illinois	• Provides culturally and linguistically appropriate health education to South Asian women. • Provides support services such as transportation for screening appointments. • Outreached to grassroots agencies such as the Muslim Resource Center, providing free mammograms and access to treatment. • Cancer education materials available in English, Gujarati, Hindi, and Urdu.	
Susan G. Komen Foundation in developed videos in English with subtitle options in various languages (Komen, 2014).	Breast cancer	SAA women	National	• Videos available in Hindi and Punjabi to increase awareness of breast cancer. • Stress key cancer control messages: (a) "know your risk of breast cancer," (b) "get screened," (c) "know what is normal for you," and (d) "make healthy lifestyle choices."	

Recommendations

Overall cancer rates among the SAA population are low; however, certain subgroups within this population are masked in the existing data. In order to fully understand disparities among the SAA community, the following recommendations are presented:

- Further disaggregated data are needed. This includes disaggregation of data separating SAA from the larger AAPI research and within the SAA community. Within the South Asian subcontinent, there are several differences with regard to culture, language, religion, and food—all of which can impact cancer-related health behaviors. Additionally, Asian Indians have higher household incomes and levels of educational attainment than Bangladeshis, Pakistanis, and Sri Lankans, which may further lead to health disparities (Asian and Pacific Islander American Health Forum, 2006).
- More epidemiological research is needed for the SAA population to determine the incidence and prevalence of cancer at the national level. Studies should include large samples of underserved SAA subgroups, such as Bangladeshis and Pakistanis, in order to understand the nuances among South Asian subgroup cancer rates. These data would help in allocating limited funding to subgroups that are most in need of screening and education efforts.
- More research is needed to track cancer screening rates of breast, cervical, and colorectal cancers among South Asian subgroups. Current research on SAA subgroups focuses on using purposive and convenience sampling. Future research should focus on more rigorous research methodology and using random sampling in order to be more representative of the community. This is a large task, as funding and community support are required in order to truly capture a large enough sample size to address differences within SAA subgroups. The return on investment may not be high if representative samples of SAA subgroups are not acquired. Currently, this may only be possible in states with large SAA populations, including California, New Jersey, and New York.
- Qualitative research should be conducted in order to better understand and address potential barriers to cancer screening. At the local level, researchers need to work with communities to document and disseminate information about efforts already in place for cancer prevention and screening among SAAs. A major research gap includes the lack of information regarding cancer survivorship among SAAs. Qualitative research aimed at

understanding barriers faced by cancer survivors is needed in order to fully understand the resources that are required by this community both before and after cancer treatment.

■ More research is needed regarding behavioral changes that may occur during immigration and living in the United States. Further research should focus on cancers that are preventable through lifestyle modifications.

■ Community-based participatory research that involves leaders, including those at faith-based institutions, is imperative for engaging the community and understanding culturally appropriate lifestyle behavior changes. More focused evaluation research is needed in order to advance the community work that has been conducted to date. Without proper evaluation of community-based programs, it is possible that failed interventions may be repeated, and effective programs may not have the proper impact in changing behaviors and screening practices.

■ Existing community organizations should create a network for cancer surveillance and screening, and work to share existing materials, so as not to recreate the wheel. Organizations such as the South Asian Public Health Association (SAPHA) can facilitate these conversations, allowing for greater access to educational materials.

■ Evaluation components should also be added with collaborators from research institutions to further determine the effectiveness and efficacy of existing programs and materials. Through a collaborative effort, strides can be made in preventing cancers such as breast and oral cancers, which disproportionally impact the SAA community.

Conclusions

Despite recent gains in research among the SAA population, much work remains. There are very few cancer education programs that have proven to be effective in the United States and that specifically target the SAA communities. In addition, more stringent research is needed to understand cancer prevention and screening behaviors among the growing subpopulation of SAAs. Finally, there is a need for better cancer surveillance and prevention with disaggregated data that focus on trends among the various subgroups that make up the South Asian population. By closely examining cancer risk, prevention, and screening practices among SAAs, and evaluating existing resources, better progress can be made toward the prevention of cancer in this population.

References

Ahluwalia, K. P. (2005). Assessing the oral cancer risk of South-Asian immigrants in New York City. *Cancer, 104*(S12), 2959–2961.

American Cancer Society. (2014). *Cancer facts & figures 2014.* Retrieved from http://www.cancer.org/acs/groups/content/@research/documents/webcontent/acspc-042151.pdf

Asian and Pacific Islander American Health Forum. (2006). *APIAHF health brief: South Asians in the United States.* Retrieved from http://www.apiahf.org/sites/default/files/APIAHF_Healthbrief08g_2006.pdf

Asian Health Coalition. (2012). *Pink Pashmina Project.* Retrieved from http://www.asianhealth.org/the-issues/cancer/educational-materials/

Ballard-Barbash, R., Friedenreich, C., Slattery, M., & Thune, I. (2006). Obesity and body composition. In D. Schottenfeld & J. F. Fraumeni Jr. (Eds.), *Cancer epidemiology and prevention* (3rd ed., pp. 422–448). New York, NY: Oxford University Press.

Hoefel, E. M., Rastogi, S., Kim, M. O., Shahid, H. (2012). *The Asian population 2000: Census 2010 brief.* Retrieved from https://www.census.gov/prod/cen2010/briefs/c2010br-11.pdf

Bharmal, N., & Chaudhry, S. (2012). Preventive health services delivery to South Asians in the United States. *Journal of Immigrant and Minority Health, 14*(5), 797–802.

Bianchini, F., Kaaks, R., & Vainio, H. (2002). Weight control and physical activity in cancer prevention. *Obesity Reviews, 3*(1), 5–8.

Bottorff, J. L., Johnson, J. L., Bhagat, R., Grewal, S., Balneaves, L. G., Clarke, H., & Hilton, B. (1998). Beliefs related to breast health practices: The perceptions of South Asian women living in Canada. *Social Science & Medicine, 47*(12), 2075–2085.

Bottorff, J. L., Johnson, J. L., Bhagat, R., Grewal, S., Balneaves, L. G., Hilton, B. A., & Clarke, H. (1999). Breast health practices and South Asian women. *The Canadian Nurse, 95*(9), 24–27.

Changrani, J., Cruz, G., Kerr, R., Katz, R., & Gany, F. M. (2006). Paan and gutka use in the United States: A pilot study in Bangladeshi and Indian-Gujarati immigrants in New York City. *Journal of Immigrant & Refugee Studies, 4*(1), 99–109.

Cui, X., Dai, Q., Tseng, M., Shu, X.-O., Gao, Y.-T., & Zheng, W. (2007). Dietary patterns and breast cancer risk in the Shanghai Breast Cancer Study. *Cancer Epidemiology Biomarkers & Prevention, 16*(7), 1443–1448.

Deapen, D., Liu, L., Perkins, C., Bernstein, L., & Ross, R. K. (2002). Rapidly rising breast cancer incidence rates among Asian-American women. *International Journal of Cancer, 99*(5), 747–750.

Delnevo, C. D., Steinberg, M. B., Hudson, S. V., Ulpe, R., & DiPaola, R. S. (2011). Epidemiology of cigarette and smokeless tobacco use among South Asian immigrants in the Northeastern United States. *Journal of Oncology, 2011.* doi: 10.1155/2011/252675. Epub 2011 May 17.

Divan, H. (2002). Cancer incidence and mortality in Asian Indians: A review of literature from the United States, South Asia, and beyond. *Asian American and Pacific Islander Journal of Health, 10*(2), 73–85.

Dos Santos Silva, S. (1999). *Cancer epidemiology, principles and methods.* Lyon, France: International Agency for Research on Cancer. Retrieved from http://www.iarc.fr/en/publications/pdfs-online/epi/cancerepi/CancerEpi.pdf

Giddings, B. H., Kwong, S. L., Parikh-Patel, A., Bates, J. H., & Snipes, K.P. (2012). Going against the tide: Increasing incidence of colorectal cancer among Koreans, Filipinos, and South Asians in California, 1988–2007. *Cancer Causes & Control, 23*(5), 691–702.

Glenn, B. A., Chawla, N., Surani, Z., & Bastani, R. (2009). Rates and sociodemographic correlates of cancer screening among South Asians. *Journal of Community Health, 34*(2), 113–121.

Gomez, S., Tan, S., Keegan, T., & Clarke, C. (2007). Disparities in mammographic screening for Asian women in California: A cross-sectional analysis to identify meaningful groups for targeted intervention. *BMC Cancer, 7*(1), 201.

Gomez, S. L., Noone, A.-M., Lichtensztajn, D. Y., Scoppa, S., Gibson, J. T., Liu, L., . . . Wilkens, L. R. (2013). Cancer incidence trends among Asian American populations in the United States, 1990 to 2008. *Journal of the National Cancer Institute, 105*(15), 1096–1110. doi: 10.1093/jnci/djt157. Epub 2013 Jul 22.

Hasnain, M., Menon, U., Szalacha, L., Ferrans, C.E. (2014) Breast cancer screening practices among first-generation immigrant Muslim women. *Journal of Women's Health* (Larchmt). Jul;23(7):602–12. doi: 10.1089/jwh.2013.4569. Epub 2014 May 27.

Islam, N., Kwon, S. C., Senie, R., & Kathuria, N. (2006). Breast and cervical cancer screening among South Asian women in New York City. *Journal of Immigrant and Minority Health, 8*(3), 211–221.

Jain, R. V., Mills, P. K., & Parikh-Patel, A. (2005). Cancer incidence in the south Asian population of California, 1988–2000. *Journal of Carcinogenesis, 4*(1), 21.

Keegan, T. H., Gomez, S. L., Clarke, C. A., Chan, J. K., & Glaser, S. L. (2007). Recent trends in breast cancer incidence among 6 Asian groups in the Greater Bay Area of Northern California. *International Journal of Cancer, 120*(6), 1324–1329.

Komen, S. G. (2014). *Translated Komen educational materials.* Retrieved from http://ww5.komen.org/translations.html

Lee, H. Y., Lundquist, M., Ju, E., Luo, X., & Townsend, A. (2011). Colorectal cancer screening disparities in Asian Americans and Pacific Islanders: Which groups are most vulnerable? *Ethnicity & Health, 16*(6), 501–518.

Lee, I., & Oguma, Y. (2006). Physical activity. *Cancer Epidemiology and Prevention,* 449–467. doi: 10.1371/journal.pone.0088495. eCollection 2014.

McCarthy, W. J., Divan, H., Shah, D., Maxwell, A., Freed, B., Bastani, B., . . . Surani, Z. (2005). *California Asian Indian Tobacco Survey— 2004.* Sacramento, CA: Department of Health Services. Retrieved from https://www.cdph.ca.gov/programs/tobacco/Documents/Resources/Publications/CTCPAsianIndianTobaccoStudy.pdf

McCracken, M., Olsen, M., Chen, M. S., Jemal, A., Thun, M., Cokkinides, V., . . . Ward, E. (2007). Cancer incidence, mortality, and associated risk factors among Asian Americans of Chinese, Filipino, Vietnamese, Korean, and Japanese ethnicities. *CA: A Cancer Journal for Clinicians, 57*(4), 190–205.

Mehrotra, N. (2010). *South Asian Total Health Initial (SATHI)—Improving the health, well being, and quality of life of the South Asian Community.* Retrieved from http://www.state.nj.us/njsncc/documents/sathi_feb10.pdf

Menon, U., Szalacha, L. A., & Prabhughate, A. (2012). Breast and cervical cancer screening among South Asian immigrants in the United States. *Cancer Nursing, 35*(4), 278–287.

Menon, U., Szalacha, L., Prabhughate, A., & Kue, J. (2014). Correlates of colorectal cancer screening among South Asian immigrants in the United States. *Cancer Nursing, 37*(1), E19–E27.

Misra, R., Menon, U., Vadaparampil, S. T., & BeLue, R. (2011). Age-and sex-specific cancer prevention and screening practices among Asian Indian immigrants in the United States. *Journal of Investigative Medicine, 59*(5), 787–792.

Moran, M. S., Gonsalves, L., Goss, D. M., & Ma, S. (2011). Breast cancers in US residing Indian-Pakistani versus non-Hispanic White women: Comparative analysis of clinical-pathologic features, treatment, and survival. *Breast Cancer Research and Treatment, 128*(2), 543–551.

Mukherjea, A, Modayil, M. V., & Tong, E. K. (2011, October). Moving towards a true depiction of tobacco use among South Asians: Analyses from the California Asian Indian Tobacco Use Survey. Poster session presented at the APHA 139th Annual Meeting and Exposition (APHA 2011, poster 247219), Washington, DC.

Mukherjea, A., & Modayil, M. V. (2013). Culturally specific tobacco use and South Asians in the United States: A review of the literature and promising strategies for intervention. *Health Promotion Practice, 14*(5 Suppl.), 48S–60S. doi: 10.1177/1524839913485585. Epub 2013 May 20.

Mukherjea, A., Wackowski, O. A., Lee, Y. O., & Delnevo, C. D. (2014). Asian American, Native Hawaiian and Pacific Islander tobacco use patterns. *American Journal of Health Behavior, 38*(3), 362–369.

Napolitano, E. (2013). *Reducing health disparities in US South Asian population.* Retrieved from http://www.mskcc.org/blog/reducing-health-disparities-us-south-asian-population

Office of Minority Health. (2014). *Cancer and Asians/Pacific Islanders.* Retrieved from http://minorityhealth.hhs.gov/omh/browse.aspx?lvl=4&lvlid=46

Parikh-Patel, A., Mills, P. K., & Jain, R. V. (2006). Breast cancer survival among South Asian women in California (United States). *Cancer Causes & Control, 17*(3), 267–272.

Patel, M., & McCarthy, W. (2011, October). *Ethnic enclaves, acculturation, mental health, and tobacco use among California Asian Indian immigrants.* Poster session presented at the APHA 139th Annual Meeting and Exposition (APHA 2011, poster 247601), Washington, DC.

Ponce, N., Gatchell, M. E., & Brown, R. (2003). *Cancer screening rates among Asian ethnic groups.* Los Angeles, CA: UCLA Center for Health Policy Research.

Pourat, N., Kagawa-Singer, M., Breen, N., & Sripipatana, A. (2010). Access versus acculturation: Identifying modifiable factors to promote cancer screening among Asian American women. *Medical Care, 48*(12), 1088–1096.

Qiu, Y., Ni, H. (2003). Utilization of dental care services by Asians and native Hawaiian or other Pacific Islanders: United States, 1997–2000. *Advance Data,* (336), 1–11.

Rashidi, A., & Rajaram, S. S. (2000). Middle Eastern Asian Islamic women and breast self-examination: Needs assessment. *Cancer Nursing, 23*(1), 64–70.

Rastogi, T., Devesa, S., Mangtani, P., Mathew, A., Cooper, N., Kao, R., & Sinha, R. (2008). Cancer incidence rates among South Asians in four geographic regions: India, Singapore, UK and US. *International Journal of Epidemiology, 37*(1), 147–160.

Saath-USA. (2008). *Saath: Together we build a healthier tomorrow.* Retrieved from http://www.saathusa.org/

Sadler, G. R., Dhanjal, S. K., Shah, N. B., Shah, R. B., Ko, C., Anghel, M., & Harshburger, R. (2001). Asian Indian women: Knowledge, attitudes and behaviors toward breast cancer early detection. *Public Health Nursing, 18*(5), 357–363.

SAHI. (2015). *South Asian Health Initiative.* Retrieved from http://www.mskcc.org/research/immigrant-health-disparities-service/south-asian-health-initiative

SAPHA. (2002). *South Asian Public Health Association—A brown paper: The Health of South Asians in the United States.* Retrieved from http://www.sapha.org/pages.php?id=42

Slattery, M. L. (2004). Physical activity and colorectal cancer. *Sports Medicine, 34*(4), 239–252.

Spratt, J. S. (1981). The primary and secondary prevention of cancer. *Journal of Surgical Oncology, 18*(3), 219–230.

Surani, Z., Baezconde-Garbanati, L., Bastani, R., & Montano, B. (2003). Improving community capacity to develop cancer awareness programs. *American Journal of Health Studies, 18*(4), 203–210.

Surani, Z., Agustin, A. L., Lally, K., Kashiwagi, C., & Barnett, E. (2012, October). *Cancer prevention and screening among South Asian women: Utilization of a culturally and linguistically appropriate health education strategy.* Poster session presented at the APHA 140th Annual Meeting and Exposition (APHA 2012, poster 268014), San Francisco.

Tardon, A., Lee, W. J., Delgado-Rodriguez, M., Dosemeci, M., Albanes, D., Hoover, R., & Blair, A. (2005). Leisure-time physical activity and lung cancer: A meta-analysis. *Cancer Causes & Control, 16*(4), 389–397.

Thune, I., & Furberg, A.-S. (2001). Physical activity and cancer risk: Dose-response and cancer, all sites and site-specific. *Medicine and Science in Sports and Exercise, 33*(6 Suppl.), S530–550; discussion S609–610.

Ward, E., Jemal, A., Cokkinides, V., Singh, G. K., Cardinez, C., Ghafoor, A., & Thun, M. (2004). Cancer disparities by race/ethnicity and socioeconomic status. *CA: A Cancer Journal for Clinicians, 54*(2), 78–93.

Chapter 4

Diabetes

Anita Mudan and Amitasrigowri Murthy

Contents

Abstract

Objective: To review the current literature on diabetes mellitus (DM) and gestational diabetes in the South Asian American (SAA) population, detailing the pathophysiology, risk factors, and impact on overall health. The chapter concludes with a summary of ongoing research and community-based interventions to address diabetes in the SAA community and provides recommendations on future directions.

Key Findings: The rates of diabetes are significantly higher in SAAs compared to other ethnic groups with similar risk factor profiles. One theory suggests the cause is a combination of lifestyle choices and an adverse metabolic profile, culminating in the clinical picture of insulin resistance. Other theories focus on genetic risk factors. Similar to DM, gestational diabetes is also found in a higher proportion of SAA pregnancies, and is thought to stem from pregestational insulin resistance. Subsequently, this poses an increased risk of diabetes developing in both the mother and child.

Recommendations: Lifestyle modifications remain the most effective means of disease prevention with culturally adapted dietary recommendations yielding the greatest compliance. Increased physical activity to at least 60 minutes daily is also recommended. More research needs to be done on the impact of gestational diabetes in offspring in order for more targeted screening and intervention programs to be implemented.

Introduction

Diabetes has become a common disease in today's society. Worldwide, there are more than 387 million people with diabetes, or 8.3% of the global population, with another 316 million, or 6.9%, who have impaired glucose tolerance, a precursor of diabetes (International Diabetes Federation, 2014). Diabetes mellitus (DM) is present across all ethnic groups, but it is found in significantly higher proportions in the South Asian population. Globally, India ranks second behind China in the number of people with diabetes, amounting to 66.8 million people, with the United States third, with 25.7 million people (International Diabetes Federation, 2014).

In general, South Asians tend to develop diabetes 10–15 years earlier, around age 45, and at a weight that is 20–30 pounds less when compared with other ethnic groups (Enas & Kannan, 2005). In fact, fewer than 30% of diabetic individuals in India are considered obese according to the World Health

Organization body mass index (WHO BMI) criteria. However, even with a mild degree of abdominal adiposity, South Asians develop diabetes. Data from a multisite study in India found an average hemoglobin A1C (a marker of blood sugar levels over several months) of 8.9%, where the normal value is less than 5.6% (Mohan et al., 2014). In New York City, the rate of diabetes in South Asians is 13.6%, compared to 7.4% in other Asians and 5.4% in Caucasians (Gupta, Wu, Young, & Perlman, 2011). 14.1% had a normal BMI using the traditional WHO criteria but this dropped to 10.2% when using the modified Asian BMI criteria (Gupta et al., 2011). In the greater Atlanta area, a study of the South Asian population found the prevalence of diabetes to be 18.3% (Venkataraman, Nanda, Baweja, Parikh, & Bhatia, 2004). In a multisite study in San Francisco and Chicago, the prevalence of diabetes was found to be 23% in South Asians, compared with 13% in the Chinese population and 6% in Caucasians (Kanaya et al., 2014). Finally, a multisite study in Houston, Phoenix, Washington, DC, Boston, San Diego, Edison, and Parsippany found a diabetes prevalence rate of 17.4% in South Asians and a prediabetes prevalence of 33% (Misra et al., 2010). All of these studies illustrate an increased prevalence of diabetes in South Asians that persists with emigration.

Throughout South Asia, including India, Bangladesh, Bhutan, Maldives, Nepal, and Sri Lanka, almost half of the individuals with diabetes are undiagnosed. As a result, many complications of diabetes, such as coronary artery disease, kidney failure, retinopathy, and neuropathy develop without any opportunity for prevention (International Diabetes Federation, 2013). Diabetes is itself an independent risk factor for the development of coronary artery disease. In 2014, there were roughly 4.9 million deaths worldwide due to diabetes and its related complications, with 1.04 million of those in India alone, and over 198,000 in the United States (International Diabetes Federation, 2014). Diabetes accounts for almost 11% of total health-care expenditures worldwide (International Diabetes Federation, 2013).

In the United States, health-care costs associated with diabetes are upward of $612 billion and the average health-care cost per person with diabetes is close to $11,000 (International Diabetes Federation, 2014). The burden of disease in South Asians, in particular, is further illustrated by higher rates of hospitalization for diabetes and its related complications (heart disease and stroke) compared to other ethnic groups. In a study of immigrants in New York City, researchers found that South Asian Americans (SAAs) were more likely than other immigrant populations to be hospitalized for heart disease (risk ratio 1.02, 95% CI 1.02, 1.03), stroke (risk ratio 1.00, 95% CI 0.99, 1.01), and diabetes (risk ratio 0.96, 95% CI 0.94, 0.97) (Muennig, Jia, & Khan, 2004).

Mechanism of Disease

DM is a group of metabolic diseases in which high blood sugar levels persist over a prolonged period. There are two major types. Type 1, also known as insulin-dependent diabetes or juvenile diabetes, is caused by autoimmune destruction of the pancreatic β-cells leading to absolute insulin deficiency. It is more commonly found in younger populations (most present before age 10) and accounts for 5%–10% of all cases of diabetes (Galtier, 2010). Type 2, known as non-insulin-dependent diabetes, is caused by insulin resistance, usually presents in adults, and accounts for 90%–95% of cases (Galtier, 2010). Prediabetes is the state of impaired glucose tolerance that precedes the development of overt diabetes and is a major target for prevention of disease. The diagnostic criteria for prediabetes and type 2 diabetes are outlined in Table 4.1.

The hallmark of diabetes is impaired insulin sensitivity of tissues, leading to impaired insulin secretion by the pancreas, and ultimately resulting in an elevated blood glucose level. Understanding the stepwise progression of insulin resistance to overt diabetes, as outlined in Figure 4.1, is essential as each stage is a potential target for intervention to prevent or delay development of the disease.

Although the stepwise development of diabetes is essentially the same among all individuals, some variations exist that may predispose certain groups to developing diabetes. Bhopal (2013) has proposed a four-stage model specifically for South Asians to help explain their substantially higher prevalence of diabetes compared to other ethnic groups. The model outlines certain characteristics, including a smaller number of pancreatic β-cells present at birth, which predispose them to abnormal β-cell function, as well as a preferential accumulation of fat in sites such as deep subcutaneous tissue, and around visceral organs, which further contributes to insulin resistance in tissues (Bhopal, 2013). The presence

Table 4.1 Diagnostic Criteria for Type 2 Diabetes

	Normal	*Prediabetes*	*Diabetes*
Fasting plasma glucose	<100 mg/dL	100–125 mg/dL	>126 mg/dL
Glucose tolerance test (blood glucose 2 hours after drinking glucose solution)	<140 mg/dL	140–199 mg/dL	>200 mg/dL
Hemoglobin A1C	<5.6%	5.7%–6.4%	>6.5%

Source: Adapted from Powers, A.C. Diabetes mellitus. In D.L. Longo et al. (Eds.), *Harrison's Principles of Internal Medicine*, New York, NY, The McGraw-Hill Companies, 2012.

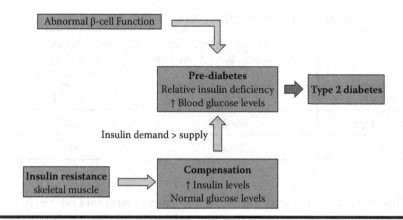

Figure 4.1 Mechanism of disease in diabetes. (Adapted from Jalili, M., Type 2 diabetes mellitus. In J.E. Tintinalli et al. [Eds.], *Tintinalli's Emergency Medicine: A Comprehensive Study Guide***, New York, NY, The McGraw-Hill Companies, 2011.)**

of these traits help explain why South Asians appear to progress through the disease stages much more quickly than other ethnic groups, resulting in the manifestation of type 2 diabetes at a younger age.

Risk Factors

Regardless of ethnicity, major risk factors for diabetes include obesity, a sedentary lifestyle, and a diet rich in simple carbohydrates and animal products. Independent of these major risk factors, however, South Asians are found to be significantly more insulin resistant and have an earlier manifestation of the insulin resistance syndrome as compared to other ethnic groups (Misra & Vikram, 2004). Current theories to explain this increased prevalence include abdominal obesity, lifestyle choices, family history of diabetes, biochemical profile, and genetic predisposition.

Obesity

BMI has long been used as a surrogate measure of body fat, as it is easy to calculate using simple measurements and is closely associated with health risk and mortality. As with all other ethnic groups, obesity in South Asians is defined as an elevated BMI and is a risk factor for diabetes. It was found, however, that when using the traditional WHO criteria, South Asians developed insulin resistance and diabetes at lower BMI ranges than Caucasians. This prompted the creation

Table 4.2 Body Mass Index (BMI) Criteria

	Traditional World Health Organization Body Mass Index (WHO BMI) Criteria	Revised Asian-Specific BMI Criteria (Jih et al., 2014)
Normal	18.5–24.9	18.5–22.9
Overweight	25–29.9	23–27.5
Obese	>30	>27.5

of different criteria that were specific for the Asian population (Table 4.2). The revised criteria take into account the preferential accumulation of abdominal fat, which is more highly associated with diabetes risk than fat elsewhere in the body (Gujral, Pradeepa, Weber, Narayan, & Mohan, 2013). For the Asian immigrant population living in the United States, a BMI cutoff point of 23 kg/m^2 has been proposed as a screening tool for those at the risk of developing diabetes. This has been shown to be more sensitive when compared to the American Diabetes Association's general screening questionnaire (Hsu, Araneta, Kanaya, Chiang, & Fujimoto, 2015).

Lifestyle

Major lifestyle risk factors in the SAA population stem from dietary westernization and decreased levels of physical activity that, when combined, result in abdominal obesity.

Diet

Dietary westernization is defined as modifications made to the traditional South Asian diet after immigrating to the United States. Modifications have also been noted in individuals migrating to urban cities within South Asian countries. These modifications include increased intake of simple carbohydrates, saturated and trans fats, energy dense fast foods, alcohol, and sugary beverages (Bakker, Sleddering, Schoones, Meinders, & Jazet, 2013). While the traditional South Asian diet is high in carbohydrates, the major change seen with westernization is the transition from carbohydrates with high-fiber content to those with low-fiber content (Joshi, Mohan, Joshi, Mechanick, & Marchetti, 2012). Another major change involves the transition from a vegetarian diet to one that contains animal products. This is more commonly seen in those who have lived in the United States for longer periods of time (Gadgil, Anderson, Kandula, & Kanaya, 2014).

These dietary changes contribute to the development of insulin resistance and diabetes in the urban and immigrant population.

Physical Activity

Another major lifestyle factor that impacts diabetes disease development is physical activity. Exercise decreases the concentration of fatty acid metabolites in the blood, thereby improving glucose uptake into skeletal muscle (Weber, Oza-Frank, Staimez, Ali, & Narayan, 2012). Thus, low levels of physical activity correlate with higher serum concentrations of free fatty acids and a higher degree of insulin resistance, as less glucose is taken up by tissue. Overall, very low levels of physical activity have been found in the SAA population, particularly in the area of strength training (Balasubramanyam, Rao, Misra, Sekhar, & Ballantyne, 2008). A study examining South Asians in Houston found that participants exercised fewer than two times per week and more often did aerobic exercise, such as walking, instead of muscle strength training (Balasubramanyam et al., 2008). This combination of increased caloric intake and decreased physical activity results in excess fat deposition, a key contributor to the development of diabetes.

Family History

Another relevant risk factor for disease development in the SAA population is a family history of diabetes. In fact, within the SAA population, family history has been found to be the strongest independent predictor of diabetes risk (Venkataraman et al., 2004). Family history is a combination of genetic expression and environmental interaction (Weber et al., 2012). According to Weber et al. (2012), positive family history can be defined in several ways, including two or more first-degree relatives, one first-degree relative plus two second-degree relatives, or more than three second-degree relatives.

Biochemical Factors

Several biochemical factors have been found to impact diabetes risk. Adiponectin, a polypeptide hormone that is produced and subsequently secreted by adipocytes (fat cells), has been shown to improve lipid metabolism and increase insulin sensitivity in tissue (Luo, Oza-Frank, Narayan, Gokulakrishnan, & Mohan, 2010). Low serum levels of adiponectin are associated with high insulin levels and this inverse correlation is seen independently of obesity (Barnett et al., 2006). Because the South Asian population has lower baseline serum levels of adiponectin, as compared to other ethnic groups, they are predisposed to development of insulin resistance (Webb, Khunti, Chatterjee, Jarvis, & Davies, 2013). Leptin is a serum protein that circulates at a level proportional to body fat mass. It provides information to the brain regarding nutritional status and subcutaneous fat mass, and regulates feeding behavior, appetite stimulation, and energy expenditure (Mente et al., 2010). Leptin plays a key role in the satiety response, is regulated by the hypothalamus, and is integral to energy metabolism (Webb et al., 2013). Since a high-carbohydrate diet is associated with higher leptin levels, it also correlates with larger measures of adiposity (Mente et al., 2010).

Genetics

Several developmental hypotheses have been proposed regarding the predisposition for diabetes in South Asians. These include the thrifty genotype, adipose tissue overflow, El Niño, variable disease selection, and mitochondrial efficiency (Bakker et al., 2013). All of these theories propose that certain traits initially evolved to assist with survival in the environment, and over time evolved to predispose to the development of diabetes as a result of changes that have occurred to the original environment (Bakker et al., 2013). Several genome-wide association studies have examined genetic polymorphisms (variations) associated with an increased risk of diabetes. Thus far, more than 60 genes have been isolated in the general population, and several of those are specific to the South Asian population (Gujral et al., 2013; Kooner et al., 2011). Genome studies remain an area of ongoing research, particularly those targeted at specific genetic variations in different ethnic groups correlating with diabetes risk. Several of these studies have already been completed on genes found in South Asians, but more work is needed to examine genes identified in other populations (Gujral et al., 2013).

Gestational Diabetes

Pathophysiology

Gestational diabetes is defined as glucose intolerance first recognized during pregnancy. Gestational insulin resistance is determined primarily by the metabolic action of placental hormones (Yajnik, 2004). Human placental lactogen decreases peripheral insulin sensitivity, and progesterone and estrogen act to increase tissue insulin resistance (Imam, 2012). Together, these hormones act to cause recurrent episodes of hyperglycemia in the mother, thereby altering fetal glucose and insulin levels.

Risk Factors

The risk factors for gestational diabetes are similar to those for type 2 diabetes, and include obesity (which accounts for almost half the cases of gestational diabetes), history of gestational diabetes, polycystic ovarian syndrome, family history of type 2 diabetes, and prediabetes (Galtier, 2010). Other risk factors unique to gestational diabetes include increasing maternal age, parity, history of infertility, and a history of prior large birth-weight babies (Berkowitz, Lapinski, Wein, & Lee, 1992; Kale et al., 2005). Certain ethnic groups, including South Asians, are at a high risk of developing gestational diabetes, with rates close to 17% in South Asians, as compared to 7% in the general population (Galtier, 2010; Imam, 2012; Smith-Morris, 2005). In 2013, there were 21.4 million (or 16.8%) live births affected by hyperglycemia worldwide, and the rates among South Asians approached 25%, which was the highest of any ethnic group (International Diabetes Federation, 2014). In New York City, rates of gestational diabetes increased dramatically in SAAs between 1990, when it was 5.7%, and 2001, when it increased to 11.1%, the highest rate of increase among any ethnic group (Thorpe et al., 2005).

Complications

Gestational diabetes can lead to numerous complications for both the mother and fetus. It is an independent risk factor for developing type 2 diabetes later in life, accounting for 30% of type 2 diabetes cases (Imam, 2012). Other serious maternal complications of gestational diabetes include hypertension, complicating approximately 10% of pregnancies, and preeclampsia, affecting 12% of diabetic pregnancies, as compared to 8% in unaffected pregnancies (Imam, 2012). These increased risks are further compounded by maternal obesity, which is in itself a risk factor for developing hypertension and type 2 diabetes.

It has been established that having better glycemic control before conception and for the duration of the pregnancy improves pregnancy outcome (Kinsley, 2007). Poor glycemic control during pregnancy has been associated with an increased incidence of spontaneous abortion, as well as an increased rate of anatomic anomalies—specifically cardiac anomalies. The risk of spontaneous abortion or malformation in a pregnancy complicated by gestational diabetes is directly correlated with the severity of hyperglycemia (Kinsley, 2007). It has also been found that babies born to mothers with gestational diabetes have a higher birth weight and more overall adipose tissue compared to those born to nondiabetic mothers (Kale et al., 2005).

Fetal macrosomia, defined as a birth weight above the 90th percentile for gestational age, or greater than 4000 g, is thought to result from maternal hyperglycemia. Hyperglycemia is known to stimulate excess growth of the fetus during the latter half of gestation, thereby increasing the risk of shoulder dystocia, and the rate of cesarean section due to labor dysfunction (Cunningham et al., 2010; Imam, 2012). Among women in developed countries, diabetes during pregnancy is the most common cause of congenital malformations, which in turn are the most important cause of perinatal death among infants (McElvy et al., 2000). Overall, both perinatal and neonatal mortality rates are higher among diabetic pregnancies when compared to nondiabetic pregnancies (Shefali, Kavitha, Deepa, & Mohan, 2006).

South Asian Population

Within the South Asian population, gestational diabetes occurs most frequently in young, urban mothers with a family history of type 2 diabetes and a high degree of adiposity (Kale et al., 2005). A Norwegian study found a higher prevalence of pregestational diabetes among immigrants born in Pakistan, India, Bangladesh, Sri Lanka, Morocco, Tunisia, and Algeria, as compared to the native population (Vangen et al., 2003). In California, Kim et al. found the highest prevalence of gestational diabetes to be in the SAA population, with 14% compared to 5.4% among Caucasians (Kim et al., 2013). It is important to note that this same study also found that gestational diabetes among SAAs had the least correlation with BMI, suggesting it was not attributable to obesity (Kim et al., 2013).

Given the high prevalence of diabetes outside of pregnancy within the South Asian population, both native and immigrant, several studies have examined the impact of pregestational diabetes on maternal and fetal outcomes. In reviewing a large population of South Asians in the United Kingdom, a higher rate of adverse birth outcomes, including stillbirths, infant deaths, and congenital malformations, were found in mothers with pregestational type 1 and type 2 diabetes (Verheijen, Critchley, Whitelaw, & Tuffnell, 2005). Women in the Asian immigrant group (Pakistani, Bangladeshi, Chinese, and Indian) made up the majority of the pregnancies affected by type 2 diabetes and were more likely to have an adverse birth outcome (Verheijen et al., 2005). This study suggests that more severe fetal complications are associated with pregestational diabetes, as compared with gestational diabetes. Although the study was conducted on immigrant populations in the United Kingdom, the findings and implications regarding pregestational diabetes and fetal complications may be applicable to South Asian immigrants within the United States, given that pregestational type 1 and type 2 diabetes are diagnosed and managed similarly in both countries.

Current Research

Several studies have examined large-scale implementation of culturally sensitive lifestyle modifications as well as medication use in South Asian disease prevention and management. These include the globally accepted use of metformin, an effective blood glucose-lowering drug, used in South Asian countries. The Indian Diabetes Prevention Program compared metformin and/or lifestyle modifications to no intervention and found that there was less progression to diabetes in both treatment groups, even in the absence of weight loss (Tillin and Chaturvedi, 2014). Several other studies have also looked at interventions in South Asians in Western countries. The Prevention of Diabetes and Obesity in South Asians (PODOSA) study in Scotland examined the impact of culturally sensitive dietary recommendations and increased physical activity on weight loss, with the aim of preventing the onset of diabetes (Wallia et al., 2013). Over a 3-year study period, the researchers found increased weight loss in the intervention group, whose participants had 15 visits from a dietitian to address culturally specific dietary modifications to traditional recipes, grocery shopping tips, and portion control. This was compared to the control group, which had four visits in the same period (Bhopal et al., 2014). In the United States, the South Asian Health and Prevention Education (SHAPE) study looked at implementing culturally sensitive lifestyle interventions in patients with prediabetes, with the goal of preventing disease progression (Shah & Kanaya, 2014). In New York City, the Diabetes Research, Education, and Action for Minorities (DREAM) project is ongoing with a goal of training community health workers to help improve diabetes control and manage related complications within the immigrant Bangladeshi community (NYU Center for the Study of Asian American Health, 2014).

The common theme in all of these studies is when lifestyle modifications, both dietary and exercise, are specifically tailored for South Asians, and take into account their specific cultural requirements, the interventions are more effective with respect to patient satisfaction and clinical outcomes, despite feasibility challenges.

Lifestyle Modifications

The mainstay of diabetes prevention and management continues to be lifestyle modification, particularly when implemented in the prediabetes stage of disease development. To prevent development of diabetes, or to improve the overall health of people with diabetes, proposed guidelines for physical activity call for a minimum of 60 minutes per day, including 30 minutes of moderate intensity aerobic exercise and at least 15 minutes of strength training (Joshi et al.,

2012). One of the most important tenets of any proposed lifestyle modification is its cultural sensitivity and specificity. Thus, rather than eliminating traditional foods, the focus should instead be on alternate preparations or portion control (Mukherjea, Underwood, Stewart, Ivey, & Kanaya, 2013). These modifications center around dietary changes such as increased whole grains, fruits, and vegetables, and decreased fats, sugars, and refined carbohydrates (Gujral et al., 2013). The studies outlined earlier provide strong groundwork and compelling evidence for the effectiveness of culturally appropriate lifestyle interventions in South Asians.

It is also important to recognize that in order to implement these lifestyle modifications, more focused screening by health-care providers is needed. Diabetes develops in a stepwise fashion, with each step a potential target for intervention. The goal of the health-care provider is to impart patient education for primary prevention as well as to detect the disease at either the insulin resistance or prediabetes stage. They then work collaboratively with and empower the patient to implement necessary lifestyle modifications to avert diabetes and its complications. This approach is based on the chronic disease self-management model which found that patient centered self-management education programs initiated by primary care providers improved outcomes and reduced health-care costs associated with chronic diseases (Bodenheimer, 2002). In particular, knowing that SAAs are predisposed to developing diabetes, health-care providers should begin measuring fasting glucose or hemoglobin A1C in younger ages and screening for diabetes if BMI is greater than 23 kg/m^2, even in the absence of obesity (Hsu et al., 2015). In order to do this, and to better screen these patients, health-care providers need to be educated on the specifics of diabetes as it relates to the SAA population.

Screening for gestational diabetes is routinely done late in the second trimester; however, given that this population is at such an increased risk, it makes sense to initiate preventative lifestyle and dietary measures prior to pregnancy, so more women can enter pregnancy at an optimal weight and with controlled blood sugars (Hedderson et al., 2012). This requires earlier focused screening in SAA women by primary care clinicians and education by gynecologists at preconception visits. In Canada, the South Asian Birth Cohort Study trial compared an immigrant population to a native Indian population and examined the impact of intrauterine risk factors on birth weight, neonatal adiposity, and postnatal growth patterns (Anand et al., 2013). A similar study on migrant populations in the United States would be valuable, given the differences in prenatal screening, as well as different factors affecting pregestational health in U.S. immigrants. Finally, after giving birth, more frequent screening for diabetes in the mother is also suggested. The child's growth should be monitored closely to prevent the development of obesity.

Major next steps in diabetes research focus on continued large-scale implementation of culturally appropriate patient-centered interventions. Preliminary findings from studies in other countries have shown significant success; thus, large-scale studies within the United States would be interesting to follow. The chronic disease self-management model predicts that these interventions are likely to offer the best approach to improve long-term outcomes in patients with chronic diseases like diabetes.

Recommendations

Based on available evidence, the following are recommended for the prevention and management of diabetes among SAAs.

■ Adopt culturally specific dietary modifications combined with portion control and increased whole grains, fruits, and vegetables.
■ Engage in at least 60 minutes of physical activity daily, including at least 30 minutes of moderate intensity aerobic exercise and 15 minutes of strength training.
■ Obtain annual diabetes screening (fasting glucose or hemoglobin A1C) for those with BMI >23 kg/m².
■ Provide education to SAA women with regard to risk factors, screening tests, and complications of gestational diabetes prior to pregnancy.
■ Implement culturally specific lifestyle modifications early in pregnancy, and combine these with initial gestational diabetes screening during the first trimester.

Conclusions

The global disease burden associated with diabetes is tremendous, accounting for significant morbidity, mortality, and individual and societal health-care costs. As a chronic disease, diabetes is associated with multiorgan complications, including neuropathy, peripheral vascular disease, nephropathy, coronary artery disease, and retinopathy. With a significantly higher prevalence in the SAA population, diabetes is a major health concern. The etiology of this increased prevalence is multifactorial, combining a genetic predisposition with adverse lifestyle choices, and ultimately leading to abdominal obesity and development of an adverse metabolic profile. A related concern is the increased prevalence of gestational diabetes within the SAA population, which is associated with significant maternal and fetal complications. Successful interventions have focused on targeted culturally specific lifestyle modifications aimed at altering the traditional South Asian diet and increasing physical activity. The significant disease burden within SAAs, and the associated morbidity and mortality associated with diabetes, make this a key population who would benefit from continued culturally appropriate, patient-centered lifestyle interventions, along with continued research into genetic factors that contribute to their specific predisposition for disease development.

References

Anand, S. S., Vasudevan, A., Gupta, M., Morrison, K., Kurpad, A., Teo, K. K., & Srinivasan, K. (2013). Rationale and design of South Asian Birth Cohort (START): A Canada-India collaborative study. *BMC Public Health, 13*, 79. doi: 10.1186/1471-2458-13-79

Bakker, L. E., Sleddering, M. A., Schoones, J. W., Meinders, A. E., & Jazet, I. M. (2013). Pathogenesis of type 2 diabetes in South Asians. *Eur J Endocrinol, 169*(5), R99–R114. doi: 10.1530/eje-13-0307

Balasubramanyam, A., Rao, S., Misra, R., Sekhar, R. V., & Ballantyne, C. M. (2008). Prevalence of metabolic syndrome and associated risk factors in Asian Indians. *J Immigr Minor Health, 10*(4), 313–323. doi: 10.1007/s10903-007-9092-4

Barnett, A. H., Dixon, A. N., Bellary, S., Hanif, M. W., O'Hare, J. P., Raymond, N. T., & Kumar, S. (2006). Type 2 diabetes and cardiovascular risk in the UK south Asian community. *Diabetologia, 49*(10), 2234–2246. doi: 10.1007/s00125-006-0325-1

Berkowitz, G. S., Lapinski, R. H., Wein, R., & Lee, D. (1992). Race/ethnicity and other risk factors for gestational diabetes. *Am J Epidemiol, 135*(9), 965–973.

Bhopal, R. S. (2013). A four-stage model explaining the higher risk of type 2 diabetes mellitus in South Asians compared with European populations. *Diabet Med, 30*(1), 35–42. doi: 10.1111/dme.12016

Bhopal, R. S., Douglas, A., Wallia, S., Forbes, J. F., Lean, M. E., Gill, J. M., . . . Murray, G. D. (2014). Effect of a lifestyle intervention on weight change in south Asian individuals in the UK at high risk of type 2 diabetes: A family-cluster randomised controlled trial. *Lancet Diabetes Endocrinol, 2*(3), 218–227. doi: 10.1016/s2213-8587(13)70204-3

Bodenheimer, T. (2002). Patient self-management of chronic disease in primary care. *JAMA, 288*(19), 2469. doi: 10.1001/jama.288.19.2469

Cunningham, F. G., Leveno, K. J., Bloom, S. L., Hauth, J. C., Rouse, D. J., & Spong, C. Y. (2010). Diabetes. In C. Y. Spong (Ed.), *Williams Obstetrics* (23 ed., pp. 1104–1125). New York, NY: Mc-Graw Hill Education.

Enas, E. A., & Kannan, S. (2005). *How to Beat the Heart Disease Epidemic among South Asians.* Downers Grove, IL: Advanced Heart Lipid Clinic.

Gadgil, M. D., Anderson, C. A., Kandula, N. R., & Kanaya, A. M. (2014). Dietary patterns in Asian Indians in the United States: An analysis of the metabolic syndrome and atherosclerosis in South Asians Living in America study. *J Acad Nutr Diet, 114*(2), 238–243. doi: 10.1016/j.jand.2013.09.021

Galtier, F. (2010). Definition, epidemiology, risk factors. *Diabetes & Metabolism, 36*(6, Part 2), 628–651. doi: http://dx.doi.org/10.1016/j.diabet.2010.11.014

Gujral, U. P., Pradeepa, R., Weber, M. B., Narayan, K. M., & Mohan, V. (2013). Type 2 diabetes in South Asians: Similarities and differences with white Caucasian and other populations. *Ann NY Acad Sci, 1281*, 51–63. doi: 10.1111/j.1749-6632.2012.06838.x

Gupta, L. S., Wu, C. C., Young, S., & Perlman, S. E. (2011). Prevalence of diabetes in New York City, 2002–2008: Comparing foreign-born South Asians and other Asians with U.S.-born whites, blacks, and Hispanics. *Diabetes Care, 34*(8), 1791–1793. doi: 10.2337/dc11-0088

Hedderson, M., Ehrlich, S., Sridhar, S., Darbinian, J., Moore, S., & Ferrara, A. (2012). Racial/ethnic disparities in the prevalence of gestational diabetes mellitus by BMI. *Diabetes Care, 35*(7), 1492–1498. doi: 10.2337/dc11-2267

Hsu, W. C., Araneta, M. R., Kanaya, A. M., Chiang, J. L., & Fujimoto, W. (2015). BMI cut points to identify at-risk Asian Americans for type 2 diabetes screening. *Diabetes Care, 38*(1), 150–158. doi: 10.2337/dc14-2391

Imam, K. (2012). Gestational diabetes mellitus. *Adv Exp Med Biol, 771*, 24–34.

International Diabetes Federation. (2013). *IDF Diabetes Atlas.* 6. Retrieved August 3, 2015, from http://www.idf.org/diabetesatlas

International Diabetes Federation. (2014). *IDF Diabetes Atlas Update Poster.* 6. Retrieved August 3, 2015.

Jalili, M. (2011). Type 2 diabetes mellitus. In J. E. Tintinalli, J. S. Stapczynski, O. J. Ma, D. M. Cline, R. K. Cydulka, G. D. Meckler, & The American College of Emergency Physicians (Eds.), *Tintinalli's Emergency Medicine: A Comprehensive Study Guide* (7th ed., Chapter 219). New York, NY: The McGraw-Hill Companies.

Jih, J., Mukherjea, A., Vittinghoff, E., Nguyen, T. T., Tsoh, J. Y., Fukuoka, Y., . . . Kanaya, A. M. (2014). Using appropriate body mass index cut points for overweight and obesity among Asian Americans. *Prev Med, 65*, 1–6. doi: 10.1016/j.ypmed.2014.04.010

Joshi, S. R., Mohan, V., Joshi, S. S., Mechanick, J. I., & Marchetti, A. (2012). Transcultural diabetes nutrition therapy algorithm: The Asian Indian application. *Curr Diab Rep, 12*(2), 204–212. doi: 10.1007/s11892-012-0260-0

Kale, S. D., Kulkarni, S. R., Lubree, H. G., Meenakumari, K., Deshpande, V. U., Rege, S. S., . . . Yajnik, C. S. (2005). Characteristics of gestational diabetic mothers and their babies in an Indian diabetes clinic. *J Assoc Phys India, 53*, 857–863.

Kanaya, A. M., Herrington, D., Vittinghoff, E., Ewing, S. K., Liu, K., Blaha, M. J., . . . Kandula, N. R. (2014). Understanding the high prevalence of diabetes in U.S. south Asians compared with four racial/ethnic groups: The MASALA and MESA studies. *Diabetes Care, 37*(6), 1621–1628. doi: 10.2337/dc13-2656

Kim, S. Y., Saraiva, C., Curtis, M., Wilson, H. G., Troyan, J., & Sharma, A. J. (2013). Fraction of gestational diabetes mellitus attributable to overweight and obesity by race/ethnicity, California, 2007–2009. *Am J Public Health, 103*(10), e65–e72. doi: 10.2105/AJPH.2013.301469

Kinsley, B. (2007). Achieving better outcomes in pregnancies complicated by type 1 and type 2 diabetes mellitus. *Clin Ther, 29*(Suppl. D), S153–S160. doi: 10.1016/j.clinthera.2007.12.015

Kooner, J. S., Saleheen, D., Sim, X., Sehmi, J., Zhang, W., Frossard, P., . . . Chambers, J. C. (2011). Genome-wide association study in individuals of South Asian ancestry identifies six new type 2 diabetes susceptibility loci. *Nat Genet, 43*(10), 984–989. doi: 10.1038/ng.921

Luo, M., Oza-Frank, R., Narayan, K. M., Gokulakrishnan, K., & Mohan, V. (2010). Serum total adiponectin is associated with impaired glucose tolerance in Asian Indian females but not in males. *J Diabetes Sci Technol, 4*(3), 645–651.

McElvy, S. S., Miodovnik, M., Rosenn, B., Khoury, J. C., Siddiqi, T., Dignan, P. S., & Tsang, R. C. (2000). A focused preconceptional and early pregnancy program in women with type 1 diabetes reduces perinatal mortality and malformation rates to general population levels. *J Matern Fetal Med, 9*(1), 14–20. doi: 10.1002/(sici)1520-6661(200001/02)9:1<14::aid-mfm5>3.0.co;2-k

Mente, A., Razak, F., Blankenberg, S., Vuksan, V., Davis, A. D., Miller, R., . . . Anand, S. S. (2010). Ethnic variation in adiponectin and leptin levels and their association with adiposity and insulin resistance. *Diabetes Care, 33*(7), 1629–1634. doi: 10.2337/dc09-1392

Misra, A., & Vikram, N. K. (2004). Insulin resistance syndrome (metabolic syndrome) and obesity in Asian Indians: Evidence and implications. *Nutrition, 20*(5), 482–491. doi: 10.1016/j.nut.2004.01.020

Misra, R., Patel, T., Kotha, P., Raji, A., Ganda, O., Banerji, M., . . . Balasubramanyam, A. (2010). Prevalence of diabetes, metabolic syndrome, and cardiovascular risk factors in US Asian Indians: Results from a national study. *J Diabetes Complications, 24*(3), 145–153. doi: 10.1016/j.jdiacomp.2009.01.003

Mohan, V., Shah, S. N., Joshi, S. R., Seshiah, V., Sahay, B. K., Banerjee, S., . . . DiabCare India Study Group. (2014). Current status of management, control, complications and psychosocial aspects of patients with diabetes in India: Results from the DiabCare India 2011 Study. *Indian J Endocrinol Metab, 18*(3), 370–378. doi: 10.4103/2230-8210.129715

Muennig, P., Jia, H., & Khan, K. (2004). Hospitalization for heart disease, stroke, and diabetes mellitus among Indian-born persons: A small area analysis. *BMC Cardiovasc Disord, 4*(1), 19. doi: 10.1186/1471-2261-4-19

Mukherjea, A., Underwood, K. C., Stewart, A. L., Ivey, S. L., & Kanaya, A. M. (2013). Asian Indian views on diet and health in the United States: Importance of understanding cultural and social factors to address disparities. *Fam Community Health, 36*(4), 311–323. doi: 10.1097/FCH.0b013e31829d2549

NYU Center for the Study of Asian American Health. (2014). *DREAM: Diabetes Research, Education, and Action for Minorities.* Retrieved August 10, 2015.

Powers, A. C. (2012). Diabetes mellitus. In D. L. Longo, A. S. Fauci, D. L. Kasper, S. L. Hauser, J. L. Jameson, & J. Loscalzo (Eds.), *Harrison's Principles of Internal Medicine* (18 ed., Chapter 344). New York, NY: The McGraw-Hill Companies.

Shah, A., & Kanaya, A. M. (2014). Diabetes and associated complications in the South Asian population. *Curr Cardiol Rep, 16*(5), 476. doi: 10.1007/s11886-014-0476-5

Shefali, A. K., Kavitha, M., Deepa, R., & Mohan, V. (2006). Pregnancy outcomes in pre-gestational and gestational diabetic women in comparison to non-diabetic women—A prospective study in Asian Indian mothers (CURES-35). *J Assoc Phys India, 54*, 613–618.

Smith-Morris, C. M. (2005). Diagnostic controversy: Gestational diabetes and the meaning of risk for Pima Indian women. *Medical Anthropology, 24*(2), 145–177. doi: 10.1080/01459740590933902

Thorpe, L. E., Berger, D., Ellis, J. A., Bettegowda, V. R., Brown, G., Matte, T., . . . Frieden, T. R. (2005). Trends and racial/ethnic disparities in gestational diabetes among pregnant women in New York City, 1990–2001. *Am J Public Health, 95*(9), 1536–1539. doi: 10.2105/ajph.2005.066100

Tillin, T., & Chaturvedi, N. (2014). Stemming the tide of type 2 diabetes and its consequences in south Asian individuals. *Lancet Diabetes Endocrinol, 2*(3), 186–188. doi: http://dx.doi.org/10.1016/S2213-8587(13)70210–9

Vangen, S., Stoltenberg, C., Holan, S., Moe, N., Magnus, P., Harris, J. R., & Stray-Pedersen, B. (2003). Outcome of pregnancy among immigrant women with diabetes. *Diabetes Care, 26*(2), 327–332.

Venkataraman, R., Nanda, N. C., Baweja, G., Parikh, N., & Bhatia, V. (2004). Prevalence of diabetes mellitus and related conditions in Asian Indians living in the United States. *Am J Cardiol, 94*(7), 977–980. doi: http://dx.doi.org/10.1016/j.amjcard.2004.06.048

Verheijen, E. C., Critchley, J. A., Whitelaw, D. C., & Tuffnell, D. J. (2005). Outcomes of pregnancies in women with pre-existing type 1 or type 2 diabetes, in an ethnically mixed population. *BJOG, 112*(11), 1500–1503. doi: 10.1111/j.1471-0528.2005.00747.x

Wallia, S., Bhopal, R. S., Douglas, A., Bhopal, R., Sharma, A., Hutchison, A., . . . Sheikh, A. (2013). Culturally adapting the prevention of diabetes and obesity in South Asians (PODOSA) trial. *Health Promot Int.* doi: 10.1093/heapro/dat015

Webb, D. R., Khunti, K., Chatterjee, S., Jarvis, J., & Davies, M. J. (2013). Adipocytokine associations with insulin resistance in British South Asians. *J Diab Res, 2013*(561016), 7 p. doi: 10.1155/2013/561016

Weber, M. B., Oza-Frank, R., Staimez, L. R., Ali, M. K., & Narayan, K. M. (2012). Type 2 diabetes in Asians: Prevalence, risk factors, and effectiveness of behavioral intervention at individual and population levels. *Annu Rev Nutr, 32*, 417–439. doi: 10.1146/annurev-nutr-071811-150630

Yajnik, C. S. (2004). Obesity epidemic in India: Intrauterine origins? *Proc Nutr Soc, 63*(3), 387–396.

LIFESTYLE AND HEALTH

Chapter 5

Nutrition

Kasuen Mauldin, Sadhna Diwan,
and Satya S. Jonnalagadda

Contents

Abstract

Objective: The authors review South Asian American immigrant dietary practices and report on the implications for chronic disease and the nutritional and dietary recommendations to decrease this risk.

Key Findings: South Asians who immigrate to Western countries tend to have higher total carbohydrate intake as a result of refined grains and hidden sugars, higher unhealthy fat intake, and lower fiber consumption. Overall, South Asians have a higher susceptibility to metabolic and cardiovascular diseases and their dietary habits further increase the risk for chronic disease.

Recommendations: Targeted nutrition education messages should be provided to South Asian American populations. Dietary recommendations should include (1) limiting refined carbohydrates and hidden sugar intake; (2) replacing unhealthy trans-fat and saturated fat intake with healthier unsaturated fats, including omega-3 fatty acids; and (3) increasing fiber intake by eating more vegetables. Additionally, the new Asian-specific body mass index (BMI) reference values and waist-based measurements should be used when performing nutritional assessments. Finally, given the important role that nutrition plays in chronic disease, more resources should be devoted to research into South Asian dietary practices following immigration.

Introduction

Over the last 10 years, a growing body of research has provided evidence that South Asians are at higher risk for chronic diseases often associated with obesity, as defined by excess body fat mass (Chopra, Misra, Gulati, & Gupta, 2013; Go et al., 2013; Kanaya et al., 2010). These include central obesity, type 2 diabetes mellitus, cardiovascular disease, and metabolic syndrome (Chopra et al., 2013; Jafar et al., 2004; Misra & Khurana, 2009), defined as a group of interrelated metabolic risk factors that increase risk for cardiovascular disease (Grundy et al., 2005). Metabolic syndrome is diagnosed when an individual has three of five diagnostic criteria, which include elevated waist circumference, elevated triglycerides, reduced high-density lipoprotein (HDL)-cholesterol, elevated blood pressure, and elevated fasting glucose. The diagnostic values for each are detailed in Table 5.1 (Grundy et al., 2005). Higher susceptibility to these conditions is due to the interactions among genetic, epigenetic, and lifestyle factors (Gholap, Davies, Patel, Sattar, & Khunti, 2011; Misra & Khurana, 2011). A key lifestyle factor affecting the development of chronic disease is nutrition or dietary intake (Ishwarwal, Misra, Wasir, & Nigam, 2009; Misra, Khurana, Isharwal, & Bhardwaj, 2009; Misra, Singhal, et al., 2011). Within traditional South Asian dietary practices, there is great variety as a result of the diverse geography and heterogeneous population within the Indian subcontinent (Kittler, Sucher, & Nahikian-Nelms, 2011). Thus, this diversity persists among South Asian American immigrants (Jonnalagadda & Diwan, 2002a).

The primary driving forces behind the dietary practices of immigrants are "nutrition transition" and "dietary acculturation" (Holmboe-Ottesen & Wandel, 2012; Satia, 2010). Nutrition transition refers to the industrialization

Table 5.1   Diagnostic Criteria and Values for Metabolic Syndrome

Diagnostic Criteria	Diagnostic Value
Elevated waist circumference	≥102 cm or 40 inches in men ≥88 cm or 35 inches in women
Elevated triglycerides	≥150 mg/dL or on drug treatment for elevated triglycerides
Reduced HDL-cholesterol	<40 mg/dL in men <50 mg/dL in women
Elevated blood pressure	≥130 mm Hg systolic, ≥85 mm Hg diastolic or on antihypertensive drug treatment
Elevated fasting glucose	≥100 mg/dL or on drug treatment for elevated glucose

and globalization of the international food market and the subsequent increased availability of ultra-processed, energy-dense food products (Popkin, 2009; Satia, 2010). Nutrition transition began as a phenomenon in high-income developed countries and has since spread to low-income countries, and from urban to rural areas (Popkin, 2009; Satia, 2010). The processed food products associated with nutrition transition often contain more unhealthy fats, added caloric sweeteners, and increased animal-source foods (Pingali, 2007; Popkin, 2009). Dietary acculturation refers to the process where immigrants adopt the dietary practices of the host country (Satia-Abouta, Patterson, Neuhouser, & Elder, 2002). The degree of nutrition transition in the country of origin can affect the speed at which dietary acculturation occurs after immigrating.

To date, millions of South Asians have migrated to other countries, including the United States and Canada, which have the greatest number of South Asian immigrants (OECD, 2011). With this immigration, South Asians have undergone shifts in lifestyle factors that can lead to changes in dietary habits. The speed and degree of these changes are dependent upon many factors, including the reason for migration, income level, work status, level of education, religion, food beliefs, and/or length of residence (Holmboe-Ottesen & Wandel, 2012; Wandel, Råberg, Kumar, & Holmboe-Ottesen, 2008). The focus of this chapter is to summarize trends in South Asian American dietary practices following immigration to Western countries and to review the effects of South Asian diets on chronic disease risk.

Summary of Evidence/Review of Literature

Trends in Dietary Practices

Because there are many geographic and climatic variations and heterogeneous populations within each South Asian country, there exists much diversity in dietary intake and practices among South Asians based on their places of origin (Kittler et al., 2011). For example, the main staple in Northern and Western India is wheat, while the main staple in Southern and Eastern India is rice. In Pakistan, the main staples are wheat, rice, and corn (Kittler et al., 2011). One generalization regarding the modern Asian Indian diet is that, compared with other cultures, it tends to be high in carbohydrates (70%–80% of total daily caloric intake) and low in protein (9%–10% of total daily caloric intake) (Dixit, Azar, Gardner, & Palaniappan, 2011). Contributing to this high carbohydrate intake are refined carbohydrates including white rice, white flour, hidden sugars in sweets and processed foods, dairy products, and fruits.

The term "hidden sugar" refers to sugars and syrups such as high-fructose corn syrup, maltose, cane sugar, corn sweetener, honey, and molasses that are added to processed foods including *lassi* (a yogurt-based drink), soft drinks, juices, candies, cakes, desserts, fruit drinks, pastries, cereals, and even nonsweet foods like chips (American Heart Association, 2014a).

As mentioned earlier in the Introduction, evidence from the scientific literature suggests that when South Asians immigrate to Western countries such as the United States, Canada, or countries in Europe, changes in dietary intake occur (Anderson et al., 2005; Dixit et al., 2011; Gilbert & Khokhar, 2008; Holmboe-Ottesen & Wandel, 2012; Mahadevan & Blair, 2009). It is important to note, however, that the majority of these studies have largely examined first-generation Asian Indian adult immigrants. In fact, age is a major factor contributing to changes in dietary habits (Gilbert & Khokhar, 2008). Trends show that younger immigrants more readily adopt Western foods, often viewed as convenient and reflective of autonomy associated with the host country (Gilbert & Khokhar, 2008; Holmboe-Ottesen & Wandel, 2012; Mahadevan & Blair, 2009). Food items that are the first to see changed in one's diet are the "accessory foods"—for example, snacks, sweets, and foods that are high in hidden sugars and saturated fats (Anderson et al., 2005; Holmboe-Ottesen & Wandel, 2012). College-age immigrants have reported replacing traditional carbohydrate foods such as lentils and *chapati* (unleavened flat bread) with common host-country carbohydrate foods such as pasta, bread, muffins, bagels, and ready-to-eat cereal (Mahadevan & Blair, 2009). Additionally, because of their convenience, modified and prepared frozen or canned items have replaced recipes such as curry that traditionally use fresh produce (Mahadevan & Blair, 2009). Younger South Asian immigrants also tend to eat fewer fruits and vegetables following migration (Gilbert & Khokhar, 2008; Kumar, Holmboe-Ottesen, Lien, & Wandel, 2004).

Conversely, older immigrants are less likely to change their traditional dietary practices compared with younger ones. This is likely due to fewer interactions with the mainstream population. Regardless of age, however, traditional staple foods often remain in the diet or remain unchanged for the longest period of time following migration (Gilbert & Khokhar, 2008). These staples include lentils, flatbreads, and rice, all of which tend to be carbohydrate based and result in carbohydrate consumption that accounts for approximately 60%–70% of total food intake (Jonnalagadda & Khosla, 2007; Misra, Rastogi, & Joshi, 2009). Also contributing to this high carbohydrate intake are highly sweetened South Asian desserts that are often served at festivals and celebrations (Kittler et al., 2011). Traditional cuisines also incorporate the use of many different spices and include dairy products such as yogurt, milk, and butter or ghee (a clarified butter) (Kittler et al., 2011). Thus, in addition to some of the traditional foods of South Asians not being nutrient-dense, they can also be more energy-dense than is desirable.

The vegetarian diet. Some South Asians, upon migration, modify their vegetarian status. This is often done as a result of the amount of exposure to Western foods and culture, as well as the convenience, cost, and availability of traditional food items (Mahadevan & Blair, 2009). Even those who choose to remain vegetarians after immigration still seem to consume a higher total carbohydrate and higher fat diet (Jonnalagadda & Diwan, 2002b). The typical South Asian vegetarian diet differs from the ideal vegetarian diet, which is higher in vegetable intake and includes high-quality plant-based protein sources. The general postimmigration trend for South Asians is bicultural food intake with a high consumption of total carbohydrates. These high carbohydrates come from refined sources, unhealthy fats, particularly from processed foods, meat, and a decreased fiber intake (Anderson et al., 2005; Holmboe-Ottesen & Wandel, 2012; Wandel et al., 2008). Taken together, these changes to dietary practices following immigration only help to exacerbate South Asians' risk for development of diet-related chronic diseases such as metabolic syndrome, type 2 diabetes mellitus, and cardiovascular disease.

Globalization influences. It is worth noting that these changing dietary trends are not unique to South Asian immigrants. Globalization influences have also altered the dietary practices of South Asians living on the Indian subcontinent (Gupta et al., 2010; Isharwal et al., 2008; Misra, Singhal, et al., 2011; Pingali, 2007). In fact, as a result of nutrition transition in South Asian countries, people with higher socioeconomic status living in India have seen an increase in refined carbohydrate intake in the form of Western foods like burgers, pizzas, french fries, and chips (Misra, Rastogi, et al., 2009). Among Asian

Indians with lower socioeconomic status, diets tend to be more cereal based with low levels of fruit and vegetable intake (Misra, Rastogi, et al., 2009). Other dietary imbalances in native South Asian diets include low levels of fiber and healthy fats such as omega-3 polyunsaturated fatty acid intakes, high saturated fat and carbohydrate intakes, and the consumption of trans fatty acids that are often found in processed foods (Misra, Khurana, et al., 2009).

In line with these global dietary trends, rates of chronic diseases among South Asians worldwide have increased. India is among the top "23 high-burden countries," defined as low- and middle-income countries with a high burden of chronic disease (Alwan et al., 2010).

Effects of Dietary Trends on Risk of Chronic Diseases

Regardless of immigration status, the South Asian American diet in general includes an excess intake of calories, simple carbohydrates, saturated fats, and trans fats, and a low intake of fiber (Misra, Sharma, et al., 2011). These changes in nutrient intake have contributed to increased rates of obesity and diet-related chronic diseases among South Asians. Additionally, high levels of saturated fat consumption in the context of altered metabolism (such as in those with metabolic syndrome) contribute to postprandial (after meal) sustained high triglyceride levels, inflammation, and insulin resistance (Kennedy, Martinez, Chuang, LaPoint, & McIntosh, 2009; Margioris, 2009). Excess refined or simple carbohydrates in the diet further contribute to an increased risk for altered metabolism, and the intake of trans fats has been associated with an unfavorable lipid profile and cardiovascular disease (Gupta et al., 2010; Isharwal, Misra, Wasir, & Nigam, 2009; Misra, Khurana, et al., 2009; Misra, Rastogi, et al. , 2009; Misra & Khurana, 2009).

Numerous clinical trials have shown that replacing saturated fat intake with healthy unsaturated fatty acids and complex carbohydrates, which contain fiber, will help decrease cardiovascular disease risk (Siri-Tarino, Sun, Hu, & Krauss, 2010). Therefore, the goal of any nutrition intervention focused on the South Asian population should be to prevent and effectively treat chronic diseases by reversing the unhealthy dietary trends that have been adopted.

Recent Research Findings Impacting the Nutritional Assessment of the South Asian Community

Because South Asians tend to carry adiposity in their upper body and abdominal regions, new BMI (= kg/m^2) reference values have been developed and recommended for use for Asian populations (Hsu, Araneta, Kanaya, Chiang, & Fujimoto, 2015). These new values take into account the increased suscepti-bility of this population for obesity-related comorbidities at lower BMIs com-pared with other ethnicities (WHO Expert Consultation, 2004; Snehalatha, Viswanathan, & Ramachandran, 2003). Thus, whereas the cutoff for the clas-sification of "overweight" starts at 25.0 for the general Western population, cur-rent guidelines recommend a BMI cutoff of 23.0 among Asians, particularly South Asian Americans (Snehalatha et al., 2003). This BMI reference value allows public health professionals to better identify individuals who may benefit from early nutrition education and interventions in order to prevent develop-ment of chronic disease such as type 2 diabetes.

Of course, while BMI is a useful screening tool, it does have its limitations. It does not give information about an individual's body weight distribution (i.e., where weight is distributed on the body) or body composition (i.e., percent body fat). In fact, because waist-based measurements provide insight into an individ-ual's abdominal adiposity, waist circumference and waist-to-hip ratio are better indicators of chronic disease risk. Clinicians should consider using waist-based measurements to assess South Asian Americans since many South Asians have normal Asian-adjusted BMIs (as described in the previous paragraph) but still have abdominal obesity and increased risk for chronic disease.

Researchers have also been investigating South Asian body composition (directly measuring adiposity and lean body mass) as yet another nutrition-assessment marker to identify at-risk individuals (Goel et al., 2008; Goel, Misra, Vikram, Poddar, & Gupta, 2010; Joseph et al., 2011). Though the direct mea-sure of adiposity in the public health setting is not practical, work to support possible alternate body composition reference values should be considered in the research and clinical settings (Goel et al., 2008; Joseph et al., 2011).

There has been some progress in developing nutrition assessment and edu-cation tools that are specific to South Asians living in Western countries. A food frequency questionnaire (FFQ) that includes common ethnic foods was created in order to assess macro- and micronutrient intake among South Asian Americans (Sevak et al., 2004). While a 24-hour recall is the preferred method of collecting nutrient intake information, FFQs are nonetheless useful for larger epidemiological studies, due mainly to their lower cost and ease of use. The validation of a South Asian–specific FFQ allows researchers to have a stan-dardized method of capturing dietary nutrient intake in this high-risk popu-lation (Kelemen et al., 2003). Additionally, as a result of increased awareness of the South Asian population's susceptibility to chronic diseases, many online resources are now available to provide nutrition education aimed at prevention and management of metabolic and cardiovascular diseases. Examples of these specific dietary education tools are listed in Appendix A.

As growing numbers of South Asians continue to immigrate to the United States, additional research efforts have been devoted to serving the needs of this at-risk population, particularly in regions of high concentration. In 2006, the Metabolic Syndrome and Atherosclerosis in South Asians Living in America (MASALA) Study was initiated in the San Francisco Bay Area as a long-term study to identify factors, including nutrition, that lead to heart disease in South Asian Americans (MASALA, 2006). By 2013, the MASALA Study had more than 900 participants and researchers are hopeful that information gathered will be instrumental in the prevention and treatment of heart disease in South Asians (MASALA, 2006).

Recommendations

For health professionals working with South Asians in the United States, it is recommended to first use the new Asian-specific BMI reference values in nutrition assessment. This will help to ensure that at-risk individuals are appropriately identified. Additionally, when possible, clinicians should also collect waist-based measurements including waist circumference and waist-to-hip ratio, both of which can better assess body weight distribution. This may require additional physician education and training initiatives.

With regard to nutritional interventions, clinicians should encourage mindful eating and a balanced diet to include micronutrient-dense foods such as fruits and vegetables, and healthy protein sources. Specific dietary guidelines should also focus on the following (Misra, Sharma, et al., 2011):

- Limiting refined carbohydrates and "hidden" sugars
- Replacing unhealthy trans and saturated fat intake with healthy unsaturated fats, such as monounsaturated and omega-3 fatty acids (nuts and fish are dietary sources of healthy fats)
- Increasing fiber intake from vegetables

Finally, although the focus of this chapter is on nutrition, one cannot ignore the integral role that physical activity plays in a person's metabolic health. South Asian Americans tend to have lower physical activity levels, which may also contribute to their increased risk of chronic disease (Fischbacher, Hunt, & Alexander, 2004). Recommendations for regular physical activity, including taking a brisk walk after eating, should be made in conjunction with dietary guidelines. The current American Heart Association recommendations regarding physical activity for overall cardiovascular health are as follows (2014b):

■ A minimum of 30 minutes of moderate intensity aerobic activity at least 5 days per week; or a minimum of 25 minutes of vigorous aerobic activity at least 3 days per week; or a combination of moderate- and vigorous-intensity aerobic activity; *and* moderate- to high-intensity muscle-strengthening activity at least 2 days per week for additional health benefits.
■ For lowering blood pressure and cholesterol, recommendations suggest an average of 40 minutes of moderate- to vigorous-intensity aerobic activity three to four times per week.

Conclusions

A person's risk for chronic disease is largely dependent on the interaction between genetics and environment. Given the South Asian population's genetic susceptibility for metabolic and cardiovascular diseases, this group of immigrants must work even harder to change lifestyle factors that can help lower their risk for chronic diseases (Jonnalagadda & Khosla, 2007). Thankfully, there has been heightened awareness regarding the increased risk of chronic disease in the South Asian American population.

Given the important role that nutrition plays in chronic disease risk, additional resources should be dedicated to the review of South Asian dietary practices after immigration. While there have been a number of publications investigating the South Asian population's increased risk for chronic disease, there is still only limited research focusing on their changes in dietary habits after immigration, particularly research that focuses on gender- and/or age-specific differences. More investigation is needed into the changing dietary patterns of South Asian immigrants based on gender, age, and degree of acculturation. It would also be of interest to research dietary practices over one's life span, particularly during key developmental events such as pregnancy.

References

Alwan, A., Maclean, D. R., Riley, L. M., d'Espaignet, E. T., Mathers, C. D., Stevens, G. A., & Bettcher, D. (2010). Monitoring and surveillance of chronic noncommunicable diseases: Progress and capacity in high-burden countries. *Lancet, 376*(9755), 1861–1868.

American Heart Association. (2014a). Added Sugars. Retrieved from http://www.heart.org/HEARTORG/GettingHealthy/NutritionCenter/HealthyEating/Added-Sugars_UCM_305858_Article.jsp

American Heart Association. (2014b). American Heart Association Recommendations for Physical Activity in Adults. Retrieved from http://www.heart.org/HEARTORG/GettingHealthy/PhysicalActivity/FitnessBasics/American-Heart-Association-Recommendations-for-Physical-Activity-in-Adults_UCM_307976_Article.jsp

Anderson, A. S., Bush, H., Lean, M., Bradby, H., Williams, R., & Lea, E. (2005). Evolution of atherogenic diets in South Asian and Italian women after migration to a higher risk region. *Journal of Human Nutrition and Dietetics, 18*(1), 33–43.

Chopra, S. M., Misra, A., Gulati, S., & Gupta, R. (2013). Overweight, obesity and related non-communicable diseases in Asian Indian girls and women. *European Journal of Clinical Nutrition, 67*(7), 688–696.

Dixit, A. A., Azar, K. M., Gardner, C. D., & Palaniappan, L. P. (2011). Incorporation of whole, ancient grains into a modern Asian Indian diet to reduce the burden of chronic disease. *Nutrition Reviews, 69*(8), 479–488.

Fischbacher, C. M., Hunt, S., & Alexander, L. (2004). How physically active are South Asians in the United Kingdom? A literature review. *Journal of Public Health (Oxford, England), 26*(3), 250–258.

Gholap, N., Davies, M., Patel, K., Sattar, N., & Khunti, K. (2011). Type 2 diabetes and cardiovascular disease in South Asians. *Primary Care Diabetes, 5*(1), 45–56.

Gilbert, P. A., & Khokhar, S. (2008). Changing dietary habits of ethnic groups in Europe and implications for health. *Nutrition Reviews, 66*(4), 203–215.

Go, A.S., Mozaffarian D., Roger, V. L., Benjamin, E. J., Berry, J. D., Borden, W. B., . . . American Heart Association Statistics Committee and Stroke Statistics Subcommittee. (2013). Heart disease and stroke statistics—2013 update: A report from the American Heart Association. *Circulation, 127*(1), e6–e245.

Goel, K., Gupta, N., Misra, A., Poddar, P., Pandey, R. M., Vikram, N. K., & Wasir, J. S. (2008). Predictive equations for body fat and abdominal fat with DXA and MRI as reference in Asian Indians. *Obesity (Silver Spring), 16*(2), 451–456.

Goel, K., Misra, A., Vikram, N. K., Poddar, P., & Gupta, N. (2010). Subcutaneous abdominal adipose tissue is associated with the metabolic syndrome in Asian Indians independent of intra-abdominal and total body fat. *Heart, 96*(8), 579–583.

Grundy, S. M., Cleeman, J. I., Daniels, S. R., Donato, K. A., Eckel, R. H., Franklin, B. A., . . . National Heart, Lung, and Blood Institute. (2005). Diagnosis and management of the metabolic syndrome: An American Heart Association/National Heart, Lung, and Blood Institute Scientific Statement. *Circulation, 112*(17), 2735–2752.

Gupta, N., Shah, P., Goel, K., Misra, A., Rastogi, K., Vikram, N. K., . . . Gulati, S. (2010). Imbalanced dietary profile, anthropometry, and lipids in urban Asian Indian adolescents and young adults. *Journal of the American College of Nutrition, 29*(2), 81–91.

Holmboe-Ottesen, G., & Wandel, M. (2012). Changes in dietary habits after migration and consequences for health: A focus on South Asians in Europe. *Food and Nutrition Research, 56* 18891.

Hsu, W. C., Araneta, M. R. G., Kanaya, A. M., Chiang, J. L., & Fujimoto, W. (2015). BMI cut points to identify at-risk Asian Americans for type 2 diabetes screening. *Diabetes Care, 38*(1), 150–158.

Isharwal, S., Arya, S., Misra, A., Wasir, J. S., Pandey, R. M., Rastogi, K., . . . Sharma, R. (2008). Dietary nutrients and insulin resistance in urban Asian Indian adolescents and young adults. *Annals of Nutrition and Metabolism, 52*(2), 145–151.

Isharwal, S., Misra, A., Wasir, J. S., & Nigam, P. (2009). Diet & insulin resistance: A review & Asian Indian perspective. *Indian Journal of Medical Research, 129*(5), 485–499.

Jafar, T.H., Levey, A.S., White, F.M., Gul, A., Jessani, S., Khan, A.Q., . . . Chaturvedi, N. (2004). Ethnic differences and determinants of diabetes and central obesity among South Asians of Pakistan. *Diabetic Medicine, 21*(7), 716–723.

Jonnalagadda, S. S., & Diwan, S. (2002a). Regional variations in dietary intake and body mass index of first-generation Asian-Indian immigrants in the United States. *Journal of the American Dietetic Association, 102*(9), 1286–1289.

Jonnalagadda, S. S., & Diwan, S. (2002b). Nutrient intake of first generation Gujarati Asian Indian immigrants in the U.S. *Journal of the American College of Nutrition, 21*(5), 372–380.

Jonnalagadda, S. S., & Khosla, P. (2007). Nutrient intake, body composition, blood cholesterol and glucose levels among adult Asian Indians in the United States. *Journal of Immigrant and Minority Health, 9*(3), 171–178.

Joseph, L., Wasir, J. S., Misra, A., Vikram, N. K., Goel, K., Pandey, R. M., . . . Kondal, D. (2011). Appropriate values of adiposity and lean body mass indices to detect cardiovascular risk factors in Asian Indians. *Diabetes Technology and Therapeutics, 13*(9), 899–906.

Kanaya, A. M., Wassel, C.L., Mathur, D., Stewart, A., Herrington, D., Budoff, M.J., . . . Liu, K. (2010). Prevalence and correlates of diabetes in South Asian Indians in the United States: Findings from the Metabolic Syndrome and Atherosclerosis in South Asians Living in America Study and the Multi-Ethnic Study of Atherosclerosis. *Metabolic Syndrome and Related Disorders, 8*(2), 157–164.

Kelemen, L. E., Anand, S. S., Vuksan, V., Yi, Q., Teo, K. K., Devanesen, S., . . . SHARE Investigators. (2003). Development and evaluation of cultural food frequency questionnaires for South Asians, Chinese, and Europeans in North America. *Journal of the American Dietetic Association, 103*(9), 1178–1184.

Kennedy, A., Martinez, K., Chuang, C. C., LaPoint, K., & McIntosh, M. (2009). Saturated fatty acid-mediated inflammation and insulin resistance in adipose tissue: Mechanisms of action and implications. *Journal of Nutrition, 139*(1), 1–4.

Kittler, P. G., Sucher, K., & Nahikian-Nelms, M. (2011). *Food and culture*. Retrieved from https://www.cengagebrain.com.au/content/9781133784425.pdf

Kumar, B. N., Holmboe-Ottesen, G., Lien, N., & Wandel, M. (2004). Ethnic differences in body mass index and associated factors of adolescents from minorities in Oslo, Norway: A cross-sectional study. *Public Health Nutrition, 7*(8), 999–1008.

Mahadevan, M., & Blair, D. (2009). Changes in food habits of south Indian Hindu Brahmin immigrants in State College, PA. *Ecology of Food and Nutrition, 48*(5), 404–432.

Margioris, A. N. (2009). Fatty acids and postprandial inflammation. *Current Opinion in Clinical Nutrition and Metabolic Care, 12*(2), 129–137.

MASALA. (2006). *Metabolic Syndrome and Atherosclerosis in South Asians Living in America.* Retrieved from http://www.masalastudy.org/about/index.html

Misra, A., & Khurana, L. (2009). The metabolic syndrome in South Asians: Epidemiology, determinants, and prevention. *Metabolic Syndrome and Related Disorders, 7*(6), 497–514.

Misra, A., and Khurana, L. (2011). Obesity-related non-communicable diseases: South Asians vs White Caucasians. *International Journal of Obesity (London), 35*(2), 167–187.

Misra, A., Khurana, L., Isharwal, S., & Bhardwaj, S. (2009). South Asian diets and insulin resistance. *British Journal of Nutrition, 101*(4), 465–473.

Misra, A., Rastogi, K., & Joshi, S. R. (2009). Whole grains and health: Perspective for Asian Indians. *Journal of the Association Physicians of India, 57,* 155–162.

Misra, A., Sharma, R., Gulati, S., Joshi, S. R., Sharma, V., Ghafoorunissa, . . . National Dietary Guidelines Consensus Group. (2011). Consensus dietary guidelines for healthy living and prevention of obesity, the metabolic syndrome, diabetes, and related disorders in Asian Indians. *Diabetes Technology Therapeutics, 13*(6), 683–694.

Misra, A., Singhal, N., Sivakumar, B., Bhagat, N., Jaiswal, A., & Khurana, L. (2011). Nutrition transition in India: Secular trends in dietary intake and their relationship to diet-related non-communicable diseases. *Journal of Diabetes, 3*(4), 278–292.

OECD StatExtracts iLibrary. (2011). International Migration Database. Retrieved from http://stats.oecd.org/Index.aspx?DatasetCode=MIG

Pingali, P. (2007). Westernization of Asian diets and the transformation of food systems: Implications for research and policy. *Food Policy, 32*(3), 281–298.

Popkin, B. M. (2009). Global changes in diet and activity patterns as drivers of the nutrition transition. *Nestle Nutrition Workshop Series Pediatric Program, 63,* 1–10; discussion 10–4, 259–68.

Satia, J. A. (2010). Dietary acculturation and the nutrition transition: An overview. *Applied Physiology Nutrition Metabolism, 35*(2), 219–223.

Satia-Abouta, J., Patterson, R. E., Neuhouser, M. L., & Elder, J. (2002). Dietary acculturation: Applications to nutrition research and dietetics. *Journal of American Diet Association, 102*(8), 1105–1118.

Sevak, L., Mangtani, P., McCormack, V., Bhakta, D., Kassam-Khamis, T., & dos Santos Silva, I. (2004). Validation of a food frequency questionnaire to assess macro- and micro-nutrient intake among South Asians in the United Kingdom. *European Journal Nutrition, 43*(3), 160–168. doi: 10.1007/s00394-004-0454-6

Siri-Tarino, P. W., Sun, Q., Hu, F. B., & Krauss, R. M. (2010). Saturated fat, carbohydrate, and cardiovascular disease. *American Journal of Clinical Nutrition, 91*(3), 502–509.

Snehalatha, C., Viswanathan, V., & Ramachandran, A. (2003). Cutoff values for normal anthropometric variables in Asian Indian adults. *Diabetes Care, 26*(5), 1380–1384.

Wandel, M., Råberg, M., Kumar, B., & Holmboe-Ottesen, G. (2008). Changes in food habits after migration among South Asians settled in Oslo: The effect of demographic, socio-economic and integration factors. *Appetite, 50*(2–3), 376–385.

WHO Expert Consultation. (2004). Appropriate body-mass index for Asian populations and its implications for policy and intervention strategies. *Lancet, 363*(9403), 157–163.

Chapter 6

Obesity

Anita Mudan and Amitasrigowri Murthy

Contents

Abstract

Objective: To review different components of the obesity epidemic in the South Asian population by focusing on current guidelines, risk factors, related diseases, and interventions, and to formulate recommendations to prevent and address obesity among South Asians in the United States.

Key Findings: As a population, South Asians are more prone to abdominal obesity, which is associated with complications and related diseases. The differences in body fat distribution prompted a modification of the body mass index (BMI) guidelines for South Asians to reflect the propensity for abdominal fat, and thus better screen individuals to properly risk stratify them. Predisposition to abdominal fat is multifactorial with adverse lifestyle choices (reduced physical activity and poor diet) as well as a genetic susceptibility playing key roles.

Recommendations: More work is needed to implement and evaluate culturally-appropriate lifestyle and dietary interventions. Further research into the genetics of obesity within the South Asian population is needed to better target certain groups for interventions, as well as to improve risk calculations. Additionally, use of the South Asian consensus guidelines for BMI, waist circumference (WC), and waist-to-hip ratio (WHR) needs to be expanded in the health-care setting as well as at home.

Introduction

Obesity has become a truly global epidemic. Over the last few decades, rates of obesity in the United States have increased 119% (Rudin, Rincon, Bauman, & Barzilai, 2007). While this dramatic increase is being seen population wide, trends have emerged within certain ethnic groups. Asian Indians are the largest South Asian subgroup for which the largest amount of data exist. They comprise roughly 18.4% of the total Asian population within the United States (Taylor, 2013). Asian Indians, both globally and within the United States, have high rates of diabetes, cardiovascular disease, and dyslipidemia, all of which are considered obesity-related complications. Furthermore, they tend to develop these complications with smaller amounts of weight gain compared with other ethnic groups. Thus, obesity within the Asian Indian population, as well as the larger South Asian population, is an epidemic that requires immediate improvements in both screening and treatment.

Defining Obesity

Obesity is defined as having a body fat content greater than 25% in men and 33% in women (Enas & Kannan, 2005). There are three primary ways to measure obesity: calculating (1) body mass index (BMI), (2) waist circumference (WC), and (3) waist-to-hip ratio (WHR).

BMI is the ratio of body weight to height as measured in kilograms/meters squared. Based on the current Centers for Disease Control and Prevention (CDC) BMI guidelines, the prevalence of obesity compared with its associated complications is discordant within the South Asian population. The rates of diabetes, metabolic syndrome, and cardiovascular disease, all considered complications of obesity, are significantly higher than the rates of obesity within this group. This implies that complications tend to occur at lower BMIs in South Asians versus other ethnic groups. Given this discordance and because South Asians carry 3%–6% more body fat within any BMI level, the World Health Organization (WHO) altered the BMI classification system specifically for the South Asian population (Enas & Kannan, 2005). The modified criteria, shown in Table 6.1, demonstrate lower values for each stratum.

WC is another measure that is more specific for abdominal/truncal obesity, defined as fat accumulation around the abdomen, which can be both under the skin as well as around internal organs. The simplicity of its measurement makes it easy for patients to understand and self-monitor changes. The guidelines for WC in South Asians have also been modified to reflect the preferential accumulation of abdominal fat. WC measurements above the recommended values are consistent with abdominal obesity (Misra, Wasir, & Vikram, 2005). Compared with Caucasians who have a similar body fat percentage, the average WC of South Asians was 10 cm smaller (Misra & Khurana, 2011). The revised guidelines, shown in Table 6.2, help detect abdominal obesity earlier, and thus may serve as a good screening tool.

Table 6.1   BMI Criteria

	General BMI Guidelines (WHO, 1997)	*Consensus BMI Guidelines for South Asians (Misra et al., 2009)*
Normal	18.5–24.9	18–22.9
Overweight	25–29.9	23–24.9
Obese	>30	>25

Table 6.2   Waist Circumference (WC) Criteria

	General WC Guidelines (Lean, Han, & Morrison, 1995)	Consensus WC Guidelines for South Asians (Misra et al., 2009)
Men	>102 cm	>78 cm
Women	>88 cm	>72 cm

Table 6.3   Waist-to-Hip Ratio (WHR) Criteria

	General Guidelines for WHR (Rudin et al., 2007)	Consensus Guidelines for WHR in South Asians (Misra et al., 2009)
Men	>1.0	>0.88
Women	>0.9	>0.8

Perhaps the best measurement of abdominal fat is the WHR. WHR is the ratio of WC to hip circumference. Larger values correlate with a higher degree of abdominal adiposity and are predictive of more adverse outcomes (Rudin et al., 2007). WHR is considered a better marker of abdominal obesity compared with BMI, as BMI distributes weight based on height, and does not account for preferential fat accumulation in a single area. Similar to BMI and WC, the cutoff values to diagnose abdominal obesity for South Asians, shown in Table 6.3, have been lowered to account for preferential accumulation of abdominal fat and the resulting increase in cardio-metabolic risk factors. However, WHR is not used commonly in clinical practice due to the difficulty in explaining its measurement and use (Misra et al., 2009).

Abdominal Obesity

Abdominal fat is more predictive of developing obesity-related complications such as diabetes, dyslipidemia, and cardiovascular disease. Among South Asian adults, the prevalence of generalized obesity based on BMI is around 12%, but abdominal obesity (fat specifically deposited around the abdomen) is closer to 41%, which supports the theory that South Asians preferentially accumulate abdominal fat (Enas & Kannan, 2005). Abdominal obesity has several different subcategories based on location of fat accumulation: superficial subcutaneous (directly below the skin), deep subcutaneous (below the superficial layer—separated by the abdominal wall fascia), and visceral (surrounding the internal organs) (Anand et al., 2011). Kohli and Lear (2012) compared fat distribution and location among different ethnic groups and found that South Asians had higher amounts of subcutaneous and visceral adipose tissue (309.4 and 115.2 cm^2, respectively) compared with Caucasians (265.2 cm^2 subcutaneous and 100.8 cm^2 visceral), and Chinese (221.2 cm^2 subcutaneous and 100 cm^2 visceral). Visceral fat is especially concerning, given the associated increased risk for developing obesity-related complications.

The theory behind South Asians' tendency for preferentially developing visceral fat involves adipose tissue development in the abdomen. As fat is stored, it first accumulates in the superficial layer, then the deep layer, and finally the visceral layer. It is proposed that South Asians have a decreased storage capacity in their superficial subcutaneous layer, leading to earlier "overflow" of fat into the deep and visceral layers (Anand et al., 2011). This leads to hypertrophy (increased size) of existing adipocytes, as opposed to adipocyte hyperplasia (increased number), which is usually seen in other ethnic groups (Anand et al., 2011). This phenomenon, "ethnic lipodystrophy," can all be traced back to adipocyte hypertrophy and increased fat storage in the deep and visceral layers (Anand et al., 2011).

Apart from just storage, adipose tissue is also metabolically active, secreting the metabolites adiponectin and leptin. Low levels of adiponectin are seen in people with large amounts of adipose tissue and vice versa, with low levels resulting in insulin resistance (Shah et al., 2012). Leptin is another insulin sensitizing metabolite at normal degrees of adiposity, but as levels increase, with increasing amounts of fat tissue, it results in insulin resistance (Shah et al., 2012).

The preferential accumulation of metabolically active abdominal fat puts South Asians at an increased risk of developing obesity and its complications independent of lifestyle risk factors. Therefore, the risk factors discussed in detail in the following section become even more important targets for preventative measures.

Risk Factors for Obesity

Physical Activity

The current global obesity epidemic has been attributed to an increased caloric intake combined with a decrease in physical activity. Asian Indians have one of the lowest rates of physical activity among Asian American groups (Taylor, 2013). Looking at the emigrant population in the United States, more than 40% of Asian Indians are not getting adequate physical activity (Daniel & Wilbur, 2011). When examining specific exercise habits of participants in the Canadian Multi-Cultural Health Assessment Trial (M-CHAT) study, South Asians had lower levels of moderate and moderate-vigorous physical activity, and were 1.58 (men) and 1.66 (women) times more likely to be physically inactive compared with Europeans (Lesser, Yew, Mackey, & Lear, 2012). Since physical inactivity is an independent risk factor for obesity, increasing duration, intensity, and frequency of physical activity is an important goal for primary prevention.

Diet

The major dietary contribution to obesity stems from increased caloric intake, a phenomenon that is occurring due to a combination of a nutrition transition and acculturation. The nutrition transition, a product of industrialization and globalization of the food market, resulted in increased consumption of highly processed foods, while acculturation caused the adoption of food choices and eating habits from the host country (Holmboe-Ottesen & Wandel, 2012). In the case of South Asians, this translates to a decreased intake of traditional foods or modification of traditional foods to reflect what is readily available. The traditional South Asian diet has high regional variability, but generally includes whole grains, lentils/beans, vegetables, fruits, meat/fish (although many are vegetarian), and has low fats and sugars. One of the most common initial patterns seen upon emigration is a decrease in vegetarianism, that is, decreased consumption of traditional foods in general (Garduno-Diaz & Khokhar, 2013). The hallmarks of a Western diet include low fiber intake, and a high consumption of meat, animal fats, and processed carbohydrates (Abate & Chandalia, 2007). Modifications to the traditional diet usually start with a transition from whole grains to processed ones, decreased consumption of beans/lentils, increased meat/fish and full-fat dairy consumption, and significantly increased intake of fats and sugars (Holmboe-Ottesen & Wandel, 2012). The longer South Asians reside in their new country, the less they consume their traditional food, replacing it with fat-laden snacks and fast food, both of which are cheap and readily available (Dixit, Azar, Gardner, & Palaniappan, 2011). The other major dietary change upon emigration is increased soda consumption, which drastically increases sugar intake (Lesser, Gasevic, & Lear, 2014). Increased saturated fat and refined carbohydrate intake associated with dietary Westernization correlates with excess weight gain, specifically the accumulation of abdominal fat (Misra & Vikram, 2004).

Genetics

Since South Asians have a high predisposition to developing abdominal obesity, there has recently been a large push to examine possible genetic factors.

The fat mass and obesity-associated gene (*FTO* gene) has been shown to have the strongest link to obesity susceptibility. Genetic variation in the *FTO* gene increases the risk of obesity by 1.25 fold, increases BMI by approximately 0.26 kg/m², and increases WC by 0.51 cm (Li et al., 2012). Another study looking at the lipoprotein lipase (an enzyme involved in the metabolism of fats) gene found that genetic variants were associated with increased risk of obesity (Khanna & Mani, 2012). Both studies show promising evidence of a genetic component to the development of obesity in South Asians, which remains an area of ongoing research.

Prenatal Factors

Multiple studies have examined prenatal conditions that could impact the development of obesity later in life. Many of these studies are based on the "Barker hypothesis," which proposes that intrauterine conditions, namely maternal malnutrition, cause alterations in metabolic homeostatic mechanisms, which can lead to the development of diseases in adulthood (de Boo & Harding, 2006). Therefore, even though maternal malnutrition often results in low-birthweight infants (weight below the 10th percentile for gestational age), these infants are still at an increased risk of becoming obese later in life. Studies looking at body composition of South Asian infants with low birthweight found that even though their weight was low, there was more adipose tissue and less muscle mass compared with Caucasian infants (Misra & Khurana, 2011). Another study demonstrated that childhood BMI, central and generalized adiposity, and circulating glucose and insulin levels were higher in children with lower birthweights (Yajnik, 2004). Children who were small at birth were more likely to have "catch up obesity," defined as higher weight or fat mass as well as a larger amount of subcutaneous abdominal adipose tissue at 8 years of age, compared with those with a normal birthweight (Misra & Khurana, 2011). These findings support the hypothesis that a lower birthweight is associated with metabolic adaptations that predispose to adipose tissue formation after birth.

Cultural Perception

While not traditionally thought of as a disease risk factor, cultural beliefs play a significant role in shaping daily lifestyle, and can indirectly contribute to the development of obesity and its related diseases. These cultural beliefs seem to hold an even more important place in emigrant populations, due to concerns of being in a new environment and integrating into a different society (Patel, Phillips-Caesar, & Boutin-Foster, 2012). Within the South Asian community, there is a general lack of understanding regarding the relationship between lifestyle and its impact on disease. Developing a disease is not seen as being under one's own control. Therefore, it is not necessary to change lifestyle factors as development of disease is ultimately predetermined by fate (Patel et al., 2012).

Gender roles, specifically their influence on diet, are a major contributor to disease risk. Traditionally, women are in charge of the home, preparing food, and taking care of the household (Patel et al., 2012). Due to the strong familial and social networks among South Asians, and the resulting pressures to respect traditional beliefs, many women prioritize adhering to cultural norms regarding diet even when advised by health professionals to make changes (Lucas, Murray, & Kinra, 2013). The expectations of the family strongly influence dietary choices and preparation, making it extremely difficult to make any modifications, which could impact the whole family (Lucas et al., 2013). Furthermore, the traditional diet is seen as a cultural cornerstone, and is believed by many to be healthy because it has been passed down for generations, and ancestors did not struggle with obesity or its related diseases (Patel et al., 2012).

One of the key barriers to exercise in South Asians is a lack of leisure time (Lucas et al., 2013). Exercise does not have a firm place in traditional South Asian culture (Lucas et al., 2013). Along the same lines, cultural beliefs emphasize that any time that is available outside of work should be spent taking care of the family, instead of doing an activity alone, thereby further discouraging participation in exercise programs that would take time away from family (Patel et al., 2012).

Finally, one of the most significant cultural barriers in this group is body image. Larger body types are seen as healthier, making people less inclined to want to lose weight (Patel et al., 2012). This is reflected in perceptions of ideal body weight. In a study of South Asians in the United States, 60% of patients who were overweight and 19% who were obese by BMI considered themselves to be normal or even underweight. Even more distressing, few in the overweight/obese category believed that their health was affected by their weight (Tang et al., 2012). Lucas et al. found that many South Asian women in the United Kingdom perceived themselves to be of normal weight when they were in fact overweight by BMI (Lucas et al., 2013). This altered perception of body image is also prevalent in South Asian children, who perceive themselves as thinner than their actual body weight (Pallan, Hiam, Duda, & Adab, 2011). Given the strong cultural tradition in this population, and the significant impact it has in shaping lifestyle choices, it is easy to see why attempting to initiate changes that seek to alter these beliefs would be met with resistance. Therefore, any attempt to initiate lifestyle interventions must start by trying to reform perception of body image and highlight the direct connection between lifestyle choices, weight, and chronic diseases.

Obesity-Related Noncommunicable Diseases

In addition to being a health risk, obesity is also a risk factor for developing an array of other diseases, known collectively as obesity-related noncommunicable diseases. These include heart disease, dyslipidemia, metabolic syndrome, and obstructive sleep apnea, all of which are discussed below.

Heart Disease

South Asians are four times more likely to develop coronary artery disease (CAD) compared with Caucasians (Silbiger et al., 2013). The elevated risk of CAD is due to the higher levels of obesity in South Asians. Elevations in BMI directly lead to obesity-related diseases, which are considered independent risk factors for cardiovascular disease (Prasad, Kabir, Dash, & Das, 2013). The onset of these obesity-related diseases can occur up to a decade earlier in South Asians, directly leading to more complications. This longer duration of exposure ultimately results in greater morbidity and a diminished quality of life (Sathe et al., 2013). Moreover, cardiovascular disease in South Asians is more extensive and clinically aggressive, and leads to a 40% higher mortality rate compared with Caucasians (Silbiger et al., 2013). In a study of emigrant populations in New York City, South Asians were more likely to present with triple vessel disease compared with Caucasians, 32.5% versus 22.4%, and were twice as likely to have diffuse atherosclerotic lesions at time of presentation (Silbiger et al., 2013). This finding is consistent with the increased rates of high blood pressure, dyslipidemia, and diabetes, all contributing factors to cardiovascular disease (Bharmal et al., 2014).

Dyslipidemia

Dyslipidemia, defined by the criteria listed in Table 6.4, is one of the most common diseases associated with obesity, and is itself a risk factor for other obesity-related diseases. Dyslipidemia has been found in South Asians of a lower

Table 6.4 Dyslipidemia Criteria

Rader and Hobbs (2012)
↑ Total cholesterol
↑ Low-density lipoprotein (LDL)
↑ Triglycerides
↓ High-density lipoprotein (HDL)

BMI and body fat percentage compared with other ethnic groups (Misra & Shrivastava, 2013). The larger number of adipocytes found in overweight/obese patients directly results in higher levels of both triglycerides and low-density lipoprotein (LDL), both of which are criteria for dyslipidemia (Rader & Hobbs, 2012). The high LDL levels in South Asians tend to be predominantly composed of small, dense LDL, which is more likely to lead to atherosclerosis than other LDL subtypes (Misra & Shrivastava, 2013). Low high-density lipoprotein (HDL) levels are prevalent among South Asians, and a large percentage of the HDL found in South Asians is dysfunctional, which further exacerbates the effects of low HDL levels (Misra & Khurana, 2011). Therefore, not only are South Asians more likely to develop dyslipidemia with lower overall levels of adipose tissue, but also the specific manifestation of dyslipidemia is more likely to lead to heart disease.

Metabolic Syndrome

Metabolic syndrome encompasses an array of metabolic factors, which when combined increase the risk of developing cardiovascular disease and diabetes. A minimum three out of the five criteria listed in Table 6.5 must be fulfilled in order to make the diagnosis of metabolic syndrome (Misra & Bhardwaj, 2014). The etiology of metabolic syndrome centers around insulin resistance caused by high circulating levels of fatty acids released into the bloodstream, which cause hyperglycemia and the other components of the syndrome (Eckel, 2012). These criteria have further been adjusted for South Asians, reflecting the greater tendency for abdominal fat accumulation (Misra & Khurana, 2009). Even with the modified criteria, South Asians still have a significantly higher prevalence of metabolic syndrome in all BMI categories compared with Caucasians, shown in Table 6.6 (Palaniappan, Wong, Shin, Fortmann, & Lauderdale, 2011). The presence of metabolic syndrome increases the risk of cardiovascular disease 1.5–3 fold, and the risk of diabetes 3–5 fold compared with the general population (Eckel, 2012).

Table 6.5   Metabolic Syndrome Criteria

Misra and Khurana (2009)
Waist circumference ≥90 cm (male), ≥80 cm (female)
Fasting blood glucose ≥100 mg/dL
Blood pressure ≥130/85 mmHg
Triglycerides ≥150 mg/dL
High-density lipoprotein (HDL) ≤40 mg/dL (male), ≤50 mg/dL (female)

Table 6.6 Prevalence of Metabolic Syndrome

BMI	Palaniappan et al. (2011)	
	South Asians	Caucasians
Normal (18.5–24.9)	38%	10%
Overweight (25–29.9)	50%	24%
Class I obesity (30–34.9)	60%	42%
Class II obesity (35–39.9)	78%	58%

Other diseases, such as obstructive sleep apnea, are also significantly associated with obesity, but there are still limited data in the South Asian population.

Recommendations

The proposed recommendations below include lifestyle modifications, exercise, and increasing education regarding obesity among health-care providers and the South Asian community.

- *Exercise:* Several studies have examined various exercise regimens for South Asians to formulate ideal recommendations of time and intensity needed to influence their adverse cardio-metabolic risk profile. South Asians need to undertake higher levels of physical activity than Caucasians, 266 minutes/week versus 150 minutes/week of moderate physical activity, in order to have the same impact on their risk factors (Celis-Morales, Ghouri, Bailey, Sattar, & Gill, 2013). In adults, this translates to roughly 30 minutes of moderate aerobic exercise + 15 minutes muscle strengthening + 15 minutes work-related exercise (walking, climbing stairs, etc.) per day (Misra et al., 2012).
- *Diet/Lifestyle:* Lifestyle intervention programs, which target diet and exercise changes in families instead of individuals, are a promising method of effecting change on a multigenerational level. In order for these programs to be successful in South Asian communities, they need to be tailored to overcome the specific cultural barriers. The Prevention of Diabetes and Obesity in South Asians (PODOSA) trial in Scotland adapted dietary and exercise interventions to be administered in participants' homes by community health workers and dieticians, with a goal to try to increase weight loss and physical activity over a 3-year period (Wallia et al., 2013). They focused on a home-based approach, targeted the whole family, and most importantly,

conducted the interventions in participants' primary language. The key to success in this example is the cultural specificity to South Asians.

■ *Children:* Build interventions that can be used among children. The major goal of any intervention in children is primary prevention of obesity and instilling healthy lifestyle practices in them from an early age to prevent obesity later in life. Our recommendations for children fall under the umbrella of family-based culturally sensitive dietary/lifestyle modifications. In addition, there should be efforts placed on education regarding healthy body image for younger age groups, particularly children.

■ *Other Treatment Options:* First-line obesity interventions center around diet and lifestyle modifications. However, with increasing obesity rates, other treatment options have been studied as adjuncts to lifestyle modifications, especially in cases of refractory obesity (obesity that has not responded to lifestyle modifications alone). Pharmacologic agents have shown some benefit when used in people with BMIs > 25 with or without comorbidities (Misra et al., 2009). Bariatric surgery has also gained some popularity in those with severe obesity, BMI > 32, and multiple comorbid conditions. Malabsorptive procedures, which alter the anatomy of the gastrointestinal tract, were shown to be more effective at treating obesity and comorbid conditions compared with restrictive procedures, which simply decrease the capacity of the stomach (Misra et al., 2009). However, very little research has been done on either pharmacologic or surgical obesity treatment in South Asians. Although these treatment options are available, they are considered a last resort, and dietary and lifestyle modifications remain the preferred method of intervention for treating obesity.

Recommendations Summary

■ Utilize the consensus BMI, WC, and WHR for South Asians to screen for obesity in the outpatient health-care setting, as well as educating the South Asian community on how to self-monitor these measurements.

■ Thirty minutes of moderate intensity aerobic exercise plus an additional 15 minutes of weight training daily.

■ Culturally specific dietary modifications implemented for an entire household.

■ Institute healthy eating and exercise habits early in childhood for primary prevention of obesity.

Conclusions

Obesity is a major health-care concern in South Asians both worldwide and in the United States because it is a direct risk factor for cardiovascular disease, diabetes, dyslipidemia, and other obesity-related diseases. South Asians have a significantly higher prevalence of all obesity-related diseases compared with other ethnic groups. This is likely due to the propensity to accumulate visceral fat. Combining the predisposition for accumulating abdominal fat with a lifestyle that lacks sufficient physical activity and a diet high in empty calories only increases the risk of becoming obese and developing related complications. The interventions targeting obesity that have proved successful have focused on culturally adapted dietary and lifestyle modifications for entire families. This remains an area of continued research in order to improve the effectiveness of these programs and to target earlier generations. Given their significant risk factors and potential disease burden, South Asians are a key group that would benefit from continued targeted interventions as well as further research into their predisposition for abdominal fat accumulation and the resulting obesity-related diseases.

References

Abate, N., & Chandalia, M. (2007). Ethnicity, type 2 diabetes & migrant Asian Indians. *Indian Journal of Medical Research, 125*(3), 251–258.

Anand, S. S., Tarnopolsky, M. A., Rashid, S., Schulze, K. M., Desai, D., Mente, A., . . . Sharma, A. M. (2011). Adipocyte hypertrophy, fatty liver and metabolic risk factors in South Asians: The Molecular Study of Health and Risk in Ethnic Groups (mol-SHARE). *PLoS One, 6*(7), e22112. doi:10.1371/journal.pone.0022112

Bharmal, N., Kaplan, R. M., Shapiro, M. F., Mangione, C. M., Kagawa-Singer, M., Wong, M. D., & McCarthy, W. J. (2014). The association of duration of residence in the United States with cardiovascular disease risk factors among South Asian immigrants. *Journal of Immigrant and Minority Health*. doi:10.1007/s10903-013-9973-7

Celis-Morales, C. A., Ghouri, N., Bailey, M. E., Sattar, N., & Gill, J. M. (2013). Should physical activity recommendations be ethnicity-specific? Evidence from a cross-sectional study of South Asian and European men. *PLoS One, 8*(12), e82568. doi:10.1371/journal.pone.0082568

Daniel, M., & Wilbur, J. (2011). Physical activity among South Asian Indian immigrants: An integrative review. *Public Health Nursing, 28*(5), 389–401. doi:10.1111/j.1525-1446.2010.00932.x

de Boo, H. A., & Harding, J. E. (2006). The developmental origins of adult disease (Barker) hypothesis. *Australian and New Zealand Journal of Obstetrics and Gynaecology, 46*(1), 4–14. doi:10.1111/j.1479-828X.2006.00506.x

Dixit, A. A., Azar, K. M., Gardner, C. D., & Palaniappan, L. P. (2011). Incorporation of whole, ancient grains into a modern Asian Indian diet to reduce the burden of chronic disease. *Nutrition Reviews, 69*(8), 479–488. doi:10.1111/j.1753-4887.2011.00411.x

Eckel, R. H. (2012). The metabolic syndrome. In D. L. Longo, A. S. Fauci, D. L. Kasper, S. L. Hauser, J. L. Jameson, & J. Loscalzo (Eds.), *Harrison's principles of internal medicine* (18ed., chap. 242). New York, NY: The McGraw-Hill Companies.

Enas, E. A., & Kannan, S. (2005). *How to beat the heart disease epidemic among South Asians.* Downer's Grove, IL: Advanced Heart Lipid Clinic.

Garduno-Diaz, S. D., & Khokhar, S. (2013). South Asian dietary patterns and their association with risk factors for the metabolic syndrome. *Journal of Human Nutrition and Dietetics, 26*(2), 145–155. doi:10.1111/j.1365-277X.2012.01284.x

Holmboe-Ottesen, G., & Wandel, M. (2012). Changes in dietary habits after migration and consequences for health: A focus on South Asians in Europe. *Food and Nutrition Research, 56.* doi:10.3402/fnr.v56i0.18891

Khanna, P., & Mani, A. (2012). Prevalence of obesity and traditional cardiovascular risk factors in South Asians. *Current Cardiovascular Risk Reports, 6*(2), 112–119. doi:10.1007/s12170-012-0220-x

Kohli, S., & Lear, S. A. (2012). Differences in subcutaneous abdominal adiposity regions in four ethnic groups. *Obesity (Silver Spring), 21*(11), 2288–95. doi:10.1002/oby.20102

Lean, M. E., Han, T. S., & Morrison, C. E. (1995). Waist circumference as a measure for indicating need for weight management. *British Medical Journal, 311*(6998), 158–161.

Lesser, I. A., Gasevic, D., & Lear, S. A. (2014). The association between acculturation and dietary patterns of South Asian immigrants. *PLoS One, 9*(2), e88495. doi:10.1371/journal.pone.0088495

Lesser, I. A., Yew, A. C., Mackey, D. C., & Lear, S. A. (2012). A cross-sectional analysis of the association between physical activity and visceral adipose tissue accumulation in a multiethnic cohort. *Journal of Obesity, 2012,* 703941. doi:10.1155/2012/703941

Li, H., Kilpelainen, T. O., Liu, C., Zhu, J., Liu, Y., Hu, C., . . . Loos, R. J. (2012). Association of genetic variation in FTO with risk of obesity and type 2 diabetes with data from 96,551 East and South Asians. *Diabetologia, 55*(4), 981–995. doi:10.1007/s00125-011-2370-7

Lucas, A., Murray, E., & Kinra, S. (2013). Health beliefs of UK South Asians related to lifestyle diseases: A review of qualitative literature. *Journal of Obesity, 2013,* 827674. doi:10.1155/2013/827674

Misra, A., & Bhardwaj, S. (2014). Obesity and the metabolic syndrome in developing countries: Focus on South Asians. *Nestlé Nutrition Institute Workshop Series, 78,* 133–140. doi:10.1159/000354952

Misra, A., Chowbey, P., Makkar, B. M., Vikram, N. K., Wasir, J. S., Chadha, D., . . . Munjal, Y. P. (2009). Consensus statement for diagnosis of obesity, abdominal obesity and the metabolic syndrome for Asian Indians and recommendations for physical activity, medical and surgical management. *Journal of the Association of Physicians of India, 57,* 163–170.

Misra, A., & Khurana, L. (2009). The metabolic syndrome in South Asians: Epidemiology, determinants, and prevention. *Metabolic Syndrome and Related Disorders, 7*(6), 497–514. doi:10.1089/met.2009.0024

Misra, A., & Khurana, L. (2011). Obesity-related non-communicable diseases: South Asians vs White Caucasians. *International Journal of Obesity (London), 35*(2), 167–187. doi:10.1038/ijo.2010.135

Misra, A., Nigam, P., Hills, A. P., Chadha, D. S., Sharma, V., Deepak, K. K., . . . Gupta, S. (2012). Consensus physical activity guidelines for Asian Indians. *Diabetes Technology and Therapeutics, 14*(1), 83–98. doi:10.1089/dia.2011.0111

Misra, A., & Shrivastava, U. (2013). Obesity and dyslipidemia in South Asians. *Nutrients, 5*(7), 2708–2733. doi:10.3390/nu5072708

Misra, A., & Vikram, N. K. (2004). Insulin resistance syndrome (metabolic syndrome) and obesity in Asian Indians: Evidence and implications. *Nutrition, 20*(5), 482–491. doi:10.1016/j.nut.2004.01.020

Misra, A., Wasir, J. S., & Vikram, N. K. (2005). Waist circumference criteria for the diagnosis of abdominal obesity are not applicable uniformly to all populations and ethnic groups. *Nutrition, 21*(9), 969–976. doi:10.1016/j.nut.2005.01.007

Palaniappan, L. P., Wong, E. C., Shin, J. J., Fortmann, S. P., & Lauderdale, D. S. (2011). Asian Americans have greater prevalence of metabolic syndrome despite lower body mass index. *International Journal of Obesity (London), 35*(3), 393–400. doi:10.1038/ijo.2010.152

Pallan, M. J., Hiam, L. C., Duda, J. L., & Adab, P. (2011). Body image, body dissatisfaction and weight status in South Asian children: A cross-sectional study. *BMC Public Health, 11*, 21. doi:10.1186/1471-2458-11-21

Patel, M., Phillips-Caesar, E., & Boutin-Foster, C. (2012). Barriers to lifestyle behavioral change in migrant South Asian populations. *Journal of Immigrant and Minority Health, 14*(5), 774–785. doi:10.1007/s10903-011-9550-x

Prasad, D. S., Kabir, Z., Dash, A. K., & Das, B. C. (2013). Effect of obesity on cardiometabolic risk factors in Asian Indians. *Journal of Cardiovascular Disease Research, 4*(2), 116–122. doi:10.1016/j.jcdr.2012.09.002

Rader, D. J., & Hobbs, H. H. (2012). Chapter 356. Disorders of Lipoprotein Metabolism. In D. L. Longo, A. S. Fauci, D. L. Kasper, S. L. Hauser, J. L. Jameson, & J. Loscalzo (Eds.), *Harrison's Principles of Internal Medicine* (18th ed). New York, NY: The McGraw-Hill Companies.

Rudin, E., Rincon, M., Bauman, J., & Barzilai, N. (2007). Obesity. In E. B. James (Ed.), *Encyclopedia of gerontology* (2nd ed., pp. 277–282). New York, NY: Elsevier.

Sathe, A., Flowers, E., Mathur, A., Garcia, D. M., Kotrys, J., Gandhi, R., . . . Mathur, A. (2013). A culturally specific health coaching program targeting cardiovascular disease risk in South Asians: Rationale, design, and baseline data. *Ethnicity and Disease, 23*(3), 304–309.

Shah, A., Hernandez, A., Mathur, D., Budoff, M. J., & Kanaya, A. M. (2012). Adipokines and body fat composition in South Asians: Results of the Metabolic Syndrome and Atherosclerosis in South Asians Living in America (MASALA) study. *International Journal of Obesity (London), 36*(6), 810–816. doi:10.1038/ijo.2011.167

Silbiger, J. J., Stein, R., Roy, M., Nair, M. K., Cohen, P., Shaffer, J., . . . Kamran, M. (2013). Coronary artery disease in South Asian immigrants living in New York City: Angiographic findings and risk factor burdens. *Ethnicity and Disease, 23*(3), 292–295.

Tang, J. W., Mason, M., Kushner, R. F., Tirodkar, M. A., Khurana, N., & Kandula, N. R. (2012). South Asian American perspectives on overweight, obesity, and the relationship between weight and health. *Preventing Chronic Disease, 9,* E107.

Taylor, P. (2013). The rise of Asian Americans. *Pew Research Center.* Available at www.pewsocialtrends.org/asianamericans

Wallia, S., Bhopal, R. S., Douglas, A., Bhopal, R., Sharma, A., Hutchison, A., . . . Sheikh, A. (2013). Culturally adapting the prevention of diabetes and obesity in South Asians (PODOSA) trial. *Health Promotion International, 29*(4):768–779. doi:10.1093/heapro/dat015

World Health Organization. (1997). *Obesity: Preventing and managing the global epidemic.* Report of a WHO consultation presented at The World Health Organization, June 3–5, Geneva, Switzerland. Publication WHO/NUT/NCD/98.1.

Yajnik, C. S. (2004). Obesity epidemic in India: Intrauterine origins? *Proceedings of the Nutrition Society, 63*(3), 387–396.

Chapter 7

Tobacco Use

Arnab Mukherjea, Mary V. Modayil,
Rajiv Ulpe, and Smita C. Banerjee

Contents

Abstract

Objective: To examine patterns of tobacco use and associated factors among South Asians living in the United States. A review of existing domestic interventions to address tobacco use is provided, as well as recommendations to further understand and curb tobacco use among South Asian Americans.

119

Key Findings: Unlike mainstream tobacco use in Western countries, the South Asian population's tobacco use in the United States shows no definitive association with socioeconomic status. Current literature indicates a differential rate in use of tobacco products across all age groups and income/education levels. Cultural tobacco products, forms of tobacco that are indigenous to South Asian countries, continue to be brought into the United States through covert channels. The limited data in the United States are congruent with the larger body of international literature indicating that cultural tobacco use among South Asians is a serious health concern.

Recommendations: Continued monitoring of cultural tobacco use, including prevalence, community-based participatory methods, and qualitative inquiry, is needed to develop and evaluate public health campaigns aimed at tobacco control among South Asians in the United States. A coordinated and comprehensive strategy that encompasses research, practice, and policy should emphasize the dangers of cultural tobacco product use. Mainstream tobacco-control messaging, policy making, and programming need to be more visible in US neighborhoods with large South Asian populations, while addressing unique determinants of use. The procurement and sale of cultural tobacco products should be targeted in order to disrupt the supply-chain cycle for such products.

Introduction

South Asians consume a variety of tobacco products that can be broadly grouped into three forms: (1) smoked tobacco, (2) smokeless tobacco, and (3) tobacco products used as additives to food or health products. Smoked forms include *bidis*, cigarettes, *hookah*, *cheroots*, *chillum*, *chuttas*, cigars, *dhumti*, *hooklis*, and pipe. Smokeless forms include *paan* (betel quid) with tobacco, *paan masala* with tobacco, *gutka*, areca nut, commercial chewing tobacco, *khaini*, *mainpuri* tobacco, *mawa*, slaked lime preparations with tobacco, snus (moist commercial tobacco), and tobacco powder (Mukherjea, Modayil, & Tong, 2015; National Cancer Institute [NCI], 2002). Smokeless forms added to food or health products include *bajjar*, creamy snuff (also used as toothpaste), *gudhaku*, *gul*, *lal dantmanjan*, *mishri*, nicotine chewing gum, and tobacco water (NCI, 2002).

Studies indicate that South Asians have a greater likelihood of using multiple tobacco products concurrently than other population groups (Agaku et al., 2014). The majority of tobacco consumed by South Asians globally, however, is in smokeless form, with the most widely used products being indigenous to South Asia (Mukherjea, Morgan, Snowden, Ling, & Ivey, 2012; Reddy and Gupta, 2004; Sreeramareddy, Pradhan, Mir, & Sin, 2014). There are considerable differences in the nomenclature of smokeless forms of tobacco indigenous to

South Asia. For example, *betel quid* may refer to a product containing areca (or betel) nut, with or without tobacco. Similarly, *paan masala* usually does not have tobacco as an ingredient, but because there is no standardization in its contents, it can be branded as a smokeless tobacco product (Mukherjea et al., 2015).

Despite the wider availability of traditional tobacco products (e.g., cigarettes) in the United States, South Asian Americans appear to use or prefer the use of cultural tobacco products that originate from South Asia (World Health Organization [WHO], 2010).

The purpose of this chapter is to summarize the existing evidence in the United States combined with relevant data from other global regions. The future direction of research, as well as potential targets for interventions that promote prevention and cessation of use of tobacco-related products, are also discussed.

Literature Review of Tobacco Use

Prevalence in South Asia

A growing body of evidence indicates that in 2010 the number of tobacco users in India was close to 275 million (Giovino et al., 2012). This number eclipses the adult populations of several European nations and is more than three-fourths the size of the US population. There is considerable heterogeneity in the type and volume of tobacco use among countries in South Asia (Gilani & Leon, 2013; International Institute for Population Sciences [IPS], 2010; WHO, 2010, 2011), as well as among states in each country (see Table 7.1).

Income and Education

A plethora of studies indicate varying patterns of tobacco use across different income levels (Agrawal et al., 2013). While education is definitely a mediating factor against tobacco use in Western countries, the relationship between education and tobacco use in South Asia is not as clear, with education and tobacco use not as well correlated. For example, use of cigarettes is reported by a greater proportion of high-income households, while the use of *bidis* is reported less often in South Asia (Agrawal et al., 2013).

Tobacco-Related Disease

Use of *betel* (areca nut) without tobacco and sold as *paan masala*, or with tobacco and sold as *paan* or *betel quid,* and *gutka*, is connected with the development of oral submucous fibrosis (OSF), a chronic condition leading to progressive difficulty in mouth opening and a poorer quality of life. This condition is a precursor

Table 7.1 Current Tobacco Use Prevalence by South Asian Countries

Country	Title of Survey	Year	Age Group (Years)	Description	Prevalence (%) Male	Prevalence (%) Female	Prevalence (%) Total
Smoking Tobacco Prevalence							
Bangladesh	Global Adult Tobacco Survey (WHO, 2010)	2009	15+	Current tobacco smoking	44.7	1.5	23.0
Bhutan	Report on 2007 STEPS Survey for Risk Factors and Prevalence of Noncommunicable Diseases in Thimphu (WHO, 2011)	2007	25–74	Current tobacco smoking	8.4	4.7	6.8
Fiji	Fiji Noncommunicable Diseases STEPS Survey (WHO, 2011)	2002	15–85	Daily tobacco smoking	26.0	3.9	–
India	Global Adult Tobacco Survey (IPS, 2010)	2009	15+	Current tobacco smoking	15.0	1.9	8.7
Maldives	Maldives STEPS Survey (WHO, 2011)	2004	25–64	Current tobacco smoking	37.5	11.8	–
Nepal	Nepal Noncommunicable Disease Risk Factors Survey (WHO, 2011)	2008	15–64	Current tobacco smoking	34.5	15.9	26.3
Pakistan	Gilani and Leon, 2013	2012	≥18	Current users of cigarettes, *bidis,* hookah, or *shisha*	31.4	1.8	18.2
Sri Lanka	Sri Lanka STEPS Survey (WHO, 2011)	2006	15–64	Current tobacco smoking	29.9	0.4	15.0
Smokeless Tobacco Prevalence							
Bangladesh	Noncommunicable Disease Risk Factors Survey (WHO, 2010)	2011	25+	Current users of smokeless tobacco	27.2	32.6	30.1

Country	Title of Survey	Year	Age Group (Years)	Description	Prevalence (%) Male	Female	Total
Bhutan	STEPS Survey for Risk Factors and Prevalence of Noncommunicable Diseases in Thimphu (WHO, 2011)	2007	25–74	Current users of smokeless tobacco	21.1	17.3	19.4
India	Global Adult Tobacco Survey (IPS, 2010)	2011	15+	Current users of smokeless tobacco	32.9	18.4	25.9
Nepal	Nepal Demographic and Health Survey (WHO, 2011)	2011	15–49	Current users of smokeless tobacco	37.9	6.0	–
Pakistan	Gilani and Leon, 2013	2012	≥18	Current users of smokeless tobacco (*Naswar*/tobacco in *paan/gutka*)	15.1	4.6	10.5
Sri Lanka	Sri Lanka STEPS Survey (WHO, 2011)	2006	15–64	Current users of smokeless tobacco	24.9	6.9	15.8
Any Tobacco Prevalence							
Bangladesh	Global Adult Tobacco Survey (WHO, 2010)	2009	15+	Current users of any tobacco	58.0	28.7	43.3
India	Global Adult Tobacco Survey (IPS, 2010)	2009	15+	Current users of any tobacco	47.9	20.3	34.6
Pakistan	Gilani and Leon, 2013	2012	≥18	Current users of any tobacco	34.9	5.1	21.7
Dual Tobacco Prevalence							
India	Global Adult Tobacco Survey (IPS, 2010)	2009	15+	Current users of smoking and smokeless tobacco	9.3	1.1	5.3

Note: STEPS = WHO STEPwise Approach to Chronic Disease Risk Factor Surveillance to mouth cancer in adults and is a disease that disproportionately affects individuals who use areca nut and areca nut-blended tobacco products (Auluck, Hislop, Poh, Zhang, & Rosin, 2009; van Wyk, Stander, & Padayachee, 1993).

While it may appear to be an oversimplification of OSF trends, it seems clear that with increasing immigration of South Asians to Western countries, the use of areca nut in tobacco-related products will ultimately lead to an overall rise in the rate of OSF in Western countries (van Wyk et al., 1993). Still, data linking areca nut use with increased OSF incidence in Western countries are limited. Initial results from a study in British Columbia, Canada, indicated a higher rate of oral cancer and precancerous cases among South Asians (Auluck et al., 2009). This study showed a relative risk of 1.33 and 1.66 for South Asian men and women, respectively, compared with the general population (2009).

Social and Cultural Acceptability

Much of the tobacco use in South Asia can be attributed not only to an incomplete understanding of the harm imposed by consumption, but also by a belief that many of these products actually produce a medicinal benefit (Liu, Kumar, Sedghizadeh, Jayakar, & Shuler, 2008). Gupta, Ray, Sinha, and Singh (2011) demonstrated that in many regions of South Asia, the initiation of cultural tobacco use occurs as early as 5 years of age (Auluck et al., 2009). Often, the strongest influence for starting was the use and, in some cases, encouragement by family members. South Asian youth often attempted to emulate elders and also succumbed to pressure from peers, patterns seen in both male and female youth (Auluck et al., 2009; Ferlay, Bray, & Pisani, 2002; Mukherjea & Modayil, 2013).

In addition to interpersonal influences, other factors play a role in influencing regular use of cultural tobacco products. Tobacco is seen in many forms as integral for celebratory functions such as weddings (Hossain et al., 2014). Similarly, tobacco products are given to and received by guests as symbolic gestures of salutation, respect, companionship, and solidarity (Mukherjea & Modayil, 2013; Preeti & Raut, 2012). In parts of India, *betel quid* with tobacco is used by women for cosmetic purposes to emphasize the coloring of mouth and lips (Mukherjea & Modayil, 2013). Moreover, faith plays an important role in the persistent use of cultural tobacco. For example, the use of *paan* is highly valued within the Hindu religion and, with tobacco as a common ingredient, consumption became a convenient vehicle for the initiation and maintenance of this form of tobacco use (Majumdar, Raje, & Dandekar, 2011; McCarthy et al., 2005; Thankappan & Thresia, 2007).

Interestingly, the other two major faiths in South Asia, Islam and Sikhism, provide contrasting patterns of cultural tobacco use, despite explicit prohibitions. Whereas Sikhs demonstrate very low rates of use, those of Muslim faith in South Asia tend to exhibit prevalence incommensurate with religious doctrines (McCarthy et al., 2005; Mukherjea & Modayil, 2013). These patterns are reinforced by tobacco imagery in South Asian media, which has been shown to have an important effect on cultural tobacco use in South Asia (Chaturvedi, Arora, Dasgupta, & Patwari, 2011). For instance, adolescents in India who watched Bollywood movies with tobacco depictions were more likely to use tobacco than those who had not seen these movies (Kyain, Islam, Sinha, & Rinchen, 2011; Vishwanath, Ackerson, Sorensen, & Gupta, 2010). Thus, a confluence of unique social, cultural, and institutional factors contribute to the pervasive and persistent use of tobacco in South Asia.

Postmigration Tobacco Use by South Asians

The majority of South Asians residing in the United States are first-generation immigrants, having migrated following the relaxation of immigration restrictions in 1965 (Sorensen et al., 2013). As a result, there is an increased availability of cultural tobacco products from South Asia in the United States (Gupta et al., 2011), coupled with an exponential growth of South Asian American communities over the last decade (Gupta et al., 2011). Thus, it is important to gain a better understanding of tobacco use and tobacco-related diseases in South Asia in order to better account for and understand its use by South Asians living in the United States.

Upon migration to the West, South Asians continue to use cultural tobacco products. Studies from the United Kingdom indicate a high rate of *betel quid* use in Bangladeshi communities around London (Begh et al., 2011). Additionally, use of smokeless tobacco, particularly in the form of *paan* and *gutka*, is increasing in prevalence among immigrant populations from South Asian countries. Similar studies from Canada (Auluck et al., 2009) suggest that the use of cultural tobacco products, primarily those containing areca nut, is a routine and daily practice and constitutes an important component of social life and cultural identity in the South Asian population.

Recent studies conducted in the United States over the past 10 years have reported similar high rates of smokeless tobacco use by South Asian immigrant populations (Giovino et al., 2012; Stellman & Resnicow, 1997; WHO, 2009). For instance, in a community-based convenience sample of 138 individuals of South Asian descent in the New York metropolitan area, 35% of Bangladeshis and 31% of Gujarati Indians reported regular use of smokeless tobacco products (Giovino et al., 2012).

Separate survey data from California (McCarthy et al., 2005) and New Jersey (Delnevo, Steinberg, Hudson, Ulpe, & DiPaola, 2011) also collected information on smokeless tobacco use among South Asians. New Jersey and California surveillance and monitoring among South Asians showed smoked tobacco prevalence to be below 5%, with men smoking more than women. In New Jersey (and other parts of the Northeast United States), Delnevo et al., demonstrated that Pakistanis are overrepresented among cigarette smokers, while Asian Indians are overrepresented among smokeless tobacco users (2011).

Mainstream smokeless tobacco use is more common among younger White men and those with lower levels of education. After adjusting for education and age, this study found that South Asian men had four times higher odds of smokeless tobacco use than non-White men (Delnevo et al., 2011). The overall finding was that South Asian men have the highest rate of current smokeless tobacco use among all men compared with other regions of the country and where South Asians are separately sampled. It is worth noting that this study only surveyed the use of mainstream smokeless products. Therefore, the overall use of all forms of smokeless tobacco (including cultural tobacco products) would be considerably higher.

The California Asian Indian Tobacco Use Survey (CAITS) collected data from a random sample of Asian Indian adults in California and found higher rates of smokeless tobacco use but lower use of smoking tobacco (McCarthy et al., 2005). Subsequently, Mukherjea & Modayil reanalyzed the CAITS data and found that 14% of men and 12% of women were current users of cultural smokeless tobacco products. Unlike rates observed for mainstream tobacco smoking, those who used smokeless products tended to be college educated and had higher incomes (2013).

Given the high prevalence of smokeless tobacco use among immigrant South Asians, it is imperative that tobacco-control research focuses on preventing and reducing smokeless tobacco use among this group, especially considering the associated burden of disease in this community. Attention should also be paid to the use of products exclusively containing *betel nut* (areca nut), as studies have concluded that this ingredient is an independent carcinogen and may contribute to cancer disparities found among South Asians (Sharan, Mehrotra, Choudhry, & Asotra, 2012).

Some studies have examined religiosity among immigrants in the United States and have concluded that a fair proportion of immigrant families remain unassimilated and continue to follow native customs and practices. It is possible that the use of areca nut, regarded as an auspicious commodity in Hinduism, along with the use of *betel* leaves in ceremonies, afford a sociocultural reason behind its continued importance (Mukherjea & Modayil, 2013). It remains unclear whether the exalted status given to areca nut in culture and religion

(Hinduism) translates to smokeless tobacco use by South Asian immigrants in Western countries.

The lack of surveillance data in Canada and the United States has masked the importance of tobacco as a growing public health concern for the South Asian community. It has also resulted in limited intervention planning. The United Kingdom has a longer history of South Asian immigration and a greater presence, and has taken commendable steps to address health concerns associated with the use of tobacco and tobacco-related products (Chadda & Sengupta, 2002). These have included language access on telephone-quit lines, educational materials in South Asian languages, innovative interventions using community health workers, and targeted education efforts in areas with a large South Asian population. Research related to smokeless tobacco use among South Asians is still in its infancy in the United States and other Western countries with large South Asian populations, barring a few exploratory studies (Agaku et al., 2014; Giovino et al., 2012; WHO, 2009).

Mukherjea and Modayil (2013) conducted a literature review of tobacco use patterns and existing tobacco-control strategies among South Asian Americans. They summarized that, while limited, the studies on prevalence and determinants of culturally specific tobacco use among South Asians highlighted unique influences on use, ranging from perceptions of health benefits to degree of acculturation and religiosity. Of the six studies reviewed, one intervention study specifically evaluated the programmatic objectives related to tobacco-control efforts for minors (Jain, Mills, & Parikh-Patel, 2005). Other separate surveillance studies examined reducing the availability of tobacco products (Changrani, Cruz, Kerr, Katz, & Gany, 2006), and promoting tobacco cessation services for South Asians in Southern California (Glenn, Surani, Chawla, & Bastani, 2009). The intervention study stressed the importance of organizational and legislative policies for tobacco-control efforts by increasing provider knowledge regarding screening for cultural tobacco use and compliance with existing youth access laws.

Three additional qualitative studies that employed focus groups, investigated smokeless tobacco use among South Asian Americans (Hrywna et al., 2016; Banerjee et al., 2014; Mukherjea et al., 2012). These studies focused on cultural tobacco products (mainly *gutka* and *paan*), their use and initiation patterns by South Asians of various sociodemographic backgrounds, and perceptions of quitting and/or controlling tobacco use. Mukherjea et al. (2012) concluded that the use of smokeless tobacco products is considered an expression of South Asian ethnic identity and a mechanism to outwardly display ethnic pride (Auluck et al., 2009). Banerjee et al. noted the ease of obtaining smokeless tobacco products in South Asian residential neighborhood stores (2014). They noted several factors that promoted the initiation of smokeless tobacco use, including social networks, perceived benefits, and curiosity. Additionally, participants voiced perceptions related to the role of medical doctors and dentists in discouraging smokeless tobacco use, such as highlighting harms of cultural tobacco use. Finally, the study proposed policy-level solutions to curtailing smokeless tobacco while also acknowledging that the increased prevalence and easy accessibility are likely to expand the market for tobacco usage and undermine tobacco control. Finally, Hrywna et al. noted that there were likely gender-age differences in the types of specific cultural tobacco products used by South Asians in the United States (2016).

Yet another qualitative study examined cognitive rationalizations (termed "disengagement beliefs") to disentangle the inconsistency posed by South Asians regarding their continued use of smokeless tobacco, despite awareness of health concerns (Banerjee et al., 2013; Mukherjea et al., 2012). Five themes of disengagement beliefs emerged, including (1) skepticism about the *gutka/tambaku paan*–cancer link, (2) perceived invulnerability to *gutka/tambaku paan*–related harm, (3) compensatory beliefs, (4) faith-based rationalization, and (5) acknowledgment of addiction. The totality of the qualitative studies provide implications for improving tobacco screening and control efforts in the United States, with recommendations for developing culturally relevant, tobacco-control public health messages for South Asians living in the United States.

Unfortunately, there is not much data on the rise and severity of tobacco-related cancer incidence among South Asians in the U.S. This is due to the small number of participants who self-identify as South Asian on national cancer registries, as well as the small numbers of respondents who report lung, bronchial, esophageal, and oral cancers. In fact, most population-level US estimates currently available have excluded South Asians (from Asian subgroup analyses) or have focused on cancer disparities among Asians as a single subpopulation. Liu et al. (2008) utilized data from the California Cancer Registry (CCR) in order to calculate the age-adjusted incidence rates of invasive oral squamous cell carcinoma by sex, race/ethnicity, and anatomical subsite among residents in California from 1988 to 2001. Findings revealed that South Asians had a much higher percentage of oral cancer cases (particularly in the cheek or buccal mucosa) compared with other racial/ethnic groups (Liu et al., 2008). The following age-adjusted incidence rates were observed among California's South Asians for different oral subsites: (1) oral cavity 3.56/1,00,000 [95% confidence interval (CI) = 0.6–2.5], (2) tongue 1.94 /1,00,000 (95% CI = 0.4–2.6), (3) gum 0.17/1,00,000 (95% CI = 0.0–120.4), (4) floor of mouth 0.26/1,00,000 (95% CI = 0.0–64.5), and (5) palate 0.50/1,00,000 (95% CI = 0.0–17.1).

A more recent analysis from Gomez et al. (2013) examined 10 regions from the United States and found that lung cancer rates increased among Asian Indian/ Pakistani men over a 20-year period. The 1990–1994 age-adjusted incidence rate for lung cancer was 20.4/1,00,000 (95% CI = 15.6–26.2) compared with the 2004–2008 age-adjusted incidence rate of 30.1/1,00,000 (95% CI = 26.0–34.6). Oral cancer was not examined in this analysis (Gomez et al., 2013).

Overall, the rates of oral cancers are higher among South Asians than other groups (Auluck et al., 2009). This may be attributable to the continuation of smokeless tobacco use habits among South Asians following migration (Ferlay et al., 2002; Sushma & Sharang, 2005). Data indicate that oral cancer incidence and mortality among people of South Asian descent are almost twice those of global rates (Ferlay et al., 2002) and are largely attributable to the use of indigenous smokeless tobacco products in the South Asian community (Auluck et al., 2009; Ferlay et al., 2002). While it is clear that areca nut by itself can cause oral afflictions such as oral cancer, the addition of areca nut in blended tobacco products can result in a synergistic effect which may contribute to a higher incidence of oral cancers than by the use of areca nut alone.

Gaps in the Literature

There have been no studies documenting quit rates by South Asians in the United States. Studies from the United Kingdom for this population may not be applicable due to the different demographic distribution of South Asian subgroups in US ethnic enclaves.

It is also of note that there is a dearth of prevalence data from surveillance efforts in the United States, which speaks to the need to review data from countries of origin. There are large gaps in our understanding of South Asian tobacco use, including young adult cessation interventions that tackle the hookah culture in the United States and the rise of e-cigarettes. Given the popularity of novel products among young adults and the coadoption of mainstream products by South Asians, it would be helpful to address these issues in order to prevent an increasing health disparities related to tobacco use and its adverse outcomes among the next generation of South Asians.

Community-Level Tobacco Control Interventions

There is very little information regarding tobacco-control efforts that target South Asian Americans. On a national level, the *Asian Pacific Partners for Empowerment, Advocacy and Leadership* (APPEAL) developed a leadership training program in 1994. Since then, the program has trained more than 1000 community leaders, including South Asians, from across the United States to advocate for health justice and policy change with regard to tobacco use. Trained leaders have also launched major advocacy campaigns to counter the targeting of

Asian American and Native Hawaiian and Pacific Islander communities by the tobacco industry (Asian Pacific Partners for Empowerment [APPE], 2014). The impact of this program, however, specifically among South Asian communities has not been formally reported.

The CAITS survey examined quit rates among Asian Indians and found that for those few Californians of Indian ancestry who do become regular users of cigarettes, the 30-day quit rate is higher (63.0%) than for most smokers in California (<60%), at least among Asian Indian men (McCarthy et al., 2005). In California, from 2005 to 2008, the South Asian Network (SAN) developed a Tobacco Control Community Advisory Committee, which was funded by the California Department of Health Services Tobacco Control Section. The Advisory Committee implemented the *Communities of Excellence in Tobacco Control (CX)* process, in order to identify areas of need for tobacco-control interventions (Saath USA, 2008). The year-long planning grant led to the development of a tobacco-control program to mobilize South Asian merchants and store owners on the enforcement of the "Stop Tobacco Access to Kids Enforcement" or "STAKE Act" in Southern California. According to the program's CX assessment, many retailers in California's South Asian communities were not aware that the law also prohibited the sale of South Asian smokeless tobacco products such as *gutka*, *paan masala*, and *zarda*.

Over a period of two years, the program disseminated culturally tailored materials to 90% of store owners and consumers in areas where South Asians were concentrated. The goal was to help enforce the "STAKE Act" and materials specified South Asian tobacco products. The program also partnered with two clinics in order to increase provider counseling to South Asian tobacco users through a tobacco user identification system and the use of tailored print materials (Glenn et al., 2009). In 2008, the program ended and the California Department of Health Services Tobacco Control Section has not funded any South Asian–specific tobacco-control programs in California since. However, from 2011 to 2013, a new initiative to address tobacco use among South Asian young adults began. This was a collaborative effort between Claremont Graduate University's School of Community and Global Health (CGU) and Saath USA, funded by the California Department of Health's Tobacco-Related Diseases Research Program (Saath USA, 2008). Research from this program has helped spark the development of a new South Asian youth health network in Southern California that focuses on tobacco use prevention through outreach at local community or *desi* events such as *bhangra* nights (Saath USA, 2008).

In the city of New York, the South Asian Health Initiative (SAHI) launched tobacco education efforts from 2006 to 2008 through their "Stop *Paan*" and other community-level initiatives to educate South Asians on the impact of smokeless tobacco use and oral cancer (Changrani et al., 2006). More recently, in 2011, the Rutgers Cancer Institute of New Jersey launched the *South Asian Tobacco Cessation & Cancer Awareness Resource* (SATCCAR), funded by the NCI through an administrative supplement from the National Outreach Network of the NCI. This program included a needs assessment to determine knowledge, attitudes, behaviors, and practices regarding smoking and smokeless tobacco. The goals of the program included: (1) development of culturally appropriate messages regarding the harms of smoking, smokeless tobacco use, and cessation in the South Asian population; (2) development of an educational/outreach and message dissemination plan; and (3) implementation of a local education/ outreach activity focused on the development of a tobacco cessation curriculum tailored to the local South Asian population.

Gaps in Intervention Activities

There have been sporadic tobacco-control activities implemented at the community level in California and New York that target South Asian Americans over the last 20 years. However, no current sustainable strategies in the United States address South Asian-specific tobacco use. States where large South Asian populations live, including New York, California, Illinois, and Texas, are positioned to promote tobacco-control strategies that can benefit South Asians and significantly reduce the burden of diseases caused by tobacco use.

Recommendations

Continued monitoring of cultural tobacco use disaggregated by South Asian subgroup along with the use of community-based participatory methods and qualitative inquiry may be particularly suited to develop and examine tobacco-control public health campaigns. Such methods have been used to demonstrate the symbolic role played by the use of specific tobacco products to preserve cultural linkages to South Asia, as well as to express ethnic identity. It is particularly important that attention be paid to the uptake of tobacco by young adult and second-generation South Asians as they may exhibit unique patterns of use given their establishment of cultural identity in the United States, and the differential adoption of "native" and "dominant" cultural behavioral patterns.

Moreover, comprehensive educational interventions should be designed to emphasize the dangers of tobacco in cultural products, as well as the dangers of areca nut, which synergistically offers a greater risk for cancers of the mouth, throat, and stomach, and endocrine disorders that may lead to insulin resistance. Areca nut, in addition to worsening oral cancer risk associated with smokeless tobacco use, can contribute to oral cancer risk independently (van Wyk et al., 1993). Particular attention should be paid to the health consequences suffered by children, both acutely and later in life, due to early adoption. In addition to California, New York, and New Jersey, other states with large South Asian communities, such as Illinois and Texas, can greatly benefit from increased culturally appropriate tobacco-control initiatives developed through national collaboration and dissemination. Implementation of such programs may ultimately result in a reduced burden of tobacco-related disease unnecessarily suffered by South Asians living in the United States.

Clinicians need to be aware of the popularity of specific products among individuals of South Asian descent. They need to inquire about usage, promote cessation among users, regularly screen for health conditions associated with consumption, and use evidence-based screening and counseling approaches to empower users to quit using. In tandem, cessation protocols that address both the social and biological determinants of use need to be developed and tested so that an evidence base exists that promotes quitting. More broadly, tobacco-control messages and programming need increased visibility in neighborhoods with large South Asians populations.

Finally, it is alarming that cultural products continue to be brought into the United States through covert channels, often marked as products for religious purposes or as food. Religious leaders can play an important role in stopping this. Since Sikh and Islamic faiths prohibit tobacco use, cultural settings for both faiths can play a prominent role in promoting future tobacco-control interventions. The role of prevention in Hinduism is more complicated since *paan* plays an integral part of worship and celebrations. However, since tobacco is not a necessary ingredient, it is imperative to raise awareness about the toxic effects of adding tobacco to *paan* preparations.

It is important that the procurement and sale of cultural tobacco products be targeted to disrupt the supply-chain cycle for such products in ethnic enclaves. Efforts to educate US Customs and Immigration personnel about these products at international airports with high traffic from South Asian countries is bound to affect cultural tobacco product availability by blocking the major entry route for such products. Currently, mechanisms used by commodity traders and vendors in ethnic enclaves enable them to override strong enforcement and legal limitations set up by the US Food and Drug Administration (FDA) for the sale of tobacco products. At the same time, sales of cultural tobacco products in ethnic enclaves that is specifically marked as food products could be better regulated by the Department of Agriculture or the FDA. Specifically, they can better oversee food adulterants with carcinogens like magnesium carbonate that are often found in South Asian tobacco products.

Conclusions

Given the rapidly growing South Asian American population, particularly in New York City, Chicago, Los Angeles, and the San Francisco Bay Area, the issue of tobacco use cannot be ignored. In particular is the potential risk for South Asian smokeless tobacco products to "cross over" into a new population of non-South Asian users, or to adolescents and young adults of South Asian origin. The significance of improved smokeless tobacco-control initiatives, both in the United States and internationally, is paramount to addressing preventable tobacco-related disparities and related conditions among South Asians.

In summary, addressing the South Asian population's disproportionate burden of disease related to cultural tobacco use remains an underappreciated community health concern. A coordinated and comprehensive strategy using research, policy, and practice that includes the monitoring of all forms of tobacco (including cultural forms) is paramount to ensuring that tobacco-related disparities among South Asians are ultimately eliminated and the pursuit of optimal health and well-being is realized among this rapidly growing minority community.

References

Agaku, I. T., Filippidis, F. T., Vardavas, C. I., Odukoya, O. O., Ayo-Yusuf, O. A., & Connolly, G. N. (2014). Poly-tobacco use among adults in 44 countries during 2008–2012: Evidence for an integrative and comprehensive approach in tobacco control. *Drug and Alcohol Dependence*, *139*, 60–70. doi:10.1016/j.drugalcdep.2014.03.003

Agrawal, A., Karan, A., Selvaraj, S., Bhan, N., Subramanian, S., & Millett, C. (2013). Socio-economic patterning of tobacco use in Indian states. *The International Journal of Tuberculosis and Lung Diseases*, *17*(8), 1110–1117. doi:http://dx.doi.org/10.5588/ijtld.12.0916

Asian Pacific Partners for Empowerment. (2014). Asian Pacific Partners for Empowerment, Advocacy and Leadership—Towards Health Parity and Justice: Accomplishments. Retrieved from http://www.appealforcommunities.org/accomplishments

Auluck, A., Hislop, G., Poh, C., Zhang, L., & Rosin, M. P. (2009). Areca nut and betel quid chewing among South Asian immigrants to Western countries and its implications for oral cancer screening. *Rural Remote Health*, *9*(2), 1118.

Banerjee, S. C., Ostroff, J. S., Bari, S., D'Agostino, T. A., Khera, M., Acharya. S., Gany F. (2014). Gutka and tambaku paan use among South Asian immigrants: A focus group study. *Journal of Immigrant & Minority Health*, *16*(3), 531–539.

Banerjee, S. C., Ostroff, J. S., D'Agostino, T. A., Bari, S., Khera, M., Acharya, S., & Gany, F. (2013). Disengagement beliefs in South Asian immigrant smokeless tobacco users: A qualitative study. *Addiction Research & Theory*, *22*(3), 229–238.

Begh, R. A., Aveyard, P., Upton, P., Bhopal, R. S., White, M., & Amos, A. (2011). Promoting smoking cessation in Pakistani and Bangladeshi men in the UK: Pilot cluster randomised controlled trial of trained community outreach workers. *Trials, 12*(197). doi:10.1186/1745-6215-12-197

Chadda, R. K., & Sengupta, S. N. (2002). Tobacco use by Indian adolescents. *Tobacco Induced Disease, 1*(2), 111–119.

Changrani, J., Cruz, G., Kerr, R., Katz, R., & Gany, F. M. (2006). Paan and gutka use in the United States: A pilot study in Bangladeshi and Indian-Gujarati immigrants in New York City. *Journal of Immigrant & Refugee Studies, 4*(1), 99–109.

Chaturvedi, S., Arora, N. K., Dasgupta, R., & Patwari, A. K. (2011). Are we reluctant to talk about cultural determinants? *Indian Journal of Medical Research, 133*(361–363), 361.

Delnevo, C. D., Steinberg, M. B., Hudson, S. V., Ulpe, R., & DiPaola, R. (2011). Epidemiology of cigarette and smokeless tobacco use among South Asian immigrants in the Northeastern United States. *Journal of Oncology, 2011*(252675).

Ferlay, J., Bray, F., & Pisani, P. (2002). *GLOBOCAN 2002: Cancer Incidence, Mortality and Prevalence Worldwide*. IARC CancerBase No. 5 Version 2.0. (Vol. 5). Lyon, France: IARC.

Gilani, S. I., & Leon, D. A. (2013). Prevalence and sociodemographic determinants of tobacco use among adults in Pakistan: Findings of a nationwide survey conducted in 2012. *Population Health Metrics, 11*(1), 16. doi:10.1186/1478-7954-11-16

Giovino, G. A., Mirza, A. S., Samet, J. M., Gupta, P. C., Jarvis, M. J., & Bhala, N. (2012). Tobacco use in 3 billion individuals from 16 countries: An analysis of nationally representative cross-sectional household surveys. *Lancet, 380*(9842), 668–679. doi:10.1016/S0140-6736(12)61085-X

Glenn, B., Surani, Z., Chawla, N., & Bastani, R. (2009). Tobacco use among South Asians: Results of a community-university collaborative study. *Ethnicity & Health, 14*(2), 131–145.

Gomez, S. L., Noone, A-N., Lichtensztajn, D. Y., Scoppa, S., Gibson, J. T., Liu, L., . . . Miller, B. A. (2013). Cancer incidence trends among Asian American populations in the United States, 1990 to 2008. *Journal of the National Cancer Institute, 105* (15): 1096–1110. doi:10.1093/jnci/djt157.

Gupta, P. C., Ray, C. S., Sinha, D. N., & Singh, P. K. (2011). Smokeless tobacco: A major public health problem in the SEA region: A review. *Indian Journal of Public Health, 55*(3), 199.

Hossain, M. S., Kypri, K., Rahman, B., Arslan, I., Akter, S., & Milton, A. H. (2014). Prevalence and correlates of smokeless tobacco consumption among married women in rural Bangladesh. *PLoS ONE, 9*(1: e84470). doi:10.1371/journal.pone.0084470

Hrywna, M., Lewis, M. J., Mukherjea, A., Banerjee, S. C., Steinberg, M. B., & Delnevo, C. D. (2016). Awareness and Use of South Asian Tobacco Products Among South Asians in New Jersey. *Journal of Community Health*, 1–8.

International Institute for Population Sciences, I. (2010). *Global Adult Tobacco Survey: India (GATS INDIA), 2009–2010*. Mumbai, India: International Institute for Population Sciences.

Jain, R. V., Mills, P. K., & Parikh-Patel, A. (2005). Cancer incidence in the south Asian population of California, 1988–2000. *Journal of Carcinogenesis, 4*(21).

Kyain, N. N., Islam, M. A., Sinha, D. N., & Rinchen, S. (2011). Social, economic, and legal dimensions of tobacco and its control in South-East Asia region. *Indian Journal of Public Health*, *55*(3), 161–168.

Liu, L., Kumar, S. K., Sedghizadeh, P. P., Jayakar, A. N., & Shuler, C. F. (2008). Oral squamous cell carcinoma incidence by subsite among diverse racial and ethnic populations in California. *Oral Surgery Oral Medicine Oral Pathology Oral Radiology Endodontics*, *105*(4), 470–480. doi:10.1016/j.tripleo.2007.07.007

Majumdar, R., Raje, S. S., & Dandekar, A. (2011). Socio demographic factors associated with tobacco use in rural Maharashtra. *Medical Journal of DY Patil University*, *6*, 161–164.

McCarthy, W. J., Divan, H., Shah, D., Maxwell, A., Freed, B., Bastani, R., . . . Surani, Z. (2005). California Asian Indian Tobacco Survey—2004. Sacramento, CA: California Department of Health Services.

Mukherjea, A., & Modayil, M. V. (2013). Culturally specific tobacco use and south Asians in the United States: A review of the literature and promising strategies for intervention. *Health Promotion and Practice*, *14*, 48S–60S. doi:10.1177/1524839913485585

Mukherjea, A., Modayil, M. V., & Tong, E. K. (2015). Paan (pan) and paan (pan) masala should be considered tobacco products. *Tobacco Control*, 24:e280–e284. doi:10.1136/tobaccocontrol-2014-051700

Mukherjea, A., Morgan, P. A., Snowden, L. R., Ling, P. M., & Ivey, S. L. (2012). Social and cultural influences on tobacco-related health disparities among South Asians in the USA. *Tobacco Control*, *21*(4), 422–428. doi:10.1136/tc.2010.042309

National Cancer Institute, N. (2002). *Smokeless Tobacco Fact Sheets: A Report of the 3rd International Conference on Smokeless Tobacco*. Paper presented at the 3rd International Conference on Smokeless Tobacco, Stockholm, Sweden. Retrieved from http://cancercontrol.cancer.gov/brp/tcrb/stfact_sheet_combined10-23-02.pdf

Preeti, S., & Raut, D. K. (2012). Prevalence and pattern of tobacco consumption in India. *International Research Journal of Social Sciences*, *1*(4), 36–43.

Reddy, K. S., & Gupta, P. C. (2004). *Report on Tobacco Control in India*. New Delhi, India: Ministry of Health & Family Welfare, Ministry of Health Family Welfare, Government of India. Retrieved from http://mohfw.nic.in/WriteReadData/l892s/911379183TobaccocontroinIndia_10Dec04.pdf

Saath USA. (2008). Saath: Together we build a healthier tomorrow. Retrieved from www.saathusa.org

Sharan, R. N., Mehrotra, R., Choudhry, Y., & Asotra, K. (2012). Association of betel nut with carcinogenesis: Revisit with a clinical perspective. *PLoS ONE*, *7*(8: e42759). doi:10.1371/journal.pone.0042759

Sorensen, G., Pednekar, M. S., Sinha, D. N., Stoddard, A. M., Nagler, E., Aghi, M. B., . . . Gupta, P. C. (2013). Effects of a tobacco control intervention for teachers in India: Results of the Bihar school teachers study. *American Journal of Public Health*, *103*(11), 2035–2040. doi:10.2105/AJPH.2013.301303

Sreeramareddy, C. T., Pradhan, P. M. S., Mir, I. A., & Sin, S. (2014). Smoking and smokeless tobacco use in nine South and Southeast Asian countries: Prevalence estimates and social determinants from Demographic and Health Surveys. *Population Health Metrics*, *12*(22). doi:10.1186/s12963-014-0022-0

Stellman, C. D., & Resnicow, K. (1997). Tobacco smoking and social class. In M. Kognivenas, N. Pearce, & M. Susser (Eds.), *Social Inequalities and Cancer*, Vol. 138 (pp. 229–250). Lyon, France: IARC.

Sushma, C., & Sharang, C. (2005). Pan masala advertisements are surrogate for tobacco products. *Indian Journal of Cancer*, *42*(2), 94.

Thankappan, K. R., & Thresia, C. U. (2007). Tobacco use & social status in Kerala. *Indian Journal of Medical Research*, *126*, 300–308.

van Wyk, C. W., Stander, I., & Padayachee, A. (1993). The areca nut chewing habit and oral squamous cell carcinoma in South African Indians: A retrospective study. *South African Medical Journal*, *83*, 425–429.

Vishwanath, K., Ackerson, L. K., Sorensen, G., & Gupta, P. C. (2010). Movies and TV influence tobacco use in India: Findings from a national survey. *PLoS ONE*, *5*(6: e11365).

World Health Organization. (2009). Women and health: Today's evidence tomorrow's agenda. Retrieved from http://www.who.int/gender-equity-rights/knowledge/9789241563857/en/

World Health Organization. (2010). Global Adult Tobacco Survey Fact Sheet Bangladesh: 2009. Retrieved from http://www.who.int/tobacco/surveillance/fact_sheet_of_gats_bangladesh_2009.pdf

World Health Organization. (2011). WHO Report on the Global Tobacco Epidemic, 2011. *Warning about the Dangers of Tobacco*. Geneva: WHO. Retrieved from http://www.who.int/tobacco/global_report/2011/en/

Chapter 8

HIV/AIDS

Swagata Banik and Viraj Patel

Contents

Abstract

Objective: To highlight the sociocultural and structural factors that heighten HIV vulnerability among South Asians living in the United States.

Key Findings: Data regarding HIV in South Asians residing in the United States, including prevalence of HIV, are limited because this population is typically grouped in the category of "Asian American/Pacific Islander (API)." The limited research that is available suggests there are two South Asian subpopulations in particular with increased HIV vulnerability: men who have sex with men (MSM) and heterosexual women. South Asian MSM face stigma, racism, and internalized homophobia, which can lead to engaging in high-risk behaviors. Intimate partner violence, lack of HIV knowledge, and HIV stigma are primary risk factors for South Asian heterosexual women in the United States.

Recommendations: For all levels of HIV/AIDS data collection and reporting, South Asian Americans need to be identified specifically and accurately. Both descriptive and intervention research are needed to understand and address HIV vulnerabilities of various South Asian subgroups in the United States, including MSM, heterosexual women, adolescents, transgender individuals, and new immigrants.

Introduction

South Asian immigrants in the United States have received little attention from health researchers, particularly with regard to HIV, despite the total South Asian population numbering over three million (Asian American Federation, 2012). Because epidemiological and behavioral data that are specific to HIV in South Asian Americans (SAAs) are extremely sparse, the current review uses the limited aggregated data available for Asian and Pacific Islanders (APIs) in order to help understand HIV related issues among SAAs. Of note, APIs are often collectively categorized as a singular cultural entity, though the actual cultural "subgroups" are extremely diverse in terms of cultural attitudes, sexual norms, immigration experiences, language, religion, and so forth. Keeping this limitation in context, this chapter provides a broad overview of issues related to HIV for this population.

This chapter focuses largely on two specific subpopulations particularly vulnerable to HIV infection: men who have sex with men (MSM), and heterosexual women. However, it is important to note that there are other populations, including adolescents, transgender individuals, and recent immigrants, who may also be vulnerable to HIV acquisition, although data for these groups are even more sparse or nonexistent.

HIV Prevalence among South Asian Americans

The API population is often underrepresented in health surveys and generally consolidated into one category, raising questions of accuracy in data. Studies that highlight HIV case-reporting forms may misclassify people's race and ethnicity, either by relying on misleading information on place of birth or on inaccurate sources, such as medical record data or the subjective impression of an individual (Eckholdt, Chin, Manzon-Santos, & Kim, 1997; Kelly, Chu, Diaz, Leary, & Buehler, 1996). These further call into question the accuracy of the limited available epidemiological data. The API population accounts for approximately 1% of people living with HIV and 2% of new HIV infections in the United States, of which approximately 61%–86% occur among MSM within the API community (Adih, Campsmith, Williams, Hardnett, & Hughes, 2011; Centers for Disease Control and Prevention, 2013; Wong et al., 2011). In the context of HIV research with sexual minority men globally, the diverse identities and experiences of both homosexual and bisexual men are often combined, using the label MSM.

Between 2002 and 2005, the rate of new AIDS cases in API communities in the United States increased by 15% (RYA HIV/AIDS Program, 2008), which may underscore issues with knowledge, risk perception, safe sex practices, and access to testing and treatment. In fact, a recent analysis of data from the Centers for Disease Control and Prevention (CDC) showed that APIs were the only racial group with a statistically significant increase in new HIV diagnoses (4.4%) between 2001 and 2008 (Adih et al., 2011), while there was also a notable decline in new infections from 2007 to 2010, from 10.4 cases to 8.4 cases per 100,000 people (Adih et al., 2011). Additionally, because diagnosis and infections are often regarded as two different epidemiological concepts, making sense of these trends can be difficult. With regard to HIV, diagnosis refers to the identification of or becoming aware of the infection, and is dependent on testing for HIV. Infection, however, may occur regardless of awareness, thus, rates of diagnosis do not necessarily correlate with infection rates.

The overall lack of research and available data on HIV among APIs, and in particular the South Asian American population, highlights the challenges faced in interpreting the available data, and makes extrapolation of these trends to SAAs even more problematic. Additionally, existing data on risk behaviors among APIs suggest that the relatively low number of HIV cases may not provide a full picture of the epidemic or the issues faced by this understudied and underserved population.

Low Rate of HIV Testing among South Asian Americans

Overall, APIs are significantly less likely to report being tested for HIV in the past 12 months, despite engaging in a similar proportion of HIV risk behaviors as other racial and ethnic groups (Adih et al., 2011). In Washington, DC, the HIV testing rate in a sample of API adults was 30.8%, which is lower than the median HIV testing rate by state in the US adult population (Huang, Wong, De Leon, & Park, 2008). Meanwhile, the number of AIDS cases reported between 1999 and 2003 increased at a higher rate (35%) for APIs than for other minority groups (Choi, Han, Hudes, & Kegeles, 2002). In 2011, a CDC report indicated that nearly one in four (22.7%) Asian immigrants living with HIV were unaware of their status and over one-third of Asians developed AIDS soon after being diagnosed with HIV (CDC, 2013). This suggests that late testing becomes a missed opportunity to prevent progression to AIDS, and highlights the need for testing programs in these communities.

Among APIs, Huang et al. (2005) categorized barriers to HIV testing into two broad groups, psychosocial and structural (Huang et al., 2005). Psychosocial barriers included low perceived risk for HIV and stigma surrounding HIV as a sexually transmitted condition. Structural barriers included limited access to HIV-related information and healthcare services. Lower HIV testing rates among those with access to care are likely multifactorial and include a low per-ceived risk among South Asian patients, as well as provider-related barriers. Studies show that physicians are less likely to order tests in APIs for sexually transmitted infections (STI) or HIV compared with other races/ethnicities (Maldonado, 1999). This may be due to provider discomfort with sexual risk assessment and low perceived risk among Asian patients.

HIV Infection among MSM

According to the CDC, HIV infections among the API population are occurring predominantly among MSM (van Griensven & de Lind van Wijngaarden, 2010). This is consistent with the findings of Adih et al. (2011), who found that 61% of APIs diagnosed with HIV in the United States were MSM. In addition, CDC data reveal that sexual contact is the primary mode of transmission among 86% of MSM (CDC, 2016). Furthermore, many APIs acquire the disease after immigrating to the United States, although accurate information regarding transmission and treatment is seldom obtained and/or discussed within the API MSM community (Chin, Leung, Sheth, & Rodriguez, 2007). Still, while there are no reliable prevalence estimates for API MSM, one study from the San Francisco Bay Area found, HIV prevalence to be approximately 6% (Han, 2009). It is unknown what the prevalence rates may be among South Asian MSM.

In identifying MSM, it is important to note that not all SAA MSM self-identify as gay or bisexual for a variety of reasons, including societal and cultural stigmas associated with homosexuality across South Asian countries (Banik, 2008; Banik, Fisher, & Anand, 2014a). There may also be significant intragroup differences that influence the sexual context and sexual partnership among men and that are placed under the label of MSM. For example, in India, a subgroup of self-identified heterosexual men, known as *panthi*, engage in sexual relationships with feminine men, called *kothi*, or male to female transgender persons, locally known as *hijra*. Many of these encounters are labeled by the panthis as "biological discharge" due to lack of female sexual partners or lack of privacy at home (Banik et al., 2014a). Additionally, the sexual acts by "macho men" (*panthis*) with the effeminate men (*kothi* or *hijra*) are often believed to represent "masculinity" (Asthana & Oostvogels, 2001; Khan, 2001).

For many men across South Asia, sexual engagement with other men is considered simply mischief or play, or even a bond of friendship, and the definitions of sex and masculinity are often defined by the act of penetration (Asthana & Oostvogels, 2001; Banik, 2008). As a result, the behavior, as well as the sexuality shifts, can depend upon sociocultural and psychological contexts, and sexuality becomes gender based. Thus, while the acronym MSM is intended to focus on epidemiological aspects of behavior and potential risk, it provides few insights about culturally specific sexual contexts, gender expression, and the nuanced aspects of sexual behavior and partnership among all men who engage in sexual encounters with other men and/or transgender women. This represents a lack in our understanding about unique sociocultural factors, which can have implications for HIV vulnerability among South Asian MSM, and is an area that warrants further exploration.

High Risk Sexual Behavior among Asian and Pacific Islander MSM

While API MSM may have a lower HIV incidence and prevalence rate compared with other racial/ethnic groups in the United States, high rates of HIV-related risk behaviors do exist among API MSM (Choi et al., 2002; Operario et al., 2006; Wei et al., 2011). In fact, API MSM are as likely to engage in high-risk sexual behaviors as other MSM across the United States, including anal intercourse without use of a condom, substance use, and multiple sexual partners similar to other groups. Differences within API subgroups are, however, unknown (Centers for Disease Control and Prevention, 2008; Hou & Basen-Engquist, 1997; McFarland, Chen, Weide, Kohn, & Klausner, 2004; Zaidi et al., 2005). In a study conducted in San Francisco, 26% of API MSM reported inconsistent condom use during anal sex, while nearly half did not know their partners' HIV/STI status (Han, 2009). Another study from California reported misconceptions about HIV including the perception of someone being "safe" based either on his physical attractiveness or desirability, or if they carried lubricant and condoms with them (Nemoto, Iwamoto, Kamitani, Morris, & Sakata, 2011). The high frequency of risky sexual behaviors found among API gay and bisexual men underscores the need to better understand the drivers of both high-risk and protective behaviors with regard to HIV in API subgroups.

STIs among Asian and Pacific Islander MSM

Because STIs increase the risk of HIV transmission (Truong et al., 2006), understanding STI incidence among South Asian MSM is one way to presume HIV vulnerability and present opportunities for prevention. The limited available data on STIs show that rates of rectal gonorrhea have been increasing in Asian MSM in the United States (Raymond et al., 2007). A study based on analysis of data across the country found that between 2006 and 2007, gonorrhea incidence among Asian American men had increased by 9%, while it decreased in all other racial and ethnic groups (Sabato & Silverio, 2010). Additionally, while CDC data show that APIs are highly affected by the Hepatitis B virus (HBV) and that individuals coinfected with HIV and hepatitis B have increased adverse health outcomes, it is unknown if this holds true for South Asian populations as well (CDC, 2015).

Vulnerability of South Asian MSM to HIV

Highlighting similarities among traditional cultures within the South Asian population may obscure significant differences, such as those based on religion, region of origin, length of time since immigration, and individual differences. Still, common features of the overall South Asian culture do have bearing on HIV issues in this population, particularly when considering public health promotion and healthcare initiatives (Chng & Geliga-Vargas, 2000).

Family Factors

Family and family honor are central tenets across South Asian cultures. Much of society is organized around the need to have children and preserve resources, specifically by continuing the family through material and financial resources, as well as upholding social status (Asthana & Oostvogels, 2001; Safren et al., 2006). Thus, to a large extent, an individual's identity is formed by and embedded in the internalization of family and community expectations. In this context, stigma becomes more than an individual concern. Loyalty, commitment, and fulfilling one's duty are expressed by protecting one's family and community from shame (Asthana & Oostvogels, 2001). As a result, some MSM are likely to get married to women to hide their homosexual identity while still continuing same-sex activities. In keeping with South Asian cultural values of harmony and avoidance of unpleasant interaction, many HIV-positive MSM may also choose not to disclose their status to family members as a way to protect their family from the inherent shame that HIV carries with it (Stangl et al., 2010). Because of this, however, they are also unable to access social support from family, again because of the stigma attached to both their sexual orientation and HIV status, their desire to protect family members, and/or their parents' lack of information and understanding of HIV.

Racism, Homophobia, and Internalized Homophobia

Factors contributing to HIV risk among South Asian MSM may have less to do with a lack of information or HIV awareness than with sociocultural factors such as homophobia or sexuality stigma within the larger South Asian communities. South Asian MSM can face marginalization and discrimination from both within the South Asian community and within the broader gay community (Lee, 2014). The data from studies conducted by Lee (2014) suggest that homophobia and fear of discovery by family members, as well as potential stigmatization, may lead some API MSM to have higher levels of internalized homophobia, which can influence engagement in higher risk behaviors such as unprotected sex and drug use. Racism within the gay community can also lead API MSM to engage in unsafe sex in order to please nonracially concordant partners, if the alternative is perceived to be losing their partners (van Griensven & de Lind van Wijngaarden, 2010).

South Asian MSM may also have to navigate through multiple forms of identities including sexual orientation, ethnicity, and family identity (Lee, 2014). Because homophobia and heterosexism often lead to discrimination against self-identified gay and bisexual persons, it can create an environment in which MSM are less likely to self-identify and access relevant care including HIV testing and counseling (Wong et al., 2012). They are also less likely to take advantage of preexposure prophylaxis (PrEP), which is a once daily oral antiretroviral medication taken prior to potential exposure to HIV to prevent acquisition of the virus, and postexposure prophylaxis (PEP), which are antiretroviral medications taken after potential exposure to HIV by a seronegative individual.

Cultural Construct of Sexuality in South Asia

Given the multiple identities that are borne by South Asian men, particularly MSM in diaspora communities, it is important that cultural norms, practices, and attitudes, as they relate to their place of birth or family origin, be well understood in order to fully comprehend the sociocultural context that can create HIV vulnerability among South Asian MSM. Constructs of male sexuality across South Asia are unique in many respects (Banik et al., 2014a; Banik, 2008; Boyce & Khanna, 2011; Khan, 2001). In India, for example, homosexual orientation is not typically tied to one's identity (Asthana & Oostvogels, 2001; Banik et al., 2014a), while it might be in the United States and other places. In fact, in many South Asian cultures, there is no language that denotes identity based on sexual orientation. Additionally, marriage is not necessarily considered a sexual choice, but rather a cultural and familial obligation (Banik et al., 2014a). Finally, studies indicate that bisexual identity is more prevalent among South Asian MSM than their Caucasian counterparts (Welles et al., 2011). Most research on bisexual men in South Asia and the United States has focused narrowly on homosexual risk behavior with little recognition of other aspects of bisexuality.

Resilience and Strengths

Most research on HIV in gay and other MSM populations focuses on vulnerability to infection. Little information exists, however, on resilience against HIV in these vulnerable populations and, as with other areas of HIV research in the United States, specifically with regard to South Asian populations. Of the research that does exist, evidence suggests gay men and other MSM often form strong and innovative relationships, communities, and social support networks. Additionally, self-acceptance may be a key resilience factor for South Asian and other MSM, related to both improved mental health and decreased HIV risk (Safren, 2014); studies and interventions that explore self-acceptance and other areas of resilience for SAA sexual and gender minority populations are needed.

Vulnerability of South Asian Immigrant Women to HIV

In recent years, there has been an increasing number of HIV infections among minority women that were contracted through heterosexual transmission (CDC, 2013). Among API women in the United States, most HIV infections are the result of high-risk heterosexual contact (CDC, 2008). While epidemiological data for SAA women are unavailable, they likely face a number of societal, structural, and cultural barriers that affect their risk for HIV infection, ability to get tested, and their subsequent access to care (Hahm, Lee, Rough, & Strathdee, 2012).

Misconceptions about how the disease is transmitted also exist within South Asian immigrant communities. For example, in a study conducted in New York City, 54% of South Asians surveyed incorrectly believed that diaphragms, birth control pills, and patches provided effective protection against HIV (APICHA, 2004). In 2010, a study of Bangladeshi women who were preparing to take an overseas position found that less than half of the women were able to identify at least two modes of HIV transmission (Islam, Conigrave, Miah, & Kalam, 2010). In fact, many South Asians perceive themselves to be at low risk for HIV (Beck, Majumdar, Estcourt, & Petrak, 2005) and trust that they are safe in their monogamous relationships.

Religious and cultural beliefs about HIV as a disease and HIV-related stigma prevent many South Asians from obtaining accurate information, seeking testing, and obtaining treatment (Bhattacharya, 2004; Vlassoff & Ali, 2011). While many minority communities are affected by HIV, the collective nature of South Asian families, the taboo concerning discussion of sex, and strict gender roles for women all serve to heighten the stigma and its negative impact on HIV risk among South Asian women. Immigrant API women are also at higher risk for violence and HIV due to complex immigration restrictions and language barriers, thus increasing the risk for adverse HIV and other health outcomes.

Intimate Partner and Sexual Violence

Approximately 41%–61% of Asian women report having experienced intimate partner violence (IPV) during their lifetime (Raj & Silverman, 2002; Yoshihama, Bybee, Dabby, & Blazevski, 2011). IPV can occur in many forms, ranging from coercive behavior to physical violence, and has a significant effect on a woman's sexual and reproductive health. South Asian immigrant women appear to be at particularly high risk, with 40% reporting IPV in their current relationship (Raj & Silverman, 2002, 2003). Various factors may contribute to this higher incidence of IPV among recent immigrants, including lack of sexuality education, "arranged marriages," lack of empowerment, lack of language proficiency, lack of familiarity with policies, and a sense of helplessness (Raj & Silverman, 2003).

The association between IPV and HIV risk is well documented (Li et al., 2014), with IPV increasing vulnerability to risks associated with HIV transmission. Existing studies (Li et al., 2014; Raj & Silverman, 2003; Yoshihama et al., 2011) suggest that women in abusive relationships have lower relationship power, which can affect their risk for HIV infection. IPV, therefore, is increasingly recognized as an important predictor of poor outcomes for those women living with HIV.

Social and Cultural Barriers

Stigmatization plays a significant role in how HIV and STIs are understood, prevented, and treated. API women, in particular, face strong cultural barriers including sensitivity to discussions of sexuality, presumed heterosexuality of their husbands, homophobia, and the general perception that API communities are not at risk for HIV (Beck et al., 2005; Vlassoff & Ali, 2010). This stigma discourages individuals from openly talking about sexual health and HIV, which can create a detrimental health impact. Additionally, the taboo around discussion of sexuality-related topics, even within married couples across South Asian communities, renders HIV and other STI prevention education difficult for South Asian women to obtain. In a small sample of women, Chin (1999) described the experiences of nine Asian HIV-positive women, and found that fear of stigma, concerns of disappointing and/or burdening others, and fear of discrimination by extended family and other community members strongly influenced their decision not to disclose their HIV status to others. These barriers are contextualized in the light of the collective nature of Asian cultures, in which the behavior of a single individual is viewed in the context of his or her family and community. Further, APIs living in the United States with HIV require considerable assistance navigating the service system. This is particularly true for APIs whose primary language is not English, as well as undocumented immigrants who experience greater barriers to care and have even fewer personal resources or sources of support available to them (Chin et al., 2007). A study found that when there was accessibility to culturally competent services, there was higher probability of HIV testing among South Asian immigrants (Huang et al., 2008).

Other Subgroups of South Asian Americans Vulnerable to HIV

While limited, MSM and heterosexual women are the two primary groups studied in the context of HIV. There are other subgroups, however, that may also be vulnerable to contracting HIV due to unique sociocultural factors, including adolescents, heterosexual men, transgender women, and recent immigrants.

Adolescents

Compared with the nonimmigrant population, South Asian adolescents who experience acculturation stress and family conflict may be more vulnerable to engaging in risk-taking behaviors (Bhattacharya, Cleland, & Holland, 2000). These can include alcohol and drug abuse, which can then contribute to further risk-taking behavior such as unsafe sexual activity. South Asian traditions are often focused on young people being responsible for studying hard, preparing for adulthood, and meeting parental expectations. Individuation is not necessarily seen as one of the goals of adolescence (Banik et al., 2014a; Bhattacharya, 1998; Bhattacharya et al., 2000). These studies also suggest that open discussion of sex-related topics is avoided or discouraged in the home. As a result, there is a lack of sexual health knowledge among immigrant adolescents. In addition, stigma deters adolescents from seeking HIV information, testing, and treatment, which results in a lack of perceived risk for infection and inaccurate information among South Asian adolescents with regard to HIV (Bhattacharya et al., 2000).

Transgender and Gender Nonconforming Individuals

Several studies in the United States have revealed that transgender women (male-to-female) face a disproportionate burden of HIV infection and other STIs (Bockting, Huang, Ding, Robinson, & Rosser, 2005; Herbst et al., 2008). The majority of these studies include White and Black transgender women; thus data on API transwomen are primarily nonexistent. By extrapolating data from studies with transgender participants from the United States and limited studies with *hijras* (transwomen in India) (Banik et al., 2014b), South Asian transwomen are also more likely to have high vulnerability to HIV infection and adverse health outcomes if infected. Data for transgender men and gender nonconforming individuals of any race/ethnicity are largely nonexistent.

Recent Immigrants

HIV rates among key populations, especially sexual and gender minority communities, in South Asian countries are disproportionately higher. In India, the HIV infection rate among MSM varies between 8% and 13% (UNAIDS, 2013) compared with 0.3% in the general population. The rates of HIV prevalence among key populations are escalating in specific regions in South Asia (UNAIDS, 2013). The increasing rates among certain populations such as transgender women (male-to-female), MSM (both cis- and transgender) and drug-using youth (UNAIDS, 2013) may have implications for HIV among recent South Asian immigrants. While empirical evidence is not available, there may be opportunities for HIV-positive foreign nationals to immigrate to the United States due to the removal of the ban on HIV-based immigration in 2010 (Immigration Equality, 2010). Both globalization and the increased mobility of South Asian immigrants between the United States and their place of birth and/or country of origin warrant our understanding of the sociocultural contexts of HIV risk across South Asia. Studies across South Asia show that migrant populations, which include truck drivers, cooks, taxi drivers, and caregivers, face additional vulnerability to HIV infection due to their encounters with commercial sex workers. By extrapolating findings from migrant labors studies in Southeast Asia (Verma et al., 2010), one might assume that many recent migrants who immigrate to the United States leaving their spouses or other family members behind in their native countries would experience similar HIV risk factors. For example, given that human behavior is culturally similar, these risk factors would include alcohol abuse and opportunities for encounters with commercial sex workers in the United States. In this context, lack of health education, lack of health-care access among recent immigrants (Gomez, Kelsey, Glaser, Lee, & Sidney, 2004) may also influence risk behavior such as condomless sexual encounters.

Recommendations

The importance of culturally and ethnically appropriate public health studies, health promotion interventions, and health-care services must be recognized. Recommendations emerging from the review of extant literature are as follows:

Research

- Improve systematic collection and reporting of disaggregated health data for South Asians in the United States by federal, state, and local government agencies, as well as dissemination of surveillance data.
- Given the large and growing South Asian population, develop a reliable baseline to assess ongoing changes.
- Conduct research to understand how social networks facilitate community resiliency and how to effectively leverage these networks to enhance social capital and build resiliency against HIV and other health issues.
- Facilitate research that targets South Asian MSM and other South Asian groups to examine the unique nature, extent, and cause of HIV risk behaviors as well as the trajectory of resilience in that population.
- Develop strategies to reduce HIV and sexuality-related stigma, and increase HIV testing in South Asian communities.
- Develop evidence-based strategies to prevent IPV and its impact on South Asian women in the United States.

Clinical Practice

- Make services user friendly and available through increased language translation, cultural competency, and confidentiality assurance
- Employ a diverse pool of workers in government-funded institutions, from both within and outside of the community, who can address cultural and language barriers

Community Engagement

- Foster and strengthen partnerships between health departments and community-based organizations serving South Asian American communities, to improve data collection and impact health outcomes.
- Design education, prevention, and outreach services specific to the SAA population.
- Better engage organizations serving South Asian communities and inform them of the need to provide education on HIV risks and prevention to these communities.
- Organize community forums to strategize and eliminate negative community attitudes such as denial, taboos, stigma, and homophobia that can hinder access to and utilization of services.
- Draw upon community strengths and use the cultural concepts of "strong family values" and "family unity" to foster support rather than isolation for those living with HIV.
- Promote culturally-appropriate health education among recent immigrants.

Conclusions

While the overall documented HIV infection rate is relatively lower among API communities than in the general population, prevalence of HIV-related risk behaviors may be higher. Unfortunately, there is a lack of epidemiological and behavioral data regarding HIV in the SAA population. Systemic surveillance data are urgently needed to accurately monitor HIV trends in South Asian Americans and other API groups. Stigma against people living with HIV, engaging in same-sex behaviors and/or with homosexual/queer identities, and other sociocultural and linguistic barriers challenges efforts to mount strong HIV prevention initiatives in API populations, including SAA communities. Empirical studies addressing HIV prevention and care needs of South Asian Americans are urgently needed to inform the development and implementation of evidence-based interventions. An effective strategy is essential to reach the large and growing South Asian American population in the United States, as many individuals may be unaware of their HIV status or face barriers to accessing effective HIV screening, treatment and other health services. Key to this is the need for linguistically accessible and culturally competent HIV prevention and care information and services for the South Asian American community. Finally, because the SAA population lacks appropriate knowledge of HIV and HIV-related issues, there is an urgent need for increased government and community involvement, as well as increased research funding that specifically targets HIV in the South Asian American population.

References

Adih, W. K., Campsmith, M., Williams, C. L., Hardnett, F. P., & Hughes, D. (2011). Epidemiology of HIV among Asians and Pacific Islanders in the United States, 2001–2008. *Journal of the International Association of Physicians in AIDS Care*, *10*(3), 150–159. doi:10.1177/1545109711399805

Asian American Federation Report. (2012). *A demographic snapshot of South Asians in the United State, July 2012 Update*. Retrieved from http://saalt.org/wp-content/uploads/2012/09/Demographic-Snapshot-Asian-American-Foundation-2012.pdf

Asian and Pacific Islander Coalition on HIV/AIDS, INC (APICHA). (2004). *South Asian immigrant women's HIV/AIDS related issues: An exploratory study of New York City*. Final Report Prepared for the South Asian Communities and Department of Health and Human Services (Federal Office of Minority Health). Retrieved from http://static1.squarespace.com/static/51bf34d3e4b03b777467bd1f/t/52f02111e4b09208dee44bf1/1391468817073/021306APICHA.pdf

Asthana, S., & Oostvogels, R. (2001). The social construction of male "homosexuality" in India: Implications for HIV transmission and prevention. *Social Science and Medicine, 52*, 707–721.

Banik, S., Fisher, S. L. E., & Anand, V. R. (2014a). Experiences and expression of sexual identity among married men who have sex with men in India. *Health Education Monograph Series, 32*(2), 62–67.

Banik, S., Anand, V., Srivastava, A., Mengle, S., Dange, A., Fisher, L., & Jerajani, H. (2014b). *Role of gender transition services in HIV prevention among male-to-female transgenders in India: Preliminary findings*. Abstract presented at APHA 142nd Annual Conference, New Orleans November 2014.

Banik, S. (2008). Cultural dimension of male sexual behavior and HIV risk in South Asia with special emphasis on India: A commentary. *Journal of LGBT Health Research*, *4*(2/3), 45–50.

Beck, A., Majumdar, A., Estcourt, C., & Petrak, J. (2005). We don't really have cause to discuss these things, they don't affect us: A collaborative model for developing culturally appropriate sexual health services with Bangladeshi community of Tower Hamlets. *Sexually Transmitted Infections, 81*(2), 158–162.

Bhattacharya, G. (1998). Drug use among Asian-Indian adolescents: Identifying protective and risk factors. *Adolescence, 33*(129), 169–184.

Bhattacharya, G. (2004). Health care seeking for HIV/AIDS among South Asians in the United States. *Health and Social Work, 29*(2), 106–115.

Bhattacharya, G., Cleland, C., & Holland, S. (2000). Knowledge about HIV/AIDS, the perceived risks of infection and sources of information of Asian-Indian adolescents born in the USA. *AIDS Care, 12*(2), 203–209.

Bockting, W., Huang, C. Y., Ding, H., Robinson, B. B., & Simon-Rosser, B. R. (2005). Are transgender persons at higher risk for HIV than other sexual minorities? A comparison of HIV prevalence and risks. *International Journal of Transgenderism, 8*(2–3), 123–131. doi:10.1300/J485v08n02_11

Boyce, P., & Khanna, A. (2011). Right and representations: Querying the male-to-male sexual subject in India. *Culture, Health and Sexuality, 13*(1), 89–100.

Centers for Disease Control. (2008). *HIV/AIDS among Women, CDC HIV/AIDS Fact Sheet* (Revised August 2008). Retrieved from www.cdc.gov/hiv/topics/women/resources/factsheets/pdf/

Centers for Disease Control and Prevention. (2013). Monitoring selected national HIV prevention and care objectives by using HIV surveillance data—United States and 6 dependent areas—2011. *HIV Surveillance Supplemental Report, 18*(5). Retrieved from www.cdc.gov/hiv/library/reports/

Centers for Disease Control and Prevention. (2015). *HIV/AIDS among Asians and Pacific Islanders.* Retrieved from http://www.cdc.gov/hiv/group/racialethnic/nhopi/index.html

Centers for Disease Control and Prevention. (2016). *HIV Surveillance Report, 2015.* Retrieved from http://www.cdc.gov/hiv/library/reports/hiv-surveillance.html Published November 2016. Accessed [November 2016]

Chin, D. (1999). HIV-related sexual risk assessment among Asian/Pacific Islander American women: An inductive model. *Social Science and Medicine, 49*, 241–251.

Chin, J. J., Leung, M. C., Sheth, L., & Rodriguez, T. R. (2007). Let's not ignore a growing HIV problem for Asians and Pacific Islanders in the U.S. *Journal of Urban Health, 84*(5), 642–647.

Chng, C. L., & Geliga-Vargas, J. (2000). Ethnic identity, gay identity, sexual sensation seeking and HIV risk taking among multi-ethnic men who have sex with men. *AIDS Education and Prevention, 12*(4), 326–339.

Choi, K. H., Han, C. S., Hudes, E. S., & Kegeles, S. (2002). Unprotected sex and associated risk factors among young Asian and Pacific Islander men who have sex with men. *AIDS Education and Prevention, 14*, 472–481.

Eckholdt, H. M., Chin, J. J., Manzon-Santos, J. A., & Kim, D. D. (1997). The needs of Asians and Pacific Islanders living with HIV in New York City. *AIDS Education and Prevention, 9*, 493–504.

Gomez, S. L., Kelsey, J. L., Glaser, S. L., Lee, M. M., & Sidney, S. (2004). Immigration and acculturation in relation to health and health-related risk factors among specific Asian subgroups in a health maintenance organization. *American Journal of Public Health, 94*(11), 1977–1984. doi:10.2105/AJPH.94.11.1977

Hahm, H. C., Lee, J., Rough, K., & Strathdee, S. A. (2012). Gender power control, sexual experiences, safer sex practices, and potential HIV risk behaviors among young Asian-American Women. *AIDS and Behavior, 16*(1), 179–188. doi:10.1007/s10461-011-9885-2

Han, C. S. (2009). Chopsticks don't make it culturally competent: Addressing larger issues for HIV prevention among gay, bisexual, and queer Asian Pacific Islander men. *Health and Social Work, 34*(4), 273–281.

Herbst, J. B., Jacobs, E. D., Finlayson, T. J., McKleroy, V. S., Neumann, M. S., Crepaz, N., & HIV/AIDS Prevention Research Synthesis Team. (2008). Estimating HIV prevalence and risk behaviors of transgender persons in the United States: A systematic review. *AIDS and Behavior, 12*(1), 1–17.

Hou, S. I., & Basen-Engquist, K. (1997). Human immunodeficiency 3. Virus risk behavior among White and Asian/Pacific Islander high school students in the United States: Does culture make a difference? *Journal of Adolescent Health, 20*, 68–74.

Huang, Z. J., Wong, F. Y., De Leon, J. M., & Park, R. J. (2008). Self-reported HIV testing behaviors among a sample of Southeast Asians in urban setting in the United States. *AIDS Education and Prevention, 20*(1), 65–77.

Immigration Equality. (2010). *HIV ban end and HIV-based immigration.* Retrieved from http://www.immigrationequality.org/get-legal-help/our-legal-resources/visa-questions/hiv-ban-hiv-based-immigration-applications/. Accessed March 15, 2016.

Islam, M. M., Conigrave, K., Miah, M. D., & Kalam, K. (2010). HIV awareness of outgoing female migrant workers of Bangladesh: A pilot study. *Journal of Immigrant and Minority Health, 12*(6), 940–946.

Khan, S. (2001). Culture, sexualities, and identities: Men who have sex with men in India. *Journal of Homosexuality, 40*(3/4), 99–115.

Kelly, J., Chu, S., Diaz, T., Leary, L., & Buehler, J.W. (1996). Race/ethnicity and misclassification of persons reported with AIDS. *Ethnicity and Disease, 1*, 87–94.

Lee, J. (2014). *The relative impact of identity on LGBT API outness: A quantitative analysis.* CUNY Academic Works. Retrieved from http://academicworks.cuny.edu/gc_etds/245

Li, Y., Marshall, C. M., Rees, H. C., Nunez, A., Ezeanolue, E. E., & Ehiri, J. E. (2014). Intimate partner violence and HIV infection among women: A systematic review and meta-analysis. *Journal of the International AIDS Society, 17*, 18845. doi:10.7448/IAS.17.1.18845

Maldonado, M. (1999). *HIV/AIDS and Asians and Pacific Islanders.* Washington, DC: National Minority AIDS Council.

McFarland, W., Chen, S., Weide, D., Kohn, R. P., & Klausner, J. D. (2004). Gay Asian men in San Francisco follow the international trend: Increases in rates of unprotected anal intercourse and sexually transmitted diseases, 1999–2002. *AIDS Education and Prevention, 16*(1), 13–18.

Nemoto, T., Iwamoto, M., Kamitani, E., Morris, A., & Sakata, M. (2011). Targeted expansion project for outreach and treatment for substance abuse and HIV risk behaviors in Asian and Pacific Islander communities. *AIDS Education and Prevention, 23*(2), 175–191.

Operario, D., Choi, K. H., Chu, P. L., McFarland, W., Secura, G. M., Behel, S., . . . Valleroy, L. (2006). Prevalence and correlates of substance use among young Asian Pacific Islander men who have sex with men. *Prevention Science, 7*, 19–29.

Raj, A., & Silverman, J. (2002). Intimate partner violence against South Asian women residing in greater Boston. *Journal of the American Medical Women's Association, 57*, 111–114.

Raj, A., & Silverman, J. (2003). Immigrant South Asian women at greater risk for injury from intimate partner violence. *American Journal of Public Health, 93*(3), 435–437.

Raymond, H. F., Chen, S., Truong, H. M., Knapper, K. B., Klausner, J. D., Choi, K. H., & McFarland, W. (2007). Trends in sexually transmitted diseases, sexual risk behavior, and HIV infection among Asian/Pacific Islander men who have sex with men, San Francisco, 1999–2005. *Sexually Transmitted Diseases, 34*(5), 262–264.

The RYA HIV/AIDS Program. (2008). *Asian/Pacific Islanders and HIV/AIDS.* Retrieved from ftp://ftp.hrsa.gov/hab/Asian.Pacific.pdf. Downloaded on 1-4-2015

Sabato, T. M., & Silverio, A. Q. (2010). A forgotten population: Addressing comprehensive HIV prevention needs among American Asians and Pacific islanders. *Journal of the Association of Nurses in AIDS Care, 21*(4), 364–370.

Safren, S. A., Martin, C., Menon, S., Greer, J., Solomon, S., Mimiaga, M. J., & Mayer, K. H. (2006). A survey of MSM HIV prevention outreach workers in Chennai, India. *AIDS Education and Prevention, 18*(4), 323–332.

Stangl, A., Carr, D., Brady, L., Eckhaus, T., Claeson, M., & Nyblade, L. (2010). *Tackling HIV Related Stigma and Discrimination in South Asia* (p. 232). Washington, DC: The World Bank.

Truong, H. M., Kellogg, T., Klausner, J. D., Katz, M. H., Dilley, J., Knapper, K., & McFarland, W. (2006). Increases in sexually transmitted infections and sexual risk behaviour without a concurrent increase in HIV incidence among men who have sex with men in San Francisco: A suggestion of HIV serosorting? *Sexually Transmitted Infections, 82*(6), 461–466.

UNAIDS Report. (2013). *HIV in Asia and the Pacific.* http://www.unaids.org/sites/default/files/media_asset/2013_HIV-Asia-Pacific_en_0.pdf

van Griensven, F., & de Lind van Wijngaarden, J. W. (2010). A review of the epidemiology of HIV infection and prevention responses among MSM in Asia. *AIDS, 24*(Suppl. 3), S30–S40.

Vlassoff, C., & Ali, F. (2011). HIV-related stigma among South Asians in Toronto. *Ethnicity and Health, 16*(1), 25–42. doi:10.1080/13557858.2010.523456

Wei, C., Raymond, H. F., Wong, F. Y., Silvestre, A. J., Friedman, M. S., Documét, P., . . . Stall, R. (2011). Lower HIV prevalence among Asian/Pacific Islander men who have sex with men: A critical review for possible reasons. *AIDS and Behavior, 15*(3), 535–549.

Welles, S. W., Ross, M. W., Banik, S., Fisher, L., McFarlane, M., Kachur, R., . . . Allensworth-Davies, D. (2011). Demographic and sexual behavior comparisons of Indian and U.S. Internet samples of men who have sex with men. *International Journal of Sexual Health, 23*(2), 90–101.

Wong, F. Y., Crisostomo, V. A., Bao, D., Smith, B. D., Young, D., Huang, Z. H., . . . Frangos, S. E. (2011). Development and implementation of a collaborative, multi-stakeholder research and practice model on HIV prevention targeting Asian American and Pacific Islander men who have sex with men. *American Journal of Public Health, 101*(4), 623–631.

Wong, F. Y., Nehi, E. J., Han, J. J., Huang, Z. J., Wu, Y., Young, D., & Ross, M. W; The MATH Study consortium. (2012). HIV testing and management. Findings from a national sample of Asian and Pacific Islander men who have sex with men. *Public Health Reports, 127*(2), 186–194.

Yoshihama, M., Bybee, D., Dabby, C., & Blazevski, J. (2011). *Lifecourse experiences of intimate partner violence and help-seeking among Filipino, Indian and Pakistani women: Implications for justice system responses.* Washington, DC: National Institute of Justice.

Zaidi, I. F., Crepaz, N., Song, R., Wan, C. K., Lin, L. S., Hu, D. J., & Sy, F. S. (2005). Epidemiology of HIV/AIDS among Asians and Pacific Islanders in the United States. *AIDS Education and Prevention, 17,* 405–417.

HEALTH OF VULNERABLE POPULATIONS

VI

HEALTH OF VULNERABLE POPULATIONS

Chapter 9

Women's Health

Rashmi Kudesia, Sundes Kazmir,
Divya Talwar, and Amitasrigowri Murthy

Contents

Abstract

Objective: To review and summarize the evidence regarding the uptake of preventive health services among South Asian American (SAA) women, and delineate important health concerns for this population from adolescence through the reproductive years, into menopause, and during postmenopausal years.

Key Findings: South Asian women have specific biological and cultural risk factors that should be considered by healthcare providers when caring for South Asian women born in the United States or abroad. Important health concerns involving SAA women include barriers to care, elevated metabolic risks, excess body fat in adolescents, and higher rates of polycystic ovarian disease and diabetes in reproductive-aged women. Additionally, certain cultural traditions have been found to lead to stigma and shame with regard to reproduction and sexuality.

Recommendations: As a result of these findings, more culturally sensitive outreach and research are needed in order to understand the full impact of immigration and differences among the SAA population. There is also a need to identify best practices in the provision of health care as it relates to South Asian women.

Introduction

South Asian American (SAA) women represent a unique population with specific health-related concerns and risks. This is due to both biological and cultural factors. Because the SAA population in general tends to have reduced uptake of appropriate health care, this chapter begins by detailing barriers to preventive care for SAA women. Specific diseases and cultural topics are then addressed according to their particular relevance to SAA women. Similar to the American College of Obstetricians and Gynecologists (ACOG), a life-stage approach (adolescence, reproductive years, menopause and beyond) was used to identify topics in order of relevance.

SAAs are one of the fastest growing minority populations in the United States (South Asian Americans Leading Together [SAALT], 2015). Unfortunately, SAAs are often categorized with other Asian Americans who have different health profiles, and literature specifically relating to SAAs is sparse. The objective of this chapter is to detail the current state of medical knowledge regarding SAA women's health. Where possible, the authors draw on insights from research conducted in South Asia, Canada, and the United Kingdom, where the immigrant South Asian population is a much more visible and well-studied minority.

Preventive Care

In the United States, regular preventive check-ups, including screening for hypertension, diabetes, and elevated lipids are recommended for all adults; along with screenings for breast and cervical cancer for women (Bharmal & Chaudhry, 2012).

Among the SAA population, however, there is a lower adherence to screening guidelines, which is thought to be related to health insurance status, lower socio-economic status (SES), and shorter length of stay in the United States (Boxwala, Bridgemohan, Griffith, & Soliman, 2010; Glenn, Chawla, Surani, & Bastani, 2009; Islam, Kwon, Senie, & Kathuria, 2006). In fact, studies exploring preventive health behavior found more than half of the SAA population examined did not receive the recommended services, with women faring significantly worse (Bharmal & Chaudhry, 2012).

These findings are clearly illustrated when looking at specific screenings. Mammography rates among South Asian women living in the United States have generally been reported in the range of 47% – 70%, which is well below the Healthy People 2020 target goal of 81.1% (Gomez, Tan, Keegan, & Clarke, 2007; Islam et al., 2006; Rahman & Rahman, 2008; Sadler et al., 2001; Wu, West, Chen, & Hergert, 2006; Menon, Szalacha & Prabhughate, 2012; Hasnain, Menon, Szalacha & Ferrans, 2014. Reasons for not receiving a mammography include age less than 50 years, unemployed, non-US citizen, and uninsured. Cultural reasons for low mammography rates include modesty, embarrassment during breast examination, and lack of a physician's recommendation for breast examination. Similar low rates can also be seen for Pap testing for cervical cancer (De Alba, Ngo-Metzger, Sweningson, & Hubbell, 2005). Likewise, a cross-sectional study of osteoporosis screening in Dallas showed that despite knowledge of calcium intake and bone density scans, only a small number of South Asian women living in the United States followed preventive guidelines (Shakil et al., 2010). A large study of only Indian Americans demonstrated somewhat higher rates of screening (81.2% mammography, 74.2% Pap test) but also found that education and access to care increased the odds of receiving cancer screening two- to six-fold (Misra, Menon, Vadaparampil, & BeLue 2011). Thus, both immigrant status and cultural practices contribute to the overall lower utilization of preventive services by South Asian women living in the United States.

When attempting to adopt a healthy lifestyle, South Asian immigrant women face specific barriers (Patel, Phillips-Caesar, & Boutin-Foster, 2012). These barriers include a decreased awareness regarding the availability of and need for organized exercise classes, discomfort in Western exercise facilities, and a lack of counseling and role modeling from health-care providers and cultural leaders; all of which contribute to lower rates of physical activity seen in the SAA population, particularly women (Abbasi, 2014; Allender, Cowburn, & Foster, 2006; Kandula & Lauderdale, 2005; Lawton, Ahmad, Hanna, Douglas, & Hallowell, 2006; Sriskantharajah & Kai, 2007). Conversely, South Asian women who were born in the United States are more aware of preventive health services and perceive a greater benefit from them, which is associated with greater uptake of services (Ahmad et al., 2004). Still, several factors may inhibit increased uptake, including limited social support, high cost of medical care, and job uncertainty (Ahmad et al., 2004; Tirodkar et al., 2011).

Puberty

Puberty in girls is defined as the time at which an adolescent begins developing secondary sexual characteristics, including breast buds followed by underarm and pubic hair. Menarche, or the first menstrual period, usually follows within a few years of puberty (Styne, 2004). Two papers in the 1990s evaluated age of menarche, with a study of an urban Punjabi population showing a median age at menarche of 13.2 in 709 girls, while a study of 9951 affluent girls from eight Indian states showed a mean menarcheal age of 12.6 (Agarwal et al., 1992; Sharma, 1990). These ages are roughly similar to the data reported for US girls of all ethnicities. The *U.S. National Health and Nutrition Examination Survey III* demonstrated a mean menarcheal age of 12.4 (Wu, Mendola, & Buck, 2002). Still, reports demonstrate that the average age of menarche has dropped by several years, a trend believed to be related to higher body fat or body mass indices (BMIs) (Kaplowitz, Slora, Wasserman, Pedlow, & Herman-Giddens, 2001). Early puberty can lead to lower final heights and short- and long-term psychosocial distress due to early debut to sexuality (Johansson & Ritzén, 2005).

Data related specifically to puberty among South Asian girls are limited. Even in the United Kingdom, where South Asians are more represented in research, menarcheal data remain underreported. Additional data show that South Asian individuals have higher body fat per unit BMI when compared to Caucasian individuals. Differences between South Asian countries may exist as well, with some data suggesting that Indian children and adolescents may have greater predisposition to central adiposity than those from Pakistan or Bangladesh (Harding, Maynard, Cruickshank, & Gray, 2006; Shaw, Crabtree, Kibirige, & Fordham, 2007). Further, the *Add Health Study* reported significant increases in obesity levels for second- (26.9%) and third-generation (27.6%) compared with first-generation (11.6%) SAA children (Popkin & Udry, 1998).

As girls enter puberty, the majority of them seek to learn more about the changes occurring in their bodies and they believe these questions should be answered by their physician (Ackard & Neumark-Sztainer, 2001). However, cultural beliefs and traditions surrounding reproduction still contribute to inaccurate information reported by native South Asian girls (Goel & Kundan, 2011) and may also be propagated by mothers. The available literature suggests significant variation in how immigrant SAA mothers handle discussion of sex and marriage (Deepak, 2005). This can impede an adolescent's ability to receive appropriate care and counseling (McKee, O'Sullivan, & Weber, 2006). As such, providers caring for immigrant adolescents must provide accurate and thorough information without alienating traditional parents.

Adolescents and parents should be reassured that ACOG recommends the first gynecologic visit to occur between the ages of 13 and 15 in order for adolescents to receive age-appropriate care and counseling (American College of Obstetricians & Gynecologists [ACOG], 2012). Further, gynecologic visits allow for education on sex and wellness (American Academy of Pediatrics [AAP], 1998).

Contraception and Safe Sex

Discussing sexual health with SAA patients can be challenging for clinicians and must be approached with sensitivity. For many South Asian women, sexual health is a delicate topic, regardless of religion or whether they are immigrants or born in the United States. Sexuality is rarely discussed at home and is often only seen as an appropriate topic to address just prior to marriage (Fisher, Bowman, & Thomas, 2003). In fact, many South Asian religions and cultures idealize a woman's virginity and believe that discussion of reproductive health among unmarried women is unnecessary. Families also believe that women will learn about their bodies through experience once they are married or from friends (Farid, Siddique, Bachmann, Janevic, & Pichika, 2013; Fisher et al., 2003). As a result of these beliefs, the health-care provider becomes a critical source for accurate and clear information.

In 2007, a Canadian study examined cervical cancer screening among immigrant Sikh women aged 21–65 years. The study illustrated the highly private nature of sexual and reproductive health issues (Oelke & Vollman, 2007). Women in the study described the cervix as "an unseen, unknown" part of the body, and far less important than the visible external body. In terms of issues and potential areas for improvement with health-care provider relationships, many cited a preference for same-sex providers, with privacy and embarrassment concerns serving as impediments to seeing a male physician. Further, while many in the Canadian study stated that a female, Sikh, Punjabi-speaking physician would be ideal, others were more receptive to seeing a physician from outside their community. This was due to fear that in the small, close-knit Sikh community their medical information may not be kept truly confidential.

In the United Kingdom, approximately 8% (4.6 million) of the population is of South Asian descent, constituting the largest ethnic group. A literature review examining the sexual and reproductive health of this particular population identified areas of concern, particularly among young and unmarried people (Griffiths, Prost, & Hart, 2008). The review showed that young, unmarried South Asians consistently perform more poorly than their peers when questioned about sexually transmitted infections, symptoms, and prevention (Coleman & Testa, 2008; Sinha, Curtis, Jayakody, Viner, & Roberts, 2006). Other studies comparing ethnic variations in sexual behavior in the United Kingdom have shown that fewer Indian and Pakistani women report sexual activity compared with other ethnic groups (Fenton et al., 2005). South Asian women also report an older age of first intercourse and a lower number of lifetime partners (Saxena et al., 2006). It is important to note, however, that populations in these studies tended to be older and married. The major gap in research is still on the behavior of unmarried, second-generation South Asian women aged 16–30 years. One study addressing this group found that upon leaving home, young women do begin to enter into sexual relationships outside of marriage (Griffiths et al., 2008).

It is important to understand that an environment of sexual shame and secrecy can put women at risk for undesired pregnancy, manipulative relationships, and sexual assault. This is illustrated by the case of a 25-year-old single US Indian woman who initially denied using birth control or being sexually active for several years before finally admitting to having boyfriends who would "do something to me down there" (Fisher et al., 2003). Fisher et al. reported that this patient had assumed this was what boyfriends did and did not realize she had the right to say no. Furthermore, she had no knowledge of what birth control was or how children were conceived (Fisher et al., 2003).

Indeed, studies conducted in Canada, the United Kingdom, and the United States have shown that South Asian women tend to use contraception at varying frequencies, but generally less often than their non-South Asian counterparts. A recent study at two women's clinics in New Jersey examined attitudes toward family planning among SAA immigrants, as compared to non-South Asian women (Farid et al., 2013). In this study, the SAA women were Indian or Pakistani, with 12% born in the United States. They had a higher level of education, which correlated to higher contraception use (Farid et al., 2013). These results are consistent with prior observations in the United Kingdom that less educated women have little knowledge of contraception until just prior to marriage or even after the birth of their first child (Griffiths et al., 2008).

The New Jersey study also found that non-South Asian women were more likely to use contraception (85% vs. 68%) and, among SAA women, Muslims were less likely to use contraception (Farid et al., 2013). Additionally, the study found that SAA women were less likely to learn about family planning from parents, and instead relied on doctors as their source for contraceptive knowledge. Of the SAA respondents surveyed at the two clinics, 13% indicated that they would not discuss contraception with their own daughters due to their belief that contraception was "unnatural" and inconsistent with their religious beliefs. Participants in the study identified barriers to contraceptive use, including culture, lack of education, and family opposition. South Asian couples are often expected to procreate soon after marriage; thus, while some may have immigrated to a Western nation, many still abide by South Asian cultural norms. Another barrier identified by respondents in this study was misinformation and fear about the side effects of birth control (Farid et al., 2013). In the United Kingdom, research has also shown that South Asian women use a more limited range of contraceptive options, generally preferring barrier methods such as condoms, with some use of oral contraceptives or intrauterine devices (Saxena et al., 2006). Fear of side effects or a lack of understanding are reasons often cited for discontinuation of family planning methods (Griffiths et al., 2008).

Irregular Menstruation

Menstrual disorders can be common in South Asian women. Conditions reported most often include dysmenorrhea (painful menses), long or irregular menstrual cycles, and premenstrual syndrome. The timing of these disorders is of utmost importance when assessing the causes of irregular menstruation. Within the first three years of menarche, irregular menses are usually due to immaturity of the hypothalamic–pituitary–ovarian axis. By the end of the third year after menarche, most women have menstrual cycles within the normal range of 21–35 days. Despite this, up to 20% of women can have an underlying disorder causing irregular menses. This requires a careful history and examination to determine the exact cause, as well as an evaluation for anemia in women with heavy or prolonged bleeding patterns.

In South Asian women, the most common cause of irregular menses is polycystic ovarian syndrome (PCOS). The prevalence of other conditions leading to irregular menses among SAA women has not yet been clearly established. In the United Kingdom, however, abnormal uterine bleeding has been shown to be a main cause for anemia in South Asian women, and may be more severe or persistent without treatment due to their propensity for low-iron vegetarian diets (Chapple, 1998; Fischbacher et al., 2001).

PCOS and Metabolic Disease

PCOS is a hormone disorder characterized by irregular or absent periods, ovaries that have many small follicles on ultrasound, and/or elevated levels of male hormones, often leading to hirsutism (excess body hair). South Asian women are at elevated risk of developing this disorder, although the underlying mechanism for PCOS development remains unclear. In addition to hormonal disruptions, PCOS is also associated with cardiovascular risk factors including hypertension, high cholesterol, insulin resistance, and diabetes mellitus. SAA women, like all South Asians, are already genetically predisposed to developing these metabolic conditions, and it is concerning that young South Asian women with PCOS are at elevated metabolic risk compared to similarly aged PCOS women of other ethnicities (Wijeyaratne, Balen, Barth, & Belchetz, 2002).

Though data are limited on the prevalence of PCOS in the general South Asian population, a study from the United Kingdom found polycystic ovaries in 52% of a random sample of South Asian women living in the United Kingdom (Rodin, Bano, Bland, Taylor, & Nussey, 1998). Other studies have shown that South Asian women with PCOS had more severe symptoms and higher rates of metabolic disturbance (Mehta, Kamdar, & Dumesic, 2013; Wijeyaratne et al., 2002, 2011). Among infertility patients, PCOS appears to be a particularly predominant cause in the South Asian population. A 2008 study of 2270 infertility patients in India indicated a 46.5% prevalence rate of PCOS (Rajashekar, Krishna, & Patil, 2008). This percentage is substantially higher than baseline population rates of up to 15% or the 7% of infertility patients who are pursuing in-vitro fertilization and have an ovulatory dysfunction (Fauser et al., 2012; Centers for Disease Control [CDC], 2013).

Smaller studies have demonstrated that South Asian infertility patients are more likely to present with PCOS than Caucasian infertility patients (44.2% vs. 11.5%) (Kudesia, Illions, & Lieman, 2016). Additionally, South Asian women with PCOS have been found to have reduced fertilization and live birth rates when undergoing in vitro fertilization (Palep-Singh, Picton, Vrotsou, Maruthini, & Balen, 2007). Further work in this area is needed. It has been postulated that geographic location, ethnic origin, and cultural practices are likely contributors to the differing manifestation of PCOS (Fauser et al., 2012). Attention must also be paid to differences in US-born versus foreign-born South Asians, as well as women within certain South Asian subcategories.

In addition to the impact that PCOS has on a woman's body, it is important to note its impact on a woman's quality of life, as measured by a broad subjective assessment of the positive and negative aspects of one's life (Fauser et al., 2012; Kumarapeli, Seneviratne Rde, & Wijeyaratne, 2011). Hirsutism, one of the components of PCOS, was found to be more prevalent in South Asian women with PCOS (Mehta et al., 2013) and has been cited as a major instigator of distress.

In summary, expert consensus acknowledges major gaps in the understanding of PCOS. As a result, PCOS has been identified as a major issue of concern for South Asian women across the globe. It is one that must be diagnosed and managed appropriately, not only because of its reproductive consequences but also because of its metabolic consequences.

Fertility and Pregnancy

Though PCOS is a leading cause of infertility among South Asian women, it is certainly not the only cause. While there are no data to suggest that SAA couples experience infertility at higher rates than Caucasian couples, the success rates for treatment cycles are lower (Butts & Seifer, 2010; Shahine et al., 2009). It may also be more difficult to treat infertility in South Asian patients with PCOS because they exhibit different sensitivity to ovarian stimulation medications than those with differing ethnic backgrounds (Palep-Singh et al., 2007). An evaluation of ovarian reserve by anti-Müllerian hormone demonstrates higher levels in South Asian women, although this variation was not significant after controlling for age, BMI, and smoking status (Bhide, Gudi, Shah, & Homburg, 2014).

Because of these variations, it is important for health-care providers to be aware that South Asian patients presenting for fertility care may represent a patient population that is typically younger and more likely to have PCOS, as well as one that may also require individualized stimulation protocols to optimize outcomes. Additionally, women with preexisting illnesses or other pregnancy-related concerns should be encouraged to seek the care of an obstetrician or primary care provider prior to attempting conception.

Preconception counseling can ensure that maternal health is optimal for carrying a successful pregnancy to term. As part of this counseling, consanguinity is one area that may be difficult for some South Asian families to discuss. Some communities, often those of Islamic faith, encourage marriage within the family. In fact, the rate of first-cousin marriage among British Pakistanis is estimated at 55%, thereby making invaluable the use of appropriate genetic counseling prior to pregnancy (Khan, Benson, Macleod, & Kingston, 2010). The prevalence of congenital and genetic disorders among offspring of consanguineous couples is approximately twice that of nonconsanguineous couples, in addition to a higher prevalence for miscarriage and neonatal death (Bundey & Alam, 1993).

The need to actively encourage genetic counseling in South Asians is appropriate, as some data suggest that ethnic minorities are less likely to participate in prenatal screening (Fransen et al., 2009). Because of this, less is known about the normative values for these populations and further research is needed to determine ethnically specific cutoffs for testing analytes (Spencer, Heath, El-Sheikhah, Ong, & Nicolaides, 2005). Prenatal screening should also include testing for thalassemia, a common cause of anemia in South Asians, as well as for cystic fibrosis, which is now increasingly recognized in India (Kabra, Kabra, Lodha, & Shastri, 2007).

Once pregnant, cultural notions of modesty, as well as issues of access and insurance, may predispose South Asian women living in the United States to delay or forgo prenatal care, likely contributing to the observation that SAA women tend to breastfeed at lower rates than Caucasian women (Brar et al., 2009; Douglas, 2012). Intuitively, as South Asian immigrant women become more acculturated to Western lifestyles, some of these trends may diminish, and therefore it should not be assumed that they apply to all South Asian women. Still, in more traditional or secluded communities, there is important outreach work required in order to engage women and encourage them to seek the best reproductive care possible.

Given the elevated risk of the development of diabetes, all pregnant South Asian women should undergo early screening for gestational diabetes for each pregnancy. This is consistent with ACOG guidelines and includes a glucose challenge test in the first trimester and, if the result is normal, a routine screening in the second trimester. In a UK study of pregnant women with gestational diabetes mellitus, those of South Asian descent had higher glucose levels, were more likely to have a family history of diabetes, and were diagnosed with gestational diabetes mellitus early in their pregnancy (Wong, 2012). If diagnosed, women should pay close attention to dietary and exercise recommendations to avoid morbidity for themselves as well as their unborn child.

When discussing pregnancy among South Asian women, it is also important to consider the phenomenon of sex selection. In South Asian societies, tradition has instilled a strong preference for sons for a variety of reasons, including the economic utility of male offsprings, the contribution to elder care, and the avoidance of a future dowry expense. The Indian government has passed multiple laws limiting the use of biomedical technology for sex selection. In the United States, eight states have passed restrictive legislation prohibiting sex-selective abortion, though preimplantation genetic diagnosis for sex selection remains legal. In a study of 65 foreign-born South Asian women who were living in California, New Jersey, or New York, participants spoke of intense pressure from in-laws and husbands to have sons, including verbal and physical abuse (Puri, Adams, Ivey, & Nachtigall, 2011). In this study, 40% had terminated prior pregnancies with female fetuses, while 89% of women carrying female fetuses in a current pregnancy were pursuing abortion. In direct contrast, the National Asian American Survey, a poll conducted among Asian Americans, reveals that Asian Americans do not have a preference for sons over daughters (Ramakrishnan, Junn, Lee, & Wong, 2012). Regardless, healthcare providers should strive to provide nonjudgmental services and referrals while, at the same time, screening as appropriate for coercive or abusive situations.

In summary, South Asian women have unique physical and cultural factors that are relevant to their reproductive care. More research and outreach are needed to increase understanding and provide for their care.

Menopause and Osteoporosis

A women is considered to have reached menopause when menstrual periods have been absent for 12 consecutive months. The preceding years may be characterized by symptoms that include hot flashes, vaginal dryness, mood changes, fatigue, and poor sleep quality. In the United States, the average age of menopause is 51. Studies in South Asia have shown the average menopausal age to be younger, ranging from 45.02 to 48.7, with less exercise and higher socioeconomic status predicting a later age (Bairy, Adiga, Bhat, & Bhat, 2009; Kakkar, Kaur, Chopra, Kaur, & Kaur, 2007; Kapur, Sinha, & Pereira, 2009; Kriplani & Banerjee, 2005; Singh, 2012). Hot flashes are among the most bothersome of menopausal symptoms, and are easier to study than more multifactorial complaints such as mood or sleep changes.

A study in Bangladesh showed the average age at menopause of 51.1, though with a lower incidence of symptoms, such as hot flashes, than was seen in Western populations (Rahman, Salehin, & Iqbal, 2011). A multiethnic US study also showed that Indian-American women had among the lowest rates (31.3%) of hot flashes compared with the highest rate of 61.4% seen in Black participants (Reed et al., 2014). A similar rate (34%) was seen in a multicenter urban study in India, which associated hot flash prevalence with higher anxiety, spicy food intake, older age, and more frequent exercise (Stefanopoulou et al., 2013). This study also found hot flashes to be more problematic for women who were in poorer general health and had more negative views of menopause. In a South Asian cohort in the United Kingdom, less acculturation accompanied by poor general health and anxiety were identified as predictors of hot flashes (Hunter, Gupta, Papitsch-Clark, & Sturdee, 2009). Thus, the available literature suggests that the symptomatology and triggers for menopausal symptoms may be ethnic specific.

As one might expect, rural residence and lower socioeconomic status have been linked to a poorer understanding of menopause with employment and education status also impacting a woman's experience of menopausal symptoms (Borker, Venugopalan, & Bhat, 2013; Kakkar et al., 2007; Wani & Gupta, 2013).

There is some evidence to suggest that yoga practice may ameliorate the manifestations of menopause (Chattha, Raghuram, Venkatram, & Hongasandra, 2008). In the United Kingdom, a study of South Asian women showed no difference compared with Caucasian women with regard to their fears and concerns related to menopause and hormone replacement therapy, though uptake did appear to be lower (Sethi & Pitkin, 2000). Since then, the release of the Women's Health Initiative findings has led to a more limited use of hormone replacement therapy (Majumdar, Almasi, & Stafford, 2004). The authors believe, however, that this only serves to increase the need for thorough counseling and discussion in the management of menopausal symptoms.

A major health concern for postmenopausal women is osteoporosis, defined as loss of bone mass that predisposes women to fractures. Hip fractures are associated with major morbidity and can impact subsequent quality of life. In India, it has been estimated that 50%–70% of postmenopausal women may suffer from osteoporosis, while diasporic South Asian women are at an elevated risk for osteoporosis and/or fracture (Darling, Hakim, et al., 2013a; Khandelwal, Chandra, & Lo, 2012). These differences are believed to be due, at least in part, to the lower vitamin D levels seen in diasporic pre- and postmenopausal South Asian women (Darling, Hart, et al., 2013b; Hart et al., 2013; Lowe, Mitra, Foster, Bhojani, & McCann, 2010). Thus, lower dietary intake of calcium and lower frequency of exercise are also important risk factors in developing low bone mineral density in both native and diasporic South Asians (Aggarwal et al., 2011). As a result, it has been suggested that replacement values of calcium and vitamin D should be greater than those recommended by the United States Preventive Services Task Force, although to date there is no evidence of benefit to support this suggestion (Gooneratne, 2013).

Recommendations

To improve the health of SAA women based on the literature reviewed for this chapter, the following set of recommendations is offered for those interested in the research or clinical care of this particular patient population:

■ Though there has been an increase in the number of studies that include South Asian women, most are limited to regions where South Asians form a large ethnic minority. Hence, more studies that are geographically representative of the United States are needed. These findings can then be used to develop education interventions for use in major South Asian languages.
■ Many studies employed qualitative research design or used quantitative designs but were limited by small samples. Thus, not only is more

work needed, but studies should also include a separate category for the South Asian ethnicity, along with consideration of oversampling, in order to achieve a representative study population. Findings from studies that conflate distinct South Asian subpopulations or combine South Asians with other Asian ethnicities must be closely inspected as each contains vastly different health risks and cultural influences.

■ Cultural competency training should be required for health-care providers. The major barriers for South Asian women seeking appropriate care revolves around modesty and presumed appropriate behavior for girls and women. It is pivotal for providers to understand this and consider these cultural aspects when caring for South Asian patients.

■ Most preventive care studies have focused on knowledge and attitudes. Though the pervasive model minority myth may lead providers to assume high compliance with health guidelines, there are many South Asian subpopulations that struggle financially and have low education or socioeconomic status. Specific outreach and education for South Asian communities is necessary.

■ Collaboration with South Asian community-based organizations is recommended, especially to dispel cultural taboos and stigmas. This partnership can be particularly effective for sensitive topics such as puberty, sexual activity, domestic violence, and mental health. In general, however, such joint efforts will be most productive in improving uptake of preventive care, dispelling myths, and dissuading harmful cultural traditions, as well as encouraging adoption of healthy lifestyle choices.

Conclusions

This chapter has outlined the state of current understanding as it relates to the health of South Asian women throughout the various stages of reproductive life. Much work remains in order to fully understand the impact of immigration and acculturation to a Western lifestyle and to confidently extrapolate findings in native South Asian women to both immigrant and US-born South Asian women. Furthermore, biologic and/or cultural forces exist that propagate variations among those hailing from different South Asian countries as has been observed in the large South Asian immigrant population in the United Kingdom. Nonetheless, the current understanding includes many health-related issues of particular relevance to South Asian women and their health-care providers. Those issues of greatest impact include (1) barriers to care, (2) elevated metabolic risks manifesting as excess body fat in adolescents and higher rates of polycystic ovarian disease and diabetes in reproductive-aged women, and (3) cultural traditions propagating secrecy and shame around reproduction and sexuality. The most culturally sensitive approach would combine an awareness of these general patterns with a patient-centered approach focused on individual health risks.

References

Abbasi, I. N. (2014). Socio-cultural barriers to attaining recommended levels of physical activity among females: A review of literature. *Quest, 66*(4), 448–467. doi:10.1080/00336297.2014.955118

Ackard, D. M., & Neumark-Sztainer, D. (2001). Health care information sources for adolescents: Age and gender differences on use, concerns, and needs. *Journal of Adolescent Health, 29*(3), 170–176.

Agarwal, D. K., Agarwal, K. N., Upadhyay, S. K., Mittal, R., Prakash, R., & Rai, S. (1992). Physical and sexual growth pattern of affluent Indian children from 5 to 18 years of age. *Indian Pediatrics, 29*(10), 1203–1282.

Aggarwal, N., Raveendran, A., Khandelwal, N., Sen, R. K., Thakur, J. S., Dhaliwal, L. K., ... Manoharan, S. R. (2011). Prevalence and related risk factors of osteoporosis in peri- and postmenopausal Indian women. *Journal of Midlife Health, 2*(2), 81–85. doi:10.4103/0976-7800.92537

Ahmad, F., Shik, A., Vanza, R., Cheung, A. M., George, U., & Stewart, D. E. (2004). Voices of South Asian women: Immigration and mental health. *Women Health, 40*(4), 113–130.

Allender, S., Cowburn, G., & Foster, C. (2006). Understanding participation in sport and physical activity among children and adults: A review of qualitative studies. *Health Education Research, 21*(6), 826–835. doi:10.1093/her/cyl063

American Academy of Pediatrics (AAP). (1998). Counseling the adolescent about pregnancy options. *Pediatrics, 101*(5), 938–940. doi:10.1542/peds.101.5.938

American College of Obstetricians & Gynecologists (ACOG). (2012). Committee Opinion No. 534: Well-woman visit. *Obstetrics & Gynecology, 120*(2 Pt. 1), 421–424. doi:10.1097/AOG.0b013e3182680517

Bairy, L., Adiga, S., Bhat, P., & Bhat, R. (2009). Prevalence of menopausal symptoms and quality of life after menopause in women from South India. *Australian and New Zealand Journal of Obstetrics, 49*(1), 106–109. doi 10.1111/j.1479-828X.2009.00955.x

Bharmal, N., & Chaudhry, S. (2012). Preventive health services delivery to South Asians in the United States. *Journal of Immigrant and Minority Health, 14*(5), 797–802. doi:10.1007/s10903-012-9610-x

Bhide, P., Gudi, A., Shah, A., & Homburg, R. (2014). Serum anti-Mullerian hormone levels across different ethnic groups: A cross-sectional study. *British Journal of Obstetrics and Gynaecology, 122*(12), 1625–1629. doi:10.1111/1471-0528.13103

Borker, S. A., Venugopalan, P. P., & Bhat, S. N. (2013). Study of menopausal symptoms, and perceptions about menopause among women at a rural community in Kerala. *Journal of Midlife Health, 4*(3), 182–187. doi:10.4103/0976-7800.118997

Boxwala, F. I., Bridgemohan, A., Griffith, D. M., & Soliman, A. S. (2010). Factors associated with breast cancer screening in Asian Indian women in metro-Detroit. *Journal of Immigrant and Minority Health, 12*(4), 534–543. doi:10.1007/s10903-009-9277-0

Brar, S., Tang, S., Drummond, N., Palacios-Derflingher, L., Clark, V., John, M., & Ross, S. (2009). Perinatal care for South Asian immigrant women and women born in Canada: Telephone survey of users. *Journal of Obstetrics & Gynaecology Canada, 31*(8), 708–716.

Bundey, S., & Alam, H. (1993). A five-year prospective study of the health of children in different ethnic groups, with particular reference to the effect of inbreeding. *European Journal of Human Genetics, 1*(3), 206–219.

Butts, S. F., & Seifer, D. B. (2010). Racial and ethnic differences in reproductive potential across the life cycle. *Fertility and Sterility, 93*(3), 681–690. doi:http://dx.doi.org/10.1016/j.fertnstert.2009.10.047

Chapple, A. (1998). Iron deficiency anaemia in women of South Asian descent: A qualitative study. *Ethnicity & Health, 3*(3), 199–212. doi:10.1080/13557858.1998.9961862

Chattha, R., Raghuram, N., Venkatram, P., & Hongasandra, N. R. (2008). Treating the climacteric symptoms in Indian women with an integrated approach to yoga therapy: A randomized control study. *Menopause, 15*(5), 862–870. doi:10.1097/gme.0b013e318167b902

Centers for Disease Control and Prevention (CDC) (2013, August 13). *National ART Success Rates.* Retrieved from https://www.sartcorsonline.com/rptCSR_PublicMultYear.aspx?ClinicPKID=0

Coleman, L. M., & Testa, A. (2008). Sexual health knowledge, attitudes and behaviours: Variations among a religiously diverse sample of young people in London, UK. *Ethnicity & Health, 13*(1), 55–72. doi:10.1080/13557850701803163

Darling, A. L., Hakim, O. A., Horton, K., Gibbs, M. A., Cui, L., Berry, J. L., ... Hart, K. H. (2013). Adaptations in tibial cortical thickness and total volumetric bone density in postmenopausal South Asian women with small bone size. *Bone, 55*(1), 36–43. doi:10.1016/j.bone.2013.03.006

Darling, A. L., Hart, K. H., Macdonald, H. M., Horton, K., Kang'ombe, A. R., Berry, J. L., & Lanham-New, S. A. (2013). Vitamin D deficiency in UK South Asian Women of childbearing age: A comparative longitudinal investigation with UK Caucasian women. *Osteoporos is International, 24*(2), 477–488. doi:10.1007/s00198-012-1973-2

De Alba, I., Ngo-Metzger, Q., Sweningson, J. M., & Hubbell, F. A. (2005). Pap smear use in California: Are we closing the racial/ethnic gap? *Preventive Medicine, 40*(6), 747–755. doi:10.1016/j.ypmed.2004.09.018

Deepak, A.C. (2005). Parenting and the process of migration: Possibilities within South Asian families. *Child Welfare, 84*(5), 585–606.

Douglas, N. (2012). Befriending breastfeeding: A home-based antenatal pilot for south Asian families. *Community Practitioner, 85*(6), 28–31.

Farid, H., Siddique, S. M., Bachmann, G., Janevic, T., & Pichika, A. (2013). Practice of and attitudes towards family planning among South Asian American immigrants. *Contraception, 88*(4), 518–522. doi:10.1016/j.contraception.2013.03.011

Fauser, B. C., Tarlatzis, B. C., Rebar, R. W., Legro, R. S., Balen, A. H., Lobo, R., ... Barnhart, K. (2012). Consensus on women's health aspects of polycystic ovary syndrome (PCOS): The Amsterdam ESHRE/ASRM-Sponsored 3rd PCOS Consensus Workshop Group. *Fertility and Sterility, 97*(1), 28–38.e25. doi:10.1016/j.fertnstert.2011.09.024

Fenton, K. A., Mercer, C. H., McManus, S., Erens, B., Wellings, K., Macdowall, W., ... Johnson, A. M. (2005). Ethnic variations in sexual behaviour in Great Britain and risk of sexually transmitted infections: A probability survey. *Lancet, 365*(9466), 1246–1255. doi:10.1016/s0140-6736(05)74813-3

Fischbacher, C., Bhopal, R., Patel, S., White, M., Unwin, N., & Alberti, K. G. (2001). Anaemia in Chinese, South Asian, and European populations in Newcastle upon Tyne: Cross sectional study. *British Medical Journal, 322*(7292), 958–959.

Fisher, J. A., Bowman, M., & Thomas, T. (2003). Issues for South Asian Indian patients surrounding sexuality, fertility, and childbirth in the US health care system. *The Journal of the American Board of Family Practice, 16*(2), 151–155.

Fransen, M. P., Wildschut, H. I., Vogel, I., Mackenbach, J. P., Steegers, E. A., & Essink-Bot, M. L. (2009). Ethnic differences in considerations whether or not to participate in prenatal screening for Down syndrome. *Prenatal Diagnosis, 29*(13), 1262–1269. doi:10.1002/pd.2391

Glenn, B. A., Chawla, N., Surani, Z., & Bastani, R. (2009). Rates and sociodemographic correlates of cancer screening among South Asians. *Journal of Community Health, 34*(2), 113–121. doi:10.1007/s10900-008-9129-1

Goel, M. K., & Kundan, M. (2011). Psycho-social behaviour of urban indian adolescent girls during menstruation. *Australasian Medical Journal, 4*(1), 49–52. doi:10.4066/amj.2011.534

Gomez, S. L., Tan, S., Keegan, T. H., & Clarke, C. A. (2007). Disparities in mammographic screening for Asian women in California: A cross-sectional analysis to identify meaningful groups for targeted intervention. *BMC Cancer, 7*, 201. doi:10.1186/1471-2407-7-201

Gooneratne, P. (2013). Commentary on guidelines on postmenopausal osteoporosis—Indian Menopause Society. *Journal of Midlife Health, 4*(2), 133–135.

Griffiths, C., Prost, A., & Hart, G. (2008). Sexual and reproductive health of South Asians in the UK: An overview. *Journal of Family Planning and Reproductive Health Care, 34*(4), 251–260.

Harding, S., Maynard, M., Cruickshank, J. K., & Gray, L. (2006). Anthropometry and blood pressure differences in black Caribbean, African, South Asian and white adolescents: The MRC DASH study. *Journal of Hypertension, 24*(8), 1507–1514. doi:10.1097/01.hjh.0000239285.20315.4d

Hasnain, M., Menon, U., Szalacha, L., Ferrans, C. E. (2014) Breast cancer screening practices among first-generation immigrant Muslim women. *Journal of Women's Health (Larchmt)*, Jul;23(7):602-12. doi: 10.1089/jwh.2013.4569. Epub 2014 May 27.

Hunter, M. S., Gupta, P., Papitsch-Clark, A., & Sturdee, D. W. (2009). Mid-aged health in women from the Indian subcontinent (MAHWIS): A further quantitative and qualitative investigation of experience of menopause in UK Asian women, compared to UK Caucasian women and women living in Delhi. *Climacteric, 12*(1), 26–37. doi:10.1080/13697130802556304

Islam, N., Kwon, S. C., Senie, R., & Kathuria, N. (2006). Breast and cervical cancer screening among South Asian women in New York City. *Journal of Immigrant and Minority Health, 8*(3), 211–221. doi:10.1007/s10903-006-9325-y

Johansson, T., & Ritzén, E. M. (2005). Very long-term follow-up of girls with early and late menarche. *Endocrine Development, 8*, 126–136.

Kabra, S. K., Kabra, M., Lodha, R., & Shastri, S. (2007). Cystic fibrosis in India. *Pediatric Pulmonology, 42*(12), 1087–1094.

Kakkar, V., Kaur, D., Chopra, K., Kaur, A., & Kaur, I. P. (2007). Assessment of the variation in menopausal symptoms with age, education and working/non-working status in north-Indian sub population using menopause rating scale (MRS). *Maturitas, 57*(3), 306–314. doi:10.1016/j.maturitas.2007.02.026

Kaplowitz, P. B., Slora, E. J., Wasserman, R. C., Pedlow, S. E., & Herman-Giddens, M. E. (2001). Earlier onset of puberty in girls: Relation to increased body mass index and race. *Pediatrics, 108*(2), 347–353. doi:10.1542/peds.108.2.347

Kandula, N. R., & Lauderdale, D. S. (2005). Leisure time, non-leisure time, and occupational physical activity in Asian Americans. *Annals of Epidemiology, 15*(4), 257–265. doi:http://dx.doi.org/10.1016/j.annepidem.2004.06.006

Kapur, P., Sinha, B., & Pereira, B. M. (2009). Measuring climacteric symptoms and age at natural menopause in an Indian population using the Greene Climacteric Scale. *Menopause, 16*(2), 378–384. doi:10.1097/gme.0b013e31818a2be9

Khan, N., Benson, J., Macleod, R., & Kingston, H. (2010). Developing and evaluating a culturally appropriate genetic service for consanguineous South Asian families. *Journal of Community Genetics, 1*(2), 73–81. doi:10.1007/s12687-010-0012-2

Khandelwal, S., Chandra, M., & Lo, J. C. (2012). Clinical characteristics, bone mineral density and non-vertebral osteoporotic fracture outcomes among postmenopausal U.S. South Asian Women. *Bone, 51*(6), 1025–1028. doi:10.1016/j.bone.2012.08.118

Kriplani, A., & Banerjee, K. (2005). An overview of age of onset of menopause in northern India. *Maturitas, 52*(3-4), 199–204. doi:10.1016/j.maturitas.2005.02.001

Kudesia, R., Illions, E. H., & Lieman, H. J. (2016). Elevated prevalence of polycystic ovary syndrome and cardiometabolic disease in South Asian infertility patients. *Journal of Immigrant and Minority Health*, epub ahead of print, doi: https://dx.doi.org/10.1007/s10903-016-0454-7

Kumarapeli, V., Seneviratne Rde, A., & Wijeyaratne, C. (2011). Health-related quality of life and psychological distress in polycystic ovary syndrome: A hidden facet in South Asian women. *British Journal of Obstetrics and Gynaecology, 118*(3), 319–328. doi:10.1111/j.1471-0528.2010.02799.x

Lawton, J., Ahmad, N., Hanna, L., Douglas, M., & Hallowell, N. (2006). I can't do any serious exercise: Barriers to physical activity amongst people of Pakistani and Indian origin with Type 2 diabetes. *Health Education Research, 21*(1), 43–54. doi:10.1093/her/cyh042

Lowe, N. M., Mitra, S. R., Foster, P. C., Bhojani, I., & McCann, J. F. (2010). Vitamin D status and markers of bone turnover in Caucasian and South Asian postmenopausal women living in the UK. *British Journal of Nutrition, 103*(12), 1706–1710. doi:10.1017/s0007114509993850

McKee, M. D., O'Sullivan, L. F., & Weber, C. M. (2006). Perspectives on confidential care for adolescent girls. *Annals of Family Medicine, 4*(6), 519–526. doi:10.1370/afm.601

Majumdar, S., Almasi, E., & Stafford, R. (2004). Promotion and prescribing of hormone therapy after report of harm by the Women's Health Initiative. *Journal of the American Medical Association, 292*, 1983–1988. doi:10.1001/jama.292.16.1983

Mehta, J., Kamdar, V., & Dumesic, D. (2013). Phenotypic expression of polycystic ovary syndrome in South Asian women. *Obstetrical and Gynecological Survey, 68*(3), 228–234. doi:10.1097/OGX.0b013e318280a30f

Menon, U., Szalacha, L. A., & Prabhughate, A. (2012). Breast and cervical cancer screening among South Asian immigrants in the United States. *Cancer Nursing,* 35(4), 278–287.

Misra, R., Menon, U., Vadaparampil, S. T., & BeLue, R. (2011). Age-and sex-specific cancer prevention and screening practices among Asian Indian immigrants in the United States. *Journal of Investigative Medicine, 59*(5), 787–792.

Oelke, N. D., & Vollman, A. R. (2007). Inside and outside: Sikh women's perspectives on cervical cancer screening. *Canadian Journal of Nursing Research, 39*(1), 174–189.

Palep-Singh, M., Picton, H. M., Vrotsou, K., Maruthini, D., & Balen, A. H. (2007). South Asian women with polycystic ovary syndrome exhibit greater sensitivity to gonadotropin stimulation with reduced fertilization and ongoing pregnancy rates than their Caucasian counterparts. *European Journal of Obstetrics, Gynecology, and Reproductive Biology, 134*(2), 202–207. doi:10.1016/j.ejogrb.2007.02.005

Patel, M., Phillips-Caesar, E., & Boutin-Foster, C. (2012). Barriers to lifestyle behavioral change in migrant South Asian populations. *Journal of Immigrant and Minority Health, 14*(5), 774–785. doi:10.1007/s10903-011-9550-x

Popkin, B. M., & Udry, J. R. (1998). Adolescent obesity increases significantly in second and third generation U.S. immigrants: The National Longitudinal Study of Adolescent Health. *Journal of Nutrition, 128*(4), 701–706.

Puri, S., Adams, V., Ivey, S., & Nachtigall, R. D. (2011). There is such a thing as too many daughters, but not too many sons: A qualitative study of son preference and fetal sex selection among Indian immigrants in the United States. *Social Science Medicine, 72*(7), 1169–1176.

Rahman, S., Salehin, F., & Iqbal, A. (2011). Menopausal symptoms assessment among middle age women in Kushtia, Bangladesh. *BMC Research Notes, 4,* 188. doi:10.1186/1756-0500-4-188

Rahman, S. M., & Rahman, S. (2008). Breast cancer perceptions, knowledge and behavioral practices among women living in a rural community. *International Journal of Cancer Prevention, 2*(6), 415–425.

Rajashekar, L., Krishna, D., & Patil, M. (2008). Polycystic ovaries and infertility: Our experience. *Journal of Human Reproductive Sciences, 1*(2), 65–72.

Ramakrishnan, K., Junn, J., Lee, T., & Wong, J. (2012). *National Asian American Survey, 2008.* Retrieved from http://doi.org/10.3886/ICPSR31481.v2

Reed, S. D., Lampe, J. W., Qu, C., Copeland, W. K., Gundersen, G., Fuller, S., & Newton, K. M. (2014). Premenopausal vasomotor symptoms in an ethnically diverse population. *Menopause, 21*(2), 153–158. doi:10.1097/GME.0b013e3182952228

Rodin, D. A., Bano, G., Bland, J. M., Taylor, K., & Nussey, S. S. (1998). Polycystic ovaries and associated metabolic abnormalities in Indian subcontinent Asian women. *Clinical Endocrinology (Oxford), 49*(1), 91–99.

Sadler, G. R., Dhanjal, S. K., Shah, N. B., Shah, R. B., Ko, C., Anghel, M., & Harshburger, R. (2001). Asian Indian women: Knowledge, attitudes and behaviors toward breast cancer early detection. *Public Health Nursing, 18*(5), 357–363.

Saxena, S., Copas, A. J., Mercer, C., Johnson, A. M., Fenton, K., Erens, B., ... Wellings, K. (2006). Ethnic variations in sexual activity and contraceptive use: National cross-sectional survey. *Contraception, 74*(3), 224–233. doi:10.1016/j.contraception.2006.03.025

Sethi, K., & Pitkin, J. (2000). British-Asian women's views on and attitudes towards menopause and hormone replacement therapy. *Climacteric, 3*(4), 248–253.

Shahine, L. K., Lamb, J. D., Lathi, R. B., Milki, A. A., Langen, E., & Westphal, L. M. (2009). Poor prognosis with in vitro fertilization in Indian women compared to Caucasian women despite similar embryo quality. *PLoS One, 4*(10), e7599. doi:10.1371/journal.pone.0007599

Shakil, A., Gimpel, N. E., Rizvi, H., Siddiqui, Z., Ohagi, E., Billmeier, T. M., & Foster, B. (2010). Awareness and prevention of osteoporosis among South Asian women. *Journal of Community Health, 35*(4), 392–397. doi:10.1007/s10900-010-9263-4

Sharma, K. (1990). Age at menarche in northwest Indian females and a review of Indian data. *Annals of Human Biology, 17*(2), 159–162.

Shaw, N. J., Crabtree, N. J., Kibirige, M. S., & Fordham, J. N. (2007). Ethnic and gender differences in body fat in British schoolchildren as measured by DXA. *Archives of Disease in Childhood, 92*(10), 872–875. doi:10.1136/adc.2007.117911

Singh, M. (2012). Early age of natural menopause in India, a biological marker for early preventive health programs. *Climacteric, 15*(6), 581–586. doi:10.3109/13697137.2011.643514

Sinha, S., Curtis, K., Jayakody, A., Viner, R., & Roberts, H. (2006). Family and peer networks in intimate and sexual relationships amongst teenagers in a multicultural area of East London. *Sociological Research Online, 11*(1). Retrieved from http://www.socresonline.org.uk/11/1/sinha/sinha.pdf

South Asian Americans Leading Together. (2015). *A demographic snapshot of South Asians in the United States*. Retrieved from http://saalt.org/wp-content/uploads/2016/01/Demographic-Snapshot-updated_Dec-2015.pdf

Spencer, K., Heath, V., El-Sheikhah, A., Ong, C. Y., & Nicolaides, K. H. (2005). Ethnicity and the need for correction of biochemical and ultrasound markers of chromosomal anomalies in the first trimester: A study of Oriental, Asian and Afro-Caribbean populations. *Prenatal Diagnosis, 25*(5), 365–369. doi:10.1002/pd.1153

Sriskantharajah, J., & Kai, J. (2007). Promoting physical activity among South Asian women with coronary heart disease and diabetes: What might help? *Family Practice, 24*(1), 71–76. doi:10.1093/fampra/cml066

Stefanopoulou, E., Shah, D., Shah, R., Gupta, P., Sturdee, D. W., & Hunter, M. S. (2013). An International Menopause Society study of Climate, Altitude, Temperature (IMS-CAT) and vasomotor symptoms in urban Indian regions. *Climacteric, 14*(4), 417–424. doi:10.3109/13697137.2013.852169

Styne, D. M. (2004). Puberty, obesity and ethnicity. *Trends in Endocrinology and Metabolism, 15*(10), 472–478. doi:10.1016/j.tem.2004.10.008

Tirodkar, M. A., Baker, D. W., Makoul, G. T., Khurana, N., Paracha, M. W., & Kandula, N. R. (2011). Explanatory models of health and disease among South Asian immigrants in Chicago. *Journal of Immigrant and Minority Health, 13*(2), 385–394. doi:10.1007/s10903-009-9304-1

Wani, R. J., & Gupta, A. S. (2013). Money & Menopause: The relationship between socioeconomic class and awareness about menopause in women in Mumbai, India. *Journal of Obstetrics and Gynaecology of India, 63*(3), 199–202. doi:10.1007/s13224-012-0323-9

Wijeyaratne, C. N., Balen, A. H., Barth, J. H., & Belchetz, P. E. (2002). Clinical manifestations and insulin resistance (IR) in polycystic ovary syndrome (PCOS) among South Asians and Caucasians: Is there a difference? *Clinical Endocrinology (Oxford), 57*(3), 343–350.

Wijeyaratne, C. N., Seneviratne Rde, A., Dahanayake, S., Kumarapeli, V., Palipane, E., Kuruppu, N., ... Balen, A. H. (2011). Phenotype and metabolic profile of South Asian women with polycystic ovary syndrome (PCOS): Results of a large database from a specialist endocrine clinic. *Human Reproduction, 26*(1), 202–213. doi:10.1093/humrep/deq310

Wong, V. W. (2012). Gestational diabetes mellitus in five ethnic groups: A comparison of their clinical characteristics. *Diabetic Medicine, 29*(3), 366–371. doi:10.1111/j.1464-5491.2011.03439.x

Wu, T., Mendola, P., & Buck, G. M. (2002). Ethnic differences in the presence of secondary sex characteristics and menarche among US girls: The Third National Health and Nutrition Examination Survey, 1988–1994. *Pediatrics, 110*(4), 752–757.

Wu, T. Y., West, B., Chen, Y. W., & Hergert, C. (2006). Health beliefs and practices related to breast cancer screening in Filipino, Chinese and Asian-Indian women. *Cancer Detection and Prevention, 30*(1), 58–66.

Chapter 10

Lesbian, Gay, Bisexual, Transgender, and Questioning (LGBTQ) Health

Sindhura Kodali, Monideepa Becerra, and Ken Coelho

Contents

---

* In this chapter, the term LGBTQ will be used as an umbrella term, to capture the broad range of identities and behaviors among sexual and gender minorities, including lesbian/bisexual women, gay/bisexual men, transgender, and questioning people.

Abstract

Objective: To review the available literature on South Asian American (SAA) lesbian, gay, bisexual, transgender, and questioning (LGBTQ) individuals living in the United States, including the primary health issues that affect this population. Recommendations to effectively address the health needs of this subpopulation of SAAs are provided.

Key Findings: While a review of the literature revealed that the health concerns of SAA LGBTQ individuals are generally similar to those of the general population, a unique set of psychosocial concerns was also found in relation to this group. These include heterosexism, homophobia and internalized homophobia, racism, barriers to acculturation, and specific cultural pressures such as internalized heterosexism, all of which collectively influence their health status. These concerns also create barriers to self-identification and health-seeking behaviors which, in turn, may create specific health risks for this subpopulation of SAAs. This is most commonly seen in the areas of mental health, sexually transmitted infection screening and treatment, interpersonal violence, and utilization of preventive health services.

Recommendations: Community and grassroots organizations should continue to spearhead advocacy and training in order to increase awareness of and access to services for the SAA LGBTQ population. Service agencies and healthcare providers can play a valuable role by receiving and offering culturally appropriate training, improving education and outreach, and establishing psychosocial support services.

Introduction

While the body of literature regarding the health of lesbian, gay, bisexual, transgender, and questioning (LGBTQ) people living in the United States has continued to grow, there remains a gap in the literature focusing on this group within the South Asian American (SAA) population. Though their health needs likely parallel those of the larger LGBTQ population, the combination of being both a racial and sexual minority poses unique challenges and leads to different health outcomes (McKeown, Nelson, Anderson, Low, & Elford, 2010).

Although the exact number of South Asians living in the United States and identifying as LGBTQ is unknown, a rough extrapolation can be derived from statistical models that have been used to estimate the national percentage of individuals who are LGBTQ Asian Pacific Islanders (APIs). Lieb et al. (2011) used statistical modeling to develop state-by-state and national estimates of particular demographics related to men who have sex with men (MSM). They calculated that, of an estimated 7.1 million MSM residing in the United States in 2007, 2.7% were APIs. Additional information on how many of these men are SAAs can be derived from the national survey of API LGBTQ individuals in the United States conducted by Dang and Vianney (2007). This is the largest survey conducted on this group and includes data from 860 respondents from 38 states. Of these, approximately 20% were identified as Asian Indian, Pakistani, Sri Lankan, or Bangladeshi, with the distribution of individual groups reflecting similar trends of API groups reported in Census data (Dang & Vianney, 2007). This gives us an estimate of 50,000–100,000 South Asian LGBTQ individuals living in the United States. The survey also found that respondents resided primarily in California (37%), the greater New York area (18%), Chicago (5%), Boston (5%), and Washington, DC (4%), which tend to correlate with dense SAA populations (Dang & Vianney, 2007).

Because the sample in this survey over-represents US-born and naturalized citizens, it likely fails to capture accurate numbers of immigrant APIs and, by corollary, SAA LGBTQ individuals. Thus, the actual numbers of SAA LGBTQ men and women are likely higher than estimates suggest. Such limited quantitative data highlight the need for continued collection of disaggregated demographic data in order to better characterize the actual population. As such, this chapter aims to identify key findings from current research related to the health of SAA LGBTQ people living in the United States. This includes a review of the scientific literature and additional resources including surveys administered by community-based organizations, as well as information from relevant websites.

Defining LGBTQ in the SAA Context

A major challenge in conducting research and writing about SAAs who identify as LGBTQ is defining the term LGBTQ in the South Asian context. In 2011, the University of Chicago hosted a roundtable discussion on *Sexual Identity, Health and Stigma in India: Traditional Statuses and Western Influences* (University of Chicago, 2011). Experts involved in this roundtable discussion noted that the standard Western heterosexual/homosexual dichotomy did not align with norms in India where terms such as "the other" or *Hijra** are utilized. Because

---

* *Hijra* is a term used in South Asia—to refer to transwomen (male-to-female transsexual or transgender individuals).

this concept may also apply to other South Asian countries, the traditional Western categorization might make it difficult for SAA immigrants to identify according to Western definitions of sexual minority identities. Roundtable participants also found this to be true for the term MSM, which has been viewed as an unknown term, thus further escalating the difficulty of identifying the SAA LGBTQ population.

Adherence to the Asian culture has also been shown to be negatively associated with internalized heterosexism, defined as a system of attitudes, bias, and discrimination in favor of opposite-sex sexuality and relationships (Szymanski & Sung, 2010). Subsequently, researchers have found that those with low internalized heterosexism, and thus presumably adherence to Asian cultural norms were more likely to disclose their sexual orientation (Szymanski & Sung, 2010). Fundamentally, SAA LGBTQ individuals may not be as open to disclosing their orientation, making the population difficult to define and quantify.

The term LGBTQ has no single definition and encompasses a broad community of individuals with unique identities and experiences. For the purposes of discussing health outcomes, LGBTQ will be used to refer to individuals who self-identify a sexual orientation or attraction toward the same sex or both sexes. The term transgender includes those who identify with a gender that is different from their sex at birth (Committee on Lesbian, Gay, Bisexual, and Transgender Health Issues and Research, Gaps and Opportunities; Board on the Health of Select Populations; Institute of Medicine, 2011). The authors recognize that sexual orientation does not necessarily translate to behavior and behavior does not necessarily translate to sexual orientation, particularly for those who do not openly disclose their orientation. For the purposes of discussing health outcomes, it will be assumed that the SAA LGBTQ population shares similar risks as other LGBTQ populations, particularly those comprised of ethnic minorities. This assumption includes the caveat that in certain populations who engage in particular sexual behaviors without identifying as LGBTQ, such as MSM, the risks may be even higher.

Key Health Issues

Mental Health

Qualitative research on the health of LGBTQ individuals in general has identified key mental health issues that commonly affect the LGBTQ population, including major depression and anxiety disorders (Clements-Nolle, Marx, Guzman, & Katz, 2001; Meyer & Northridge, 2007; Mayer et al., 2008; Wolitski, Stall, & Valdiserri, 2008). Although there is little information specifically about SAA LGBTQ individuals, the minority stress model offers a useful framework to consider the impact of belonging to a racial minority while also being LGBTQ in America, particularly with regard to mental health (Meyer, 1995). This theoretical framework, previously outlined by Virginia Brooks, posits that "membership in a stigmatized group exposes individuals to chronic stressors and may predispose minority group members to a variety of mental health concerns" (Brooks, 1981). In this research, Meyer (1995) also identified three specific processes thought to contribute to higher rates of mental illness in minority groups: (1) internalized negative attitudes and stereotypes regarding one's minority status, (2) expectations of stigma from the environment, and (3) actual prejudicial events.

Minority stress constructs have been shown empirically to be associated with social anxiety in gay men (Burns, Kamen, Lehman, & Beach, 2012). In a 2007 report on LGBTQ APIs, the National LGBTQ Task Force found that an overwhelming majority of respondents experienced verbal harassment at one time in their lives for being of API descent (77%) or LGBT (74%) (Dang & Vianney, 2007). This report lends further credence to the concept of dual stress that can potentially lead to adverse mental health outcomes for LGBTQ individuals of South Asian descent. More recently, an in-depth analysis of minority stress in the SAA LGBTQ population found that participants experienced more racist events and heterosexism, as well as internalized heterosexism, and reported higher levels of psychological distress (Sandil, Robinson, Brewster, Wong, & Geiger, 2015). This finding correlates with findings in API communities where racist events and heterosexism, both internalized and external, positively correlated with psychological distress (Szymanski & Sung, 2010; Yoshikawa, Wilson, Chae, & Cheng, 2004). The analysis also found that SAA LGBTQ individuals experienced stressors similar to other LGBTQ groups, particularly LGBTQ API individuals, and other groups of color (Sandil et al., 2015).

In 2006, the *Southern California South Asian Lesbian, Gay, Bisexual, Transgender, Intersex, Queer, and Questioning (LGBTIQ) South Asian Needs Assessment* was conducted (Satrang and South Asian Network, 2006). The assessment involved a survey of a volunteer-driven snowball sample of 80 participants regarding social and health issues and found that 90% of respondents experienced mental health issues, including suicidal ideation and substance abuse, while 45% experienced suicidal thoughts, 36% experienced abuse from family members, and 34% engaged in unsafe sex. More than two-thirds of the survey respondents reported feelings of loneliness and isolation and felt like they were leading a "double life." Younger respondents (17–25 years old) were substantially more likely to have experienced mental health issues (100%) and suicidal thoughts (85%) than those 26–40 years old (94% and 38%, respectively) or those 41 years and older (75% and 35%, respectively). A greater proportion of US-born respondents reported experiencing suicidal thoughts, abuse from family members, and sexual assault, as compared to immigrant respondents, though this finding may be limited by their willingness to report. These findings suggest a potential unmet mental health need in the SAA LGBTQ population. However, given the small sample size, these results should be extrapolated to larger populations with caution (Satrang and South Asian Network, 2006).

In 2013, a study on mental health in minority MSM in California found a positive association between anxiety and perceived racism within the LGBTQ API community that did not appear to exist for African Americans or Latinos (Choi, Paul, Ayala, Boylan, & Gregorich, 2013). Interestingly, API MSM were also more likely to report racism within the gay community than were African American and Latino MSM. It can be extrapolated from these findings that varying cultural contexts are likely to interact differently with the experiences of racism, heterosexism, and perceived homophobia. Ultimately, this can precipitate psychological distress, depression, and anxiety in SAA LGBTQ individuals.

Data on API lesbian and bisexual women also suggest an increased incidence of depression and suicidal behaviors. In a Boston-based study, Lee and Hahm (2012) found the proportion of lifetime suicidal ideation to be double among lesbian and bisexual API women when compared with heterosexual API women (15% vs. 31%). They also found the proportion of lifetime suicide attempts was substantially greater (5.8% vs. 13.2%) in the lesbian and bisexual API group. These results are consistent with findings from the National Latino and Asian American Survey that reported a higher prevalence of suicide in lesbian and bisexual API women when compared with non-API heterosexual women (Cochran, Mays, Alegria, Ortega, & Takeuchi, 2007). It is important to note that these data are not specific to SAA lesbian women or even to SAA LGBTQ women. However, because the strongest predictor of suicide is a previous attempt any findings suggestive of increased suicidality or suicide attempts within a certain population are important for clinicians and mental health practitioners to consider when treating these populations and certainly warrants further investigation (Haukka, Suominen, Partonen, & Lönnqvist, 2008).

Substance Abuse

Despite the lack of specific quantitative data, substance abuse disorders remain a significant health concern among LGBTQ people in general and is an area of additional concern among SAA LGBTQ individuals. LGBTQ individuals who experience perceived discrimination often display higher levels of substance abuse, including binge drinking, and have a greater likelihood of being a smoker with a greater number of cigarettes smoked per day (Burgess, Lee, Tran, & van Ryn, 2008). In the Southern California LGBTIQ South Asian Needs Assessment Survey, 29% of respondents reported having experienced issues with alcohol, tobacco, or other drugs (Satrang and South Asian Network, 2006).

Of these, 52% reported seeking help for this problem with shame or embarrassment, being unsure as to whether they had a problem, or not knowing where to look for help if they did believe they had a problem with substance abuse.

Among Lesbian and bisexual API women, Lee and Hahm (2012) found greater odds of doing hard drugs, smoking marijuana, or binge drinking (1.5–3 times higher) than their heterosexual counterparts. Here again, while there were no SAA women included in the study, this finding may extend to this population given the similar implications of mental health, depression, and gender on substance abuse. The findings are also consistent with other studies of substance abuse behavior among lesbian and bisexual women, which suggest it may indeed apply and certainly should be kept in mind by health-care professionals when considering baseline risk (Cochran & Cauce, 2006; Drabble & Trocki, 2005; Stevens, 2012).

Intimate Partner Violence

Intimate partner violence (IPV) is a pervasive problem in the general API and SAA community and is also a major concern in the general and SAA LGBTQ communities. Rates of IPV on LGBTQ individuals are equal to or higher than those seen in heterosexual relationships. This is due to a number of factors, including minority stress (e.g., internalized homonegativity), reluctance to seek help, difficulty leaving an abusive relationship, and difficulty disclosing orientation and openly discussing same-sex relationships with friends and family (Edwards, Sylaska, & Neal, 2015). Common characteristics of IPV in the API LGBTQ population include perpetrators who use control, intimidation, and fear; sexual jealousy and possessiveness; shaming; and, for victims, limited access to social and community networks (Kanuha, 2013).

Studies on IPV in the South Asian LGBTQ community are significantly lacking. The few that do exist identify several challenges and barriers to health care for victims of IPV in the South Asian, API, and general LGBTQ communities throughout North America. These include society, self, family, relationships, the external environment, structure of society or institutions, the legal system, stigma, anti-homosexuality, and inequity. In 2010, St. Pierre and Senn (2010) conducted a descriptive mixed-methods study using a sample of 280 LGBTQ individuals who were living in Canada and were victims of IPV. The study highlighted three key barriers to help-seeking behavior: (1) non-disclosure or suppression of LGBTQ status, (2) lack of available LGBTQ-specific services for victims of IPV, and (3) the perception of a lower understanding of LGBTQ issues within mainstream services, exacerbated by homophobia and heterosexism in society.

In a more recent study, researchers also identified three major barriers for LGBTQ individuals seeking help for IPV: (1) lack of knowledge or understanding of IPV in the LGBTQ community, (2) the stigma of homosexuality or being associated with a member of the LGBTQ community, and (3) inequality in the criminal justice system (Calton, Cattaneo, & Gebhard, 2015). Also in 2015, Parry and O'Neal found major barriers for LGBTQ IPV victims who sought care via social services. These included relationship, societal, institutional, and legal barriers. Other studies on IPV in the LGBTQ population have identified isolation as a serious barrier for victims seeking help (Bornstein, Fawcett, Sullivan, Senturia, & Shiu-Thornton, 2006; Calton et al., 2015). Again, while these findings are not specific to South Asian populations, they do represent important IPV issues for the LGBTQ community as a whole, hence, they likely play a role in SAA LGBTQ relationships as well.

There is a clear need for interventions and services to address barriers to seeking care and services for LGBTQ IPV survivors. These also must be culturally appropriate and accessible. Duke and Davidson (2009) recommend that agencies providing LGBTQ IPV-specific services to victims of IPV should identify themselves as being inclusive agencies. More high-quality research is required in the South Asian LGBTQ population that can provide a basis for understanding the key challenges and barriers to seeking healthcare services, as well as the intersection of ethnicity, gender, and sexual identity for South Asian LGBTQ victims of IPV (Inman, Devdas, Spektor, & Pendse, 2014).

Sexually Transmitted Infections

One of the most significant health challenges facing the LGBTQ community is the impact of sexually transmitted infections (STIs), most notably the HIV/AIDS epidemic. Specific data among the SAA LGBTQ population have, however, been sparse. Existing data from Canada and the United Kingdom point to higher rates of high-risk sexual behavior in this group, which may also warrant an increased clinical index of suspicion and additional screening. In the United Kingdom, a study on black and minority ethnic (BME) MSM, which specifically evaluated South Asian subsets, found that BME populations as a whole reported higher rates of unprotected anal intercourse than their White MSM counterparts (Soni, Bond, Fox, Grieve, & Sethi, 2008). These trends remained similar across minority subsets, including South Asians, although prior studies have suggested that South Asians are less likely to report unprotected anal intercourse (Hickson et al., 2004). Rates of STIs in both BME and White counterparts were similar in the study from the United Kingdom. This suggests that the rate of STIs in South Asian MSM may also be consistent with the rate of STIs in the larger LGBTQ community in the United States, though it is difficult to extrapolate data from the United Kingdom to the United States.

In Canada, a study of sexual behavior in South Asian and European Canadian homosexual men found no difference between the two groups in how likely they were to engage in high-risk behavior such as unprotected anal intercourse (Ratti, Bakeman, & Peterson, 2000). While these findings do not provide clear quantitative information on rates of STIs, they do suggest that trends within South Asian subsets of these groups may in fact parallel those of the larger community. Still, these findings must be interpreted in the context of STI prevalence, particularly because HIV prevalence among minority populations is quite different among populations in the United States, United Kingdom, and Canada.

In the United States, there are little demographic data on the rates of specific STIs in the SAA population, but the rates of STIs in API populations may contain some of these data and point to a trend. In 2005, APIs represented 1.1% of all reported AIDS patients in the United States. That same year, the Centers for Disease Control and Prevention (CDC) reported that, among APIs, the number of MSM accounted for 67% of cumulative AIDS cases (CDC, 2008). More recent studies have noted that API MSM engage in high levels of HIV-related risk behaviors, including substance abuse and unprotected anal intercourse (Operario et al., 2006). Surprisingly, HIV prevalence and incidence rates have been much lower among API MSM than rates among the general population, specifically when compared to other racial/ethnic minority MSM. The Urban Men's Health Study found that HIV prevalence was 16% among API MSM in San Francisco compared to 25% among Whites, 38% among Blacks, and 31% among Latinos (Schwarcz et al., 2007). In the larger API population, a 2007 study of approximately 1200 young API adults found that 13% of females and 4% of males had an STI previously (Hahm, Lee, Ozonoff, & Amodeo, 2007). Thus, while the rates of male STI prevalence appear to be consistent with rates among the general population, rates in female APIs were significantly higher. In comparison, however, studies examining rates of STIs in the general population found no marked disparity between men and women in their study groups (Ford, Jaccard, Millstein, Bardsley, & Miller, 2004).

In addition to these demographics, Hahm et al. (2007) found that being of Indian origin was also associated with increased odds of having an STI. Though this research was not specific to the LGBTQ community, the identification of a correlation between Indian origin and having an STI is new and worth noting, especially when considering STIs in SAA populations. Hahm et al. (2007) also postulated that ethnic differences in rates of STIs may be related to the rapid rise of documented cases of HIV in India over the last several decades, which coincides with the rapid rise of the Indian immigrant population in the

United States, which grew 124% from 1990 to 2000, and the frequent rates of travel between the United States and India. This hypothesis needs more robust analysis and comparison with data from other populations, but it is worth noting for both clinicians and future researchers that it is a point that requires further exploration.

Studies also indicate that APIs are more likely than all other ethnic groups in the United States to be diagnosed with AIDS at the time of HIV testing (Wong, Campsmith, Nakamura, Crepaz, & Begley, 2004). In fact, up to 45.6% of APIs in the United States with AIDS cite an opportunistic infection such as *Pneumocystis carinii* pneumonia as their initial presenting problem (CDC, 2002; Eckholdt, Chin, Manzon-Santos, & Kim, 1997; Wong et al., 2004). In 2011, this finding was further corroborated by data collected from 2001–2008 which found an increase in HIV diagnoses among APIs compared to other ethnic minorities, as well as a shorter HIV to AIDS interval, particularly among API MSM (Adih, Campsmith, Williams, Hardnett, & Hughes, 2011). Delay in presentation, diagnosis, and treatment among APIs are consistent with general trends indicating that healthcare access, presentation, diagnosis, and treatment are often delayed, particularly with respect to stigmatized diseases such as STIs. It is therefore reasonable to suspect that similar trends may exist regarding STIs among the South Asian LGBTQ population.

Other important trends regarding HIV in the API LGBTQ population do exist. Although difficult to interpret without larger context, they are worth mentioning as possible areas of research and data collection in the future. In a study of sexual behaviors of MSM from different minority groups, API men displayed higher rates of condom use when compared to men from other minority backgrounds (Calabrese, Rosenberger, Schick, Novak, & Reece, 2013). Lesbian and bisexual API women showed a significantly higher risk for HIV than exclusively heterosexual Asian American women, as evidenced by higher rates of multiple sex partners, anal sex, sex while drinking or taking drugs, and sex with high-risk sexual partners (Lee & Hahm, 2012). Though these studies examined small cohorts, the findings are consistent with larger trends within the LGBTQ community, suggesting that they may also point to important health trends in STIs in the South Asian LGBTQ population.

Barriers to Care

General health needs, particularly with respect to preventive health and screening, are not vastly different in the SAA LGBTQ population versus the larger SAA population. Barriers to accessing care do, however, exist and can include limited language proficiency, fear of the medical establishment, and stigma associated with disclosing sexual orientation to family members or health-care providers. Together, these barriers likely play a role in the SAA LGBTQ population accessing healthcare resources less often than other vulnerable populations who are without the fear of sexual orientation stigmatization.

In 2006, the *Southern California LGBTIQ South Asian Needs Assessment Survey* (Satrang and South Asian Network) provided one of the first comprehensive evaluations of this population. Results showed that while much of the study population reported being "out" to immediate family, friends, or healthcare providers, they were less likely to be open about their sexual identity to the larger community (religions/spiritual or ethnic) or extended family. Interestingly, most young respondents (under 26 years of age) reported not being "out" to anyone, including healthcare professionals. This is the opposite of what was found in the general LGBTQ population in the United States, where younger populations were more likely to be "out" than older populations (Williams, 2010). This finding further demonstrates a significant public health concern for the young SAA LGBTQ community who may be more likely to lack adequate care or access to services because they are not able to openly discuss their sexuality. Also of note is that older SAA LGBTQ respondents were more likely to report feeling alienated by the South Asian community than younger respondents. One in four respondents also reported being alienated and friends were cited as a source of emotional support (Satrang and South Asian Network, 2006).

Results such as these highlight the need for culturally competent social support programs for the SAA LGBTQ community in order to ensure they are receiving adequate mental health support (Satrang and South Asian Network, 2006). Researchers have also found significant disparities in terms of access to and utilization of healthcare. While nearly 80% of respondents reported having access to mental health services, only 30% reported using such services, with a higher percent being those born in the United States as opposed to their foreign-born counterparts (Satrang and South Asian Network, 2006). Such trends highlight an imperative need to increase mental health service utilization within the community, particularly the firstgeneration immigrants.

Access to reproductive health care is also critical. Despite California's Family PACT initiative to provide free access to reproductive health care, only three-quarters of the women studied in the South Asian Needs Assessment Survey reported having access and less than two-thirds reported utilization of reproductive health care (Satrang and South Asian Network, 2006). Undoubtedly, public health efforts for the SAA LGBTQ community are much needed, with a particular need for adequate reproductive health care for women. While such efforts are in place, few are specifically targeted toward the South Asian LGBTQ population which represents yet another area of unmet need.

Similar trends were identified with regard to access and utilization of HIV and other STI testing. The survey noted that 40% of the population who had access reported such testing in the past year (Satrang and South Asian Network, 2006). Younger South Asian LGBTQ individuals reported even lower trends of healthcare utilization, as did those without a college degree (Satrang and South Asian Network, 2006). Given that younger LGBTQ members of the South Asian population reported a lower likelihood of being "out," even to healthcare professionals, such results on the lack of adequate HIV/STI screening warrants further public health efforts to increase the use of such services (Satrang and South Asian Network, 2006). The researchers further noted a higher prevalence of HIV among the respondents when compared to the general Asian American population in the area. For example, 6% of the population reported HIV and 2% with another STI, while the HIV rate among the general Asian American population is 2% (CDC, 2015) While the needs assessment such as the one highlighted here is limited to one geographic area, few studies of similar comprehensive assessment of this population exist, and the results have significant implications for the larger South Asian LGBTQ population (Satrang and South Asian Network, 2006).

Adding to this research is the *2008 California Transgender Economic Health Survey* which demonstrated that 11% of the Asian (defined by respondent self-identification) LGBTQ population reported lack of health insurance, with higher rates reported for women as compared to men (Hartzell, Frazer, Wertz, & Davis, 2009). In addition, transgender people reported a significant lack of adequate health insurance, partly due to their transgender status because most health insurance companies do not include transition-related care. Furthermore, despite having health insurance, 42% of transgender people reported delaying care due to financial constraints, while 26% reported that such a delay in care worsened their health though fear of discrimination was not evaluated (Hartzell et al., 2009) While similar large-scale studies of the SAA LGBTQ population are lacking, given the low cultural acceptance and subsequent low social support, similar prevalence is expected in the SAA LGBTQ population.

The recent strike down of Section Three of the Defense of Marriage Act in the United States, which prohibited the federal government from recognizing same-sex marriage, has significant implications for the LGBTQ population, including SAA LGBTQ individuals. In the 2015 landmark case, *Obergefell v. Hodges*, the United States Supreme Court ruled that the fundamental right to marry is guaranteed to same-sex couples and therefore requires all states to issue marriage licenses and recognize same-sex marriages performed in other jurisdictions (Supreme Court of the United States, 2015). This ruling has the potential to improve healthcare access and affords same sex couples the ability to make medical decisions.

Recommendations

The following are a broad set of recommendations to address the gaps in the health status of the SAA LGBTQ population:

- Promote high-quality primary research to provide the basis for understanding the key challenges and barriers to seeking healthcare services, as well as the intersection of ethnicity, gender, and sexual identity for all SAA LGBTQ.
- Increase community-based grassroots programs that focus on reducing stigma, homophobia, and inequities; and address issues related to the legal system for victims of IPV within the SAA LGBTQ population.
- Train healthcare professionals to recognize the range of diversity and provide culturally and linguistically appropriate services to SAA LGBTQ populations.
- Train healthcare professionals who provide services to SAA LGBTQ populations to identify and recognize high-risk issues such as mental health, substance abuse, STIs, and interpersonal violence.
- Provide local and national support for program guidelines that target SAA LGBTQ IPV outreach services and advocacy training.
- Target efforts of community-based programs to promote knowledge and utilization of healthcare services among the SAA LGBTQ population.
- Develop programs to help the SAA LGBTQ population identify healthcare discrimination.
- Create a directory of community resources and organizations for the LGBTQ population in the SAA community.
- Hold national conferences to bring together community organizations and to focus on coordinating efforts related to SAA LGBTQ education, equality, rights, immigration, health, and culture.

Conclusions

The current literature indicates that SAA LGBTQ individuals are significantly understudied. Despite the paucity of data, a review of qualitative studies conducted by community organizations and quantitative information on the general LGBTQ and API LGBTQ populations suggests that the health risks of South Asian LGBTQ individuals largely parallel those of their heterosexual, other non-API LGBTQ and API counterparts. Specific areas of disparity include mental health, substance abuse, interpersonal violence, and heightened risk for sexually transmitted infections, including HIV and AIDS, in the setting of decreased access to preventive screening services.

Such a vulnerable population remains underserved due to the lack of both epidemiologic and social research addressing barriers to adequate health care and in turn resulting in limited data on health disparities in this population.

Factors such as heterosexism, homophobia, and internalized homophobia, racism, acculturation, and specific cultural pressures all work together and lead to specific health disparities in this population. For the South Asian LGBTQ population, this also includes access to healthcare at lower rates as a result of a variety of cultural, financial, and structural barriers such as stigma and unwillingness to disclose sexual orientation. Further research is needed to better understand and address the health needs of this population. While community-based grassroots organizations have driven advocacy and provision of services for this group, continued advocacy is needed to increase support and provision of services to this population.

Community Resources

A number of community resources exist for South Asian LGBTQ people living in the United States:

- Satrang, Los Angeles, CA—www.satrang.org
- API Equality, Los Angeles, CA—apiequalityla.org
- Desi-LGBTQ Hotline (908-FOR-DEQH) (908-367-3374)—deqh.org
- Q&A Space—qaspace.apiequalityla.org
- Trikone, San Francisco Bay Area, CA—www.trikone.org
- Massachusetts Area SA Lambda Association (MASALA), Boston, MA—bostonmasala.wordpress.com
- SA Lesbian and Gay Association (SALGA), New York City and Philadelphia—www.salganyc.org/
- Khush, Texas & Washington, DC—khushtexas.org, khushdc.blogspot.com

References

Adih, W. K., Campsmith, R., Williams, C. L., Hardnett, F. P., & Hughes, D. (2011). Epidemiology of HIV among Asians and Pacific Islanders in the United States, 2001–2008. *Journal of the International Association of Physicians in AIDS Care, 10*(3), 150–159. doi:10.1177/1545109711399805

Bornstein, D. R., Fawcett, J., Sullivan, M., Senturia, K. D., & Shiu-Thornton, S. (2006). Understanding the experiences of lesbian, bisexual and trans survivors of domestic violence: A qualitative study. *Journal of Homosexuality, 51*(1), 159–181.

Brooks, V. R. (1981). *Minority stress and lesbian women.* Lexington, MA: Lexington Books, D.C. Health and Co, Washington, DC. ISBN-10: 0669039535.

Burgess, D., Lee, R., Tran, A., & van Ryn, M. (2008). Effects of perceived discrimination on mental health and mental health services utilization among gay, lesbian, bisexual and transgender persons. *Journal of LGBT Health Research, 3*(4), 1–14. doi:10.1080/15574090802226626

Burns, M. K., Kamen, C., Lehman, K. A., & Beach, S. (2012). Minority stress and attributions for discriminatory events predict social anxiety in gay men. *Cognitive Therapy and Research, 36*, 25–35. doi:10.1007/s10608-010-9302-6

Calabrese, S. K., Rosenberger, J. G., Schick, V. R., Novak, D. S., & Reece, M. (2013). An event-level comparison of risk-related sexual practices between black and other-race men who have sex with men: Condoms, semen, lubricant, and rectal douching. *AIDS Patient Care and STDs, 27*(2), 77–84. doi:10.1089/apc.2012.0355

Calton, J. M., Cattaneo, L. B., & Gebhard, K. T. (2015). Barriers to help seeking for lesbian, gay, bisexual, transgender, and queer survivors of intimate partner violence. *Trauma, Violence & Abuse*, May 15. [Epub ahead of print]1524838015585318. doi:10.1177/1524838015585318

Centers for Disease Control (CDC). (2002). Diagnosis and reporting of HIV and AIDs in states with HIV/AIDS surveillance—United States, 1994–2000. *Morbidity and Mortality Weekly Report, 51*(27), 595–598.

Centers for Disease Control. (2008). *HIV/AIDS among Asians and Pacific Islanders.* Retrieved from www.cdc.gov/hiv/resources/factsheets/PDF/API.pdf

Centers for Disease Control. (2015). *HIV among Asians.* Retrieved from http://www.cdc.gov/hiv/pdf/group/racialethnic/asians/cdc-hiv-asians.pdf

Choi, K., Paul, J., Ayala, G., Boylan, R., & Gregorich, S. E. (2013). Experiences of discrimination and their impact on the mental health among African American, Asian and Pacific Islander, and Latino men who have sex with men. *American Journal of Public Health, 103*(5), 868–874. doi:10.2105/AJPH.2012.301052

Clements-Nolle, K., Marx, R., Guzman, R., & Katz, M. (2001). HIV prevalence, risk behaviors, health care use, and mental health status of transgender persons: Implications for public health interventions. *American Journal of Public Health, 91*(6), 915–921.

Cochran, B. N., & Cauce, A. M. (2006). Characteristics of lesbian, gay, bisexual, and transgender individuals entering substance abuse treatment. *Journal of Substance Abuse Treatment, 30*(2), 135–146.

Cochran, S., Mays, V., Alegria, M., Ortega, A., & Takeuchi, D. (2007). Mental health and substance use disorders among Latino and Asian American lesbian, gay, and bisexual adults. *Journal of Consulting and Clinical Psychology, 75*(5), 785–794. doi:10.1037/0022-006X.75.5.785

Committee on Lesbian, Gay, Bisexual, and Transgender Health Issues and Research, Gaps and Opportunities; Board on the Health of Select Populations; Institute of Medicine. (2011). *The health of lesbian, gay, bisexual, and transgender people: Building a foundation for better understanding.* Washington, DC: The National Academies Press. doi:10.17226/13128

Dang, A., & Vianney C. (2007). *Living in the margins: A national survey of lesbian, gay, bisexual and transgender Asian American and Pacific Islanders.* New York, NY: National Gay and Lesbian Task Force Policy Institute.

Drabble, L., & Trocki, K. (2005). Alcohol consumption, alcohol-related problems, and other substance use among lesbian and bisexual women. *Journal of Lesbian Studies, 9*(3), 19–30.

Duke, A., & Davidson, M. M. (2009). Same-sex intimate partner violence: Lesbian, gay, and bisexual affirmative outreach and advocacy. *Journal of Aggression, Maltreatment & Trauma, 18*(8), 795–816.

Eckholdt, H. M., Chin, J. J., Manzon-Santos, J. A., & Kim D. D. (1997). The needs of Asians and Pacific Islanders living in New York City. *AIDS Education and Prevention, 9*(6), 493–504.

Edwards, K. M., Sylaska, K. M., & Neal, A. M. (2015). Intimate partner violence among sexual minority populations: A critical review of the literature and agenda for future research. *Psychology of Violence, 5*(2), 112–121. doi:10.1037/a0038656

Ford, C. A., Jaccard, J., Millstein, S. G., Bardsley, P. E., & Miller, W. C. (2004). Perceived risk of chlamydial and gonococcal infection among sexually experienced young adults in the United States. *Perspectives on Sexual and Reproductive Health, 36*(6), 258–264.

Hahm, H. C., Lee, J., Ozonoff, A., & Amodeo, M. (2007). Predictors of STDs among Asian and Pacific Islander young adults. *Perspectives on Sexual and Reproductive Health, 39*(4), 231–239.

Hartzell, E., Frazer, M. S., Wertz, K., & Davis, M. (2009). *The state of transgendered California: Results from the 2008 California Transgender Economic Health Survey.* San Francisco, CA: Transgender Law Center.

Haukka, J., Suominen, K., Partonen, T., & Lönnqvist, J. (2008). Determinants and outcomes of serious attempted suicide: A nationwide study in Finland, 1996–2003. *American Journal of Epidemiology, 167*(10), 1155–1163.

Hickson, F., Reid, D., Weatherburn, P., Stephens, M., Nutland, W., & Boakye, P. (2004). HIV, sexual risk, and ethnicity among men in England who have sex with men. *Sexually Transmitted Infections, 80*(6), 443–450.

Inman, A. G., Devdas, L., Spektor, V., & Pendse, A. (2014). Psychological research on SA Americans: A three-decade content analysis. *Asian American Journal of Psychology, 5*(4), 364–372. doi:10.1037/a0035633

Lee, J., & Hahm, H. C. (2012). HIV risk, substance use and suicidal behaviors among Asian American lesbian and bisexual women. *AIDS Education and Prevention, 24*(6), 549–563.

Lieb, S., Fallon, S. J., Friedman, S. R., Thompson, D. R., Gates, G. J., Libertia, T. M., & Malow, R. M. (2011). *Statewide estimation of racial/ethnic populations of men who have sex with men in the U.S. public health reports.* January–February 2011. Vol. 126. Retrieved from www.publichealthreports.org/issueopen.cfm?articleID=2577.

Kanuha, V. K. (2013). Relationships so loving and so hurtful: The constructed duality of sexual and racial/ethnic intimacy in the context of violence in Asian and Pacific Islander lesbian and queer women's relationships. *Violence Against Women, 19*(9), 1175–1196. doi:10.1177/1077801213501897

Mayer, K. H., Bradford, J. B., Makadon, H. J., Stall, R., Goldhammer, H., & Landers, S. (2008). Sexual and gender minority health: What we know and what needs to be done. *American Journal of Public Health, 98*, 989–995.

McKeown, E., Nelson, S., Anderson, J., Low, N., & Elford, J. (2010). Disclosure, discrimination and desire: Experiences of Black and South Asian gay men in Britain. *Culture, Health & Sexuality, 12*(7), 843–856. doi:10.1080/13691058.2010 .499963

Meyer, I. H. (1995). Minority stress and mental health in gay men. *Journal of Health and Social Behavior, 36*(1), 38–56.

Meyer, I. L., & Northridge, M. E. (Eds.). (2007). *The health of sexual minorities: Public health perspectives on lesbian, gay, bisexual and transgender populations.* New York, NY: Springer.

Operario, D., Choi, K. H., Chu, P. L., McFarland, W., Secura, G. M., Behel, S., . . . Valleroy, L. (2006). Prevalence and correlates of substance use among young Asian Pacific Islander men who have sex with men. *Prevention Science, 7,* 19–29.

Parry, M. M., & O'Neal, E. N. (2015). Help-seeking behavior among same-sex intimate partner violence victims: An intersectional argument. *Criminology, Criminal Justice Law & Society, 16,* 51–67.

Ratti, R., Bakeman, R., & Peterson, J. (2000). Correlates of high-risk sexual behaviour among Canadian men of South Asian and European origin who have sex with men. *AIDS Care, 12*(2), 193–202.

Sandil, R., Robinson, M., Brewster, M., Wong, S., & Geiger, E. (2015). Negotiating multiple marginalizations: Experiences of South Asian LGBQ individuals. *Cultural Diversity and Ethnic Minority Psychology, 21*(1), 76–88.

Satrang and South Asian Network. (2006). *No more denial! Giving visibility to the needs of the South Asian LGBTIQ community in Southern California.* Retrieved from http:// southasiannetwork.org/wp-content/uploads/2010/06/No_More_Denial.pdf

Schwarcz, S., Scheer, S., McFarland, W., Katz, M., Valleroy, L., Chen, S., & Catania, J. (2007). Prevalence of HIV infection and predictors of high-transmission sexual risk behaviors among men who have sex with men. *American Journal of Public Health, 97*(6), 1067–1075.

Soni, S., Bond, K., Fox, E., Grieve, A., & Sethi, G. (2008). Black and minority ethnic men who have sex with men: A London genitourinary medicine clinic experience. *International Journal of STD & AIDS, 19*(9), 617–619.

Stevens, S. (2012). Meeting the substance abuse treatment needs of lesbian, bisexual and transgender women: Implications from research to practice. *Substance Abuse and Rehabilitation, 3*(Suppl. 1), 27–36. doi:10.2147/SAR.S26430

St. Pierre, M., & Senn, C. Y. (2010). External barriers to help-seeking encountered by Canadian gay and lesbian victims of intimate partner abuse: An application of the barriers model. *Violence and Victims, 25*(4), 536–552.

Supreme Court of the United States. (2015). *Obergefell et al. v. Hodges, Director, Ohio Department of Health, et al.* Retrieved from www.supremecourt.gov/ opinions/14pdf/14-556_3204.pdf

Szymanski, D. M., & Sung, M. R. (2010). Minority stress and psychological distress among Asian American sexual minority persons. *The Counseling Psychologist, 38,* 848–872.

University of Chicago. (2011). *Sexual identity, health and stigma in India: Traditional statuses and Western influences.* Retrieved from www.ssa.uchicago.edu/sexual-identity-india-rountable-discussion

Williams, R. (2010). People coming out as gay at younger age, research show. *The Guardian*. Retrieved from www.theguardian.com/world/2010/nov/15/gay-people-coming-out-younger-age

Wolitski, R. J., Stall, R., & Valdiserri, R. O. (Eds.). (2008). *Unequal opportunity: Health disparities affecting gay and bisexual men in the United States*. New York, NY: Oxford University Press.

Wong, F. Y., Campsmith, M. L., Nakamura, G. V., Crepaz, N., & Begley, E. (2004). Reasons for testing and awareness of care-related services among a group of HIV-positive Asian Americans and Pacific Islanders in the United States: Findings from a supplemental HIV/AIDS surveillance project. *AIDS Education and Prevention, 16*(5), 440–447.

Yoshikawa, H., Wilson, P. A., Chae, D. H., & Cheng, J. F. (2004). Do family and friend-ship networks protect against the influence of discrimination on mental health and HIV risk among Asian and Pacific Islander gay men? *AIDS Education and Prevention, 16*, 84–100.

Chapter 11

Care of Older Adults

Neelum T. Aggarwal and Kala M. Mehta

Contents

Abstract

Objective: To review the healthcare trends and needs of South Asian adults 65 years or older, who are residing in the United States and to make appropriate recommendations for future research, interventions, and programs for this subpopulation of South Asian Americans.

Key Findings: Older South Asian Americans are a diverse group. They are primarily persons who immigrated early and "aged in place" and newer immigrants who often followed their adult children. The mortality profile of older South Asian Americans shows high lung cancer rates in men and high breast cancer rates in women. Additionally, as with the general South Asian population, rates of chronic diseases, such as cardiovascular disease and diabetes mellitus are extremely high for older South Asians in the United States. Though formal studies of cognitive disorders in the United States have not been conducted among South Asians, based on their risk profile, this population may have up to twice the rate of cognitive disorders including Alzheimer's disease. Additionally, physical function, diet, and exercise are often poor among South Asian American adults.

Recommendations: This chapter is a call to action to address the research and practice gaps identified. The highest priorities are neurocognitive disorders, elder abuse, and the healthcare access needs of noncitizen South Asian older adults. In the realm of lifestyle modifications, increased exercise and dietary changes can play an important role in improving diabetes mellitus, cardiovascular, and other health conditions. More culturally acceptable and culture-specific diets and exercise programs tailored to older South Asians are needed. Family-centered approaches, in-home support services that focus on geriatric syndromes such as depression and falls, and the caregiving burden related to dementia are also required. Finally, older South Asians may have unique, family-centered requests as they age, so there is a need to address preferences for end-of-life care.

Introduction

This chapter presents the current health research as it pertains to South Asian Americans (SAAs) who are 65 years of age or older and whose country of origin is Bangladesh, Bhutan, India, Nepal, Pakistan, Sri Lanka, or the Maldives. Much of the research presented in this chapter focuses on Asian Indian older adults.

Of the older SAAs, there are two distinct groups: early immigrants (those who have "aged in place" and are now older and more acculturated) and emerging immigrants (those who have joined their adult children and who are recently settled in the United States). In 1965, the *Immigration & Nationality Act* included family reunification preferences that not only enabled educated South Asian professionals (e.g., doctors, engineers, and scientists) to immigrate to the United States but also permitted immigration of close family members, including parents. This resulted in a large wave of South Asian migration that included older adults (Immigration Policy Center, 2002). By 2010, according to the U.S. Census, there were 3,863,963 South Asians living in the United States (individuals indicated this race/ethnic group alone or in combination with another race/ethnic group). Of these, an estimated 226,000, or 6%, were age 65 or older (U.S. Census Bureau, 2010) (Figure 11.1).

The older SAA population is very diverse with regard to language and religion. Similar to the general SAA population, older SAAs have varied regional affiliations with languages, including Hindi, Urdu, Tamil, Gujarati, Telugu, Bengali, Punjabi, and Malayalam (Ryan, 2013). Language barriers may exist for the older SAA population, particularly if the elder is monolingual in a South Asian language. This can affect access to healthcare. In terms of religion, older SAAs have varied religious affiliations, including Hindu (51%), Muslim (11%), Christian (18%), Sikh (5%), Jain (2%), Buddhist (1%), other (1%), and unaffiliated/don't know (11%) (Pew Research Center's Forum on Religion & Public Life, 2012). Thus, when engaging older SAAs, it is important to underscore the immense diversity in South Asia and to understand that they may speak a wide variety of languages and come from one of many religions.

Due to the "silvering" of the SAA population and projected population growth for all Asian groups in the United States, the number of SAAs who are 65 years or older is projected to double between 2010 and 2060 (U.S. Census Bureau, 2012a). Thus, it is important to investigate the health needs of this subgroup in order to ensure informed policy decisions, improved current and future clinical research, and culturally appropriate medical and health services to address a variety of health conditions.

Cause-Specific Mortality

Between 1990 and 2000, mortality data of Asian Indians in California showed that the leading causes of death for men and women who were 65 years and older were the following: (1) cardiovascular disease; (2) cancer, all-cause (lung cancer was primary cancer in men and breast cancer was primary cancer cause in women); (3) cerebrovascular disease; (4) pneumonia; and (5) diabetes mellitus (predominantly type 2) (Palaniappan, Mukherjea, Holland, & Ivey, 2010). The first three causes of death are similar to the overall older population in the

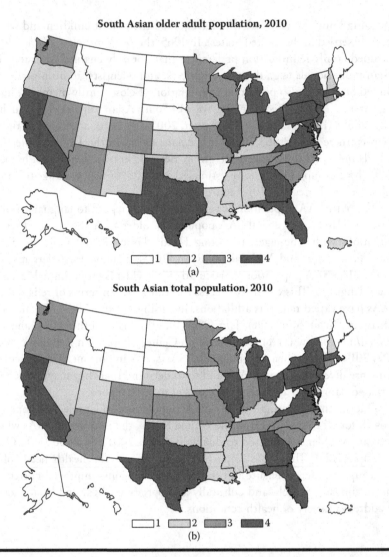

Figure 11.1 Older South Asian and overall population in the United States. (a) Total South Asian older adult population: 226,000. 1, (white): 0–400 older adults; 2, (light gray): 401–1,000 older adults; 3, (medium gray): 1,001–4,000 older adults; 4, (dark gray): 4,001–46,210 older adults. (b) Total South Asian population: 3,863,963.1, (white): 0–6,584 South Asians; 2, (light gray): 6,585–18,646 South Asians; 3 (medium gray): 18,647–79,091 South Asians; 4 (dark gray): 79,092–688,358 South Asians. (From U.S. Census Bureau, *The Asian Population: 2010 Census Briefs*, 2012b, Retrieved from www.census.gov/prod/cen2010/briefs/c2010br-11.pdf.)

United States. Pneumonia and diabetes mellitus, however, are ranked higher as causes of death for older SAAs as compared to the overall 65 years and older population in the United States.

Prevalence of Health Conditions

There have been limited studies conducted to date in the United States on the older South Asian population, with only one cohort study devoted solely to older SAAs. That study began in 2011 and consisted of interviews of approximately 400 South Asian elders in Houston, TX. Unfortunately, the results from this study have not been published. A large needs assessment conducted by Vyas et al. on the SAA population found that older SAAs were less likely to be insured and less likely to exercise than comparable age populations in the United States (Vyas, Chaudhary, Ramiah, & Landry, 2013).

The statewide California Health Interview Survey (CHIS 2007–2012) (Table 11.1) data were analyzed for this chapter. Among the sample surveyed,

Table 11.1 South Asian Older Adult Profile: Data from the California Health Interview Survey (2011–2012)

	Older South Asians
Demographics	
Age (range)	65–106 years
Male	66.8%
Married	74.6%
Geriatric Measures	
Self-Rated General Health	
Excellent	7.3%
Very Good	28.1%
Good	44.9%
Fair	14.8%
Poor	4.9%
Disability Status due to Physical, Mental, or Emotional Condition	52.6%

(*Continued*)

Table 11.1 South Asian Older Adult Profile: Data from the California Health Interview Survey (2011–2012) (Continued)

	Older South Asians
Household Chores Impairment	
Moderate	9.3%
Severe	5.7%
Fell More than Once in the Past Year	6.9%
Health Conditions (Ever Diagnosed with)	
Arthritis, gout, lupus, or fibromyalgia	38.4%
Heart disease	51.5%
Diabetes mellitus	27.1%
Borderline or pre-diabetes	23.0%
Stroke	12.7%
High blood pressure	48.2%
Serious psychological distress in past year	14.0%
Lifestyle Factors	
Current smoker	3.9%
Obese or overweight	47.5%
Vigorous activity at least 20 minutes/day and 3 days/week (excludes walking)	19.1%
Volunteered in past year	9.1%
Access	
Had a usual place to go to for health care	97%

Note: These data were obtained from the 2011–2012 California Health Interview Survey. All South Asian respondents aged 65–106 years were included in these analyses.

60 respondents self-identified as older South Asian adults (65 years and older). Two-thirds of the 60 respondents identified themselves as men and three-quarters were married. A high prevalence of heart disease (51.5%) was found, along with high blood pressure (48.5%). Approximately half of the older SAAs

in California had either pre-diabetes (23%) or a self-reported diagnosis of diabetes mellitus (27%). There was a 12.7% prevalence of stroke, and the combined rate of arthritis, gout, lupus, or fibromyalgia was 38.4%. Nearly half (47.5%) of the CHIS sample was overweight or obese, based on self-reported height and weight. It should be noted that participants in CHIS are English-speaking, highly educated, have spent time in the United States, and are of higher socioeconomic status (SES) than the larger South Asian population. Given this, these health indicators may underreport the true health profile of the larger, older South Asian population.

Although research on older South Asians is limited, there have been several studies conducted on the general South Asian population that show high prevalence of cardiovascular disease (Hajra et al., 2013). In fact, South Asians carry more than twice the risk for developing cardiovascular disease and diabetes mellitus than non-Hispanic Whites, with the greatest risk found among the middle-aged population (age range 35–64 years) (Khattar, Swales, Dore, Senior, & Lahiri, 2001; Venkataraman, Nanda, Baweja, Parikh, & Bhatia, 2004). Immigrant SAA men have particularly high rates of coronary heart disease, hypertriglyceridemia, non-insulin-dependent diabetes mellitus, and lower high-density lipoprotein cholesterol levels, as compared to non-Hispanic White men.

Diabetes mellitus is another significant disease, with SAA nearly three times more likely to report having a history of diabetes mellitus as compared to non-Hispanic Whites (Oza-Frank, Ali, Vaccarino, & Narayan, 2009). Data from the *National Health Interview Survey* showed that South Asians had the highest prevalence of diabetes mellitus among Asian ethnic groups, specifically when compared to Chinese and Japanese populations (Barnes, Adams, & Powell-Griner, 2010). Diabetes mellitus becomes more significant for South Asians as they age because it is associated with increased comorbid illnesses, such as cardiovascular disease and stroke, and can lead to poor quality of life. The high rates of chronic disease in the South Asian population are due to underlying lifestyle-associated risk factors that are also applicable to older South Asians and are described in the following sections.

Physical Activity and Diet

Much of the high rates of chronic disease among the SAA population are a result of lifestyle. The prevalence of sedentary lifestyles in the SAA population has been reported to be as high as 50% (Bharmal et al., 2015). Additionally, analyses of the CHIS data found that 47% of older South Asians are obese or overweight (California Health Interview Survey, 2007–2012). This rate is higher than that found in other Asian populations but lower than that found in non-Latino Whites of the same age.

Diets vary for older South Asians. In a study (Gadgil, Anderson, Kandula, & Kanaya, 2014) of 892 SAA adults (half of whom were older adults, age 65 years or over, residing in California), three major dietary patterns were identified: (1) animal proteins; (2) fried snacks, sweets, and high-fat dairy products; and (3) fruits, vegetables, nuts, and legumes. The authors found that consumption of animal proteins was associated with higher body mass index (mean = 0.73 m/kg^2), waist circumference (mean = 0.84 cm), total cholesterol (mean = 8.16 mg/dL), and low-density lipoprotein cholesterol (mean = 5.69 mg/dL) (all $p < .05$). Conversely, consumption of fruits, vegetables, nuts, and legumes was associated with lower odds of hypertension (odds ratio [OR] = 0.63) and metabolic syndrome (OR = 0.53). Thus, the authors found that animal proteins, fried snacks, sweets, and high-fat dairy products were associated with adverse metabolic risk factors in SAA adults, whereas consumption of fruits, vegetables, nuts, and legumes was linked to a better health profile (Gadgil et al., 2014; Mukherjea, Underwood, Stewart, Ivey, & Kanaya, 2013). This includes ensuring they are meeting the required protein and nutrient needs.

Currently, there is one culturally specific trial aimed at improving diet and exercise for older SAAs (Kandula et al., 2013). The *South Asian Heart Lifestyle Intervention* (SAHELI) is designed to improve cardiovascular risk factors in a community setting. It remains to be seen, however, whether it will result in improvement in dietary outcomes for this subpopulation.

Social determinants of health that lead to lifestyle choices, including diet and physical activity, can be related to community factors including environment and acculturation, and may be compounded when there is a lack of social support and sense of community (Jonnalagadda & Diwan, 2005). For example, when older adults are isolated, they may choose a poor diet and remain sedentary, choosing not to engage in exercise. Also compounding the dietary issues for South Asians is the increased Westernization of diet and low physical activity, which result in increased weight in newer immigrants (Kalavar, Kolt, Giles, & Driver, 2005). Thus, the choice of diet and physical activity are very important for maintaining the health of the older SAA population.

Studies differ regarding rates of exercise in the older SAA population. On the basis of the CHIS data (California Health Interview Survey, 2007–2012), 1 in 5 older South Asians performed vigorous physical activity three times per week, as compared to 1 in 10 for older non-Hispanic Whites. Other reports, however, suggest that older South Asians engage in less exercise (Gadgil et al., 2014). In a systematic review of South Asians living in the United Kingdom, several factors were identified as contributors to physical activity. According to patients' self-reports, the most salient factor that promoted exercise was that it was part of their social group norm (Horne & Tierney, 2012). In this instance, group norms referred to the notion that the social network surrounding older South Asians participated in some form of regular exercise. In addition, South Asian adults with higher education and better self-efficacy, as well as lower perceived discrimination, were more likely to exercise. Findings of this review from the United Kingdom can be extrapolated to SAAs until we have more direct and conclusive evidence from the United States.

Research has shown that pairing exercise with a social component, particularly in the United States, has been successful (Sathe et al., 2013). One study found that step counts were uniformly low for South Asians as a group, when compared to non-Hispanic Whites (Daniel, Wilbur, Fogg, & Miller, 2013; Daniel, Wilbur, Marquez, & Farran, 2013). The authors noted that this could possibly be improved on in a social setting, such as a group walking for exercise or as a means of getting to a group activity. In addition to promoting exercise in the South Asian community at large, one study in Chicago focused on creating public health messages to encourage exercise (Kandula, Khurana, Makoul, Glass, & Baker, 2012). Recommendations were taken from South Asian participants about how to create effective public announcements for their community. Participants suggested that effective messages recognize the heterogeneity of the South Asian community, engage communities in each phase of the design, incorporate culturally appropriate explanatory models, and address economic and structural barriers (Kandula et al., 2012).

Physical Function and Mobility

It is important to note that being overweight or obese can not only lead to other comorbidities such as heart disease and diabetes mellitus, but it can also negatively impact physical functioning later in life. The prevalence of a sedentary lifestyle in South Asians has been reported to be as high as 50% in the United States (Bharmal et al., 2015) and analyses of the CHIS data show that 47% of older South Asians are either obese or overweight (California Health Interview Survey, 2007–2012). Another population-based study in California (Gee & Ponce, 2010) found that activity limitations were a significant problem for older South Asians. In fact, for older South Asians residing in California, the analysis of the CHIS data found that 50% of older adults self-reported disability, whereas 15% indicated they had moderate-to-severe impairment in performing household chores. In the same study, 6.9% of older South Asians reported falling more than once in the past year (Table 11.1). Thus, older South Asians are often overweight and have activity limitations that can precipitate poor outcomes such as falls. To date, however, no formal study related to falls has been conducted among older South Asian Americans.

Neurocognitive Disorders

Neurocognitive disorders such as Alzheimer's disease are among the most prevalent illnesses of older adulthood, particularly at advanced ages. It is surprising then that very little is known about the risk for neurocognitive disorders in the South Asian population. In India, prevalence rates from distinct regional community-based studies of dementia have varied from 1.02% to 3.36% in adults older than 65 years of age (Chandra et al., 1998; Rajkumar & Kumar, 1996; Rajkumar, Kumar, & Thara, 1997; Shaji, Bose, & Verghese, 2005; Shaji, Promodu, Abraham, Roy, & Verghese, 1996).

Reasons for the low reported prevalence rates include the importance of cultural consideration when assessing patients and their families regarding cognitive symptoms. This cultural consideration includes low literacy and language barriers. For example, the spoken version of many Indian languages lacks a term for dementia, whereas the term "memory impairment" is often used as a catchall phrase to describe other non-memory-related health/medical concerns. As a result, prevalence of dementia has gone underreported or even underdiagnosed in this community. Despite these issues, recent estimates have shown that over the last two decades, the prevalence of dementia in India has increased, ranging from 1.4%–3.5% among those 65 years and older in rural settings to 2.4% among those 65 years and older in urban settings (Llibre et al., 2008). Although higher than earlier studies, these prevalence rates are still much lower than the estimated 11% dementia rate reported in the United States (Alzheimer's Association, 2014). It remains to be seen whether this is a result of underdiagnosis and/or underreporting or is truly a lower rate. Similar differences in rates have been noted for mild cognitive impairment, a diagnosis considered a precursor to Alzheimer's disease in some instances, in urban versus rural settings. When compared to other low- and middle-income countries, the Indian population appears to have higher rates of amnestic mild cognitive impairment (Sosa et al., 2012). The bibliography at the end of the chapter includes references to the Mini-Mental State Exam (MMSE) in Hindi and Gujarati, which can serve as resources for those looking for culturally and linguistically appropriate assessment tools (Tiwari, Tripathi, & Kumar, 2009; Ganguli et al., 1995).

To our knowledge, no studies of neurocognitive disorders in older South Asians have been undertaken in the United States. However, using known indices to project Alzheimer's prevalence (Aggarwal, Tripathi, Dodge, Alladi, & Anstey, 2012; Anstey, Cherbuin, & Herath, 2013), one can extrapolate, based on the current rates of low exercise, low fish intake, high cholesterol, high levels of type 2 diabetes mellitus, and moderate levels of depressive symptoms, that older South Asian adults will be at least twice as likely to develop dementia, when compared with older non-Hispanic Whites in the United States.

Quality of Life and Mental Health

Quality of life is just as important an issue for older South Asians as it is with the overall older adult population. According to the CHIS, 20% of older South Asians who were surveyed rated their health as "fair" or "poor" (California Health Interview Survey, 2007–2012). A study conducted by Nandan (2007) found differences in quality of life based on whether the older adult was a new immigrant or an immigrant who had aged in place. This was further exemplified in a study of 109 South Asian seniors, conducted in California (Mukherjee, 2013). Using the WHOQOL-BREF, a quality-of-life assessment instrument developed by the World Health Organization Quality of Life project, older adults in the third wave (followers of adult children) had a lower rated quality of life when compared with older adults who had aged in place (Mukherjee, 2013). In another study of older Asian Indian immigrants in New York, female immigrants were three times more likely to report poor self-rated health than male immigrants (Shibusawa & Mui, 2010). These adults also had low self-reported mastery, were more often financially dependent on their children or the government, and perceived more often that a language barrier limited their access to services and transportation while residing in the United States, as compared with their lives in India (Shibusawa & Mui, 2010). Personal mastery covers an individual's beliefs regarding the extent to which outcomes can be controlled or influenced (Schultz, Heckhausen, and O'Brian, 1994). In part, these individuals were less isolated and had higher levels of social support in India, as compared to their lives in the United States.

The study by Mukherjee (2013) also measured rates of depression using the *Center for Epidemiologic Studies Depression Scale* (CES-D) and found rates that were somewhat higher than those in older SAAs who became U.S. citizens. Another study, conducted in Atlanta, found similar rates of depression in immigrants who had limited English proficiency (Gujarati-speaking) as compared to older, more acculturated Asian Indians (Diwan, Lee, & Sen, 2011). In this study, however, the authors found that social networks for new immigrants were similar to those who had lived in the United States longer.

Screening Instruments

Screening instruments are important for regular monitoring of cognitive functioning and mental health for older South Asians. Some instruments have been translated into South Asian languages. Screening instruments for cognitive function include the MMSE in Gujarati and Hindi (Ganguli et al., 1995; Lindesay et al., 1997). For depressive symptoms, the Patient Health Questionnaire-9 is available at www.PHQScreeners.com for the following Indian languages: Gujarati, Hindi, Kannada, Malayalam, Punjabi, Tamil, and Telugu.

Living Preferences and Caregiving

As with other populations, the social structure for older South Asians has profound potential to impact their health. One common issue for older South Asians is whether they choose to live with their adult children or live on their own. The preferred choices for living arrangements include moving closer to children, moving to a retirement community, and less preferred, moving in with children (Diwan, 2008; Diwan et al., 2011). For those who prefer a retirement community, there is a strong preference for a culture-centered facility, though few exist. Other preferences included not moving at all and returning to South Asia. These expectations also varied with endorsement of self-rated health, length of residence in the United States, and filial piety (Diwan, 2008; Diwan et al., 2011). Filial piety is a concept in Asian cultures that underscores the primary duty of respect, obedience, and care for one's parents and elderly family members. Thus, the decision of where to live can be complicated and it is critically important for South Asian families with older family members to learn about their community, including available senior resources, and preferably before a health crisis arises.

To date, few studies have been conducted on caregiving for the older SAA population. For many older South Asians, the activities of social workers and home-care nurses are unfamiliar and possibly unwelcome. Home visits by these providers are not always acceptable to the care recipient. Additionally, family members caring for their elders often seek help from family and friends and are unlikely to place an elder in a nursing home, except as a last resort. As is similar worldwide, the caregiver is often a spouse, daughter, or daughter-in-law. In a recent study of caregiving in India (Gupta, 2009), a systematic framework was developed to examine the role of caregiving in light of the caregivers' adherence to Asian cultural norms and their rank in the family, as well as the presence of behavioral symptoms in the patient.

In January 2016, an evaluation of an Internet-based caregiver intervention module for Asian Indian adults was launched in Bengaluru, India (Gallagher-Thompson et al., 2016). The modules include information on how caregivers can take care of themselves, as well as how they can handle common situations such as wandering and agitation, both common occurrences in patients with dementia. This trial will provide baseline information about beliefs, practices, occurrence of caregiving burden, and whether an Internet-based approach affects the perceived stress and depression of these caregivers. This approach (using an Internet portal) is important because it will fill a huge gap in service provision/caregiver burden reduction where these resources do not currently exist for most South Asians.

Alternative Medicine and Health Beliefs

Older South Asians may engage in alternative medicine practices that are used widely in South Asia. The decision to use alternative medicine may also impact whether older SAAs use Western allopathic medicine and, if so, whether instructions regarding these medicines are followed. Many older South Asians believe in using alternative or complementary medicine approaches to health. One such approach is an intricate healing system that originated in India, called *Ayurveda.** Within *Ayurveda*, the concept of dementia is acknowledged in South Asian culture, and studies have reported the use of Ayurvedic therapies in the management of dementia (Tiwari & Tripathi, 2013).

With regard to health beliefs for followers of the Hindu religion, specific aspects may affect decision-making as it relates to health care. Tiwari and Tripathi (2013) found that fatalism (karma), along with renunciation of material issues, affected how older adults addressed or acknowledged their health and disease conditions. Thus, many older SAAs may balance treating their health issues with a combination of Western and alternative medicine and approaches (particularly those who are Hindu and use Ayurveda or are Muslim and use other health belief systems). This can have important implications for the SAA population (Hasnain, Connell, Menon, & Tranmer, 2011; Tirodkar et al., 2011). The implications for SAA from all religious groups need further study.

Healthcare Access and Utilization

For older South Asians who do not have citizenship or permanent residency in the United States, access to care continues to be a documented challenge. One particular study noted that recent immigrants face a lack of access to insurance

---

*Ayurveda is made up of two Sanskrit words: *ayu* meaning "life" and *veda* meaning "the knowledge of." It is a science that relates to the complete human being (body, mind, senses, and soul). It explains how balance can be attained physically, mentally, and spiritually. Accordingly, each individual is thought to be made up of three *doshas* (*vata*, *pitta*, or *kapha*) and each *dosha* represents a certain bodily activity. The ratio of *doshas* varies in each individual. When any of these *doshas* accumulates strength, *ayurveda* suggests specific lifestyle and nutrition guidelines to assist in reducing the *dosha* that has become excessive. Specific *ayurvedic* medicines are formulated to balance these *doshas*.

because they do not qualify for Medicare (Shibusawa & Mui, 2010). It should be noted that access to the U.S. healthcare system varies by state and local governance. Shibusawa and Mui's study of older Asian Indian immigrants living in New York found that less than 50% were enrolled in Medicare, whereas up to 20% had used an emergency department within the past year (2010). They did not, however, note whether these visits were for primary care or emergency reasons. In contrast, in the CHIS population (which has a high level of education and SES), 97% had a regular place to go to for their healthcare needs. Still, even with access to basic health insurance in some instances, equitable access and low utilization remains a challenge for older South Asians (Akhtar, Hipkiss, & Stoves, 2014; Khosla, Washington, & Regunath, 2015; Kristiansen et al., 2014). In the San Francisco Bay Area, a community ambassador program successfully connected seniors to available resources and improved healthcare access (Community Ambassador Program, 2016).

End of Life and Decision-Making

Cultural beliefs play a large role in decision-making at the end of life. Older South Asians can have vastly different beliefs about death and dying than other cultural groups. They are also less likely to be autonomous in their decision-making and more likely to subscribe to family-centered decision-making. Many older South Asian patients also prefer to die at home and each religious community has specific rituals and practices related to this occurrence. One focus group study was conducted with first- and second-generation South Asian adults residing in the Chicago area (Sharma, Khosla, Tulsky, & Carrese, 2012). Common themes that were identified included family duty, lack of explicit discussion between patients and their family about preferences, and tensions between wanting to meet traditional expectations and the challenges in doing so. In addition, there is also the issue of SAAs' preference for being buried or having their ashes dispersed in their places of origin or their home countries. This may also impact end-of-life decisions.

Elder Abuse

Although exact prevalence rates are lacking, there is increasing recognition that older South Asians are vulnerable to elder abuse, often as a result of their language and cultural isolation. The types of abuse include physical, verbal, and financial abuse, and neglect (Nagpaul, 1998; Segal, 1999; Shankardass, 2013). Groups such as Narika and Maitri in the San Francisco Bay Area and Sahara in Southern California are working toward increasing awareness about elder abuse in South Asian communities. These organizations provide awareness and prevention work in the community, legal advocacy, financial workshops, and in some instances, transitional housing.

Recommendations

Although a good deal of data have been presented on care of older South Asians living in the United States, there is still much work to be done. Gaps in population-level social service and health services research continue to exist for older South Asians in the United States. It is important that all healthcare providers practicing in the healthcare delivery system be encouraged to play a significant role in addressing these issues by using a collaborative and multiple-level approach. We offer recommendations in the following two broad categories: 1) Research: 2) Practice-based.

Research

According to government recommendations addressing the health of Asian Americans (The White House, 2011) there is a growing need to evaluate and document the health and behavioral patterns of older Asian groups, with the goal of developing better culturally tailored initiatives for these groups. Priorities for research include the following:

- Develop and conduct a national needs assessment of older South Asians, similar in structure to needs assessments conducted in Houston, TX, and Washington, DC (Vyas et al., 2013).
- Design the research with the approach that all South Asian countries of origin are represented in the needs assessment survey.
- Define whether the needs assessments include new immigrants (recent followers of adult children) or those older South Asians who have aged in place.
- Identify which older South Asian subgroups lack access to care or have low utilization.
- Establish a nationwide registry or database of the geriatric and adult health of older South Asians. This database should ask questions about cognitive functioning, assess cardiovascular disease risk factors, incidence of falls, history of elder abuse, depression and mental health, diagnoses of dementia/stroke/Alzheimer's disease, as well as which lifestyle interventions are most effective for older South Asians.

■ As the South Asian population ages, use national population-level surveys to project the need for in-home health services, long-term care services (nursing home placement), or hospice in the United States. If possible, identify language, regional, and religious needs.

■ Support researchers as they extend outreach efforts to older South Asians in order to have them fully participate in randomized controlled clinical trials on geriatric interventions.

■ Develop acceptable, feasible, and culturally relevant diet and exercise life-style interventions that are specific to older South Asians.

Healthcare Professionals and Providers

■ Increase recognition of cardiovascular, diabetes mellitus, and Alzheimer's disease risk for all South Asians, with a focus on older South Asians.

■ Work with national and local partners to ensure that patient and community resource materials are available in a variety of South Asian languages, in accordance with the monolingual South Asian population base. Languages to include, but not be limited to, are Hindi, Urdu, Tamil, Gujarati, Telugu, Bengali, Punjabi, and Malayalam. Offer specific supportive services to older South Asians as they age, from retirement communities and financial planning for retirement to South Asian–specific home supports and nursing home care.

■ Document barriers to healthcare access and utilization among older South Asians and collaborate with researchers and policy makers to share this information.

■ Encourage patients to fill out an Advance Care directive and speak to their families about end-of-life preferences (http://www.iha4health.org/our-services/advance-directive/).

■ Facilitate discussions to increase acceptance and reduce stigma for mental health, dementia, and elder abuse among older South Asians, which can ultimately lead to the development of policies and best practices.

■ For healthcare professionals serving South Asians, employ the principle of cultural humility (Tervalon & Murray-Garcia, 1998). This principle involves asking about the patient's health beliefs, preferences, and decisions without making any presumptive assertions as to what a "South Asian" patient might prefer. For those who prefer a more proscriptive approach, background, or description, utilizing teaching modules that describe religious and cultural specifications for older South Asians may be preferable (Periyakoil & Dara, 2010).

- Incorporate the principles of the MacArthur Foundation's Research Studies on Successful Aging (Rowe & Kahn, 1998) that indicate the process of aging and the rate at which it occurs are not solely related to ethnicity and genetics, but instead, point to the role of lifestyle, social environment, and social structure on the process of formal aging (Rowe & Kahn, 1998) in the future development of healthy aging programs and communities.
- Partner with South Asian senior programs that are currently in use in places of worship and community-based organizations (i.e., senior program at the Indian Community Center in Milpitas, California, and the South Asian Network's senior walking groups in Southern California.)

Conclusions

The population of South Asian adults aged 65 years and older living in the United States is growing. They are diverse in language and regional and religious affiliation. Their unique health needs include higher rates of diabetes mellitus and cardiovascular disease. Underlying these health issues are specific lifestyle factors such as diet and exercise. As South Asians age, these risk factors become even more important as they can lead to a variety of geriatric issues, including mobility limitation, increased risk for falls, increased severity of cardiovascular disease and diabetes mellitus, and higher risk for neurocognitive disorders such as Alzheimer's disease and stroke. It is important to take advantage of the evidence available on these and other important issues, such as falls, elder abuse, depression, mental health, and end-of-life care, as well as on which lifestyle interventions are most effective for older South Asians. In summary, as the population of older South Asians continues to grow, it is increasingly important to determine the most effective interventions available that can promote successful aging among this population.

References

Aggarwal, N. T., Tripathi, M., Dodge, H. H., Alladi, S., & Anstey, K. J. (2012). Trends in Alzheimer's disease and dementia in the Asian-Pacific region. *International Journal of Alzheimer's Disease, 2012*, 171327. doi: 10.1155/2012/171327

Akhtar, T., Hipkiss, V., & Stoves, J. (2014). Improving the quality of communication and service provision for renal patients of South Asian origin: The contribution of a cultural and health improvement officer. *Journal of Renal Care, 40*(Suppl. 1), 41–46. doi: 10.1111/jorc.12086

Alzheimer's Association. (2014). Alzheimer's disease facts and figures. *Alzheimer's & Dementia: The Journal of the Alzheimer's Association, 10*(2), e47–e92.

Anstey, K. J., Cherbuin, N., & Herath, P. M. (2013). Development of a new method for assessing global risk of Alzheimer's disease for use in population health approaches to prevention. *Prevention Science, 14*(4), 411–421.

Barnes, P. M., Adams, P. F., & Powell-Griner, E. (2010). *Health Characteristics of the American Indian or Alaska Native Adult Population: United States, 2004–2008.* National Health Statistics Report. Retrieved from www.cdc.gov/nchs/data/nhsr/nhsr020.pdf.

Bharmal, N., Kaplan, R. M., Shapiro, M. F., Mangione, C. M., Kagawa-Singer, M., Wong, M. D., & McCarthy, W.J. (2015). The association of duration of residence in the United States with cardiovascular disease risk factors among South Asian immigrants. *Journal of Immigrant and Minority Health, 17*(3), 781–790. doi: 10.1007/s10903-013-9973-7

California Health Interview Survey. (2007–2012). UCLA Center for Health Policy Research, Los Angeles, CA: CHIS 2007, 2009, 2011–2012 Adult Public Use Files. [Computer File]

Chandra, V., Ganguli, M., Pandav, R., Johnston, J., Belle, S., & DeKosky, S. T. (1998). Prevalence of Alzheimer's disease and other dementias in rural India: The Indo-US study. *Neurology, 51*(4), 1000–1008.

Community Ambassador Program. (2016). Retrieved from http://capseniors.org/

Daniel, M., Wilbur, J., Fogg, L. F., & Miller, A. M. (2013). Correlates of lifestyle: Physical activity among South Asian Indian immigrants. *Journal of Community Health Nursing, 30*(4), 185–200. doi: 10.1080/07370016.2013.838482

Daniel, M., Wilbur, J., Marquez, D., & Farran, C. (2013). Lifestyle physical activity behavior among South Asian Indian immigrants. *Journal of Immigrant and Minority Health, 15*(6), 1082–1089. doi: 10.1007/s10903-013-9842-4

Diwan, S. (2008). Limited English proficiency, social network characteristics, and depressive symptoms among older immigrants. *Journals of Gerontology. Series B, Psychological Sciences and Social Sciences, 63*(3), S184–S191.

Diwan, S., Lee, S. E., & Sen, S. (2011). Expectations of filial obligation and their impact on preferences for future living arrangements of middle-aged and older Asian Indian immigrants. *Journal of Cross-Cultural Gerontology, 26*(1), 55–69. doi: 10.1007/s10823-010-9134-6

Gadgil, M. D., Anderson, C. A., Kandula, N. R., & Kanaya, A. M. (2014). Dietary patterns in Asian Indians in the United States: An analysis of the metabolic syndrome and atherosclerosis in South Asians living in America study. *Journal of the Academy of Nutrition and Dietetics, 114*(2), 238–243. doi: 10.1016/j.jand.2013.09.021

Gallagher-Thompson, D., Mehta, K. M., Pot, A. M., Dua, T., Zandi, D., Varghese, M., and Santosh, I. (2016). iSupport: An Internet caregiver intervention for South Asians. Poster presentation. Stanford Center for Innovation in Global Health Research Retreat, January 22, 2016.

Ganguli, M., Ratcliff, G., Chandra, V., Sharma, S., Gilby, J., Pandav, R., Belle, S., Ryan, C., Baker, C., Seaberg, E., and DeKosky, S. (1995). A Hindi version of the MMSE: The development of a cognitive screening instrument for a largely illiterate rural elderly population in India. *International Journal of Geriatric Psychiatry, 10*(5), 367–377.

Gee, G. C., & Ponce, N. (2010). Associations between racial discrimination, limited English proficiency, and health-related quality of life among 6 Asian ethnic groups in California. *American Journal of Public Health, 100*(5), 888–895. doi: 10.2105/ AJPH.2009.178012

Gupta, R. (2009). Systems perspective: Understanding care giving of the elderly in India. *Health Care for Women International, 30*(12), 1040–1054. doi: 10.1080/07399330903199334

Hajra, A., Li, Y., Siu, S., Udaltsova, N., Armstrong, M. A., Friedman, G. D., & Klatsky A. L. (2013). Risk of coronary disease in the South Asian American population. *Journal of the American College of Cardiology, 62*, 644–645.

Hasnain, M., Connell, K. J., Menon, U., & Tranmer, P. A. (2011). Patient-centered care for Muslim women: Provider and patient perspectives. *Journal of Women's Health, 20*(1), 73–83. doi: 10.1089/jwh.2010.2197

Horne, M., & Tierney, S. (2012). What are the barriers and facilitators to exercise and physical activity uptake and adherence among South Asian older adults: A systematic review of qualitative studies. *Preventive Medicine, 55*(4), 276–284. doi: 10.1016/j.ypmed.2012.07.016

Immigration Policy Center. (2002). *The Passage from India.* Retrieved from http:// www.issuelab.org/resource/the_passage_from_india_a_brief_history_of_indian_ immigration_to_the_u_s

Jonnalagadda, S. S., & Diwan, S. (2005). Health behaviors, chronic disease prevalence and self-rated health of older Asian Indian immigrants in the U.S. *Journal of Immigrant Health, 7*(2), 75–83.

Kalavar, J. M., Kolt, G. S., Giles, L. C., & Driver, R. P. (2005). Physical activity in older Asian Indians living in the United States: Barriers and motives. *Activities, Adaptation & Aging, 29*, 47–67. doi: 10.1300/J016v29n01_04

Kandula, N. R., Khurana, N. R., Makoul, G., Glass, S., & Baker, D. W. (2012). A community and culture-centered approach to developing effective cardiovascular health messages. *Journal of General Internal Medicine, 27*(10), 1308–1316.

Kandula, N. R., Patel, Y., Dave, S., Seguil, P., Kumar, S., Baker, D. W., & Siddique, J. (2013). The South Asian Heart Lifestyle Intervention (SAHELI) study to improve cardiovascular risk factors in a community setting: Design and methods. *Contemporary Clinical Trials, 36*(2), 479–487. doi: 10.1016/j.cct.2013.09.007

Khattar, R. S., Swales, J. D., Dore, C., Senior, R., & Lahiri, A. (2001). Effect of aging on the prognostic significance of ambulatory systolic, diastolic, and pulse pressure in essential hypertension. *Circulation, 104*(7), 783–789.

Khosla, N., Washington, K. T., and Regunath, H. (2016). Perspectives of health care providers on US South Asians' attitudes toward pain management at end of life. *American Journal of Hospice & Palliative Care, 33*(9), 849–857.

Kristiansen, M., Irshad, T., Worth, A., Bhopal, R., Lawton, J., & Sheikh, A. (2014). The practice of hope: A longitudinal, multi-perspective qualitative study among South Asian Sikhs and Muslims with life-limiting illness in Scotland. *Ethnicity & Health, 19*(1), 1–19. doi: 10.1080/13557858.2013.858108

Lindesay, J., Jagger, C., Mlynik-Szmid, A., Sinorwala, A., Peet, S., & Moledina, F. (1997). The Mini-Mental State Examination (MMSE) in an elderly immigrant Gujarati population in the United Kingdom. *International Journal of Geriatric Psychiatry, 12*(12), 1155–1167.

Llibre, R. J. J., Ferri, C. P., Acosta, D., Guerra, M., Huang, Y., Jacob, K. S., . . . 10/66 Dementia Research Group. (2008). Prevalence of dementia in Latin America, India, and China: A population-based cross-sectional survey. *Lancet, 372*(9637), 464–474. doi: 10.1016/S0140-6736(08)61002-8

Mukherjea, A., Underwood, K. C., Stewart, A. L., Ivey, S. L., & Kanaya, A. M. (2013). Asian Indian views on diet and health in the United States: Importance of understanding cultural and social factors to address disparities. *Family & Community Health, 36*(4), 311–323. doi: 10.1097/FCH.0b013e31829d2549

Mukherjee, A. (2013). *Asian Indian older adults in Silicon Valley: Quality of life of parents who immigrate to reunite with their children.* San Jose, CA: CreateSpace Independent Publishing Platform.

Nagpaul, K. (1998). Elder abuse among Asian Indians: Traditional versus modern perspectives. *Journal of Elder Abuse & Neglect, 9*(2), 77–92.

Nandan, M. (2007). "Waves" of Asian Indian elderly immigrants: What can practitioners learn? *Journal of Cross-Cultural Gerontology, 22*(4), 389–404.

Oza-Frank, R., Ali, M. K., Vaccarino, V., & Narayan, K. M. (2009). Asian Americans: Diabetes prevalence across U.S. and World Health Organization weight classifications. *Diabetes Care, 32*(9), 1644–1646. doi: 10.2337/dc09-0573

Palaniappan, L., Mukherjea, A., Holland, A., & Ivey, S. L. (2010). Leading causes of mortality of Asian Indians in California. *Ethnicity & Disease, 20*(1), 53–57.

Periyakoil, V. J., & Dara, S. (2010). *Health and Health Care of Asian Indian American Older Adults.* Retrieved from http://geriatrics.stanford.edu/ethnomed/asian_indian

Pew Research Center's Forum on Religion & Public Life. (2012). *Asian Americans: A Mosaic of Faiths.* Retrieved from http://www.pewforum.org/2012/07/19/asian-americans-a-mosaic-of-faiths-overview/

PHQScreeners.com. Pfizer Website. Retrieved from www.PHQScreeners.com; Pfizer. Accessed 2016.

Rajkumar, S., & Kumar, S. (1996). Prevalence of dementia in the community: A rural-urban comparison from Madras, India. *Australasian Journal on Ageing, 15*, 9–13.

Rajkumar, S., Kumar, S., & Thara, R. (1997). Prevalence of dementia in a rural setting: A report from India. *International Journal of Geriatric Psychiatry, 12*, 702–707.

Rowe, J. W., & Kahn, R. L. (1998). Successful aging. *Aging (Milano), 10*(2), 142–144.

Ryan, C. (2013). *Language Use in the United States, 2011 American Community Survey Reports.* Washington, DC: U.S. Department of Commerce.

Sathe, A., Flowers, E., Mathur, A., Garcia, D. M., Kotrys, J., Gandhi, R., . . . Mathur, A. (2013). A culturally specific health coaching program targeting cardiovascular disease risk in South Asians: Rationale, design, and baseline data. *Ethnicity & Disease, 23*(3), 304–309.

Schultz, R., Heckhausen, J., & O'Brian, A. T. (1994). Control and the disablement process in the elderly. *Journal of Social Behavior and Personality, 9,* 139–152.

Segal, U. (1999). Family violence: A focus on India. *Aggression and Violent Behavior, 4*(2), 213–231. doi: 10.1016/S1359-1789(97)00051-7

Shaji, S., Bose, S., & Verghese, A. (2005). Prevalence of dementia in an urban population in Kerala, India. *British Journal of Psychiatry, 186,* 136–140.

Shaji, S., Promodu, K., Abraham, T., Roy, K. J., & Verghese, A. (1996). An epidemiological study of dementia in a rural community in Kerala, India. *British Journal of Psychiatry, 168,* 745–749.

Shankardass, M. K. (2013). Addressing elder abuse: Review of societal responses in India and selected Asian countries. *International Psychogeriatrics, 25*(8), 1229–1234. doi: 10.1017/S104161021300063X

Sharma, R. K., Khosla, N., Tulsky, J. A., & Carrese, J. A. (2012). Traditional expectations versus US realities: First- and second-generation Asian Indian perspectives on end-of-life care. *Journal of General Internal Medicine, 27*(3), 311–317. doi: 10.1007/s11606-011-1890-7

Shibusawa, T., & Mui, A. C. (2010). Health status and health services utilization among older Asian Indian immigrants. *Journal of Immigrant and Minority Health, 12*(4), 527–533.

Sosa, A. L., Albanese, E., Stephan, B. C., Dewey, M., Acosta, D., Ferri, C. P., . . . Stewart, R. (2012). Prevalence, distribution, and impact of mild cognitive impairment in Latin America, China, and India: A 10/66 population-based study. *PLoS Medicine, 9*(2), e1001170.

Tervalon, M., & Murray-Garcia, J. (1998). Cultural humility versus cultural competence: A critical distinction in defining physician training outcomes in multicultural education. *Journal of Health Care for the Poor and Underserved, 9*(2), 117–125.

The White House. (2011). *Winning the Future: President Obama's Agenda and the Asian American and Pacific Islander Community.* Retrieved from http://permanent.access.gpo.gov/gpo7538/AAPI_WinningtheFuture.pdf

Tirodkar, M. A., Baker, D. W., Makoul, G. T., Khurana, N., Paracha, M.W., & Kandula, N. R. (2011). Explanatory models of health and disease among South Asian immigrants in Chicago. *Journal of Immigrant and Minority Health, 13*(2), 385–394.

Tiwari, R. S., & Tripathi, J. S. (2013). A critical appraisal of dementia with special reference to Smritibuddhihrass. *Ayu, 34*(3), 235–242.

Tiwari, S. C., Tripathi, R. K., & Kumar, A. (2009). Applicability of the Mini-mental State Examination (MMSE) and the Hindi Mental State Examination (HMSE) to the urban elderly in India: A pilot study. *International Psychogeriatrics, 21*(1), 123–128.

U.S. Census Bureau. (2010). *US Census, DP-1, Profile of General Population and Housing Characteristics.* Retrieved from factfinder2.census.gov. Accessed December 3, 2013.

U.S. Census Bureau. (2012a). *2012 National Population Projections.* Retrieved from https://www.census.gov/population/projections/data/national/2012.html

U.S. Census Bureau. (2012b). *The Asian Population: 2010 Census Briefs.* Retrieved from www.census.gov/prod/cen2010/briefs/c2010br-11.pdf.

Venkataraman, R., Nanda, N. C., Baweja, G., Parikh, N., & Bhatia, V. (2004). Prevalence of diabetes mellitus and related conditions in Asian Indians living in the United States. *American Journal of Cardiology, 94*(7), 977–980.

Vyas, A. N., Chaudhary, N., Ramiah, K., & Landry, M. (2013). Addressing a growing community's health needs: Project SAHNA (South Asian Health Needs Assessment). *Journal of Immigrant and Minority Health, 15*(3), 577–583.

SPECIAL ISSUES IN WELL-BEING

Chapter 12

Mental Health

Alison Karasz

Contents

Abstract

Objective: This chapter examines issues related to research and policy on common mental disorders in South Asian communities in Western countries, including depression, anxiety, and somatic distress. The prevalence, social context, symptom expression, treatment utilization, and conceptual representations of common mental disorders are reviewed, as well as the relevance of current treatment approaches. Strategies are suggested for creating culturally appropriate treatments that address the social adversity underlying common mental disorders in South Asian Americans.

Key Findings: Several key findings emerge from current research. First, multiple social factors have been shown to be associated with common mental disorders, including low acculturation, discrimination, and immigration stress. Second, evidence suggests differential vulnerability of subgroups within the South Asian community. For example, South Asian American children are more psychologically resilient as compared to White children, which is likely to do with benefits associated with traditional extended family life. Evidence also shows that South Asian women experience higher rates of depression, anxiety, and somatic distress, in addition to self-harm and completed suicide rates, when compared to White women and South Asian men. Social factors, particularly marital and family conflict, are the key cause of a woman's increased burden of distress and disorder. A third key finding indicates very low mental health treatment utilization among South Asian immigrants. Review of the evidence suggests that the key factor underlying low utilization is a lack of "match" between the types of treatments currently available—psychotherapy and medication—and the social models of distress and suffering held by many South Asian immigrants. The weakness of current treatment models to address social suffering in low-income South Asian groups is also highlighted.

Recommendations: There is an urgent need to adapt current mental health treatment models to better address the public health burden of common mental disorders in vulnerable subgroups. A promising strategy is the development of culturally appropriate treatment models that can achieve a conceptual match with South Asian models of distress and address underlying social causes of common mental disorders. This chapter describes innovative treatment models currently under development in both the United Kingdom and the United States.

Introduction

In 2002, authors of the *Brown Paper*'s chapter on mental health deplored the lack of data on South Asian mental health issues in the United States and emphasized the need for more research (Rastogi, Suthakaran, & Thayil, 2002). Nearly 15 years later, however, little has changed in this regard, even while the South Asian community in the United States has continued to grow substantially. In fact, from 2000 to 2010, the number of South Asian Americans (SAAs) increased by 81%, and has now reached more than 3.4 million (South Asian Americans Leading Together [SAALT], 2012). Despite this growth, the SAA population receives little attention from the public health community and only a small fraction of research dollars from the National Institutes of Health.

In seeking to report on issues informing research and policy on mental health in South Asian communities in the United States, this chapter draws, by necessity, on the substantial research literature from Canada and the United Kingdom, as well as the available US studies. This chapter focuses on common mental disorders (CMDs), which include everyday symptoms of psychological and physical distress that are common in societies across the developed and developing world. The CMD approach does not distinguish between diagnostic categories such as major depression or generalized anxiety disorder because it is not clear whether such diagnostic categories are comparable and valid across cultural settings (Beals, Manson, Mitchell, Spicer, & AI-SUPERPFP Team, 2003; Bhugra & Hicks, 2004; Cheng, 1989; Marsella, 1987), or if they represent different disorders (Slade & Watson, 2006). It is perhaps for these reasons that the CMD classification has been widely used internationally in cross-cultural mental health research.

Despite its wide prevalence, CMD is a toxic condition associated with social and psychological dysfunction and adverse health outcomes, and is a leading factor in the global burden of disease (Ferrari et al., 2013; Patel & Kleinman, 2003). It is also, however, a local phenomenon, one that is best understood in its social context. CMD arises from disturbances in what anthropologists have called "local worlds," or communities and social networks such as families, workplaces, schools, and neighborhoods. Loss, deprivation, social conflict, and violations of moral codes underlying everyday experiences in local worlds create the conditions for CMD (Kirmayer, Young, & Robbins, 1994; Kleinman & Good, 1985; Ware & Kleinman, 1992).

As the South Asian population in the United States becomes increasingly varied, South Asian immigrants today have come to occupy vastly disparate local worlds. Examples include the local worlds of the Silicon Valley engineer versus the new immigrant taxi driver; the elderly Gujarati couple living with adult children in an Atlanta suburb versus the teenager struggling with language barriers in an urban high school; or the second-generation physician married to a classmate from medical school versus the young village woman brought to the home of a husband she has never met. Just as social roles, resources, and privilege vary across individuals' local worlds, so too does mental disorder. These differences are not only in the prevalence of CMD but also in the multitude of symptoms, the ways in which symptoms are conceptualized and understood, and in the types of solutions sought to manage the disorder.

Prevalence of Common Mental Disorders

Few population-based health studies in the United States report findings on the health and mental health of the SAA population. In fact, those who are most likely to be at high risk for CMD—recent immigrants, non-English speakers, and undocumented residents—are also those who are least likely to be included in these studies. As a result, findings are difficult to interpret. In two population-based surveys from the United States, the *2004 National Latino and Asian American Study* and the *California Health Interview Study*, lower rates of mental health symptoms were found among affluent, highly educated South Asian samples, when compared with several other Asian groups, and with rates similar to White respondents (Masood, Okazaki, & Takeuchi, 2009; Sorkin, Nguyen, & Ngo-Metzger, 2011). In the United Kingdom, population-based studies examined the prevalence of CMD but reported varied results with no clear pattern. This included two large-scale surveys that found few differences in prevalence between South Asians and Whites (Nazroo, 1997; Weich et al., 2004).

Conversely, community-based studies in low-income areas have consistently found higher levels of distress in women, a key subgroup, when compared with their White counterparts (Bhui, Bhugra, Goldberg, Sauer, & Tylee, 2004; Williams, Eley, Hunt, & Bhatt, 1997). In the U.K. studies, Pakistani women, in particular, tended to report more distress (Anand & Cochrane, 2005; Creed et al., 1999). Varying results may be due in part to differences in the communities under study, as well as the lack of cross-cultural validity of measurement tools and strategies across studies (Anand & Cochrane, 2005). South Asians tend to underreport psychological symptoms in survey studies, when compared with Whites (Williams et al., 1997), thus common psychological measures of CMD likely underestimate true prevalence.

Social Context and Precipitants of CMD

In this section, social factors that are believed to account for CMD in South Asians are discussed.

Acculturation

Acculturation research indicates that the process of acculturation takes different trajectories in different social contexts. According to a widely cited model by Berry (1997), individuals who choose an "integrative" path toward acculturation seek to maintain their ethnic identity while seeking active engagement with the host culture. As a result, they enjoy better adjustment than those who reject either of these options (Berry, 1997). Empirical evidence comparing measures of acculturative adaptation also supports this view (Berry, 1997; Krishnan & Berry, 1992). In a study of South Asian children in the United Kingdom, results showed that those who made "integrated" choices regarding clothing and friendships—choices that reflected an identification with both the host culture and their own ethnic group—reported fewer mental health issues (Bhui et al., 2005). Other research also suggests that those with a strong ethnic identity enjoy greater well-being (Heim, Hunter, & Jones, 2011). Overall, those who have stronger ties and greater engagement with the majority community are younger, better educated, and higher income individuals. They enjoy greater language fluency, and experience less distress (Maker, Mittal, & Rastogi, 2006).

Racism and Discrimination

South Asian immigrant groups in the West have long been the target of racism in their host societies. In the United States, in particular, post-9/11 racist persecution and violence have been widely experienced across South Asian immigrant communities, directed specifically toward Muslims and Sikhs (South Asian Youth Action, 2013). Thus, the hypothesis that racism and discrimination have an adverse effect on CMD is a highly plausible one. A substantial literature on perceived racism/discrimination and mental health, including a large-scale population-based study (Kessler, Mickelson, & Williams, 1999), documents a strong relationship between the two (Chakraborty & McKenzie, 2002; Heim et al., 2011).

These studies do, however, share a common weakness in their cross-sectional design, which limits the ability to establish causality. The correlation between perceived racism and mental health problems does not mean that racism causes mental problems. In fact, it could just as easily mean the opposite—that people experiencing depression, anxiety, and psychosis are more likely to perceive racism and discrimination in their everyday lives. In order to untangle the causal association, more intensive and costly research approaches are needed, including longitudinal designs or nonsubjective indicators of racism/discrimination.

Immigration

In recent years, many middle- and lower-income South Asian families have immigrated to the United States. Unfortunately, they come unfamiliar with the realities of life in postrecession America, including unemployment, crime, and affordable housing shortages. As a result, many immigrants are profoundly shocked and unsettled by the reality of their new lives. In a study of new South Asian immigrants living in New York City, researchers examined social status indicators of parents prior to and following immigration. They identified a pattern of downward mobility. Fathers who had been bank managers and business owners in South Asia were now driving taxis, whereas mothers who had been teachers or housewives were working at menial jobs. Immigrants were shocked to learn they did not have the resources to seek higher education or training in the United States in order to better their circumstances (Bhattacharya & Schoppelrey, 2004). Adding to these difficulties was the burden of family expectations from their homeland. In many cases, relatives who provided funds for travel to the United States anticipated repayment in the form of ongoing financial support. Sending remittances home is a common practice and places a significant burden on struggling families (Kulkarni, 2013; South Asian Council for Social Services, 2004).

The immigration experience can be especially stressful especially for women. Women are less likely than men to speak English or to have marketable job skills (South Asian Council for Social Services, 2004). In New York City, studies conducted with Bangladeshi women found that the immigration experience was associated with disappointment, isolation, and a sense of loss. Separated from family and friendship networks in their home country, these women were now caring for small children in small crowded apartments, with no access to employment or education, and facing an uncertain future. Not surprisingly, depression, somatic distress, and other health problems are common among recent female South Asian immigrants (Gupta, 1999; Karasz, 2005; Khanlou & Peter, 2005; Naidoo & Davis, 1988; Raj & Silverman, 2003).

CMD among South Asian Subgroups

Children

Studies from the United Kingdom suggest that school-aged South Asian children experience better psychological adjustment and fewer behavioral problems than White children (Cochrane, 1979; Hackett, Hackett, & Taylor, 1991; Newth & Corbett, 1993). A number of cultural factors seem to account for this finding, one of which is a less punitive disciplinary style in South Asian households (Newth & Corbett, 1993). Traditional extended family structure has also been shown to be beneficial for South Asian children (Shah & Sonuga-Barke, 1995).

Adolescents

For adolescents, defined as ages 10–19 years (Sacks, 2003), the protective effects of traditional extended family life may not extend to them—at least, not to adolescent girls. In South Asian and White adolescent girls, rates of self-harm and suicide attempts are similar and are far higher than those among adolescent boys (Bhugra, Thompson, Singh, & Fellow-Smith, 2003). In fact, evidence suggests that these differences are related to higher rates of parental coercion directed toward adolescent daughters. In keeping with the cultural concept of *izzat*, or honor, some conservative parents may impose restrictive gender role norms on girls as they approach the end of childhood. In extreme and rare cases, forced marriages and forced emigration back to the home country have been documented (Abraham, 2000; Ayyub, 2000).

A study of women's explanatory models of depression found that conflict with parents regarding marriage was a common explanation for depressive symptoms (Karasz, 2005). Further research found that such conflicts can push young women who are dependent on their parents to desperation (Naidoo, 2003), which can lead to suicide attempts (Bhugra, 2002; Cooper et al., 2006).

Adult Women

Across cultures, women are characterized by very high rates of CMD as compared to men, including depression, anxiety, and somatic distress (Ferrari et al., 2013). Evidence suggests, however, that there is a wider mental health gender gap in South Asian societies than is found in the West. For example, a recent review of studies examining the prevalence of depression in Pakistan found an astonishing average prevalence rate of 45% for depressive symptoms among women, compared to 21% among men (Mirza & Jenkins, 2004). Evidence also suggests that South Asian women immigrants continue to experience very high rates of CMD compared to their male counterparts (Sorkin et al., 2011). Consequently, immigrant women are more likely to engage in self-harm and suicidal behaviors, including completed suicides, than either South Asian men or White women (Bhugra, Corridan, Rudge, Leff, & Mallett, 1999; Cooper et al., 2006; Nathan Kline Institute, 2005).

Studies have consistently found that family conflict is most strongly associated with CMD in adult women. In a U.K. study, Gater et al. (2009) found a prevalence rate of 65% for depression in elderly Pakistani women, compared to 21% in White women of the same age, even when controlling for age and socioeconomic status. Excess distress was associated with isolation, family conflict, and a lack of social support (Gater et al., 2009). Other studies have found that domestic violence is also a factor in a woman's suffering (Abraham, 2000, 2005; Ayyub, 2000; Kallivayalil, 2010). Results of the *California Health Interview Survey* indicated that although demographic risk factors, such as poverty, explained depressive symptoms in South Asian men, psychological distress among women was more often explained by social factors, particularly family problems (Sorkin et al., 2011).

Traditionally, early married life is a vulnerable time for South Asian women (Rastogi, 2007). The mother-in-law and daughter-in-law relationship is often a conflictual one in which the daughter-in-law experiences a considerable disadvantage. As the newest and lowest status member of the family, a young married woman in a joint family is expected to devote herself to her husband and his parents, while her own well-being is dependent upon securing their affection. When she is mistreated by these significant authority figures, the sense of shame, isolation, and despair can be overwhelming (Abraham, 2000, 2005; Kallivayalil, 2010). Joint family settings are associated with more distress and symptoms for married women than nuclear family settings (Sonuga-Barke & Mistry, 2000; Sonuga-Barke, Mistry, & Qureshi, 1998).

Because there are few culturally sanctioned avenues of escape for newly married women, women in coercive and conflictual family situations often feel trapped (Gask, Aseem, Waquas, & Waheed, 2011). Suicide attempts may be seen as a rational strategy for escaping a hopeless and unbearable situation (Chew-Graham, Bashir, Chantler, Burman, & Batsleer, 2002). In fact, South Asian women who have attempted suicide are much less likely to carry a diagnosis of depression or other mental disorder than White women (Cooper et al., 2006; van Bergen, van Balkom, Smit, & Saharso, 2012).

Postpartum Women

Across cultures, the postpartum period is a vulnerable period for women. Studies in South Asia identify very high rates of postpartum depression in new mothers (American Psychological Association, n.d.). Not surprisingly, postpartum depression in South Asia is associated with poverty, hunger, giving birth to a female child, a lack of social support, and marital conflict (Patel, Rodrigues, & DeSouza, 2002). Studies of immigrant communities in Western societies have found a similar association with poverty, substandard housing, enforced isolation, coercion, marital conflict, and a lack of social support (Husain et al., 2012; Husain, Gater, Tomenson, & Creed, 2004; Parvin, Jones, & Hull, 2004; Zelkowitz et al., 2004).

Somatization

Many studies have found that, like many non-Western, non-White, or non-middle-class individuals, South Asians are more likely to present with physical symptoms such as pain or fatigue when they are feeling distressed than are Western, White middle-class individuals (Lin, Carter, & Kleinman, 1985; Weiss, Raguram, & Channabasavanna, 1995; Weiss et al., 1986). Physical symptoms may be understood as an idiom, or language for communicating distress and social problems, also known as somatization (Bhugra & Hicks, 2004; Nichter, 1981). Of note, South Asians who express distress physically are usually fully aware of psychological symptoms as well (Rastogi, 2009a). In a study comparing emotional responses to stressful situations, researchers found that South Asian women and White women reported similar feelings of anxiety, sadness, and hopelessness when interviewed about their feelings (Karasz, Dempsey, & Fallek, 2007). However, when telling stories about these events, South Asian women were more likely than White women to include physical symptoms in their illness narratives. Symptoms including fainting, dizziness, and sensations of hot and cold were all used to emphasize the impact of these stressful situations and the moral culpability of those persons responsible for the narrator's distress (Karasz et al., 2007).

Treatment Utilization

An abundance of evidence indicates that South Asian immigrants underutilize mental health treatment when compared to Whites. They are less likely to consult or be referred to a mental health professional (Commander, Odell, Surtees, & Sashidharan, 2004; Karasz & Dempsey, 2008; Lloyd, 1992; Sorkin et al., 2011), less likely to share their mental health problems with a physician (Gillam, Jarman, White, & Law, 1989; Sorkin et al., 2011), and less likely to take antidepressants (Cooper, Booth, & Gill, 2003; Hull, Aquino, & Cotter, 2005). Among patients engaged in mental health treatment, South Asians receive less treatment (Cornwell & Hull, 1998), miss more appointments, and accept fewer prescriptions than Whites (Agius, Talwar, Murphy, & Zaman, 2010).

A variety of explanations have been suggested for the low rates of treatment utilization in South Asian communities. One is the lack of access to services, particularly in the United States, where financial and structural barriers limit access to care (Grote, Swartz, & Zuckoff, 2008). Still, even in Canada and the United Kingdom, where most people have access to mental health referrals and treatment, utilization among South Asians remains much lower than in the general population.

There is a broad perception that the use of folk treatments, including prayers, faith healing, and culturally specific medicinal treatments, serve as a barrier to treatment for mental health disorders. Yet while use of such healers and treatments is quite high in countries of origin (Halliburton, 2004; Shankar, Saravanan, & Jacob, 2006), studies of immigrant communities in Western societies have found that the usage of traditional treatments for mental disorders is low and that these treatments do not appear to serve as a barrier to care (Bhopal, 1986; Commander et al., 2004).

Stigma associated with mental illness is another common explanation for low utilization. Research shows that stigma associated with mental illness is a reality in many South Asian communities (Nieuwsma, Pepper, Maack, & Birgenheir, 2011; Rastogi et al., 2014; Sadavoy, Meier, & Ong, 2004). Research suggests that South Asian families with mentally ill members may be concerned with gossip, sometimes fearing that this may affect their social standing or ability to marry off their children (Bradby et al., 2007). As a result, South Asian patients who are concerned with stigma in the community are less willing to seek mental health treatment (Cinnirella & Loewenthal, 1999).

Explanatory Models of CMD

An important factor that can explain low rates of treatment utilization is the explanatory models of CMD common among South Asians (Chaudhury, 2011) that are at odds with explanatory models prevalent in the West. Standard mental health treatments available in Western societies are predicated on a biopsychiatric model of illness. According to this explanatory model, symptoms of distress are viewed as evidence of underlying pathology—dysfunction and disorder at the brain or behavioral level (Bolam, Murphy, & Gleeson, 2004; Saltonstall, 1993; Shilling, 2002). These "Western" assumptions are, however, at odds with explanatory models of CMDs in many South Asian societies. Emotional experiences in South Asian communities, including depression and anxiety, are generally characterized as a relatively normal response to life's problems and situations.

In 2014, a review of 19 studies of explanatory models of depression in South Asia found that biological and behavioral/cognitive explanations for symptoms were rare among participants experiencing these conditions (Aggarwal et al., 2014). Depression was attributed most frequently to familial issues including marital problems, lack of social support, social isolation, financial problems, and health issues. Notably, supernatural or "folk" explanations for depressive illness were rare. Additionally, although a similar review does not exist for the South Asian diaspora, numerous qualitative studies, as well as theoretical papers from counseling literature, reflect similar themes (Bhui, Bhugra, & Goldberg, 2002;

Chew-Graham et al., 2002; Ekanayake, Ahmad, & McKenzie, 2012; Karasz, 2005; Rastogi, 2007; Shankar et al., 2006).

A number of researchers have examined conceptual representations of depressive symptoms. These studies identify South Asian conceptual models of depression as problems of the social world, due largely to disruptions in core relationships. They suggest that conceptual representations of depression as a problem of social origin are a major reason that professional and psychological treatment are not viewed as appropriate strategies for managing depressive illness.

As an example, when asked about suitable treatments or management strategies for managing depression, participants in a vignette study conducted in the United States suggested pragmatic solutions rather than professional treatment (Karasz, 2005; Karasz et al., 2007). For example, in the case of a depressed woman dealing with marital conflicts, participants suggested that she ask for help from influential family members who could influence her husband's behavior. Likewise, depression caused by humiliating financial dependence might be addressed by finding a way for her to have an income.

These findings regarding conceptual models of depression have important implications for the design of interventions that address CMD. As the evidence suggests, the answer to solving the problem of untreated CMD does not lie simply in providing better access to conventional mental health services. As seen in therapeutic healing practices around the world, conceptual congruence between patients and healers is necessary in order for psychological therapies to be effective (Benish, Quintana, & Wampold, 2011; Kleinman, 1980). Unfortunately, this type of congruence does not always occur in Western treatment settings. Patients who conceptualize their depression in social and situational terms are skeptical of the efficacy of conventional technical treatments that focus on the individual (Karasz, Patel, Kabita, & Shimu, 2013; Karasz, Ragavan, Patel, Akhter, & Kabita, in press; Karasz & Watkins, 2006; Nadeem, Lange, & Miranda, 2009). As a result, they see less need for care (Karasz & Dempsey, 2008; Karasz et al., 2012). Though this is often labeled pejoratively as a problem with mental health literacy (Lauber, Nordt, Falcato, & Rossler, 2003), it should instead be recognized as a lack of conceptual synchrony—a clash between western 'scientific' models of mental disorder and the situational models that are common in many communities (Karasz et al., in press).

Studies suggest that South Asian immigrants conceptualize CMD symptoms as a natural or unavoidable reaction to problems in the social world. For South Asian immigrants, treatments that involve medication or talk therapy appear inadequate to address such problems especially when they relate to conflicts within hierarchical relationships. Whether the precipitating factor is marital abuse, coercion from in-laws, or separation from close family members, conventional biopsychiatric treatments that are aimed at correcting thoughts and behaviors or balancing neurotransmitters often seem inadequate. Similarly, when the problem is poverty and deprivation, medication and therapy may not be as effective as directly addressing the problem at hand (Karasz et al., 2013; Karasz et al., in press; Karasz, 1998).

New Directions in Treatment

It can be argued that new models of mental health treatment are needed in order to effectively address the widespread problem of CMD among vulnerable South Asian subgroups. Evidence has been presented that conventional mental health treatments lack relevance for South Asian immigrants who are experiencing CMD. Still, even if the conceptual gap between community models and current treatment paradigms did not exist, there would be good reason to propose that new treatment models are needed.

Growing evidence suggests that conventional treatment models for CMD, including antidepressants or psychotherapy, are much less effective than were previously thought. For example, commonly prescribed antidepressant medications are largely ineffective in treating CMD, particularly when compared to placebos (Kirsch, 2000, 2009; Moncrieff & Kirsch, 2005). Additionally, evidence suggests that standard mental health treatments currently available may be inadequate to address depression among the socially and economically vulnerable. In fact, evidence from large comparative trials in the United States found a strong link between socioeconomic status and treatment response, with patients with lower socioeconomic status achieving worse outcomes than other groups (Howland, 2008; Trivedi et al., 2006; Warden et al., 2009). Other large research studies have also found that poverty-related factors such as unemployment, economic adversity, and isolation all serve to reduce the effectiveness of both pharmacological and psychotherapeutic treatments (Brown et al., 2010; Kendrick, 2000).

Promising New Treatment Models

On the basis of the evidence among South Asian groups who are vulnerable to CMD, standard treatment approaches show limited effectiveness. As an example, clinical anecdotal evidence suggests that when distress and dysfunction are due to family disturbances, these may sometimes be addressed through marriage and family therapy. When relevant, such therapy can be culturally tailored without necessarily challenging traditional familial hierarchies (Rastogi, 2009a, 2009b).

Other novel treatment models for CMD have been described in the literature as well, including treatments that seek to address social–contextual stresses. One model, based on research demonstrating the role of social isolation in depression, uses a "befriending" model to provide companionship to depressed individuals (Harris, Brown, & Robinson, 1999). Similarly, another promising model developed in the United Kingdom for South Asian women uses social support and network-building strategies to address loneliness and isolation (Chaudhry, Waheed, Husain, Bhatti, & Creed, 2009; Gater et al., 2010).

In the United States, a partnership consisting of South Asian immigrant women, clinicians, activists, and health researchers developed a depression treatment intervention model that addresses both social isolation and financial dependence among low-income women. The model, called "Action to improve Selfesteem and Health through Asset building" (ASHA) provides depression treatment while helping women to build friendship networks. At the beginning of the program, participants open bank accounts, many for the first time in their lives, and begin saving money. Savings are matched at the end of the 6-month program and participants may use their funds to purchase assets that will contribute to their financial independence, such as job training or education. The program has shown promising results in both reducing depression and retaining women in treatment. Some graduates of the program have pooled assets to start business cooperatives (Karasz et al., 2015).

Recommendations

■ *More research.* Due to the limited research on South Asians in the United States, this review drew largely on research from Canada and the United Kingdom. Although many inferences can be drawn from these studies, the need for more research on the SAA population is clear. Both quantitative and qualitative research is needed to better understand the risks, the contextual dynamics—including racism and discrimination—and the effective interventions needed to address mental health problems in South Asian communities, particularly among newer immigrants, poorer communities, and vulnerable sub-groups described in this chapter.

■ *Better measurement tools.* More attention should be paid to developing valid clinical tools, including those that measure cultural idioms of distress (Karasz et al., 2013). Without more data from psychometrically rigorous measurement tools, it will be difficult to draw the attention of public health researchers and policy makers or to attract the resources needed to address the current gap in services.

■ *Stronger, more culturally relevant interventions.* The research reviewed in this chapter points to the need for a fresh approach to the development of clinical interventions. Conventional mental health treatments are based on the faulty assumption that such treatments are universally effective and equally well suited to diverse communities. The novel programs described in the chapter take a different approach. A common theme across these interventions is the attention to specific social and contextual antecedents that cause distress and mental disorder within the target population. It can be argued that such a contextual approach is necessary in order to address the problem of CMDs in South Asian immigrant populations. The authors hope that this chapter provides evidence to further support efforts to develop and test this approach.

Conclusions

This chapter summarizes themes that are key to understanding CMD in South Asian immigrant communities in the United States. These include the prevalence, manifestations, and some of the contextual and social issues shaping the CMD epidemic. Overall, this chapter highlights the vulnerability of some subgroups of the population, particularly adolescents and adult women. Key social precipitants include poverty, discrimination, oppressive gender roles, and the stress and loss associated with immigration. South Asians who experience CMDs such as depression utilize treatments at very low rates. This underutilization may be due to the lack of conceptual match between social models of CMD that are common in South Asian communities, and the individual focus of standard Western treatments. Thus, the weakness of current mental health treatment models in addressing CMD is largely a problem of social concordance and relevance and, again, calls for new treatment models that can better address these limitations.

References

Abraham, M. (2000). Isolation as a form of marital violence: The South Asian immigrant experience. *Journal of Social Distress & the Homeless, 9*(3), 221–236.

Abraham, M. (2005). Fighting back: Abused South Asian women's strategies of resistance. In N. J. Sokoloff & C. Pratt (Eds.), *Domestic violence at the margins: Readings on race, class, gender, and culture* (pp. 253–271). New Brunswick, NJ: Rutgers University Press.

Aggarwal, N. K., Balaji, M., Kumar, S., Mohanraj, R., Rahman, A., Verdeli, H., . . . Patel, V. (2014). Using consumer perspectives to inform the cultural adaptation of psychological treatments for depression: A mixed methods study from South Asia. *Journal of Affective Disorders, 163*, 88–101. doi: 10.1016/j.jad.2014.03.036

Agius, M., Talwar, A., Murphy, S., & Zaman, R. (2010). Issues regarding the delivery of early intervention psychiatric services to the South Asian population in England. *Psychiatria Danubina, 22*(2), 266–269.

American Psychological Association (APA). *What is postpartum depression & anxiety?* Retrieved from www.apa.org/pi/women/resources/reports/postpartum-dep.aspx

Anand, A., & Cochrane, R. (2005). The mental health status of South Asian women in Britain: A review of the UK literature. *Psychology Developing Societies, 17*(2), 195–214.

Ayyub, R. (2000). Domestic violence in the South Asian Muslim immigrant population in the United States. *Journal of Social Distress & the Homeless, 9*(3), 237–248.

Beals, J., Manson, S. M., Mitchell, C. M., Spicer, P., & AI-SUPERPFP Team. (2003). Cultural specificity and comparison in psychiatric epidemiology: Walking the tightrope in American Indian research. *Culture, Medicine and Psychiatry, 27*(3), 259–289.

Benish, S. G., Quintana, S., & Wampold, B. E. (2011). Culturally adapted psychotherapy and the legitimacy of myth: A direct-comparison meta-analysis. *Journal of Counseling Psychology, 58*(3), 279–289. doi: 10.1037/a0023626

Berry, J. W. (1997). Immigration, acculturation, and adaptation. *Applied Psychology: An International Review, 46*(1), 5–68.

Bhattacharya, G., & Schoppelrey, S. L. (2004). Preimmigration beliefs of life success, postimmigration experiences, and acculturative stress: South Asian immigrants in the United States. *Journal of Immigrant Health, 6*(2), 83–92. doi: 10.1023/B:JOIH.0000019168.75062.36

Bhopal, R. S. (1986). Asians' knowledge and behaviour on preventive health issues: Smoking, alcohol, heart disease, pregnancy, rickets, malaria prophylaxis and surma. *Community Medicine, 8*(4), 315–321.

Bhugra, D. (2002). Suicidal behavior in South Asians in the UK. *Crisis, 23*(3), 108–113.

Bhugra, D., & Hicks, M. H. (2004). Effect of an educational pamphlet on help-seeking attitudes for depression among British South Asian women. *Psychiatric Services: A Journal of the American Psychiatric Association, 55*(7), 827–829.

Bhugra, D., Corridan, B., Rudge, S., Leff, J., & Mallett, R. (1999). Social factors and first onset schizophrenia among Asians and whites. *International Journal of Social Psychiatry, 45*(3), 162–170.

Bhugra, D., Thompson, N., Singh, J., & Fellow-Smith, E. (2003). Inception rates of deliberate self-harm among adolescents in West London. *International Journal of Social Psychiatry, 49*(4), 247–250.

Bhui, K., Bhugra, D., & Goldberg, D. (2002). Causal explanations of distress and general practitioners' assessments of common mental disorder among Punjabi and English attendees. *Social Psychiatry and Psychiatric Epidemiology, 37*(1), 38–45.

Bhui, K., Bhugra, D., Goldberg, D., Sauer, J., & Tylee, A. (2004). Assessing the prevalence of depression in Punjabi and English primary care attenders: The role of culture, physical illness and somatic symptoms. *Transcultural Psychiatry, 41*(3), 307–322.

Bhui, K., Stansfeld, S., Head, J., Haines, M., Hillier, S., Taylor, S., . . . Booy, R. (2005). Cultural identity, acculturation, and mental health among adolescents in east London's multiethnic community. *Journal of Epidemiology & Community Health*, 59, 296–302.

Bolam, B., Murphy, S., & Gleeson, K. (2004). Individualization and inequalities in health: A qualitative study of class identity and health. *Social Science & Medicine*, 59(7), 1355–1365.

Bradby, H., Varyani, M., Oglethorpe, R., Raine, W., White, I., & Helen, M. (2007). British Asian families and the use of child and adolescent mental health services: A qualitative study of a hard to reach group. *Social Science & Medicine*, 65(12), 2413–2424.

Brown, G. W., Harris, T. O., Kendrick, T., Chatwin, J., Craig, T. K., Kelly, V., . . . Thread Study Group. (2010). Antidepressants, social adversity and outcome of depression in general practice. *Journal of Affective Disorders*, 121(3), 239–246. doi: 10.1016/j.jad.2009.06.004

Chakraborty, A., & McKenzie, K. (2002). Does racial discrimination cause mental illness? *British Journal of Psychiatry*, 180, 475–477.

Chaudhry, N., Waheed, W., Husain, N., Bhatti, S., & Creed, F. (2009). Development and pilot testing of a social intervention for depressed women of Pakistani family origin in the UK. *Journal of Mental Health*, 18(6), 504–509. doi: 10.1080/09638230902968209

Chaudhury, S. (2011). *Attitudes towards the diagnosis and treatment of depression among South Asian Muslim Americans* (Doctor of Philosophy). Columbia University, New York City.

Cheng, T. A. (1989). Symptomatology of minor psychiatric morbidity: A crosscultural comparison. *Psychological Medicine*, 19(3), 697–708.

Chew-Graham, C., Bashir, C., Chantler, K., Burman, E., & Batsleer, J. (2002). South Asian women, psychological distress and self-harm: Lessons for primary care trusts. *Health & Social Care in the Community*, 10(5), 339–347.

Cinnirella, M., & Loewenthal, K. M. (1999). Religious and ethnic group influences on beliefs about mental illness: A qualitative interview study. *British Journal of Medical Psychology*, 72(Pt. 4), 505–524.

Cochrane, R. (1979). Psychological and behavioural disturbance in West Indians, Indians and Pakistanis in Britain: A comparison of rates among children and adults. *British Journal of Psychiatry*, 134, 201–210.

Commander, M. J., Odell, S. M., Surtees, P. G., & Sashidharan, S. P. (2004). Care pathways for south Asian and white people with depressive and anxiety disorders in the community. *Social Psychiatry and Psychiatric Epidemiology*, 39(4), 259–264.

Cooper, H. C., Booth, K., & Gill, G. (2003). Patients' perspectives on diabetes health care education. *Health Education Research*, 18(2), 191–206.

Cooper, J., Husain, N., Webb, R., Waheed, W., Kapur, N., Guthrie, E., & Appleby, L. (2006). Self-harm in the UK: Differences between South Asians and Whites in rates, characteristics, provision of service and repetition. *Social Psychiatry and Psychiatric Epidemiology*, 41(10), 782–788.

Cornwell, J., & Hull, S. (1998). Do GPs prescribe antidepressants differently for South Asian patients? *Family Practice*, 15(1), S16–S18.

Creed, F., Winterbottom, M., Tomenson, B., Britt, R., Anand, I. S., Wander, G. S., & Chandrashekhar, Y. (1999). Preliminary study of non-psychotic disorders in people from the Indian subcontinent living in the UK and India. *Acta Psychiatrica Scandinavica, 99*(4), 257–260.

Ekanayake, S., Ahmad, F., & McKenzie, K. (2012). Qualitative cross-sectional study of the perceived causes of depression in South Asian origin women in Toronto. *BMJ Open, 2*(1), e000641. doi: 10.1136/bmjopen-2011-000641

Ferrari, A. J., Charlson, F. J., Norman, R. E., Patten, S. B., Freedman, G., Murray, C. J., . . . Whiteford, H. A. (2013). Burden of depressive disorders by country, sex, age, and year: Findings from the Global Burden of Disease study 2010. *PLoS Medicine, 10*(11), e1001547. doi: 10.1371/journal.pmed.1001547

Gask, L., Aseem, S., Waquas, A., & Waheed, W. (2011). Isolation, feeling "stuck" and loss of control: Understanding persistence of depression in British Pakistani women. *Journal of Affective Disorders, 128*(1–2), 49–55. doi: 10.1016/j.jad.2010.06.023

Gater, R., Tomenson, B., Percival, C., Chaudhry, N., Waheed, W., Dunn, G., . . . Creed, F. (2009). Persistent depressive disorders and social stress in people of Pakistani origin and white Europeans in UK. *Social Psychiatry and Psychiatric Epidemiology, 44*(3), 198–207. doi: 10.1007/s00127-008-0426-x

Gater, R., Waheed, W., Husain, N., Tomenson, B., Aseem, S., & Creed, F. (2010). Social intervention for British Pakistani women with depression: Randomised controlled trial. *British Journal of Psychiatry, 197*(3), 227–233. doi: 10.1192/bjp.bp.109.066845

Gillam, S. J., Jarman, B., White, P., & Law, R. (1989). Ethnic differences in consultation rates in urban general practice. *British Medical Journal, 299*(6705), 953–957.

Grote, N. K., Swartz, H. A., & Zuckoff, A. (2008). Enhancing interpersonal psychotherapy for mothers and expectant mothers on low incomes: Adaptations and additions. *Journal of Contemporary Psychotherapy, 38*(1), 23–33. doi: 10.1007/s10879-007-9065-x

Gupta, S. R. (1999). *Emerging voices: South Asian American women redefine self, family, and community.* Walnut Creek, CA: AltaMira Press.

Hackett, L., Hackett, R., & Taylor, D. C. (1991). Psychological disturbance and its associations in the children of the Gujarati community. *Journal of Child Psychology and Psychiatry, 32*(5), 851–856. doi: 10.1111/j.1469-7610.1991.tb01907.x

Halliburton, M. (2004). Finding a fit: Psychiatric pluralism in south India and its implications for WHO studies of mental disorder. *Transcultural Psychiatry, 41*(1), 80–98.

Harris, T., Brown, G. W., & Robinson, R. (1999). Befriending as an intervention for chronic depression among women in an inner city. 1: Randomised controlled trial. *British Journal of Psychiatry, 174*, 219–224.

Heim, D., Hunter, S. C., & Jones, R. (2011). Perceived discrimination, identification, social capital and well-being: Relationships with physical health and psychological distress in a UK minority sample. *Journal of Cross-Cultural Psychology, 42*(7), 1145–1164.

Howland, R. H. (2008). Sequenced Treatment Alternatives to Relieve Depression (STAR*D). Part 2: Study outcomes. *Journal of Psychosocial Nursing and Mental Health Services, 46*(10), 21–24.

Hull, S. A., Aquino, P., & Cotter, S. (2005). Explaining variation in antidepressant prescribing rates in east London: A cross sectional study. *Family Practice, 22*(1), 37–42.

Husain, N., Cruickshank, K., Husain, M., Khan, S., Tomenson, B., & Rahman, A. (2012). Social stress and depression during pregnancy and in the postnatal period in British Pakistani mothers: A cohort study. *Journal of Affective Disorders, 140*(3), 268–276. doi: 10.1016/j.jad.2012.02.009

Husain, N., Gater, R., Tomenson, B., & Creed, F. (2004). Social factors associated with chronic depression among a population-based sample of women in rural Pakistan. *Social Psychiatry and Psychiatric Epidemiology, 39*(8), 618–624. doi: 10.1007/s00127-004-0781-1

Kallivayalil, D. (2010). Narratives of suffering of South Asian immigrant survivors of domestic violence. *Violence Against Women, 16*(7), 789–811. doi: 10.1177/1077801210374209

Karasz, A. (2005). Cultural differences in conceptual models of depression. *Social Science & Medicine, 60*(7), 1625–1635.

Karasz, A. K. (1998). *Role strain and symptoms in a group of Pakistani immigrant women.* (Dissertation/Thesis), City University of New York, New York, NY.

Karasz, A., & Dempsey, K. (2008). Health seeking for ambiguous symptoms in two cultural groups: A comparative study. *Transcultural Psychiatry, 45*(3), 415–438.

Karasz, A., & Watkins, L. (2006). Conceptual models of treatment in depressed Hispanic patients. *Annals of Family Medicine, 4*(6), 527–533.

Karasz, A., Dempsey, K., & Fallek, R. (2007). Cultural differences in the experience of everyday symptoms: A comparative study of South Asian and European American women. *Culture, Medicine and Psychiatry, 31*(4), 473–497.

Karasz, A., Dowrick, C., Byng, R., Buszewicz, M., Ferri, L., Olde Hartman, T. C., . . . Reeve, J. (2012). What we talk about when we talk about depression: Doctor-patient conversations and treatment decision outcomes. *British Journal of General Practice, 62*(594), e55–63. doi: 10.3399/bjgp12X616373

Karasz, A., Patel, V., Kabita, M., & Shimu, P. (2013). "Tension" in South Asian women: Developing a measure of common mental disorder using participatory methods. *Progress in Community Health Partnerships, 7*(4), 429–441. doi: 10.1353/cpr.2013.0046

Karasz, A., Raghavan, S., Patel, V., Zaman, M., Akhter, L., & Kabita, M. (2015). ASHA: Using participatory methods to develop an asset-building mental health intervention for Bangladeshi immigrant women. *Progress in Community Health Partnerships.*

Kendrick, T. (2000). Why can't GPs follow guidelines on depression? We must question the basis of the guidelines themselves. *British Medical Journal, 320*(7229), 200–201.

Kessler, R. C., Mickelson, K. D., & Williams, D. R. (1999). The prevalence, distribution, and mental health correlates of perceived discrimination in the United States. *Journal of Health and Social Behavior, 40*(3), 208–230.

Khanlou, N., & Peter, E. (2005). Participatory action research: Considerations for ethical review. *Social Science & Medicine, 60*, 2333–2340.

Kirmayer, L. J., Young, A., & Robbins, J. M. (1994). Symptom attribution in cultural perspective. *Canadian Journal of Psychiatry, 39*(10), 584–595.

Kirsch, I. (2000). Are drug and placebo effects in depression additive? *Biological Psychiatry, 47*(8), 733–735.

Kirsch, I. (2009). Antidepressants and the placebo response. *Epidemiologia e Psichiatria Sociale, 18*(4), 318–322.

Kleinman, A. (1980). *Patients and healers in the context of culture: An exploration of the borderland between anthropology, medicine, and psychiatry.* Berkeley, CA: University of California Press.

Kleinman, A., & Good, B. (1985). *Culture and Depression: Studies in the Anthropology and Cross-Cultural Psychiatry of Affect and Disorder.* Berkeley, CA: University of California Press.

Krishnan, A., & Berry, J. W. (1992). Acculturative stress and acculturation attitudes among Indian immigrants to the United States. *Psychology & Developing Societies, 4*, 187–212.

Kulkarni, N. K. (2013). Worker migration from South Asia. *Searchlight Newsletter of the Rockefeller Foundation, 4*, 1–6.

Lauber, C., Nordt, C., Falcato, L., & Rossler, W. (2003). Do people recognize mental illness? Factors influencing mental health literacy. *European Archives of Psychiatry and Clinical Neuroscience, 253*(5), 248–251.

Lin, E. H., Carter, W. B., & Kleinman, A. M. (1985). An exploration of somatization among Asian refugees and immigrants in primary care. *American Journal of Public Health, 75*(9), 1080–1084.

Lloyd, K. (1992). Ethnicity, primary care and non-psychotic disorders. *International Review of Psychiatry, 4*(3–4), 257–265.

Maker, A., Mittal, M., & Rastogi, M. (2006). South Asians in the United States: Developing a systemic and empirically based mental health assessment model. In R. Rastogi & E. Wizling (Eds.), *Voices of color* (pp. 233–254). Thousand Oaks, CA: Sage Publishing.

Marsella, A. J. (1987). The measurement of depressive experience and disorder across cultures. In A. J. Marsella, R. Hirschfeld, & M. Katz (Eds.), *The measurement of depression* (pp. 376–399). New York, NY: Guilford.

Masood, N., Okazaki, S., & Takeuchi, D. T. (2009). Gender, family, and community correlates of mental health in South Asian Americans. *Cultural Diversity & Ethnic Minority Psychology, 15*(3), 265–274. doi: 10.1037/a0014301

Mirza, I., & Jenkins, R. (2004). Risk factors, prevalence, and treatment of anxiety and depressive disorders in Pakistan: Systematic review. *British Medical Journal, 328*(7443), 794. doi: 10.1136/bmj.328.7443.794

Moncrieff, J., & Kirsch, I. (2005). Efficacy of antidepressants in adults. *British Medical Journal, 331*(7509), 155–157.

Nadeem, E., Lange, J. M., & Miranda, J. (2009). Perceived need for care among low-income immigrant and U.S.-born black and Latina women with depression. *Journal of Women's Health, 18*(3), 369–375. doi: 10.1089/jwh.2008.0898

Naidoo, J. C. (2003). South Asian Canadian women: A contemporary portrait. *Psychology and Developing Societies, 15*(1), 51–67. doi: 10.1177/097133360301500104

Naidoo, J. C., & Davis, J. C. (1988). Canadian South Asian women in transition: A dualistic view of life. *Journal of Comparative Family Studies, 19*, 311–327.

Nathan Kline Institute. (2005). *Asian Indians and other South Asian Americans.* Retrieved from ssrdqst.rfmh.org/cecc/index.php?q=node/61

Nazroo, J. Y. (1997). *Ethnicity and mental health.* London: Policy Studies Institute.

Newth, S. J., & Corbett, J. (1993). Behaviour and emotional problems in three-year-old children of Asian parentage. *Journal of Child Psychology and Psychiatry, and Allied Disciplines, 34*(3), 333–352.

Nichter, M. (1981). Idioms of distress: Alternatives in the expression of psychosocial distress: A case study from South India. *Culture, Medicine, and Psychiatry, 5*(4), 379–408.

Nieuwsma, J. A., Pepper, C. M., Maack, D. J., & Birgenheir, D. G. (2011). Indigenous perspectives on depression in rural regions of India and the United States. *Transcultural Psychiatry, 48*(5), 539–568. doi: 10.1177/1363461511419274

Parvin, A., Jones, C. E., & Hull, S. A. (2004). Experiences and understandings of social and emotional distress in the postnatal period among Bangladeshi women living in Tower Hamlets. *Family Practice, 21*(3), 254–260.

Patel, V., & Kleinman, A. (2003). Poverty and common mental disorders in developing countries. *Bulletin of the World Health Organization, 81*(8), 609–615.

Patel, V., Rodrigues, M., & DeSouza, N. (2002). Gender, poverty, and postnatal depression: A study of mothers in Goa, India. *American Journal of Psychiatry, 159*(1), 43–47.

Raj, A., & Silverman, J. G. (2003). Immigrant South Asian women at greater risk for injury from intimate partner violence. *American Journal of Public Health, 93*(3), 435–437.

Rastogi, M. (2007). Coping with transitions in Asian Indian families: Systemic clinical interventions with immigrants. *Journal of Systemic Therapies, 26*(2), 55–67.

Rastogi, M. (2009a). Asian Indians in intercultural marriages: Intersections of acculturation, gender, and exogamy. In T. Karris & K. Killiam (Eds.), *Intercultural couples.* New York, NY: Routledge.

Rastogi, M. (2009b). Drawing gender to the foreground: Couple therapy with South Asians in the United States. In M. Rastogi & V. Thomas (Eds.), *Multicultural couple therapy.* Thousand Oaks, CA: Sage Publishing.

Rastogi, M., Khushalani, S., Dhawan, S., Goga, J., Hemanth, N., Kosi, R., . . . Rao, V. (2014). Understanding clinician perception of common presentations in South Asians seeking mental health treatment and determining barriers and facilitators to treatment. *Asian Journal of Psychiatry, 7*(1), 15–21. doi: 10.1016/j.ajp.2013.09.005

Rastogi, M., Suthakaran, & Thayil, C. K. (2002). South Asian American community mental health. *A Brown Paper: The Health of South Asians in the United States, 2002.* South Asian Public Health Association.

Sacks D. (2003). Age limits and adolescents. *Paediatrics & Child Health, 8*(9), 577.

Sadavoy, J., Meier, R., & Ong, A. Y. (2004). Barriers to access to mental health services for ethnic seniors: The Toronto study. *Canadian Journal of Psychiatry, 49*(3), 192–199.

Saltonstall, R. (1993). Healthy bodies, social bodies: Men's and women's concepts and practices of health in everyday life. *Social Science & Medicine, 36*(1), 7–14.

Shah, Q., & Sonuga-Barke, E. (1995). Family structure and the mental health of Pakistani Muslim mothers and their children living in Britain. *British Journal of Clinical Psychology, 34*(Pt. 1), 79–81.

Shankar, B. R., Saravanan, B., & Jacob, K. S. (2006). Explanatory models of common mental disorders among traditional healers and their patients in rural south India. *International Journal of Social Psychiatry, 52*(3), 221–233.

Shilling, C. (2002). Culture, the "sick role" and the consumption of health. *British Journal of Sociology, 53*(4), 621–638.

Slade, T., & Watson, D. (2006). The structure of common DSM-IV and ICD-10 mental disorders in the Australian general population. *Psychological Medicine, 36*(11), 1593–1600. doi: 10.1017/S0033291706008452

Sonuga-Barke, E. J., & Mistry, M. (2000). The effect of extended family living on the mental health of three generations within two Asian communities. *British Journal of Clinical Psychology, 39*(Pt. 2), 129–141.

Sonuga-Barke, E. J., Mistry, M., & Qureshi, S. (1998). The mental health of Muslim mothers in extended families living in Britain: The impact of intergenerational disagreement on anxiety and depression. *British Journal of Clinical Psychology, 37*(Pt.4), 399–408.

Sorkin, D. H., Nguyen, H., & Ngo-Metzger, Q. (2011). Assessing the mental health needs and barriers to care among a diverse sample of Asian American older adults. *Journal of General Internal Medicine, 26*(6), 595–602. doi: 10.1007/s11606-010-1612-6

South Asian Americans Leading Together. (2012, July). *A demographic snapshot of South Asians in the United States.* Retrieved from saalt.org/wp-content/uploads/2012/09/Demographic-Snapshot-Asian-American-Foundation-2012.pdf

South Asian Council for Social Services. (2004). *Unlocking the golden door: A report on the needs of South Asian New Yorkers.* Retrieved from sacssny.org/wp-content/uploads/2013/02/SACSS-UnlockingGoldenDoor_web.pdf

South Asian Youth Action. (2013). *New York City South Asian youth: Critical mass, urgent needs.* Retrieved from www.issuelab.org/permalink/resource/16968

Trivedi, M. H., Rush, A. J., Wisniewski, S. R., Nierenberg, A. A., Warden, D., Ritz, L., . . . Team, S. D. S. (2006). Evaluation of outcomes with citalopram for depression using measurement-based care in STAR*D: Implications for clinical practice. *American Journal of Psychiatry, 163*(1), 28–40.

van Bergen, D. D., van Balkom, A. J., Smit, J. H., & Saharso, S. (2012). "I felt so hurt and lonely": Suicidal behavior in South Asian-Surinamese, Turkish, and Moroccan women in the Netherlands. *Transcultural Psychiatry, 49*(1), 69–86. doi: 10.1177/1363461511427353

Warden, D., Rush, A. J., Wisniewski, S. R., Lesser, I. M., Thase, M. E., Balasubramani, G. K., . . . Trivedi, M. H. (2009). Income and attrition in the treatment of depression: A STAR*D report. *Depression and Anxiety, 26*(7), 622–633. doi: 10.1002/da.20541

Ware, N. C., & Kleinman, A. (1992). Culture and somatic experience: The social course of illness in neurasthenia and chronic fatigue syndrome. *Psychosomatic Medicine, 54*(5), 546–560.

Weich, S., Nazroo, J., Sproston, K., McManus, S., Blanchard, M., Erens, B., . . . Tyrer, P. (2004). Common mental disorders and ethnicity in England: The EMPIRIC study. *Psychological Medicine, 34*(8), 1543–1551.

Weiss, M. G., Raguram, R., & Channabasavanna, S. M. (1995). Cultural dimensions of psychiatric diagnosis. A comparison of DSM-III-R and illness explanatory models in south India. *British Journal of Psychiatry, 166*(3), 353–359.

Weiss, M. G., Sharma, S. D., Gaur, R. K., Sharma, J. S., Desai, A., & Doongaji, D. R. (1986). Traditional concepts of mental disorder among Indian psychiatric patients: Preliminary report of work in progress. *Social Science & Medicine, 23*(4), 379–386.

Williams, R., Eley, S., Hunt, K., & Bhatt, S. (1997). Has psychological distress among UK South Asians been under-estimated? A comparison of three measures in the west of Scotland population. *Ethnicity & Health, 2*(1–2), 21–29.

Zelkowitz, P., Schinazi, J., Katofsky, L., Saucier, J. F., Valenzuela, M., Westreich, R., & Dayan, J. (2004). Factors associated with depression in pregnant immigrant women. *Transcultural Psychiatry, 41*(4), 445–464.

Chapter 13

Maternal Mental Health

Deepika Goyal and Bindu Garapaty

Contents

Abstract

Objective: To review and summarize the evidence about prevalence and types of maternal mental health conditions and help-seeking behaviors among South Asian American women; the unique cultural values and practices surrounding the perinatal period; and perinatal mood disorders among South Asian mothers around the globe. The authors discuss the barriers South Asian American women face in seeking and utilizing mental health care during the perinatal period, and offer recommendations for addressing the identified gaps through changes in practice, research and policies.

Key Findings: Several research studies have noted that perinatal mood disorder is a concern among South Asian women living in other countries. To date, however, very few studies in the United States have included South Asian women in their study samples when investigating this disorder. Cultural issues associated with perinatal mood disorder include infant gender (male preferred over females) and lack of social support. The stigma of mental illness also remains an important theme throughout many studies and has been noted as a key barrier to seeking and utilizing mental health-care services. Finally, the signs and symptoms of perinatal mood disorder are difficult to decipher and South Asian cultural values, traditions, and practices may further complicate timely identification and treatment of the disorder.

Recommendations: The growing South Asian population in the United States requires attention toward a greater understanding of perinatal mood disorder within the context of their unique cultural values, traditions, and practices. Future research must include larger, more diverse samples of South Asian women with the addition of qualitative research, in order to further understand the complexities interwoven within cultural traditions and practices that may limit South Asian families from seeking help for mental health needs. Due to the diversity within South Asian subcultures, there is also a need to reframe the examination of perinatal mood disorder for this population. These findings will support health-care providers in further understanding the needs of this population and may also assist local, state, and federal agencies in establishing future funding priorities.

Introduction

The period surrounding pregnancy and childbirth is a time of joy and excitement for many new parents and families. New mothers, however, are at an increased risk of developing a range of perinatal mood disorders (PMDs), which can include antenatal depression, postpartum "baby" or "maternity" blues, postpartum psychosis, and postpartum depression (PPD). Each of these disorders has a unique constellation of symptoms and recommended treatment methodologies. The perinatal period is defined as the time from early pregnancy through the first 12 months following childbirth.

To date, the majority of research in the United States regarding PMD has been conducted among non-Hispanic White mothers, with very little research that includes South Asian women in study samples. With a growing South Asian American (SAA) population, clinicians need to be made more aware of cultural issues that may hinder timely identification and timely treatment of this potentially devastating disease. The aim of this chapter is to provide a brief overview of mental health and help-seeking behaviors among SAA women, the unique cultural values and practices surrounding the perinatal period, and the literature regarding PMD among South Asian mothers around the globe. This includes a review of the state of the science regarding PMD among SAA women. Findings will offer implications for practice and recommendations for future research that can, potentially, assist local, state, and federal health-care providers and agencies in establishing funding priorities in this area.

Perinatal Mood Disorders

Antenatal Depression

Antenatal depression is defined as the onset of depression during pregnancy until childbirth and affects up to 18% women worldwide (Gavin et al., 2005). It may be triggered by the pregnancy itself, with symptoms ranging from fatigue and insomnia to excessive worry, panic attacks, and repeated thoughts or images of frightening things happening to the baby such as miscarriage, stillbirth, and birth defects (Abramowitz, Schwartz, Moore, & Luenzmann, 2003). For many women, antenatal depression often goes unrecognized, as symptoms such as fatigue and insomnia are similar to the typical symptoms of pregnancy. It is important, however, to recognize and treat antenatal depression, because it is associated with a higher risk of fetal growth delay and premature birth (Field, 2011). Antenatal depression also places women at an increased risk for developing PPD (Williams, 2005).

Maternity Blues

Maternity blues is the most common PMD affecting up to 84% of all new mothers (Gaynes et al., 2005; Vesga-Lopez et al., 2008). Symptoms of a self-limiting disorder usually present in the first postpartum week and include labile mood, tearfulness, anxiety, loss of appetite, and irritability. Symptoms often resolve within 7–14 days, without any treatment required (O'Hara, Schlechte, Lewis, & Wright, 1991). Symptoms lasting 2 weeks or longer require further evaluation for possible PPD.

Postpartum Depression

Defined as a depressive episode, postpartum depression (PPD) occurs between 2 weeks and 12 months following childbirth (O'Hara & Swain, 1996). It has gained more attention in recent years as healthcare providers have become more knowledgeable about diagnosing PPD and recognizing it as a debilitating illness that can have significant consequences for both the mother and the child. A large study evaluated 10,000 primarily White women (80%, $n = 8016$) who attended an urban obstetric hospital in the United States 4–6 weeks postpartum (Cox, Holden, & Sagovsky, 1987). Using the *Edinburgh Postnatal Depression Scale* (EPDS), the study revealed a score of ≥10 among 14% women. According to the scale, this indicated a high risk for developing PPD (Wisner et al., 2013).

When identified early, PPD can be treated with therapy, with antidepressant medication, or through the use of complementary and alternative treatments such as yoga and bright light therapy (O'Hara & Wisner, 2014), as well as uninterrupted nighttime sleep (Goyal, Gay, & Lee, 2009). Left untreated, PPD disrupts the maternal–child bond (Beck, 1996) and is associated with delayed infant language and cognitive development (Sohr-Preston & Scaramella, 2006). It also disrupts family functioning (Tammentie, Paavilainen, Astedt-Kurki, & Tarkka, 2004), leads to early breastfeeding discontinuation (Howard, Lanphear, Lanphear, Eberly, & Lawrence, 2006), child maltreatment (Reijneveld, van der Wal, Brugman, Hira Sing, & Verloove-Vanhorick, 2004), and infanticide (Spinelli, 2004).

Postpartum Psychosis

Postpartum psychosis is the most serious type of all the PMDs and affects 1/1000 women after giving birth (Sit, Rothschild, & Wisner, 2006). Symptoms include mood fluctuation, delusions, auditory hallucinations, cognitive impairment, insomnia, and confusion, presenting rapidly after birth (Wisner, Peindl, & Hanusa, 1996). Mothers with postpartum psychosis require immediate hospitalization for inpatient psychiatric care. If left untreated, postpartum psychosis can lead to suicide, suicidal ideation, and/or infanticide (Spinelli, 2004). Although it is among the more rare types of PMDs, postpartum psychosis is likely to be featured more prominently in the media due to the severity of symptoms.

Literature Review

In 2011, more than 75% of the South Asian population in the United States was foreign-born, with women accounting for almost half (46%) of this population (South Asian Americans Leading Together [SAALT], 2014). Given the growing SAA population, it is increasingly important to identify health disparities and recognize cultural influences that may have an impact on timely identification and treatment of PMD. Although the South Asian population includes several smaller subgroups, studies predominantly report on Asian Indians only. Thus, in the absence of disaggregated data for South Asian subgroups, it is common to use data on Asian Indians to make generalizations for the larger South Asian population.

Mental Health and Help-Seeking Behavior among South Asian Indians

Research suggests that although South Asian Indians living in the United States are more likely to have employer-based health-care coverage when compared with other racial and ethnic groups, they are less likely to seek mental health-care services (Kaiser Family Foundation, 2008). As a community, South Asian Indians in the United States tend to be more family-oriented, and less self-oriented when compared with the Western perspective of self and individual autonomy within the family (Tewari, Inman, & Sandhu, 2003). Additionally, the welfare and integrity of the family is held in higher regard than an individual's needs (Farver, Narang, & Bhadha, 2002). This way of thinking may contribute to mental illness being highly stigmatized in the Indian culture and accompanied by a deeply rooted attitude often combined with a fear of patients who have such illnesses (Das & Kemp, 1997; Kishore, Gupta, Jiloha, & Bantman, 2011). Research has also found that Asian Indians often present with physical symptoms rather than recognizing and reporting their psychological symptoms and how they are actually feeling (Bhui, Bhugra, Goldberg, Dunn, & Desai, 2001). Defined as somatization, patients may indicate that they have a headache or feel weak (Kishore et al., 2011) when, in fact, they have depression.

In 2005, Conrad and Pacquiao interviewed 23 predominantly female (83%, $n = 19$) mental health-care professionals regarding their experience in treating Asian Indian patients who were admitted to an acute psychiatric hospital in the United States for depression. The sample included physicians ($n = 11$), clinicians (social workers, psychologists, counselors) ($n = 6$), and registered nurses ($n = 6$). Their findings suggested that cultural factors including stigma, religious beliefs, and language barriers all contributed to the denial of depression and the delay of treatment among Asian Indians in the United States. In a similar study

(Khanna, McDowell, Perumbilly & Titus, 2009), investigators interviewed six Asian Indian counselors and therapists who were working in the United States to explore their experiences working with Asian Indian families. Asian Indians displayed strong feelings of stigma and shame toward any mental illness or treatment such as counseling. In a secondary analysis of county mental health data in Texas, it was noted that Asian Indian ($n = 136$) clients were more likely to underutilize mental health services, as compared with Vietnamese clients ($n = 398$) (Chuang, 2005).

In a review of the literature on Asian Indian immigrant women, Tewary (2005) found that many Asian Indians did not perceive mental disorders as problematic and placed a priority on physical health over mental health. In fact, this review found that mental health was seen by some as self-inflicted and attention-seeking behavior (Tewary, 2005). As a result of these views on mental health, Asian Indians tend to wait until symptoms are severe before seeking mental health care (Durvasula & Sue, 1996). Additionally, those who do seek treatment tend to drop out earlier than is needed for proper care (Akutsu, Tsuru, & Chu, 2004). Thus, understanding the South Asian perspective on mental health is vitally important and researchers caution that lower mental health service utilization among SAAs does not correspond to a lower need for such services (Sue, Yan Cheng, Saad, & Chu, 2012).

Perinatal Cultural Practices and Traditions among South Asian Indians

South Asian Indians practice several cultural traditions during the postpartum period, with the overall goal of enhancing healing and maintaining the well-being of the mother. These traditional postpartum practices include a prescribed postpartum rest period, female family support, and a specific diet.

Postpartum Rest

After the birth of a new baby, a rest period of 30–40 days is strongly encouraged. During this time, the new mother and infant are expected to stay in the home and this is believed to promote maternal healing and protect the mother and newborn from exposure to illness and evil spirits (Chalmers & Meyer, 1993; Grewal, Bhagat, & Balneaves, 2008).

Female Family Support

During the prescribed postpartum rest period, it is customary for other female family members to take over household tasks and lend a hand in taking care of the new baby (Choudhry, 1997; Galanti, 2008). Dependence on female family members for support and care is also believed to be protection against exposure to illness and evil spirits (Chalmers & Meyer, 1993; Grewal et al., 2008).

Postpartum Diet and Food Preparation

A general perception exists among Asian Indians that consuming cold foods (e.g., milk, ghee) during the postpartum period will restore the state of "hotness" generated by the pregnancy (Goyal, 2016). Other postpartum traditions include preparation of special food for the new mother in order to promote healing. This includes certain bread dishes such as *panjiri* or *katlu* (sautéed whole wheat flour in butter with almonds and pistachios), as well as wheat, rice, ghee (clarified butter), leafy vegetables, and *jaggery* (unrefined brown sugar), all of which are encouraged to promote breast milk production (Majumdar, 1983) and promote healing (Galanti, 2008; Goyal, Park, & McNiesh, 2015).

Other Postpartum Cultural Values

The preference of male infants is another cultural view generally held by South Asians (Cohen, 2000). This high regard for male children may be related to the fact that South Asian male offspring are expected to support their parents as they age (Choudhry, 1997).

To date, no studies have examined the extent to which postpartum traditions are practiced or any association these traditions have with PMD among SAAs. For immigrants with few family members close by, however, isolation from extended family in their home country becomes a very real problem. As a result, the mother's social support system is decreased, which may impact the ability for perinatal traditions to occur, thus placing her at risk for developing PPD (Foreman & Henshaw, 2002). Additionally, immigrant mothers may have a lack of financial and insurance coverage, limited childcare, inadequate transportation options, lack of English fluency, and limited access to timely and appropriate interpretation and translation services (Callister, Beckstrand, & Corbett, 2011; Conrad & Pacquiao, 2005).

PMDs among South Asian Mothers around the Globe

Studies regarding PMD among South Asian mothers are plentiful worldwide including South Asia, Canada, and the United Kingdom. In a review of 28 studies conducted worldwide, an antenatal depression prevalence rate of 18% and incidence rate of 14% was found within a largely Caucasian sample (Gavin et al., 2005). In the United Kingdom, Dhillon and MacArthur (2010) noted a 31% antenatal depression rate using the EPDS (Cox et al., 1987). Their study involved a sample of mostly married South Asian women (Indian, $n = 25$; Bangladeshi, $n = 6$; Pakistani, $n = 60$) living in the United Kingdom with a mean age of 28.6 (SD = 5.2) years. Dhillon and MacArthur also found that family preference for a male infant, previous antenatal depression, and the number of people able to provide support were all significantly associated with current antenatal depression.

In 2009, Baldwin and Griffiths interviewed eight public health nurses of various ethnic backgrounds (none of South Asian origin) living in the United Kingdom, with the goal of exploring risks and culture-specific factors among Asian Indian women in developing PPD. Their findings highlight the importance of immediate and holistic assessment, education, and intervention by health-care providers who have sensitivity to cultural nuances. For women living in India, PPD rates of up to 32% have been noted (Affonso, De, Horowitz, & Mayberry, 2000; Chandran, Tharyan, Muliyil, & Abraham, 2002; Patel, Rodrigues, & DeSouza, 2002). A 2012 study examined 506 married South Asian women, with an average age of 24.3 (SD = 3.2) years, for PPD and associated factors in a New Delhi Hospital (Dubey, Gupta, Bhasin, Muthal, & Arora, 2012). A total of 6% ($n = 31$) of the mothers scored >9 on the EPDS, suggesting a risk for developing PPD. Other associated risk factors included birth of a female child, absence of a nuclear family structure living arrangement, and poor marital relationship.

Another study of 132 predominantly upper-class pregnant women living in Bengaluru, India (Mariam & Srinivasan, 2009), found 27 women (20%) who scored above the cutoff (≥ 8) on the General Health Questionnaire (GHQ) (Goldberg, 1978), indicating the presence of antenatal psychological distress. In addition, 30% ($n = 39$) of all mothers scored >12 on the EPDS at 6–10 weeks postpartum, indicating PPD. Of mothers with a high prenatal GHQ score, 44% scored >12 on the EPDS postpartum. This supports the existing literature suggesting prenatal depression is a risk factor for PPD (Sidebottom, Hellerstedt, Harrison, & Hennrikus, 2014). Savarimuthu et al. (2010) assessed PPD among 137 mostly married, literate, low-income women who were living in a rural area in Tamil Nadu, India. Using the *International Classification of Diseases*, 10th Edition (ICD-10) criteria, 26% ($n = 36$) women were diagnosed with PPD. Several factors were associated with PPD, including female infant gender, low education level, and an unhappy marriage.

The findings of Dubey et al. (2012), Mariam and Srinivasan (2009), and Savarimuthu et al. (2010) all mirror those of earlier studies conducted in similar study samples in India (Chandran et al., 2002; Patel et al., 2002). Another study noted that South Asian mothers with PPD and living in India did not contact their physicians because they perceived their symptoms as minor and just natural consequences of childbirth (Rodrigues, Patel, Jaswal, & de Souza, 2003). Still another report included interviews of health-care workers (including South Asians) to identify barriers to seeking help for postpartum mothers living in Canada (Teng, Blackmore, & Stewart, 2007). Stigma was cited as the major barrier and was not only confined to the person diagnosed with depression but also to all female relatives in the family. The added burden of labeling other family members with the stigma of mental illness lends support as to why maternal depression tends to go unrecognized, leaving women feeling alone and isolated (Bostock, Marsen, Sarwar, & Stoltz, 1996).

Findings from the earlier-mentioned studies suggest that South Asian women do, in fact, have PMD and that social and cultural context are important in understanding PMD within these communities. Research findings also highlight cultural factors associated with the development of PPD, including a higher regard for male infants (Chandran et al., 2002; Patel et al., 2002) and the need for family social support (Jones & Coast, 2013). Findings also suggest that South Asian mothers do experience PPD but generally do not report symptoms to health-care providers due to stigma, shame, and the fear of being labeled mentally ill (Das & Kemp, 1997; Teng et al., 2007).

PMDs among South Asian American Mothers

Several researchers have included Asian American participants in study samples when examining PMD in the United States. Identifiers such as "Asian," "Other Asian," or "Pacific Islander" have often been used to classify the race and ethnicity of participants (Dietz et al., 2007; Hayes, Ta, Hurwitz, Mitchell-Box, & Fuddy, 2010; Le, Perry, & Sheng, 2009; Savitz, Stein, Ye, Kellerman, & Silverman, 2011; Sidebottom et al., 2014). Few studies, however, have specifically explored PMD in South Asian mothers living in the United States. An extensive review of the literature through January 2014 was conducted using the following electronic databases: CINAHL, PubMed, ScienceDirect, PsycINFO, Ovid, and the Cochrane Library. Articles were included if they (1) examined PMD, (2) included Asian Indian mothers living in the United States, (3) provided PMD results for Asian Indian mothers, and (4) were published in English peer-reviewed journals. Findings revealed only four studies that included Asian Indian mothers living in the United States (Goyal, Murphy, & Cohen, 2006; Goyal, Wang, Shen, Wong, & Palaniappan, 2012; Goyal et al., 2015; Huang, Wong, Ronzio, & Yu, 2007).

Goyal et al. (2006) were the first researchers to examine PMD among Asian Indian mothers in the United States. Using a quantitative, cross-sectional design, they assessed PPD in a convenience sample of 58 self-identified Asian Indian immigrants living in Northern California. All had given birth to a healthy infant within the past 12 months. With a mean age of 29 years (SD = 3.43), all the women were married, educated at college or higher level, and had lived in the United States for an average of 10 years. Using the 35-item, self-report, Postpartum Depression Screening Scale (PDSS) (Beck & Gable, 2000), scores indicated that 52% (*n* = 30) women scored in the "likelihood of depression" range. Limitations included a small sample size and no measure of acculturation. The PDSS was chosen due to its holistic nature of assessing PPD risk, though it has not yet been validated for use among Asian Indian women.

In 2007, Huang et al. (2007) conducted a secondary analysis of the *Early Childhood Longitudinal Survey-Birth Cohort* (ECLS-B) using 9-month follow-up data. The assessment of PPD was conducted in mothers (*n* = 7676) with infants who were less than 1 year of age, using a modified 12-item Center for Epidemiologic Studies Depression Scale (CES-D) (Radloff, 1977). The sample included 205 (2.7%) Asian Indian women, of whom 41 (20%) reported mild depressive symptoms. Although important, these findings are not generalizable given the relatively small number of Asian Indian women in the study sample.

In 2012, Goyal et al., examined electronic health records to identify clinical diagnosis rates of PPD among Asian American mothers (*n* = 3225), as compared with non-Hispanic white mothers (*n* = 4582). Using specific clinical diagnosis codes for depression during the 12 months following childbirth, they found that the PPD rate of the Asian American mothers (4.6%) was significantly lower than that of the non-Hispanic white mothers (9.1%, *p* < .001). Subgroup analysis revealed that Asian Indian mothers (*n* = 1264) were significantly less likely to receive a diagnosis of PPD as compared with non-Hispanic white mothers (*p* < .001). The lower PPD diagnosis rate noted in this study may be related to patients reporting other physical symptoms in the place of depressive symptoms (somatization) or patients not recognizing and reporting depressive symptoms due to the stigma and shame associated with mental illness.

More recently, Goyal et al. (2015) used a qualitative study design with in-depth interviews to explore the perspectives of PPD among Asian Indian women (*n* = 12) living in California. The authors sought to identify what participants and their families thought about depression after the birth of a baby, to whom they would report symptoms if they occurred, the type of mental health care they desired, and any barriers or facilitators they were aware of in obtaining mental health care. The findings indicated a general lack of knowledge about PPD, a desire for complementary and alternative methods before traditional medication and therapy-based treatment, and a strong sense of shame and stigma associated with mental illness. Additionally, participants verbalized a desire to take part in postpartum rituals with their families who were back in India and unable to come to the United States.

Together, these four studies represent the current body of literature regarding PMD among Asian Indian women living in the United States. Limitations of these studies include small sample sizes with a focus on selected subpopulations of South Asian women, thereby limiting the external validity of findings. The paucity of research in this area strongly emphasizes the need for more population-based studies that include all countries of origin of the South Asian population in the United States.

Recommendations

Although relatively sparse, literature to date demonstrates that SAA women do experience perinatal depression. A multilevel approach that includes health-care providers, researchers, and policy makers is essential for the timely identification and treatment of PMD in this unique population that is rich with cultural perinatal traditions. The following recommendations provide a starting point and tools for the multidisciplinary team to better identify, refer, treat, and "normalize" PMD in order to promote optimal maternal–child and family health outcomes.

Healthcare Providers

- Healthcare providers should be encouraged to obtain cultural competence training as it relates to South Asian cultural values and issues surrounding mental illness and the perinatal period.
- Healthcare providers should be encouraged to screen for postpartum mood disorders throughout the pregnancy and postpartum period.
- Extended family members should be included in education around PMDs and in treatment discussions in order to obtain "buy-in" of the whole family. This can include the mother-in-law, father-in-law, or anyone from whom the woman subjectively feels she receives the most support.
- Complementary and alternative treatment options modalities should be offered prior to traditional pharmacological and therapy-based treatment when appropriate, given the stigma related to mental illness.
- Healthcare providers can help dispel the stigma regarding PMD by initiating education at the first prenatal visit and continuing throughout the pregnancy and postpartum period.
- When treating SAA patients with postpartum mood and anxiety disorders, healthcare providers should keep in mind the role of cultural values such as stigma and the implications for mental health services.

Research

- Purposefully recruit SAA mothers who can increase our understanding of PMDs in this unique population.
- Given the diversity within South Asian subcultures, future research should strive to recruit mothers from subgroup populations in order to identify differences within these smaller groups.
- Qualitative research methods should be included as personal narratives and experiences will greatly augment quantitative findings and provide a more holistic view of PMD.
- Research should examine the role of cultural traditions and whether they are protective for the new mother at risk of developing PPD.

Policy Considerations

- Develop statewide task force groups to develop and evaluate best practices and to ensure culturally sensitive care for the vulnerable population of pregnant women and their families. For example, the *California Maternal Mental Health Collaborative* urges private and public stakeholders to address opportunities for increasing awareness of and screening for maternal mental health disorders (California Maternal Mental Health Collaborative, n.d.).
- Enact statewide laws to increase funding for PMD education and assessment. For example, Illinois's *Perinatal Mental Health Disorders Prevention and Treatment Act* provides funding for education and assessment along with prompting early detection to ensure timely treatment (Public Act 095-0469, 2008).
- Continue to collaborate with international organizations such as the Marcé Society and Postpartum Support International, which both serve to further the education, research, and sharing of knowledge in areas of perinatal mental health (The Marcé Society, n.d.; Postpartum Support International, n.d.).

Conclusions

Despite limited research findings, there is evidence that SAA mothers do, in fact, experience PPD. What still remains unknown is whether mothers are disclosing symptoms to their health-care providers and/or whether mothers are being diagnosed appropriately. It is difficult to decipher whether mothers and their families know exactly what is important to report and what should be considered expected discomforts of pregnancy and motherhood. When collecting information from the SAA population, data should be interpreted with caution and take into account that variables such as social support, partner relationship, and infant's gender may not have been factored into and evaluated with cultural sensitivity. Thus, in order for PMD to be effectively addressed among SAA mothers, several factors need to be considered. Anonymous depression screening may be preferable given the stigma and shame that are heavily intertwined with mental illness. Additionally, health-care providers caring for SAA mothers during the perinatal period must develop culturally sensitive screening protocols and be able to recognize the role that cultural differences play as women recover after childbirth (Thung & Norwitz, 2010).

During childbearing years, women struggle with nuanced societal and family pressures and challenges. Often, resources are limited and feelings of isolation due to the lack of social support make it difficult to carry out certain rituals or customs (Goyal et al., 2015). Several studies highlight the importance of the spouse and extended family in the South Asian culture. Because of this, PMD treatment planning should include all family members in the decision-making process. With continued research and shared stories, there are opportunities for advancement in the treatment and building of community resources, all of which will result in the reduction of PMD. Additionally, providing opportunities for nonjudgmental evaluation and creation of open dialogue will empower SAA communities to reduce the stigma around mental health issues during the challenging childbearing period.

References

Abramowitz, J. S., Schwartz, S. A., Moore, K. M., & Luenzmann, K. R. (2003). Obsessive-compulsive symptoms in pregnancy and the puerperium: A review of the literature. *Journal of Anxiety Disorders, 17*(4), 461–478.

Affonso, D. D., De, A. K., Horowitz, J. A., & Mayberry, L. J. (2000). An international study exploring levels of postpartum depressive symptomatology. *Journal of Psychosomatic Research, 49*(3), 207–216.

Akutsu, P. D., Tsuru, G. K., & Chu, J. P. (2004). Predictors of nonattendance of intake appointments among five Asian American client groups. *Journal of Consulting and Clinical Psychology, 72*(5), 891–896. doi:10.1037/0022-006x.72.5.891

Baldwin, S., & Griffiths, P. (2009). Do specialist community public health nurses assess risk factors for depression, suicide, and self-harm among South Asian mothers living in London? *Public Health Nursing, 26*(3), 277–289. doi:10.1111/j.1525-1446.2009.00780.x

Beck, C. T. (1996). Postpartum depressed mothers' experiences interacting with their children. *Nursing Research, 45*(2), 98–104.

Beck, C. T., & Gable, R. K. (2000). Postpartum Depression Screening Scale: Development and psychometric testing. *Nursing Research, 49*(5), 272–282.

Bhui, K., Bhugra, D., Goldberg, D., Dunn, G., & Desai, M. (2001). Cultural influences on the prevalence of common mental disorder, general practitioners' assessments and help-seeking among Punjabi and English people visiting their general practitioner. *Psychological Medicine, 31*(5), 815–825.

Bostock, J., Marsen, M., Sarwar, Z., & Stoltz, S. (1996). Postnatal depression in Asian women. *Community Nurse, 2*(10), 34–36.

California Maternal Mental Health Collaborative. (n.d.). Retrieved from http://www.2020mom.org/about

Callister, L. C., Beckstrand, R. L., & Corbett, C. (2011). Postpartum depression and help-seeking behaviors in immigrant Hispanic women. *Journal of Obstetric, Gynecologic, & Neonatal Nursing, 40*(4), 440–449. doi:10.1111/j.1552-6909.2011.01254.x

Chalmers, B., & Meyer, D. (1993). Adherence to traditional Indian customs surrounding birth. *South African Medical Journal, 83*(3), 204–206.

Chandran, M., Tharyan, P., Muliyil, J., & Abraham, S. (2002). Post-partum depression in a cohort of women from a rural area of Tamil Nadu, India. Incidence and risk factors. *British Journal of Psychiatry, 181*, 499–504.

Choudhry, U. K. (1997). Traditional practices of women from India: Pregnancy, childbirth, and newborn care. *Journal of Obstetric, Gynecologic, & Neonatal Nursing, 26*(5), 533–539.

Chuang, J. Y. (2005). An exploratory analysis of utilization patterns of Vietnamese, Chinese and Indian Americans in a Texas County mental health service agency. *Dissertation Abstracts International, 65*(10-B), 5390.

Cohen, A. (2000). Excess female mortality in India: The case of Himachal Pradesh. *American Journal of Public Health, 90*(9), 1369–1371.

Conrad, M. M., & Pacquiao, D. F. (2005). Manifestation, attribution, and coping with depression among Asian Indians from the perspectives of health care practitioners. *Journal of Transcultural Nursing, 16*(1), 32–40. doi:10.1177/1043659604271239

Cox, J. L., Holden, J. M., & Sagovsky, R. (1987). Detection of postnatal depression. Development of the 10-item Edinburgh Postnatal Depression Scale. *British Journal of Psychiatry, 150*, 782–786.

Das, A., & Kemp, S. (1997). Between two worlds: Counseling South Asian Americans. *Journal of Multicultural Counseling and Development, 25*, 23–33.

Dhillon, N., & Macarthur, C. (2010). Antenatal depression and male gender preference in Asian women in the UK. *Midwifery, 26*(3), 286–293. doi:10.1016/j.midw.2008.09.001

Dietz, P. M., Williams, S. B., Callaghan, W. M., Bachman, D. J., Whitlock, E. P., & Hornbrook, M. C. (2007). Clinically identified maternal depression before, during, and after pregnancies ending in live births. *American Journal of Psychiatry, 164*(10), 1515–1520.

Dubey, C., Gupta, N., Bhasin, S., Muthal, R. A., & Arora, R. (2012). Prevalence and associated risk factors for postpartum depression in women attending a tertiary hospital, Delhi, India. *International Journal of Social Psychiatry, 58*(6), 577–580. doi:10.1177/0020764011415210

Durvasula, R., & Sue, S. (1996). Severity of disturbance among Asian American outpatients. *Cultural Diversity and Mental Health, 2*(1), 43–51.

Farver, J. A., Narang, S. K., & Bhadha, B. R. (2002). East meets west: Ethnic identity, acculturation, and conflict in Asian Indian families. *Journal of Family Psychology, 16*(3), 338–350.

Field, T. (2011). Prenatal depression effects early development: A review. *Infant Behavior and Development, 32*(1), 1–14. dx.doi.org/10.1016/j.infbeh.2010.09.008

Foreman, D. M., & Henshaw, C. (2002). Objectivity and subjectivity in postnatally depressed mothers' perceptions of their infants. *Child Psychiatry & Human Development, 32*(4), 263–275.

Galanti, G. (2008). *Caring for patients from different cultures* (4th ed.). Philadelphia, PA: University of Pennsylvania Press.

Gavin, N. I., Gaynes, B. N., Lohr, K. N., Meltzer-Brody, S., Gartlehner, G., & Swinson, T. (2005). Perinatal depression: A systematic review of prevalence and incidence. *Obstetrics and Gynecology, 106*(5 Pt 1), 1071–1083. doi:10.1097/01.AOG .0000183597.31630.db

Gaynes, B. N., Gavin, N., Meltzer-Brody, S., Lohr, K. N., Swinson, T., Gartlehner, G., . . . Miller, W. C. (2005). Perinatal depression: Prevalence, screening accuracy, and screening outcomes. *Evidence Report/Technology Assessment, 119*, 1–8.

Goldberg, D. P. (1978). *Manual of the general health questionnaire.* Windsor, England: NFER Publishing.

Goyal, D. (2016). Perinatal practices and traditions among Asian Indian women. *MCN, The American Journal of Maternal Child Nursing, 41*(2), 90–96. doi:10.1097/ NMC.0000000000000230

Goyal, D., Gay, C., & Lee, K. (2009). Fragmented maternal sleep is more strongly correlated with depressive symptoms than infant temperament at three months postpartum. *Archives of Women's Mental Health, 12*(4), 229–237. doi:10.1007/ s00737-009-0070-9

Goyal, D., Murphy, S. O., & Cohen, J. (2006). Immigrant Asian Indian women and postpartum depression. *Journal of Obstetric, Gynecologic, and Neonatal Nursing, 35*(1), 98–104.

Goyal, D., Park, V. T., & McNiesh, S. (2015). Postpartum depression among Asian Indian mothers. *MCN, The American Journal of Maternal Child Nursing, 40*(4):256–61. doi:10.1097/NMC.0000000000000146

Goyal, D., Wang, E. J., Shen, J., Wong, E. C., & Palaniappan, L. P. (2012). Clinically identified postpartum depression in Asian American mothers. *Journal of Obstetric, Gynecologic, and Neonatal Nursing, 41*(3), 408–416. doi:10.1111/ j.1552-6909.2012.01352.x

Grewal, S. K., Bhagat, R., & Balneaves, L. G. (2008). Perinatal beliefs and practices of immigrant Punjabi women living in Canada. *Journal of Obstetric, Gynecologic, and Neonatal Nursing, 37*(3), 290–300.

Hayes, D. K., Ta, V. M., Hurwitz, E. L., Mitchell-Box, K. M., & Fuddy, L. J. (2010). Disparities in self-reported postpartum depression among Asian, Hawaiian, and Pacific Islander women in Hawaii: Pregnancy risk assessment monitoring system (PRAMS), 2004–2007. *Maternal and Child Health Journal, 14*(5), 765–773.

Howard, C. R., Lanphear, N., Lanphear, B. P., Eberly, S., & Lawrence, R. A. (2006). Parental responses to infant crying and colic: The effect on breastfeeding duration. *Breastfeeding Medicine, 1*(3), 146–155. doi:10.1089/bfm.2006.1.146

Huang, Z. J., Wong, F. Y., Ronzio, C. R., & Yu, S. M. (2007). Depressive symptomatology and mental health help-seeking patterns of U.S.- and foreign-born mothers. *Maternal and Child Health Journal, 11*(3), 257–267. doi:10.1007/s10995-006-0168-x

Jones, E., & Coast, E. (2013). Social relationships and postpartum depression in South Asia: A systematic review. *International Journal of Social Psychiatry, 59*(7), 690–700. doi:10.1177/0020764012453675

Kaiser Family Foundation. (2008). *Race, ethnicity healthcare. Asian & Pacific Islander American Health Forum.* Available at: http://kff.org/disparities-policy/fact-sheet/health-coverage-and-access-to-care-among

Khanna, A., McDowell, T., Perumbilly, S., & Titus, G. (2009). Working with Asian Indian American families: A Delphi study. *Journal of Systemic Therapies, 28*(1), 52–71.

Kishore, J., Gupta, A., Jiloha, R. C., & Bantman, P. (2011). Myths, beliefs and perceptions about mental disorders and health-seeking behavior in Delhi, India. *Indian Journal of Psychiatry, 53*(4), 324–329. doi:10.4103/0019-5545.91906

Le, H. N., Perry, D. F., & Sheng, X. (2009). Using the Internet to screen for postpartum depression. *Maternal and Child Health Journal, 13*(2), 213–221. doi:10.1007/s10995-008-0322-8

Majumdar, A. K. (1983). *Concise history of ancient India, Vol. III: Hinduism: Society, religion and philosophy.* New Delhi, India: Munshiram Manoharlal Publishers.

Marcé Society (n.d.). Retrieved from www.marcesociety.com

Mariam, K. A., & Srinivasan, K. (2009). Antenatal psychological distress and postnatal depression: A prospective study from an urban clinic. *Asian Journal of Psychiatry, 2*(2), 71–73. doi:10.1016/j.ajp.2009.04.002

O'Hara, M. W., Schlechte, J. A., Lewis, D. A., & Wright, E. J. (1991). Prospective study of postpartum blues: Biologic and psychosocial factors. *Archives of General Psychiatry, 48*, 801–806.

O'Hara, M. W., & Swain, A. M. (1996). Rates and risk of postpartum depression: A meta-analysis. *International Review of Psychiatry, 8*(1), 37–54.

O'Hara, M. W., & Wisner, K. L. (2014). Perinatal mental illness: Definition, description and aetiology. *Best Practice & Research Clinical Obstetrics & Gynaecology, 28*(1): 3–12. doi:10.1016/j.bpobgyn.2013.09.002

Patel, V., Rodrigues, M., & DeSouza, N. (2002). Gender, poverty, and postnatal depression: A study of mothers in Goa, India. *American Journal of Psychiatry, 159*(1), 43–47.

Postpartum Support International. (n.d.). Retrieved from www.postpartum.net

Public Act 095-0469. (2008). Retrieved from http://www.ilga.gov/legislation/publicacts/fulltext.asp?Name=095-0469

Radloff, L. (1977). A self-report depression scale for research in the general population. *Applied Psychological Measurement, 1*, 385–401.

Reijneveld, S. A., van der Wal, M. F., Brugman, E., Hira Sing, R. A., & Verloove-Vanhorick, S. P. (2004). [Prevalence of parental behaviour to diminish the crying of infants that may lead to abuse]. *Nederlands Tijdschrift voor Geneeskunde, 148*(45), 2227–2230.

Rodrigues, M., Patel, V., Jaswal, S., & de Souza, N. (2003). Listening to mothers: Qualitative studies on motherhood and depression from Goa, India. *Social Science Medicine*, *57*(10), 1797–1806.

Savarimuthu, R. J., Ezhilarasu, P., Charles, H., Antonisamy, B., Kurian, S., & Jacob, K. S. (2010). Post-partum depression in the community: A qualitative study from rural South India. *International Journal of Social Psychiatry*, *56*(1), 94–102. doi:10.1177/0020764008097756

Savitz, D. A., Stein, C. R., Ye, F., Kellerman, L., & Silverman, M. (2011). The epidemiology of hospitalized postpartum depression in New York State, 1995–2004. *Annals of Epidemiology*, *21*(6), 399–406. doi:10.1016/j.annepidem.2011.03.003

Sidebottom, A. C., Hellerstedt, W. L., Harrison, P. A., & Hennrikus, D. (2014). An examination of prenatal and postpartum depressive symptoms among women served by urban community health centers. *Archives of Women's Mental Health*, *17*(1):27–40. doi:10.1007/s00737-013-0378-3

Sit, D., Rothschild, A. J., & Wisner, K. L. (2006). A review of postpartum psychosis. *Journal of Women's Health (Larchmont)*, *15*(4), 352–368. doi:10.1089/jwh.2006.15.352

Sohr-Preston, S. L., & Scaramella, L. V. (2006). Implications of timing of maternal depressive symptoms for early cognitive and language development. *Clinical Child and Family Psychology Review*, *9*(1), 65–83.

South Asian Americans Leading Together. (2014). Available at: http://saalt.org/south-asians-in-the-us/demographic-information

Spinelli, M. G. (2004). Maternal infanticide associated with mental illness: Prevention and the promise of saved lives. *American Journal of Psychiatry*, *161*(9), 1548–1557.

Sue, S., Yan Cheng, J. K., Saad, C. S., & Chu, J. P. (2012). Asian American mental health: A call to action. *American Psychologist*, *67*(7), 532–544. doi:10.1037/a0028900

Tammentie, T., Paavilainen, E., Astedt-Kurki, P., & Tarkka, M. T. (2004). Family dynamics of postnatally depressed mothers—Discrepancy between expectations and reality. *Journal of Clinical Nursing*, *13*(1), 65–74.

Teng, L., Robertson Blackmore, E., & Stewart, D. E. (2007). Healthcare workers' perceptions of barriers to care by immigrant women with postpartum depression: An exploratory qualitative study. *Archives of Women's Mental Health*, *10*(3), 93–101.

Tewari, N., Inman, A., & Sandhu, D. S. (2003). South Asian Americans: Culture, concerns and therapeutic strategies. In J. M. G. Iwamasa (Ed.), *Culturally diverse mental health: The challenges of research and resistance* (pp. 191–209). New York, NY: Taylor & Francis.

Tewary, S. (2005). Asian Indian Immigrant Women. *Journal of Human Behavior in the Social Environment*, *11*(1), 1–22. doi:10.1300/J137v11n01_01

Thung, S. F., & Norwitz, E. R. (2010). Postpartum care: We can and should do better. *American Journal of Obstetrics & Gynecology*, *202*(1), 1–4. doi:10.1016/j.ajog.2009.08.028

Vesga-Lopez, O, Blanco, C., Keyes, K., Olfson, M., Grant, B. F., & Hasin, D. S. (2008). Psychiatric disorders in pregnant and postpartum women in the United States. *Archives of General Psychiatry*, *65*(7), 805–815. doi:10.1001/archpsyc.65.7.805

Williams, C. E. (2005). Review: Depression and anxiety during pregnancy are strong indicators of postpartum depression. *Evidence Based Mental Health*, *8*(1), 21.

Wisner, K. L., Peindl, K. S., & Hanusa, B. H. (1996). Effects of childbearing on the natural history of panic disorder with comorbid mood disorder. *Journal of Affective Disorders, 41*(3), 173–180.

Wisner, K. L., Sit, D. K., McShea, M. C., Rizzo, D. M., Zoretich, R. A., Hughes, C. L., . . . Hanusa, B. H. (2013). Onset timing, thoughts of self-harm, and diagnoses in postpartum women with screen-positive depression findings. *JAMA Psychiatry, 70*(5):490–498. doi:10.1001/jamapsychiatry.2013.87

Chapter 14

Intimate Partner Violence

Memoona Hasnain, Deepika Goyal, and Susan L. Ivey

Contents

Abstract

Objective: To review evidence published between 1996 and 2015 related to intimate partner violence among the South Asian population in the United States. This chapter serves as an update of work on intimate partner violence among South Asian Americans published by the South Asian Public Health Association in 2002 and aims to (1) establish the epidemiological burden and scope, (2) provide information on barriers and facilitators for seeking help for those affected, (3) identify effective interventions to address intimate partner violence, and (4) outline research and policy gaps for future directions to advance best practices for addressing this critically important public health issue.

Key Findings: Intimate partner violence is a significant public health and primary care issue for the South Asian population in the United States. There has been increased attention and recognition of this issue, as well as enhanced resources being made available in many communities. However, despite these advances, a variety of factors, particularly the South Asian culture and social norms, continue to impede those affected by intimate partner violence from seeking help in a timely and appropriate manner.

Recommendations: The issue of intimate partner violence requires a collaborative approach to ensure the safety and well-being of the South Asian American population. There is a strong need for more coordinated and concerted responses at multiple levels to address intimate partner violence through advocacy, research, education, and community outreach. Academic and community partnerships are also needed to utilize research findings and to guide the development and testing of patient- and family-centered education and community outreach for culturally appropriate models of self-empowerment for those affected.

Introduction

Intimate partner violence (IPV) is a serious, growing, and preventable public health problem that affects millions of Americans. It is a particularly relevant issue for the South Asian American (SAA) community. The term "intimate partner violence" describes physical, sexual, or psychological harm by a current or former partner or spouse. This type of violence can occur among both heterosexual and same-sex couples and does not require sexual intimacy. Additionally, other household members might enact violence against adults in the household outside of an intimate relationship. In other resources, the term "domestic violence" may be used for such situations. However, for the purposes of this chapter, the term IPV is used with the understanding that other forms of domestic abuse, e.g., abuse by in-laws, are included.

The harmful impact of IPV resonates across communities, locally and globally. A growing body of evidence highlights the health effects of IPV, including fatal and nonfatal injuries. Thus, the consequences of IPV can span a lifetime and include both individual and societal level costs. According to the U.S. Centers for Disease Control and Prevention, the cost of IPV against women exceeds an estimated $5.8 billion annually (Centers of Disease Control and Prevention, 2013). This includes approximately $4.1 billion in direct costs for medical and mental health care and nearly $1.8 billion in indirect costs for lost productivity (Centers of Disease Control and Prevention, 2013). These estimates do not include the costs associated with the criminal justice system in IPV matters; thus the actual cost of IPV is even higher. Evidence also indicates that women carry a disproportionate burden of IPV and suffer more injuries and fatalities than do men (Archer, 2000).

In this chapter, we draw on recent literature to discuss the scope of IPV, the burden, and trends, as well as the resources and possible solutions for addressing IPV among the SAA population. A detailed analysis of the problem in the host countries from where South Asians originate is beyond the scope of this chapter. The cultural context and gender norms in countries of origin are, however, important considerations in contextualizing the causes of and contributors to IPV among SAAs.

Epidemiological Trends and Women's Experiences of IPV

Limited data on Asian Americans exist from federal data sources, including insufficient information on the prevalence of IPV. The California Health Interview Survey (CHIS, 2011) is the largest state-level health survey, surveying more than 50,000 households in California on a rolling basis and reporting data approximately every 2 years. In 2009, the levels of IPV reported for Asian populations were lower than those for other populations. In the survey, 6.7% Asians reported a history of IPV since age 18, with women reporting higher levels at approximately 10% (CHIS, 2011). The sample size of Asian Americans in the 2009 CHIS included more than 4300 adults and 400 South Asians, often referred to as a subpopulation within the larger Asian American population (CHIS, 2011).

Although other studies have been conducted on IPV among the SAA population, there are virtually no other population-based samples of South Asian populations in the United States for whom this type of data exist. The lower rate of IPV among SAAs compared with other populations reported in this survey may be an artifact. No South Asian language was used in the CHIS in 2009, and some women may have been afraid to admit to IPV, even in a telephone survey; thus the reported IPV prevalence may be an underestimate.

For a more representative estimation of IPV prevalence, an additional source of population-based evidence for Asian women comes from Cho and

Kim (2012), who used data from the Collaborative Psychiatric Epidemiology Surveys to examine the use of mental health services by IPV survivors. More than 20,000 people aged 18 years or older participated in surveys that included the *Conflict Tactics Scale* (Straus, 1979), and 755 survivors of IPV were identified. Although all types of IPV were not examined in this survey and there were no subgroup data, results suggest that approximately one in five Asian Americans who admitted to IPV had experienced severe IPV, compared with approximately one in three Latinos and African Americans. Further, although there was no significant difference in perceived mental health, the odds of seeking mental health services were lower for Asian Americans than for any other racial/ethnic group after controlling for education, socioeconomic status, type of IPV, and perceived mental health status. Women were also more likely to use mental health services than men (Cho & Kim, 2012). Use of the Conflict Tactics Scale to assess IPV in this sample may limit generalizability of the findings as it provides simple counts of violent events, does not measure all aspects of IPV, and lacks context and motive information.

Research over the last decade on the prevalence of IPV among SAA communities highlights the underrepresentation of SAAs in general research as well as in research specific to IPV. In a series of studies spanning from 2002 to 2007, Raj and colleagues investigated IPV and help-seeking behavior, the association of IPV with immigration policy, and in-law abuse of new daughters-in-law (Raj, Liu, McCleary-Sills, & Silverman, 2005; Raj, Livramento, Santana, Gupta, & Silverman, 2006; Raj & Silverman, 2002, 2003, 2007; Raj, Silverman, McCleary-Sills, & Liu, 2005). The most often-cited studies (Raj & Silverman, 2002; Raj et al., 2003) draw from a community-based volunteer sample of South Asian women ($n = 160$) in Boston who were surveyed between 1998 and 1999. The women ranged in age from 18 to 62 years, were mostly immigrants (87.5%), with a large proportion (74%) who were married, and just over half (51.6%) had children. Asian Indian women represented the majority (more than 83%) of the sample with several other countries of origin represented as well, including Bangladesh, Pakistan, Nepal, and Sri Lanka. One third (37%) of women reported they had suffered some type of IPV during the past year and more than 40% stated they had experienced IPV in their current relationship. Only half (50.6%) of the women in the Boston South Asian sample were aware of IPV services and only 11.3% of women who reported IPV ever received counseling.

Another survey conducted from 2001 to 2002, from the same research group, drew a community-based sample of 208 women who were surveyed with a separate sample of 23 women with a history of IPV who underwent in-depth interviews (Hurwitz, Gupta, Liu, Silverman, & Raj, 2006). Surveys were administered to 208 women, most of whom were married ($n = 169$), of Asian Indian descent (96%), aged between 18 and 68 years, and who had reported being in a relationship with a man. Most of the women were foreign-born (91%), 37% stated they were U.S. citizens, 26% were in the United States as permanent residents, and 21% reported they were there on spousal visas. Of the 208 women surveyed, 46% reported postgraduate training and 13% had a high school education or lower. Results from the in-depth interviews of 23 women with a history of IPV showed that 21% women reported physical or sexual abuse from their current partner and 15% reported IPV in the last year. Of those who reported IPV in a current relationship, 55% reported physical assault and 91% reported sexual assault. Results revealed that IPV contributed to poor sleep, appetite, and general poor health. In particular, findings showed poor physical health (10%) or poor mental health (16%), which included depression, anxiety, and suicidal ideation. Results also showed that abused women were significantly more likely to report poor physical health, depression, and suicidality as compared with nonabused women. Additionally, this study examined the association of IPV and in-law abuse, with 5.9% reporting emotional abuse by in-laws. Raj et al. found that women who reported IPV in their current relationship were more likely to report emotional abuse from their in-laws (2006).

In 1999, Yoshioka and Dang conducted a community survey to explore IPV among several Asian American subpopulations, including Cambodian, Chinese, Korean, South Asian, and Vietnamese (2000). Participants completed a six-part survey on attitudes about family violence and also participated in focus-group interviews. Results specific to South Asian women included not seeking help to address IPV due to stigma and the inability to leave the abusive relationship due to financial dependence on husbands.

In reviewing the nature, scope, extent, and health outcomes of abuse, several researchers have qualitatively examined IPV among SAA women. Findings were unique to each study but provide a holistic view of SAA women who have experienced IPV. Dasgupta and Warrier (1996) interviewed 12 married, well-educated women from India who were between 24 and 42 years of age. When asked about their experience with domestic violence, many stated that abuse began shortly after marriage in the form of beatings and often without cause. Abraham (1999) examined the experiences of sexual abuse among 25 Pakistani, Bangladeshi, Hindu, Muslim, Christian, and Sikh women between 22 and 47 years of age. Only one quarter ($n = 6$) were U.S. citizens. The main themes included marital rape and sexual abuse, and sexual control through threats to reproductive rights. Further analysis revealed that many women felt isolated, specifically from their spouses, as well as from family and friends.

More recently, Kallivayalil (2010) interviewed eight South Asian women, aged 30–40 years in New York. The women were referred by their therapists and had all experienced IPV. They reported feeling betrayed by not being taken care of by their spouse and feeling isolated, and they expressed general self-blame for the situations they were in, believing they placed themselves there. These themes reflect the spectrum of concerns the women had and the way in which violence affects mental health and can influence how women feel about themselves.

In similar research, Chaudhuri, Morash, and Yingling (2014) interviewed 40 South Asian women, including 32 who were referred from South Asian domestic violence advocacy agencies throughout the northeastern United States and 8 who had no history of IPV and were used for comparison. Interviews were conducted by trained South Asian volunteers or staff from the agencies, using a structured interview guide. Of the 32 women (82%) who reported a history of abuse at the time of the study, fewer than half ($n = 14$; 44%) were currently living in a women's shelter. More than two-thirds ($n = 28$, 70%) had come to the United States after a recent marriage or for the purpose of an arranged marriage.

Similar to the Kallivayalil study, a spectrum of themes emerged from women's descriptions of their marriages, circumstances of migration, abuse within the husband's families, and strategies used to prevent discord. For those living apart from their husbands, the women described how they had separated. A number of the key themes could be linked to the theory about women creating patriarchal bargains (Carter, 2015; Dasgupta, 2000). This included expectations that women would get married (preferably by a certain age), the importance of having children, and beliefs that daughters are a financial burden on their parents.

Barriers to Seeking and Utilizing Support

Despite increasing attention, the issue of IPV is still an understudied and under-addressed topic in the SAA community. Since the publication of the *Brown Paper* by the South Asian Public Health Association (SAPHA, 2002), several new programs and resources have been made available to help SAA families. Unfortunately, despite the availability of enhanced resources and awareness about them, optimal utilization of resources remains low.

More recent studies have helped add to the understanding of IPV and confirm previous findings. In a large multisite study, researchers surveyed 34 Muslim women and 84 non-Muslim women regarding the nature of the interpersonal violence they had experienced (Ammar, Couture-Carron, Alvi, & San Antonio, 2013). The women had a mean age of 32 years and all had experienced IPV in the previous 12 months. They were recruited from 17 agencies working with battered women and represented 11 states, including California, New Jersey, and

Ohio. Respondents completed extensive open- and closed-ended questions. Findings resonated with those of previous studies, including a belief that husbands abused them because they believed women were inferior and that they chose to stay in the abusive relationship due to financial reasons and citizenship issues (Ahmad, Driver, McNally, & Stewart, 2009). A limitation of this study is that only 15% (*n* = 5) of the Muslim women self-identified as South Asian. Still, the findings are important and add to the growing body of literature on this understudied population of women.

A recent qualitative review (Finfgeld-Connett & Johnson, 2013) synthesized findings from 30 research reports and highlighted the finding that domestic abuse among South Asians is perpetuated by South Asian customs and compounded by the experience of migration. The review also emphasizes the situational circumstances and language barriers that pose challenges for South Asian women seeking and attempting to utilize support services.

In fact, a host of factors contribute to the persistent and ongoing set of barriers that discourage South Asian women in the United States from seeking and using support to address IPV. On the basis of the review of extant evidence, these factors include the following:

- Cultural/religious beliefs, immense stigma associated with acknowledging IPV, compounded by values of privacy, family honor, loyalty, and shame
- Family structure and involvement of in-laws and extended family members
- Fear of harm to family, particularly to children
- Lack of education
- Low awareness about legal rights and resources
- Linguistic barriers
- Financial and emotional dependency on the perpetrator of violence
- Isolation from home and family and from their adopted community
- Immigration status, and fear of deportation and/or jail

To date, most of the research regarding IPV among South Asian women has largely focused on identifying the type of help available and the barriers to seeking that help. Less research has focused on the health outcomes or long-term effects of IPV among South Asian women. Given the types of IPV, barriers, and their effect on South Asian women, it is important to note that these women are resilient and able to adapt in order to preserve their emotional and social well-being, as noted in in-depth interviews by Ahmad and colleagues (Ahmad, Rai, Petrovic, Erickson, & Stewart, 2013) with 11 South Asian immigrant women living in the United States.

Addressing IPV among South Asians

Screening for IPV is critically important for all women regardless of race or ethnic group. In the case of South Asian women, research findings suggest that they are reluctant to acknowledge and report IPV due to cultural, economic, and citizenship status issues. Given that the perpetrators of IPV in the South Asian community are largely the husbands or male partners, it is essential to include them, as well as community leaders, in conversations addressing IPV. Additionally, although cultural values may prevent South Asian women from reporting IPV, these same cultural values socialize women from a young age to accept abuse as a normal occurrence by their husbands and male household members, which in turn empowers men to continue the abuse (Yoshihama, Blazevski, & Bybee, 2014).

Research into these cultural values was reported by Yoshihama et al. (2014) in their sample of 373 South Asian Gujarati married men ($n = 186$) and married women ($n = 187$). They examined the relationship between enculturation (maintaining cultural identity by eating traditional food, speaking in native language, and attending cultural events or temple) and IPV-supporting attitudes. Findings suggested that participants with higher levels of enculturation were more likely to condone IPV as compared with those with lower enculturation levels. In fact, enculturation was the strongest predictor of IPV-supporting attitudes in this sample.

Over the past three decades, a significant and growing body of intervention work has been initiated by South Asian community-based organizations (CBOs) in the United States in an effort to address the issue of IPV in the South Asian community. There are more than two dozen CBOs in various states that are active and have consistently worked to change community attitudes, train practitioners in South Asian cultural issues, and design culturally sensitive and linguistically appropriate interventions. Many of these CBOs, such as Apna Ghar in Chicago, Illinois, do not restrict their services to only South Asian women and children, and serve women from multiple ethnicities and backgrounds. The services provided by these CBOs are also multifaceted. For example, the project "Shanti" (Yoshiama et al., 2012) addresses IPV prevention by targeting multiple areas, including (1) increasing IPV awareness, discussion about how IPV affects the whole family; (2) dispelling the myth that IPV is tied to power, control, and respect; (3) promoting education regarding mutual respect; and (4) addressing the sense of responsibility by community organizations to support and educate families in maintaining healthy relationships. An online directory of domestic violence programs serving Asians, Native Hawaiians, and Pacific Islanders is available through the Asian and Pacific Islander Institute on Gender-Based Violence (n.d.).

Recommendations

Given the complex and multifactorial etiology of IPV, including domestic abuse by nonintimate partners such as in-laws, effectively addressing the issue requires a multilevel approach that includes health-care providers, researchers, policy makers, and the community. It also appears that the health-care and legal sectors are evolving in their approach to addressing IPV. The U.S. Preventive Services Task Force (2013) recommended that clinicians screen women of child-bearing age for IPV and provide or refer these women who screen positive to appropriate intervention services. This is a "B" class recommendation which, per the nomenclature defined by the Task Force, means that there is high certainty that the net benefit is moderate or there is moderate certainty that the net benefit is moderate to substantial. Thus, the suggested practice is to offer or provide this service. New guidelines are also emerging on human trafficking and may help health-care providers better screen for all types of IPV, not just trafficking issues.

On the basis of the available evidence, the following recommendations are aimed at strengthening the knowledge and skill set of health-care providers, optimizing the contributions of researchers, developing more effective policies, and empowering the South Asian community. They are also offered as a starting point, with the understanding that empowering the South Asian community as a whole, as well as South Asian women, their partners, and families, is essential in finding long-term, viable solutions.

Recommendations for Health-Care Providers

- Educate health-care providers regarding cultural and religious traditions or beliefs inherent in the South Asian population, along with the best ways to intervene based on principles of culturally appropriate, patient-centered care (Stewart et al., 2000, 2003; Betancourt, 2006).
- Encourage and facilitate health-care providers to obtain cultural competence training specific to South Asian cultural values and other factors contributing to women staying in abusive relationships, e.g., economic issues and immigration status.
- Enhance clinicians' awareness of cultural values when discussing IPV with South Asian patients. For example, awareness that these women may see themselves as inferior and perhaps feel as though they deserve the abuse.
- Educate health-care providers on how to listen for key words when interviewing women who have experienced IPV. Such words may include "family honor," which may be indicative of current or future harm.
- Ensure adequate linguistic access through interpretation (spoken) and translation (written) services. Educate and train all health-care providers

who come into contact with female patients to screen for IPV in appropriate encounters and in all relevant settings (e.g., primary care, obstetrics and gynecology, pediatrics, and public health services).

■ Collaborate with other disciplines to provide patient-centered and holistic, interdisciplinary care, including mental health services.

■ Assess and ensure that health education materials are at appropriate reading and comprehension levels.

Recommendations for Researchers

■ Purposefully recruit South Asian women, of all ages, into research studies in order to better understand IPV and to assist in developing appropriate interventions for this unique population.

■ Develop community-based participatory research, with a focus on empowering women and their families and communities, by eliciting the views and beliefs of South Asian men with regard to IPV and including them in the dialogue to find culturally appropriate and sustainable solutions to the growing problem of IPV.

■ Update existing databases with newer statistics, specifically disaggregating South Asians from the larger Asian American community, wherever possible.

■ Conduct rigorous evaluation of the effectiveness and feasibility of current nationwide community-based IPV organizations to inform best practices and reduce duplicate efforts (Robert Wood Johnson Foundation, 2014).

Recommendations for Policy Development

■ Establish statewide task groups to develop and evaluate best practices that ensure culturally sensitive care for this vulnerable population of abused women (Centers for Disease Control and Prevention [CDC], 2008).

■ Develop IPV reporting mandates in every state. Currently, several states including Alaska, California, and New York have initiated IPV victimization reporting requirements for health-care providers (Family Violence Prevention Fund, 2008).

■ Pay special attention to larger global health issues, such as human trafficking, to address root causes of IPV.

■ Increase funding for research and programming efforts.

■ Address immigration laws that may inhibit survivors of IPV to come forward.

■ Continue application of the work of international organizations such as the World Health Organization (WHO, 2013), which serves to further the education, research, and sharing of knowledge in areas of IPV.

Recommendations for Community Empowerment

■ Educate South Asian men on IPV, including clarification that verbal and psychological abuse, as well as withholding financial support, all constitute IPV. This type of education must be integrated into community venues (places of worship, workplace) in order to educate, empower, and provide resources to both South Asian men and women, and to find viable solutions.

■ Form support groups for men who abuse their spouses, replicating successful programs such as Alcoholics Anonymous, in addition to support groups for those experiencing IPV.

■ Develop more community-based education programs, such as healthy relationship workshops, to build the foundation for nonviolent relationships. These programs should utilize frameworks from evidence-based effective models, such as the Shanti Project in California that provides emotional and practical support for vulnerable populations (Yoshihama, Ramakrishnan, Hammock, & Khaliq, 2012).

■ Develop public awareness through social media and other means to continuously inform the public about the harmful impacts of IPV.

Conclusions

Information, awareness, education, and research regarding IPV among SAA women have steadily grown. A body of evidence suggests that they continue to experience IPV more often than other racial and ethnic groups. Findings from newer studies also reflect those of previous studies identifying cultural and immigration status-associated barriers that continue to exist. These studies also confirm that SAA women feel "trapped" in abusive relationships without much-needed support and resources to empower them. Cultural issues surrounding intimate partner abuse must be taken into consideration as they likely contribute to the nondisclosure of abuse. Best practices strongly suggest that healthcare providers who have contact with South Asian women must screen for IPV, which also has implications for health policy and clinical practice guidelines. In order to successfully address the issue of IPV for the SAA community effective interventions must be developed that are multipronged, culturally appropriate, and responsive to the needs of this unique population.

References

Abraham, M. (1999). Sexual abuse in South Asian immigrant marriages. *Violence Against Women, 5*(6), 591–618.

Ahmad, F., Driver, N., McNally, M. J., & Stewart, D. (2009). Why doesn't she seek help for partner abuse? An exploratory study with South Asian immigrant women. *Journal of Social Sciences and Medicine, 69*, 613–622. doi:10.1016/j.socscimed.2009.06.011

Ahmad, F., Rai, N., Petrovic, B., Erickson, P. E., & Stewart, D. E. (2013). Resilience and resources among South Asian immigrant women as survivors of partner violence. *Journal of Immigrant Minority Health, 15*, 1057–1064. doi:10.1007/s10903-013-9836-2

Ammar, N., Couture-Carron, A., Alvi, S., & San Antonio, J. (2013). Experiences of Muslim and non-Muslim battered immigrant women with the police in the United States: A closer understanding of commonalities and differences. *Violence Against Women, 19*(12), 1449–1471.

Archer, J. (2000). Sex differences in aggression between heterosexual partners: A meta-analytic review. *Psychological Bulletin, 126*, 651–680.

Asian and Pacific Islander Institute on Gender-Based Violence. (n.d.). A directory of domestic violence programs serving Asians, native Hawaiians and Pacific Islanders. Retrieved from http://www.apiidv.org/resources/programs-serving-apis.php

Betancourt, J. R. (2006). Cultural competence and medical education: Many names, many perspectives, one goal. *Academic Medicine, 81*, 499–501.

California Health Interview Survey. (2011). *CHIS 2009 Methodology Series: Report 2—Data collection methods.* Los Angeles, CA: UCLA Center for Health Policy Research. Retrieved from http://healthpolicy.ucla.edu/Documents/Newsroom%20PDF/CHIS2009_method2.pdf

Carter, J. (2015). Patriarchy and violence against women and girls. *Lancet, 385*(9978), e40–e41. doi:10.1016/S0140-6736(14)62217-0

Centers for Disease Control and Prevention. (2008). Strategic direction for IPV prevention. Promoting respectful, nonviolent intimate partner relationships through individual, community, and societal change. Retrieved from http://www.cdc.gov/violenceprevention/pdf/IPV_Strategic_Direction_Full-Doc-a.pdf

Centers for Disease Control and Prevention. (2013). Intimate partner violence. Retrieved from http://www.cdc.gov/violenceprevention/intimatepartnerviolence/

Chaudhuri, S., Morash, M., & Yingling, J. (2014). Marriage migration, patriarchal bargains, and wife abuse. *Violence Against Women, 20*(2), 141–161.

Cho, H., & Kim, W. (2012). Intimate partner violence among Asian Americans and their use of mental health services. Comparisons with White, Black, and Latino victims. *Journal of Immigrant and Minority Health, 14*(5), 809–815.

Dasgupta, S. (2000). Charting the course: An overview of domestic violence in the South Asian community in the United States. *Journal of Social Distress and the Homeless*, *9*(3), 173–185.

Dasgupta, S., & Warrier, S. (1996). In the footsteps of "Arundhati": Asian Indian women's experience of domestic violence in the United States. *Violence Against Women*, *2*(3), 238–259.

Family Violence Prevention Fund. (2008). State codes on intimate partner violence: Victimization reporting requirements for healthcare providers. *Journal of Clinical Ethics*, *19*(4), 330–333. Retrieved from http://www.ncdsv.org/images/State%20 Codes%20on%20IPV%20Victimization%20Rep%20Req_10-07.pdf

Finfgeld-Connett, D., & Johnson, E. (2013). Abused South Asian women in westernized countries and their experiences seeking help. *Mental Health Nursing*, *34*(12), 863–873.

Hurwitz, E., Gupta, J., Liu, R., Silverman, J., & Raj, A. (2006). Intimate partner violence associated with poor health outcomes in U.S. South Asian women. *Journal of Immigrant and Minority Health*, *8*(3), 251–261.

Kallivayalil, D. (2010). Narratives of suffering of South Asian immigrant survivors of domestic violence. *Violence Against Women*, *16*(7), 789–811.

Raj, A., & Silverman, J. (2002). Intimate partner violence against South Asian women in greater Boston. *Journal of the American Medical Women's Association*, *57*(2), 111–114.

Raj, A., & Silverman, J. (2003). Immigrant South Asian women at greater risk for injury from intimate partner violence. *American Journal of Public Health*, *93*(3), 435–437.

Raj, A., & Silverman, J. (2007). Domestic violence help-seeking behaviors of South Asian battered women residing in the United States. *International Review of Victimology*, *14*, 143–170.

Raj, A., Liu, R., McCleary-Sills, J., & Silverman, J. (2005). South Asian victims of intimate partner violence more likely than non-victims to report sexual health concerns. *Journal of Immigrant Health*, *7*(2), 85–91.

Raj, A., Livramento, K., Santana, M., Gupta, J., & Silverman, J. (2006). Victims of intimate partner violence more likely to report abuse from in-laws. *Violence Against Women*, *12*(10), 936–949.

Raj, A., Silverman, J., McCleary-Sills, J., & Liu, R. (2005) Immigration policies increase South Asian immigrant women's vulnerability to intimate partner violence. *Journal of the American Medical Women's Association*, *60*(1), 26–32.

Robert Wood Johnson Foundation. (2014). Strengthening what works: Preventing intimate partner violence in immigrant and refugee communities. Retrieved from http://www.rwjf.org/en/library/research/2014/02/strengthening-what-works.html

SAPHA. (2002). South Asian Public Health Association—A brown paper: The health of South Asians in the United States. Retrieved from http://joinsapha.org/resource-list/the-brown-paper/

Stewart, M., Brown, J. B., Donner, A., McWhinney, I. R., Oates, J., Weston, W. W., & Jordan, J. (2000). The impact of patient-centered care on outcomes. *Journal of Family Practice*, *49*, 796–804.

Stewart, M., Belle-Brown, J., Weston, W. W., McWhinney, I. R., McWilliam, C. L., & Freeman, T. (2003). *Patient-centered medicine: Transforming the clinical method* (2nd ed.). Abingdon, Oxford: Radcliffe Medical Press.

Straus, M. A. (1979). Measuring intra-family conflict and violence: The conflict tactics scale. *Journal of Marriage and Family, 41*(1), 75–88.

United States Preventive Services Taskforce. (2013). Intimate partner violence and abuse of elderly and vulnerable adults: Screening. Retrieved from http://www.uspreventiveservicestaskforce.org/Page/Topic/recommendation-summary/intimate-partner-violence-and-abuse-of-elderly-and-vulnerable-adults-screening

Yoshioka, M., & Dang, Q. (2000). Asian family violence report: A study of the Cambodian, Chinese, Korean, South Asian, and Vietnamese communities in Massachusetts. Retrieved from https://www.atask.org/site/images/pdf/asianfamilyviolencereport.pdf

Yoshihama, M., Blazevski, J., & Bybee, D. (2014). Enculturation and attitudes toward intimate partner violence and gender roles in an Asian Indian population: Implications for community-based prevention. *American Journal of Community Psychology, 53*(3–4), 249–260. doi:10.1007/s10464-014-9627-5

Yoshihama, M., Ramakrishnan, A., Hammock, A., & Khaliq, M. (2012). Intimate partner violence prevention program in an Asian immigrant community: Integrating theories, data, and community. *Violence Against Women, 18*(7), 763–783.

World Health Organization. (2013). Responding to intimate partner violence and sexual violence against women. WHO clinical and policy guidelines. Retrieved from http://apps.who.int/iris/bitstream/10665/85240/1/9789241548595_eng.pdf

FUTURE DIRECTIONS

Chapter 15

From Research to Practice and Policy: Multistakeholder Translational Research Partnerships to Reduce South Asian Health Disparities

---

Lakshmi Prasad, Sehrish Bari, Jennifer Leng, Sudha Acharya, and Francesca Gany

Contents

Abstract

Objective: Health disparities exist among South Asians in the United States. In 2013, the *South Asian Health: From Research to Practice and Policy* was established to use a multistakeholder translational research partnership approach to address these disparities. Guided by framework from the National Institute on Minority Health and Health Disparities (NIMHD), a blueprint was created to address cardiovascular disease (CVD) and cancer disparities research among South Asians in the United States. This chapter describes the multistakeholder approach used for developing the blueprint, along with key findings, and presents CVD and cancer as examples of how translational research, practice, and policy can potentially address these health disparities.

Key Findings: Several findings emerged that cut across all of the working group themes, including a need for disease and risk factor surveillance that recognizes the heterogeneity of South Asians living in the United States; the need to involve migration and acculturation as factors in disease prevalence, progression, and outcomes; the need to see the role of family and community in a patient's experience of health and illness; the need to solicit participation in research, health promotion, and initiation of policy change; and the need for culturally appropriate diagnostic and treatment models.

Recommendations: This multistakeholder translational health research partnership approach was successful in engaging key South Asian health stakeholders and setting health research priorities. This framework can be applied to identifying research priorities in the context of other health conditions covered in this publication. Multistakeholder input and involvement is critical for building consensus and fostering engagement to reduce health disparities among South Asians living in the United States.

Introduction

South Asian Americans (SAA) experience high rates of morbidity and mortality as a result of cardiovascular disease (CVD) and cancer. A translational research approach that fosters the multidirectional and multidisciplinary integration of basic science research, patient-oriented research, and population-based research, combined with the long-term goal of improving the health of the public, has the potential to reduce these health disparities in minority populations (Fleming et al., 2008; Rubio et al., 2010). Translational health research relies upon the ability of researchers and practitioners from different disciplines and backgrounds to pool their knowledge, skills, and resources, and to work with communities to develop interventions that are relevant to diverse populations. The translational health research framework for addressing health disparities involves three key components of health disparities research: (1) detecting disparities, (2) examining their causes and developing interventions, and (3) implementing interventions and monitoring outcomes specific to health disparities (Fleming et al., 2008).

South Asian Health: From Research to Practice and Policy (SAH) was established by the Memorial Sloan Kettering Cancer Center (MSKCC) in 2013. It is a translational health research initiative designed to address existing CVD and cancer disparities among the SAA population. Guided by the framework from the National Institute on Minority Health and Health Disparities (NIMHD, 2014) for minority health translational and community-engaged research, SAH engaged multidisciplinary researchers, practitioners, policymakers, and community members to develop a translational research blueprint for SAH disparities research and practice in the United States. SAH focused primarily on CVD and its risk factors, but also addressed cancer and associated risks faced by the SAA population.

While CVD and cancer encompass two broad disease groups, they have several overlapping and preventable biological risk factors (diabetes, metabolic syndrome, obesity), behavioral risk factors (unhealthy diet, physical inactivity, tobacco use), and environmental exposures (Adami et al., 1991; Kannel & McGee, 1979; Salazar-Martinez et al., 2005; Sun & Kashyap, 2011; World Health Organization, 2002).

SAH was an opportunity to unite national leaders at the forefront of research and community-based interventions to address shared CVD and cancer risk factors in the SAA population. These include, but are not limited to genetics, metabolic syndrome, inflammation and infection, tobacco use, and arsenic exposure.

This chapter describes the application of SAH to the NIMHD translational and community-engaged research framework in order to produce a research blueprint for SAH disparities research and practice in the United States. Specifically, it outlines efforts through SAH to engage multiple stakeholders around thematic content areas, the subsequent findings, and research priorities. The longer-term impact of this work remains to be studied in the future.

Background

The SAA population is faced with significant health disparities. CVD and cancer risks of South Asians are particularly urgent and inadequately addressed (Enas et al., 1996; Holland, Wong, Lauderdale, & Palaniappan, 2011; National Cancer Institute, 2012; Silbiger et al., 2011). Available evidence indicates a higher prevalence of CVD in South Asians when compared with all other ethnic groups, regardless of geographic location (Patel, Phillips-Caesar, & Boutin-Foster, 2010) and highlights the disparities in CVD within the South Asian population (Palaniappan, Mukherjea, Holland, & Ivey, 2010).

South Asians have disproportionately higher rates of morbidity and mortality from chronic conditions, including heart disease, diabetes, metabolic syndrome (MetS), obesity, and certain cancers, which result in death at younger ages (Balasubramanyam et al., 2008; Barnett et al., 2006; Forouhi et al., 2006; Kousar, Burns, & Lewandowski, 2008; Ma et al., 2003; Mathews & Zachariah, 2008; McKeigue, Shah, & Marmot, 1991; Misra, Endemann, & Ayer, 2005; Palaniappan, Wong, Shin, Fortmann, & Lauderdale, 2010; Reddy et al., 2006; Sobhani et al., 2013; Tillin et al., 2013). The high prevalence of CVD among South Asians, along with its risk factors, is multifactorial (Palaniappan, Wong, 2010) and likely influenced by an interaction of genetic, environmental, and behavioral lifestyle factors (Chen et al., 2013). In particular, lifestyle and behavior have been shown to significantly contribute to these disparities (Kandula et al., 2013).

Disparities are also evident in the incidence of cancers, some of which share common risk factors with CVD, including arsenic exposure and alternative tobacco use (Sohel et al., 2009; Mostafa, McDonald, & Cherry, 2008; Yorifuji, 2011; Li et al., 2011; Liu et al., 2008). For Indian and Pakistani immigrants in the United States, the top cancer sites are prostate and breast, while the overall South Asian population also experiences increasing rates of colon and lung cancer (Hossain, Sehbai, Abraham, & Abraham, 2008). Although oral cancer has been surpassed by other cancers in terms of incidence rates, it still remains a major concern among South Asians and is largely compounded by the use of smokeless tobacco products (Bhisey et al., 1999; IARC, 2004; Willis, Popovech, Gany, & Zelikoff, 2012).

Another important health disparity facing South Asian immigrants is the high rate of mental health disorders, which often go unaddressed (Anand, 2005; Gater et al., 2009; Taylor, Brown, & Weinman, 2013). Like many immigrant groups, South Asians are susceptible to psychological distresses due to migration, subsequent pressures to acculturate, and other social determinants that have a significant impact on their functioning and quality of life (Anand, 2005; Gater et al., 2009; Taylor et al., 2013). Consequently, these disproportionately high rates of mental illness among South Asians may play a role in the disparities found in chronic illnesses among this population, since psychosocial stressors have been linked to an increase in risk for the onset of CVD and cancer (Kemp & Quintana, 2013; Mols, Husson, Roukema, & van de Poll-Franse, 2013; Rahman et al., 2013; Touvier et al., 2013; Watkins et al., 2013).

The high prevalence of CVD and cancer risk among South Asians is commonly attributed to the interaction of predisposing genetic, environmental, socioeconomic, and behavioral lifestyle factors. Barriers to health and health care, including cultural and linguistic difficulties, lack of access to transportation, stigma, institutional barriers, and economic issues such as lack of affordable health insurance, can all serve to hinder early diagnoses and proper management of chronic diseases, including CVD and cancer in this population (Boxwala, Bridgemohan, Griffith, & Soliman, 2010; Brown, Ojeda, Wyn, & Levan, 2000; DeNavas-Walt, Proctor, & Smith, 2011; Jafri, 2011; Lai & Surood, 2013; Rehman, 2010).

In order to augment the current scientific evidence on the SAA population, several community assessments, conferences, and meetings on SAH in the United States have been conducted (see Tables 15.1 and 15.2 for a selected list). These have produced significant contributions to the existing knowledge based

Table 15.1 Community Needs Assessments on South Asians in the United States

Community Needs Assessments	Organization	Year
Unlocking the Golden Door: A Report on the Needs of the South Asian and Indo-Caribbean Communities in NYC	South Asian Council for Social Services	2001
A Brown Paper: The Health of South Asians in the United States	South Asian Public Health Association	2002
A South Asian Health Needs Assessment of the Washington, DC Region	Project SAHNA	2002
Community Health Needs and Resource Assessment: An Exploratory Study of South Asians in NYC	Center for the Study of Asian American Health	2007
Addressing Health Disparities and Health Literacy Challenges in the South Asian Community	UMDNJ-Robert Wood Johnson Medical School	2010

Table 15.2 Meetings and Conferences on South Asian American health

Meetings and Conferences	Organization	Year
Bridging Communities for Better Health	University of Southern California	2005
South Asian American Health Conference	South Asian Total Health Initiative	2005
Asian American Health Initiative Conference		2006
The Study of Asian American Health (CSAAH) Conference	Center for the Study of Asian American Health	2009
Addressing Health Disparities and Health Literacy Challenges	South Asian Total Health Initiative	2010
Health Disparities in the South Asian Community Press Forum	New York's Queens Hospital Center	2011
Bi-Annual South Asian Summit	South Asian Americans Leading Together	2011

on SAH. Unfortunately, while significant progress has been made, SAH research has not advanced sufficiently. Among other research gaps, there remains a paucity of detailed data on the populations' unique cardiovascular and cancer risk profiles, etiologic mechanisms, and effective interventions to address the health disparities affecting first- and second-generation South Asians in the United States.

South Asian Health: From Research to Practice and Policy

The translational health research framework for addressing health disparities includes three key components of health disparities research: (1) detecting disparities, (2) examining their causes and developing interventions, and (3) implementing interventions and monitoring outcomes specific to health disparities. Current evidence suggests the potential of applying a systematic and collaborative approach to address existing research gaps and to bridge research, practice, and policy efforts. The NIMHD encourages collaboration among researchers and community organizations, service providers and systems, government agencies, and other stakeholders in order to ensure that research findings translate into sustainable changes that can impact minority health at the individual, community, and system levels (NIMHD, 2014). It also calls for research that examines factors such as socioeconomics, politics, discrimination, culture, and environment in relation to health disparities (NIMHD, 2014; Agency for Healthcare Research and Quality, 2009; The Office of Disease Prevention and Health Promotion, n.d.).

The SAH initiative is specifically aimed at addressing SAH disparities in the United States by collaboratively examining current literature on SAH in the United States, identifying health research gaps, and setting research priorities and creating a blueprint for SAA health research. It was established in 2013 and funded by NIMHD (1R13 MD007147-01A1). Three leading groups in the field partnered to implement SAH: (1) the South Asian Health Initiative (SAHI), a community-based participatory research program in New York, which is codirected by the Immigrant Health and Cancer Disparities Center at MSKCC; (2) the South Asian Council for Social Services (SACSS); and (3) the Palo Alto Medical Foundation Research Institute (PAMFRI) in California. All three organizations collaborated based on their involvement in SAH research and the provision of health and social services to South Asian communities in areas with large South Asian population concentrations in the United States. Specific communities were identified in the New York/New Jersey/Connecticut tristate area and Northern California. The SAH leadership reflected this distribution as well, with representatives from each of these regions. The leadership structure also represented the important role of the community and the South Asian cultural perspective, with SACSS co-leading these efforts.

Methodology

The activities and conference goals of SAH were guided by a steering committee comprised of key researchers, providers, and community groups. The expertise of the conference steering committee reflected the objectives of SAH, and included leading researchers in South Asian CVD risk/metabolic syndrome and cancer risk, translational research, community-based participatory research, and health policy. The committee members were instrumental in identifying themes, as well as in selecting working group members and facilitators to share published and preliminary data; facilitate discussions on gaps, challenges, and solutions in working sessions; and develop new collaborations to move the CVD and cancer prevention and treatment agenda forward. The steering committee nominated participants on the basis of their experience, contributions, and research activities in South Asian CVD and cancer disparities. Participants brought expertise across a wide range of domains, including basic science and clinical research, public health, community engagement, policy, and communications. They were also representative of the heterogeneity of the South Asian community and of areas with the largest South Asian communities in the United States.

The community at large was an integral part of these working groups in order to ensure an authentic community–academic partnership. All discussions took into consideration how to most effectively bridge research, practice, and policy. SAH operated as a tripartite initiative of virtual working group meetings, an in-person convening, and several academic-community forums throughout the United States. In addition, community feedback was solicited in advance of the in-person convening on CVD and cancer-related health needs and research priorities. SAH staff conducted in-depth phone interviews with representatives of community organizations throughout New York City, Atlanta, Houston, Chicago, and California. They also administered brief surveys to community members at religious organizations in New York City, Atlanta, and Houston in order to better understand community health and social priorities that required attention.

SAH participants examined literature on SAH in the United States, identified research gaps, and collectively set research priorities to create a translational health research blueprint.

Virtual working groups. Six working groups were established. Each group was dedicated to a health area that was relevant to CVD and cancer risk faced by the South Asian immigrant community in the United States. The groups/health areas created were the following:

1. Alternative tobacco products (ATP)
2. Genetics, epigenetics, epidemiology, and pathophysiology
3. Healthcare access and patient-provider readiness
4. Inflammation, infection, exposure, and the human microbiome
5. Lifestyle and behaviors
6. Mental health and stress

Through ongoing virtual meetings, each working group reviewed and catalogued the available evidence pertaining to its theme and identified pressing gaps in the available data on CVD and cancer risk in SAA communities. For the literature review, working group members searched NCBI PubMed and Scopus databases using key terms related to the theme for their particular group. Additional articles were added based on suggestions from the steering committee, as well as those identified in the bibliographies. Concurrently, SAH partners engaged community representatives to solicit their input on research priorities at the community level. The minutes from these discussions were documented and reviewed to produce a preliminary actionable report and research priority recommendations pertaining to each working group theme.

In-person convening. In September 2013, following the working group meetings, a one-day invitational meeting to synthesize and expand upon the preliminary working group findings was held at MSKCC in New York City.

The meeting included approximately 50 invited experts, who also served as working group members, from the United States, Canada, and South Asia. Also included was a group of observers who participated in the working group sessions that were convened on the six health areas identified earlier.

Working group invitees were nominated based on their experience, contributions, and research activities in South Asian CVD and cancer disparities. The steering committee conducted a systematic, exhaustive national search using a variety of Internet resources including PubMed, Google Scholar, and Web of Knowledge, as well as reviewing NIH grant awards, working papers, and conference proceedings from the South Asian Public Health Association (SAPHA). State and local departments of health, community-based organizations, cancer survivor organizations, immigrant services organizations, religious institutions, and legal, social, and economic justice organizations were also sources for finding experts in their fields.

The resulting transdisciplinary group of researchers included community members and practitioners in medicine, nursing, health policy, health outcomes, and health services research, as well as basic, social sciences, and public health. Together, the group partnered in a multifaceted research review of SAH disparities designed to identify gaps and synergies, and to develop future research priorities.

Community forums. Five postconference community town hall meetings held in New York City, the San Francisco Bay Area, and Chicago, helped extend the conference's interactions with the community. The meetings further engaged the South Asian community to identify research and service priorities, facilitate the development of the research blueprint, and disseminate conference findings.

Findings

The virtual working group sessions, in-person convening, and community town hall meetings all served as the foundation for an ongoing collaborative effort to chart a relevant and actionable translational research blueprint to reduce SAH disparities in the United States. The following overall findings emerged that cut across all working group themes:

■ Data are needed that are nationally representative and disaggregated according to South Asian subgroups. Understanding and addressing the diverse needs and health-seeking behaviors of South Asians should begin with surveillance and data that recognize the heterogeneity within the more than 3.4 million South Asians who reside in the United States. Special attention should be paid to ethnic identity, country of origin, and immigration status.

■ Migration and acculturation in the SAA population are important factors in disease prevalence and outcomes. Oftentimes differences in disease prevalence and outcomes across migration and acculturation categories are indicative of more proximal factors, including diet and lifestyle, which can then be the target of future interventions.

■ Family members and trusted sources within the community, such as religious leaders, can play important roles in facilitating participation in research, adherence to health-promoting interventions, and initiating policy change. South Asians, or culturally sensitized individuals, can carry out these tasks by serving as community health workers, health-care providers, health-care advocates, and in other roles.

■ Culturally, appropriate diagnostic and treatment models that are tailored to SAAs are lacking, which undermines the effectiveness of the care that South Asians receive.

Findings and recommendations from the working group sessions and in-person convenings are as follows. The research, practice, and policy recommendations as they pertain to each working group area are also identified.

Alternative Tobacco Products

Alternative tobacco products (ATP), including *paan* with tobacco, *gutka, bidi,* and *kretek*, are widely used in South Asian communities. These products have been linked to increased rates of oral, pancreatic, and liver cancers, cardiovascular effects, periodontal disease, and adverse pregnancy outcomes. This working group addressed available literature and gaps in data with regard to these products, including prevalence of use, product toxicology, associated risk for disease, behavioral and pharmacological quit strategies, and the impact of current and potential regulatory policies on use and cessation.

Research Recommendations

Undertake detailed community-level and population-level assessments to better understand the prevalence of ATP use across SAA communities. These should include:

■ Implement culturally appropriate population-level surveys that collect disaggregated data on ATP use, availability, and user

■ Compile a standardized bank of questions on South Asian tobacco use for researchers in order to promote consistency and comparability across findings

■ Apply culturally sensitive research methods when investigating the nature of ATP use in South Asian communities

- Apply a collaborative approach to research and intervention efforts, incorporating the input of researchers and academics, health departments, and the community, to develop culturally sensitive surveillance mechanisms, as well as preventive and intervention strategies
- Conduct further research in the following understudied areas:
  - ATP use and its health risks among youth and pregnant women
  - The link between the use of ATP and oral cancer and CVD
  - The link between South Asian genetic profiles and ATP
  - The adaption of dependency scales for South Asian ATPs
  - A compilation of individual chemical composition of products and brands that are sold in the United States, in order to understand the differences in chemical composition of available products
- Gather data from cessation programs in South Asia and the United Kingdom
- Conduct intervention studies in the United States to inform culturally appropriate and feasible cessation strategies. Interventions include contextual counseling, behavioral therapy, and pharmacological therapy

Community-Level Recommendations

This working group recommended adoption of a community-based approach that would address ATP use in South Asian communities. This approach should include the following efforts:

- Generate awareness and improve messaging among retailers, cultural leaders, health-care providers, and other key community members who can facilitate the discouragement of ATP use, identify candidates for ATP cessation interventions, and measure impact.
- Develop training programs for healthcare providers to screen and treat ATP use.
- Educate ATP retailers on regulations and address concerns as to how sales restrictions could hurt them economically.
- Develop prevention strategies that specifically target youth.

Policy Recommendations

- Bring together representatives from health departments who are implementing tobacco control programs across states and localities in order to share data and strategies and conduct impact studies jointly.
- Conduct analysis of local-level ATP policies across the United States, particularly in areas with growing and/or currently large South Asian communities (e.g., Georgia, North Carolina, and Texas).

■ Explore the impact of environmental and other laws from countries that have been successful in curbing ATP use, particularly England and India, to inform the development of similar laws in the United States. De facto ATP control policies in South Asian communities should also be explored.

■ Greater policy advocacy is needed to promote knowledge and enforcement of regulations related to ATP marketing, importation, and sales, particularly to youth. This should include ingredient and warning labels, taxation and tracking, and unit-based and online sales, with policymakers paying special attention to enforcement at the merchant level.

Genetics, Epigenetics, Epidemiology, and Pathophysiology

Research has shown disparities in CVD, diabetes, and obesity that are partially determined by underlying biological factors. This working group catalogued the available research on the intersection of environment, genetics, biomarkers, and pathophysiology to identify gaps, as well as research priorities to address these gaps.

Research Recommendations

■ Initiate multicenter studies for biomarkers among South Asians, including reference points for metabolic syndrome, BMI, waist circumference, and diabetes risk scores. Increase focus on nutritional epigenetics in South Asian populations, including omega-3 fatty acids and other nutrients as protective factors for CVD and/or cancer.

■ Compile existing data on metabolic syndrome in South Asians to determine root genetic causes, given considerable heterogeneity of the SAA population.

■ Continue research on lipoprotein(a) to clinically validate its use as a biomarker and potentially treatable risk factor for malignant heart disease.

■ Increase focus on the environmental causes of epigenetic alterations in South Asians.

■ Tailor cardiovascular risk and diagnosis guidelines to South Asian populations in order to translate research into practice.

Health-Care Access and Patient-Provider Readiness

Poor access to health care has a detrimental impact on the health of a community. This working group discussed the current state of health-care access for South Asians. The role of cultural issues, institutional barriers, and the ongoing impact of healthcare reform (Affordable Care Act) on the community were explored. The group also examined patient and provider readiness to address health-care access barriers.

Research Recommendations

■ Disaggregate existing and future data, including NHANES, NHIS, and Census data, in order to account for heterogeneity within the South Asian population, particularly across ethnic identity, country of origin, and citizenship.

■ Include questions pertaining to healthcare access in local and national population-based surveys, such as monetary remittance, circular migration, insurance resources, transportation issues, provider availability, safety net provisions, and pharmacy access.

■ Encourage multiple research approaches to include multilevel intervention research that targets individual patient, family, community, and health-care systems; mixed methods; community-based participatory research; and policy research.

■ Conduct further research on South Asian subgroups with regard to healthcare access. This should include documented immigrants, taxi drivers, and children and adults with mental disabilities.

■ Further explore social issues that impact healthcare access among South Asians, including stigma of domestic violence and mental illness, women's access to healthcare, and impact of social networks on healthcare utilization.

Clinical Recommendations

■ Develop evidence-based guidelines and best practices that are specific to the health needs and risks of the South Asian population

■ Promote culturally sensitive preventive care, particularly for cancer screening, chronic disease management (cancer, diabetes, and heart disease), mental illness, and palliative care

■ Educate patients about their rights to access care in their preferred language

■ Educate providers about how they can work effectively with medical interpreters

■ Increase and evaluate South Asian–specific culturally responsive palliative care services in the United States

Community-Level Recommendations

■ Implement additional programs at community-based clinics that seek to decrease barriers to affordable and culturally competent health-care access for South Asians.

■ Train community members to engage with local elected officials in healthcare advocacy.

■ Train interested community members to serve as health workers who can support South Asians as they seek healthcare services, mediate patient-provider interactions, educate patients about their rights to public health benefits and medical interpretation, and encourage adherence to preventive and chronic care management guidelines.

Policy Recommendations

■ Ensure that medical curriculum includes sensitization to South Asian cultural norms and stigmas, as well as instruction on delivering culturally sensitive care.

■ Provide more medical interpreters who are trained to assist multiple South Asian subgroups (with various linguistic and cultural characteristics).

■ Implement a language translation and interpretation certification process for South Asian languages.

■ Continue funding to ensure safety net health-care services for those who are ineligible under the Affordable Care Act.

Inflammation, Infection, Exposure, and the Human Microbiome

Infection and chronic inflammation can elevate CVD and cancer risk. Environmental exposures, such as arsenic and particulate matter, also pose risks in the South Asian population. This working group examined the effects of exposure to arsenic and particulate matter, as well as the impact of human papilloma virus (HPV) and Hepatitis B/C infection on CVD and cancer risks. The group also assessed emerging research on the human microbiome and the effect of microbiome changes on obesity and diabetes risk among South Asians.

Research Recommendations

■ Establish a South Asian cohort study to assess the impact of infections, exposures, microbiota, and inflammation biomarkers on cancer and CVD risk over time.

- Focus on the long-term effects of arsenic exposure in South Asian immigrants, including cancer and CVD. Evaluate arsenic levels in domestic and imported rice.
- Exposure to particulate matter among taxi drivers and other South Asian at-risk occupational groups should be quantified and links between particulate matter, inflammation, CVD, and cancer should be investigated.
- Explore the link between HPV and oropharyngeal cancer among South Asians, specifically in the context of potential changes in the microbiota with migration.

Policy Recommendations

- Implement and evaluate culturally specific HPV vaccination programs, cervical cancer screenings, and hepatitis screenings

Lifestyle and Behaviors

Lifestyle behaviors play a significant role in CVD and cancer risk. This working group examined the impact of behaviors common in the South Asian population on CVD, diabetes, and cancer. They included diet, fasting, physical activity, and circular migration. The role of complementary and alternative medicine in the treatment of chronic conditions was also covered as part of this area, and included traditional South Asian medicine such as *ayurveda*.

Research Recommendations

- Continued research on dietary patterns and cardio-metabolic risk among the SAA population is needed. Optimally, healthful diets within South Asian populations also need to be characterized for communities.
- Culturally acceptable physical activities that address the needs and preferences of diverse members of the South Asian community should be promoted and can include family-focused or unisex exercise.

Provider Recommendations

- Culturally specific continuing medical education courses on health risks and needs of South Asians should be prioritized.
- Educate providers on complementary treatments favored by South Asian immigrants for CVD and cancer.

Community-Level Recommendations

■ Encourage community leaders to not only test the impact of health intervention models, but also to implement them in the broader community once proven successful. Restaurant owners, religious leaders, coaches, and other influential individuals can use their positions as culturally and linguistically competent influencers to implement needed change.

Mental Health and Stress

Stress and poor mental health are risk factors for CVD and cancer. Among South Asian immigrants, the stress of acculturating to the American lifestyle while maintaining certain cultural values and traditions, receiving limited social support, and undergoing occupational stress and financial strain may all contribute to high stress levels and poor mental health. This working group assessed the current literature and gaps in this area.

Research Recommendations

■ Conduct analyses on the risk of and protective factors for mental illness
■ Disaggregate data sets according to immigration group, social class, and gender
■ Conduct further research on South Asian immigrants' understanding of mental illness, with a focus on changes resulting from acculturation
■ Modify treatment as needed to incorporate non-Western treatment options such as empowerment and family unit interventions

Conclusions

The findings and recommendations produced as a result of the working group meetings and in-person sessions helped in the development of a translational research blueprint for SAH disparities research in the United States. Upon finalization, the blueprint will be disseminated as a supplement in an upcoming issue of the *Journal of Immigrant and Minority Health*. Findings have been shared with stakeholders across various forums, including community meetings in New York, the San Francisco Bay Area, and Chicago. The findings have also been reported to representatives at the NIH, CDC, and various departments of health across the country. The SAH initiative plans to engage research and community partners and encourage them to disseminate findings and develop actionable plans in order to translate research into practice and policy.

The multistakeholder translational research partnership approach adapted by SAH was crucial for engaging key stakeholders around organized discussions and producing a representative blueprint of the South Asian community's CVD and cancer-related health needs and research priorities. The efforts of SAH demonstrated that collective input and communication among stakeholders across disciplines and settings is imperative in order to establish an academic/practice/policy/community translational research partnership. The input and involvement from multistakeholders was also critical for building consensus and fostering engagement for reducing SAH disparities in the United States. Finally, the NIMHD minority health translational and community-engaged research approach can be tailored and applied to identify research priorities in the context of other health and social conditions that are included in this publication.

References

Adami, H., McLaughlin, J., Ekbom, A., Berne, C., Silverman, D., Hacker, D., & Persson, I. (1991). Cancer risk in patients with diabetes mellitus. *Cancer Causes Control, 2*(5), 307–314.

Agency for Healthcare Research and Quality. (2009). *AHRQ activities to reduce racial and ethnic disparities in health care.* Retrieved from www.ahrq.gov/research/findings/factsheets/minority/disparities/index.html

Anand, A. S. (2005). The mental health status of South Asian women in Britain: A review of the UK literature. *Psychology Developing Societies, 17*(2), 195–214.

Balasubramanyam, A., Rao, S., Misra, R., Sekhar, R. V., & Ballantyne, C. M. (2008). Prevalence of metabolic syndrome and associated risk factors in Asian Indians. *Journal of Immigrant and Minority Health, 10*(4), 313–323.

Barnett, A. H., Dixon, A. N., Bellary, S., Hanif, M. W., O'Hare, J. P., Raymond, N. T., & Kumar, S. (2006). Type 2 diabetes and cardiovascular risk in the UK South Asian community. *Diabetologia, 49*(10), 2234–2246.

Bhisey, R. A., Ramchandani, A. G., D'Souza, A. V., Borges, A. M., & Notani, P. N. (1999). Long-term carcinogenicity of pan masala in Swiss mice. *International Journal of Cancer, 83*(5), 679–684.

Boxwala, F., Bridgemohan, A., Griffith, D. M., & Soliman, A. S. (2010). Factors associated with breast cancer screening in Asian Indian women in metro Detroit. *Journal of Immigrant and Minority Health, 12*(4), 534–543. doi: 10.1007/s10903-009-9277-0

Brown, E. R., Ojeda, V. O., Wyn, R., & Levan, R. (2000). *Racial and Ethnic Disparities in Access to Health Insurance and Health Care.* UCLA Center for Health Policy Research and the Henry J. Kaiser Family Foundation. Retrieved from: kaiserfamilyfoundation.files.wordpress.com/2013/01/racial-and-ethnic-disparities-in-access-to-health-insurance-and-health-care-report.pdf

Chen, Y., Copeland, W. K., Vedanthan, R., Grant, E., Lee, J. E., Gu, D., . . . Potter, J. D. (2013). Association between body mass index and cardiovascular disease mortality in east Asians and south Asians. *British Medical Journal, 347*, f5446. doi: 10.1136/bmj.f5446

DeNavas-Walt, C., Proctor, B., & Smith, J. (2011). *Income, poverty, and health insurance coverage in the United States*. Washington, DC: US Census Bureau.

Enas, E., Garg, A., Davidson, M. A., Nair, V. M., Huet, B. A., & Yusuf, S. (1996). Coronary heart disease and its risk factors in first-generation immigrant Asian Indians to the United States of America. *Indian Heart Journal, 48*(4), 343–353.

Fleming, E. S., Perkins, J., Easa, D., Conde, J. G., Baker, R. S., Southerland, W. M., . . . Norris, K. C. (2008). The role of translational research in addressing health disparities: A conceptual framework. *Ethnicity & Disease, 18*(S2), 155–160.

Forouhi, N. G., Sattar, N., Tillin, T., McKeigue, P. M., & Chaturvedi, N. (2006). Do known risk factors explain the higher coronary heart disease mortality in South Asian compared with European mean? Prospective follow-up of the Southall and Brent Studies. *Diabetologia, 49*(11), 2580–2588.

Gater, R., Tomenson, B., Percival, C., Chaudhry, N., Waheed, W., Dunn, G., . . . Creed, F. (2009). Persistent depressive disorders and social stress in people of Pakistani origin and white Europeans in the UK. *Social Psychiatry and Psychiatric Epidemiology, 44*(3), 198–207. doi: 10.1007/s00127-008-0426-x

Holland, A. T., Wong, E. C., Lauderdale, D. S., & Palaniappan, L. P. (2011). Spectrum of cardiovascular diseases in Asian-American racial/ethnic subgroups. *Annals of Epidemiology, 21*(8), 608–14. doi: 10.1016/j.annepidem.2011.04.004

Hossain, A., Sehbai, A., Abraham, R., & Abraham, J. (2008). Cancer health disparities among Indian and Pakistani immigrants in the United States: A surveillance, epidemiology and end result-based study from 1998–2003. *Cancer, 113*(6), 1423–1430.

IARC Working Group on the Evaluation of Carcinogenic Risks to Humans. (2004). Betel-quid and areca-nut chewing and some areca nut related nitrosamines. *IARC Monographs on the Evaluation of Carcinogenic Risks to Humans, 85*, 1–334.

Jafri, N. F. (2011). The role of culture and health literacy in cancer screening practices among young, middle to upper middle-class Pakistani-American women. *Asian Pacific Journal of Cancer Prevention, 12*, 2531

Kandula, N. R., Patel, Y., Dave, S., Seguil, P., Kumar, S., Baker, D. W., . . . Siddique, J. (2013). The South Asian Heart Lifestyle Intervention (SAHELI) study to improve cardiovascular risk factors in a community setting. *Contemporary Clinical Trials, 36*(2), 479–487.

Kannel, W. B., & McGee, D. L. (1979). Diabetes and glucose tolerance as risk factors for cardiovascular disease: The Framingham Study. *Diabetes Care, 2*(2), 120–126.

Kemp, A. H., & Quintana, D. S. (2013). The relationship between mental and physical health: Insights from the study of heart rate variability. *International Journal of Pathophysiology, 89*(3):288–96. doi: 10.1016/j.ijpsycho.2013.06.018

Kousar, R., Burns, C., & Lewandowski, P. (2008). A culturally appropriate diet and lifestyle intervention can successfully treat the components of metabolic syndrome in female Pakistani immigrants residing in Melbourne. *Metabolism, 57*(11), 1502–1508.

Lai, D. W., & Surood, S. (2013). Effect of service barriers on health status of aging South Asian immigrants in Calgary, Canada. *Health and Social Work*, *38*(1), 41–50.

Li, G., Sun, G. X., Williams, P. N., Nunes, L., & Zhu, Y. G. (2011). Inorganic arsenic in Chinese food and its cancer risk. *Environment International*, *37*(7), 1219–1225.

Liu, L., Kumar, S. K., Sedghizadeh, P. P., Jayakar, A. N., & Shuler, C. F. (2008). Oral squamous cell carcinoma incidence by subsite among diverse racial and ethnic populations in California. *Oral Surgery Oral Medicine Oral Pathology Oral Radiology, and Endodontics*, *105*(4), 470–480.

Ma, S., Cutter, J., Tan, C. E., Chew, S. K., & Tai, E. S. (2003). Associations of diabetes mellitus and ethnicity with mortality in a multiethnic Asian population: Data from the 1992 Singapore National Health Survey. *American Journal of Epidemiology*, *158*(6), 543–552.

Mathews, R., & Zachariah, R. (2008). Coronary heart disease in South Asian immigrants: Synthesis of research and implications for health promotion and prevention in nursing practice. *Journal of Transcultural Nursing*, *19*(3), 292–299.

McKeigue, P. M., Shah, B., & Marmot, M. G. (1991). Relation of central obesity and insulin resistance with high diabetes prevalence and cardiovascular risk in South Asians. *Lancet*, *37*(8738), 382–386.

Memorial Sloan Kettering Cancer Center. (2013). *South Asian health: From research to practice and policy*. Retrieved from www.mskcc.org/south-asian-health-research-practice-and-policy

Misra, K. B., Endemann, S. W., & Ayer, M. (2005). Leisure time physical activity and metabolic syndrome in Asian Indian immigrants residing in Northern California. *Ethnic Disparities*, *15*(4), 627–634.

Mols, F., Husson, O., Roukema, J. A., & van de Poll-Franse, L. V. (2013). Depressive symptoms are a risk factor for all-cause mortality: Results from a prospective population-based study among 3,080 cancer survivors from the PROFILES registry. *Journal of Cancer Survivorship*, *7*(3), 484–492. doi: 10.1007/s11764-013-0286-6

Mostafa, M. G., McDonald, J. C., & Cherry, N. M. (2008). Lung cancer and exposure to arsenic in rural Bangladesh. *Occupational and Environmental Medicine*, *65*(11), 765–768.

National Cancer Institute. (2012). *State cancer profiles*. Retrieved from http://statecancer-profiles.cancer.gov/

National Institute on Minority Health and Health Disparities (NIMHD). (2014). *Transdisciplinary Collaborative Centers for Health Disparities Research*. Retrieved from http://www.nimhd.nih.gov/programs/extra/tcc.html

Office of Disease Prevention and Health Promotion. (n.d.) *Healthy people 2020*. Retrieved from www.healthypeople.gov/

Palaniappan, L., Mukherjea, A., Holland, A., & Ivey, S. L. (2010). Leading causes of mortality of Asian Indians in California. *Ethnicity and Disease*, *20*(1), 53–57.

Palaniappan, L. P., Wong, E. C., Shin, J. J., Fortmann, S. P., & Lauderdale, D. S. (2010). Asian Americans have greater prevalence of metabolic syndrome despite lower body mass index. *International Journal of Obesity*, *35*(3), 393–400.

Patel, M., Phillips-Caesar, E., & Boutin-Foster, C. (2011). Barriers to lifestyle behavioral change in migrant South Asian populations. *Journal of Immigrant and Minority Health*, *14*(5), 774–785.

Rahman, I., Humphreys, K., Bennet, A. M., Ingelsson, E., Pedersen, N. L., & Magnusson, P. K. (2013). Clinical depression, anti-depressant use and risk of future cardiovascular disease. *European Journal of Epidemiology, 28*(7), 589–595. doi: 10.1007/s10654-013-9821-z

Reddy, K. S., Prabhakaran, D., Chaturvedi, V., Jeemon, P., Thankappan, K. R., Ramakrishnan, L., . . . Jaison, T. M. (2006). Methods for establishing a surveillance system for cardiovascular diseases in Indian industrial populations. *Bulletin of the World Health Organization, 84*(6), 461–469.

Rehman, T. (2010). Social stigma, cultural constraints: They're very different. *Journal of South Asians, 414–421.*

Rubio, D. M., Schoenbaum, E. E., Lee, L. S., Schteingart, D. E., Marantz, P. R., Anderson, K. E., . . . Esposito, K. (2010). Defining translational research: Implications for training. *Academic Medicine, 85*(3), 470–475.

Salazar-Martinez, E., Lazcano-Ponce, E., Sanchez-Zamorano, L. M., Gonzalez-Lira, G., Escudero-De Los Rios, P., & Hernandez-Avila, M. (2005). Dietary factors and endometrial cancer risk: Results of a case-control study in Mexico. *International Journal of Gynecological Cancer, 15*(5), 938–945.

Silbiger, J. J., Ashtiani, R., Attari, M., Spruill, T. M., Kamran, M., Reynolds, D., . . . Rubinstein, D. (2011). Atherosclerotic heart disease in Bangladeshi immigrants: Risk factors and angiographic findings. *International Journal of Cardiology, 146*(2):e38–401. doi: 10.1016/j.ijcard.2008.12.175

Sobhani, I., Amiot, A., Le Baleur, Y., Levy, M., Auriault, M. L., Van Nhieu, J. T., & Delchier, J. C. (2013). Microbial dysbiosis and colon carcinogenesis: Could colon cancer be considered a bacteria-related disease? *Therapeutic Advances in Gastroenterology, 6*(3), 215–229.

Sohel, N., Persson, L. A., Rahman, M., Streatfield, P. K., Yunus, M., Ekström, E. C., & Vahter, M. (2009). Arsenic in drinking water and adult mortality: A population-based cohort study in rural Bangladesh. *Epidemiology, 20*(6), 824–830.

South Asian Council for Social Services. (2001). *Unlocking the golden door: A report on the needs of the South Asian and Indo-Caribbean communities in NYC.*

South Asian Public Health Association. (2002). *The Brown Paper: First edition.* Retrieved from http://joinsapha.org/resource-list/the-brown-paper/

Sun, G., & Kashyap, S. R. (2011). Cancer risk in type 2 diabetes mellitus: Metabolic links and therapeutic considerations. *Journal of Nutrition and Metabolism, 2011,* 708183. doi: 10.1155/2011/708183

Taylor, R., Brown, J. S., & Weinman, J. (2013). A comparison of the illness perceptions of North Indian and white British women. *Journal of Mental Health, 22*(1), 22–32.

Tillin, T., Hughes, A. D., Mayet, J., Whincup, P., Sattar, N., Forouhi, N. G., . . . Chaturvedi, N. (2013). The relationship between metabolic risk factors and incident cardiovascular disease in Europeans, South Asians, and African Caribbeans: SABRE (Southall and Brent Revisited) — A prospective population-based study. *Journal of the American College of Cardiology, 61*(17), 1777–1786.

Touvier, M., Druesne-Pecollo, N., Kesse-Guyot, E., Andreeva, V. A., Galan, P., Hercberg, S., & Latino-Martel, P. (2014). Demographic, socioeconomic, disease history, dietary and lifestyle cancer risk factors associated with alcohol consumption. *International Journal of Cancer, 134*(2), 445–459.

Vyas, A. N., Chaudhary, N., Ramiah, K., & Landry, M. (2013). Addressing a growing community's health needs: Project SAHNA (South Asian Health Needs Assessment). *Journal of Immigrant and Minority Health, 15*(3), 577–583.

Watkins, L. L., Koch, G. G., Sherwood, A., Blumenthal, J. A., Davidson, J. R., O'Connor, C., & Sketch, M. H. (2013). Association of anxiety and depression with all-cause mortality in individuals with coronary heart disease. *Journal of the American Heart Association, 2*(2):e000068. doi:10.1161/JAHA.112.000068

Willis, D., Popovech, M., Gany, F., & Zelikoff, J. (2012). Toxicology of smokeless tobacco: Implications for immune, reproductive, and cardiovascular systems. *Journal of Toxicology and Environmental Health Part B, Critical Reviews, 15*(5), 317–331.

World Health Organization. (2002). *Reducing risks, promoting healthy life.* Retrieved from http://www.who.int/whr/2002/en/whr02_en.pdf?ua=1

Yorifuji, T., Tsuda, T., Doi, H., & Grandjean, P. (2011). Cancer excess after arsenic exposure from contaminated milk powder. *Environmental Health and Preventive Medicine, 16*(3), 164–170.

Appendix A

South Asian Nutrition Resources on the Web

American Association of Physicians of Indian Origin

AAPI's Guide to Nutrition, Health and Diabetes gives a short description of the dietary characteristics of different regions of India and illuminates the cultural context from which the ethnic foods and eating habits have evolved. It provides practical guidelines on healthy diets and understanding how to manage chronic disease states as well as information on the health benefits of spices and weight management. It is a comprehensive summary for anyone interested in improving themselves with a delicious and health-conscious diet of South Asian cuisine.

The Public Health Committee led by Dr. Thakor Patel (2010–2011) along with a team of registered dietitians and under the editorship of Ranjita Misra, PhD, CHES, FMALRC, helped compile the second edition. AAPI's goal is to reach out to the community to promote healthy lifestyles and disease prevention.

The entire book is downloadable at http://www.aapiusa.org/resources/nutrition.aspx

Palo Alto Medical Foundation's "PRANA" (Prevention and Awareness for South Asians)

Improving South Asian health and reducing disease risk through culturally tailored programs, health-related services, and educational resources.

http://www.pamf.org/southasian/
http://www.pamf.org/southasian/nutrition/

Diabetescare.Net

Nutrition Education Tools for the South Asian Population

Through its partnership with San Jose State University, DiabetesCare.net is proud to offer its visitors this web page containing culturally sensitive nutrition education tools for the South Asian population (people originating from the countries of Bangladesh, Bhutan, India, Maldives, Nepal, Pakistan, and Sri Lanka). South Asians are at highest risk for heart disease and diabetes among all ethnicities. These tools have been developed by Ashwini R. Wagle, MS, RD, together with graduate students from the Department of Nutrition, Food Science and Packaging at San Jose State University, as part of the student master's projects.

http://www.diabetescare.net/san-jose-nutrition-education-tools.asp

South Asian Nutrition (SAN) Resources

Provided by Nutrition and Diet Resources (NDR) UK, the South Asian Nutrition (SAN) Resources offers practical, culturally sensitive dietary advice for South Asian populations. A total of 13 different titles are available in English, Bengali, Gujarati, Hindi, Punjabi, Tamil, and Urdu language versions. Topics include healthy eating, heart health, and diabetes, with advice for specific dietary concerns such as meal and snack ideas, calcium, and iron intake.

South Asian Nutrition (SAN) Resources is supported by the Multicultural Group of the British Dietetic Association.

http://www.patient.co.uk/support/South-Asian-Nutrition-(SAN)-Resources.htm

Canadian Diabetes Association

The Canadian Diabetes Association's 2008 clinical practice guidelines state that people of South Asian descent are one of the populations at a higher risk to develop type 2 diabetes. People of South Asian descent include those from Bangladesh, Bhutan, India, Maldives, Pakistan, and Sri Lanka, and they may speak Hindi, Bengali, Punjabi, Tamil, Gujarati, and Urdu, among many other languages.

To help health professionals work with this population, a South Asian working group has developed the resources below. They include background information, a glossary of terms, FAQs, and the carbohydrate content of some common foods.

http://www.diabetes.ca/for-professionals/resources/nutrition/tools/
Site with list of carbohydrate content of common South Asian foods.
http://www.diabetes.ca/files/carbohydrate-content-south-asian.pdf

Index

Printed in the United States
by Baker & Taylor Publisher Services